MOVING FORWARD WITH LITERATURE
Basals, Books, and Beyond

MOVING FORWARD WITH LITERATURE

Basals, Books, and Beyond

SHELLEY B. WEPNER
JOAN T. FEELEY

THE WILLIAM PATERSON COLLEGE OF NEW JERSEY

Merrill, an imprint of
Macmillan Publishing Company
NEW YORK

Maxwell Macmillan Canada
TORONTO

Maxwell Macmillan International
NEW YORK   OXFORD   SINGAPORE   SYDNEY

Cover Art: Leslie Beaber
Editor: Linda James Scharp
Production Editor: Christine M. Harrington
Art Coordinator: Lorraine Woost
Photo Editor: Anne Vega
Text Designer: Susan E. Frankenberry
Cover Designer: Russ Maselli
Production Buyer: Patricia A. Tonneman
All photos courtesy of Cathy A. Labate

This book was set in Galliard by Compset, Inc., and was printed and bound by Book Press, Inc., a Quebecor America Book Group Company. The cover was printed by Phoenix Color Corp.

Macmillan Publishing Company
866 Third Avenue
New York, NY 10022

Macmillan Publishing Company is part of the
Maxwell Communication Group of Companies.

Maxwell Macmillan Canada, Inc.
1200 Eglinton Avenue East, Suite 200
Don Mills, Ontario M3C 3N1

Library of Congress Cataloging-in-Publication Data
Wepner, Shelley B.
    Moving forward with literature : basals, books, and beyond /
Shelley B. Wepner, Joan T. Feeley.
        p.   cm.
    Includes bibliographical references and index.
    ISBN 0-675-21414-9
    1. Basal reading instruction.   2. Reading (Elementary)
I. Feeley, Joan T.   .   II. Title.
LB1573.38.W47   1993

92-5298
CIP

Printing: 1 2 3 4 5 6 7 8 9   Year: 3 4 5 6 7

To Leslie and Meredith
who are discovering the world through literature,
and Brian, Scott, and Kelli
who are just discovering the world of literature

In Memoriam

Robert J. Feeley
December 8, 1926–March 27, 1992
Husband to Joan
Dad to John and Maura
Grandpa to Brian, Scott, and Kelli
Besides being our in-house editor and kindly critic,
he was always one of our greatest supporters
We miss you
We love you

Preface

G OOD TEACHERS—NO MATTER where or what they teach—don't need the latest and greatest bandwagons or purportedly proven panaceas to determine *how* to teach. Good teachers know what works and feel confident enough to cut and paste strategies and activities so as to glean the "best" parts of an idea or set of materials. Good teachers balance the "voices" of others in the field with their own visceral understanding of what developing readers and writers need.

Purpose

This book is about teachers who have found their own solutions for balancing philosophies, methods, and materials. Although anchored within particular configurations for using materials to teach reading and writing, they have devised their own systems for their programs.

Research

We know about these teachers firsthand. Before one word of this book was written, we surveyed teachers to ask how they perceive their teaching situations. We asked them to indicate which of the following phrases would best describe how they work

- Teach primarily with basals
- Teach with a combination of basals and trade books
- Teach with trade books only

We also asked teachers to identify whether and how often they use technology within their reading and language arts program. We did a number of things to find teachers: distributed surveys to our graduate classes; asked current leaders from our

State Department of Education to distribute surveys to teachers in their respective districts; combed the initial program guide for the International Reading Association's annual convention to identify teacher/presenters who seemed to have something to share with our audience (we then sent letters to these presenters and interviewed them during the convention); attended conferences in different geographical regions to find additional teacher presenters whose work in the classroom elicited "oohs" and "aahs" from the audience as well as us; and asked the teachers we met and the teachers we knew to help us find others who could add to our composite of teacher applications.

Once we identified our teachers, we spent the next year conducting face-to-face and telephone interviews and in-class observations of about 55 of them to find out how they work within each configuration so that we could realistically portray material usage in K through 6 American classrooms. We devised nine different in-depth interview forms (for example, basals/no computers, combination of basals and trade books/integrate computers sometimes, trade books only/integrate computers all the time) to use with our teachers so that we were asking the same questions, based on the teachers' designated configurations.

Teachers' instructional experiences—both inspiring and frustrating—became our focal point for theoretically exploring how different kinds of materials can best be used to guide students' general literacy instruction (Chapters 2 through 5). We substituted the term *textbooks* for *basals* for students' content area instruction (Chapter 6).

Goals

Organized from an evolutionary perspective—from teaching primarily with basals to teaching primarily with trade books across the curriculum—this book tries to communicate how teachers can prepare themselves to depend less on those "soup-to-nuts" types of prepackaged programs and more on their own homemade plans for accomplishing their goals for literacy instruction. In other words, we are encouraging teachers to take ownership of their reading-writing program. How this ownership can occur at different stages and to varying degrees is presented within the context of each configuration for using materials.

Contents

This book is divided into seven chapters, with Chapters 2 through 6 highlighting what teachers across the country are doing in their classrooms. Each chapter opens with a vignette about a real experience or concern for the theory and practices contained therein. Each chapter ends with a set of discussion questions and application activities that encourage critical examination and experimentation with the ideas and suggestions. Chapter 1 uses the experiences of adult readers and a preschool reader to describe the nature of literacy. Reading and writing, treated separately and together, are discussed with instructional implications for the primary and mid-elementary grades.

In contrast to the theoretical promises in the first chapter, Chapter 2 opens with a new teacher's first taste of frustration with administrative mandates about reading instruction. This vignette leads to an in-depth look at basals, including a comparison of seven basal publishers' treatment of literature, skill development versus "real" reading, and metacomprehension strategies. Rather than overload you with the details of our semester-long analysis, we include overall trends in Chapter 2 and then provide the "nitty-gritty" charts in the book's appendix.

Chapter 3 shows how teachers "in the middle" of the basal-book spectrum are creating their own teaching formulas for working with both types of materials. Chapter 4, with its opening "snapshots" of different trade book environments, describes what different teachers are doing to create their own plans for using trade books for literacy instruction. Together, Chapters 3 and 4 provide guidelines and strategies along a continuum of instructional options that depend less on basals and more on trade books.

Chapter 5 focuses on how technology can be used to support reading and writing within each of the three material configurations: basals, combinations of basals and trade books, and trade books only. Chapter 6 demonstrates, through guidelines and teacher applications, how to use the best material resources for students' content area literacy. Chapter 7 closes the book with a look at administrative and teacher initiatives for creating a climate for change.

Beliefs

Given the vast range of available reading and language arts materials, teachers need to cultivate a discerning eye for making choices about the material they use to develop readers who actually want to read and writers who actually believe they have something to say about what they read. Accordingly, five beliefs thread the chapters together: (a) authentic literature—whether from a basal or a trade book—needs to be at the heart of the instructional program; (b) no system or set of materials can ever fully satisfy the vagaries of instruction since every teacher is contending with a different set of circumstances; (c) skill development needs to be taught within the context of students' reading and writing experiences; (d) students need daily opportunities to read and write coherent text for extended periods of time; and (e) teachers, rather than materials per se, determine the quality of students' learning experiences.

While we recognize that the trade books we mention or discuss may not be the *absolute* latest and greatest in children's literature, we know that what we have included reflects what "real" teachers are using in their classrooms. In fact, the impetus for writing this book was to communicate what really is happening from varied perspectives rather than what should be happening from only one perspective. We have, though, made an effort to suggest from time to time additional current or notable books that could be used along with or in addition to what teachers are using.

Audience

Moving Forward with Literature: Basals, Books, and Beyond is intended to supplement introductory textbooks to the field of reading or serve as a primary source for those already familiar with the vernacular of our field. We admit that there's a bit of assumptive writing on our part; not every term used is defined in the body of text. However, we provide a glossary of definitions at the end of the book for any terms or concepts that we thought could be defined or explained further.

As you look for new ways to balance basals, books, and other print you select, you probably will find yourself letting go of the strictures and structures that have imprisoned you from feeling in control. You also will discover, as we did, that you will blend other teachers' successful programs and strategies for incorporating the best of children's literature into the uniqueness of your own teacher situation to create your own literature niche. We hope that you find parts of what you need in the pages that follow.

Acknowledgments

Living through this book helped us to see that without our supporters—publishers and their representatives, editors, teachers, theoreticians, family, and friends—we just couldn't do it. This book echoes the voices and honors the contributions of the following people. We thank:

John Bailey of Macmillan/McGraw-Hill; Barry Bauer of Scott, Foresman; Barry Bostian and Mary Landgraf of Harcourt Brace Jovanovich; Gary Kistner of D. C. Heath; Chris Parish of Silver Burdett & Ginn; and Jackie Poppleton of Houghton Mifflin for graciously agreeing to send us their company's basal materials for our analysis;

Cathy Labate for not only taking the wonderful photographs in this book but also for taking time away from her own teaching responsibilities to visit other school districts with us;

Jean Sawey for helping us out with typing in a pinch and with a smile;

Julia Stapleton for helping us to distribute our initial wave of surveys;

Barbara Joan McGill for helping us to discover a few more special teachers who were out of our reach;

Eileen Hudak-Huelbig, Mary Lou Keyes, Angela McClane, and Ellen Stellingwerf, graduate students at William Paterson College, for helping us to add depth and additional insights to our analysis of the seven basals. We'll never forget our eat-away-into-the-night marathons in Scotch Plains;

Virginia Crane, Dale M. Curran, Arlene French, and Arlene Lambert for helping us to identify some of the informational books for the content area learning chapter; Judith P. Mitchell, Weber State College; Sam L. Sebesta, University of Washington; Maria J. Weiss, University of Nevada, Las Vegas; Carol A. Hodges, Buffalo State College; Roberta L. Berglund, National Louis University; Carol S. Johnson, Washington State University; Janice V. Kristo, University of Maine; Victoria Hare, University of Illinois at Chicago; Lynn C. Smith, Southern Illinois University; Ray Reutzel, Brigham Young University; Patrice Werner, Southwest Texas State; and Donna J. Camp, University of Central Florida, for reviewing the book.

Jeff Johnston for opening our eyes to the idea of writing for Merrill/Macmillan and for helping us to carve out a plan for communicating our ideas; Sally MacGregor for her warm support in the beginning stages; Julie Enriquez for courteously assisting us from start to finish; Cindy Peck for her fine copyediting; Christine Harrington for guidance through the production process; and Linda Scharp for being the ultimate professional in shepherding this book to publication. Her gentle, yet firm administrative style helped us to move forward quicker and better than anticipated;

Roy Wepner for his assistance and unspoken understanding of why the family had to be robbed of recreational time together. Bob Feeley for his sharp editorial eye in proofreading our drafts;

Leslie and Meredith Wepner for their unexpected pride and excitement about their mom's book. Their mature acceptance of "Mom needs to work" was and always will be appreciated. Brian and Scott Feeley, preschoolers who love to read (and Kelli Feeley who is just brand new), for inspiring their grandmother to write this book;

All of the teachers and administrators described herein who enchanted us with their wonderful stories and creative spirit for providing the best literacy environments possible: Rosemary Alesandro, Virginia Baird, Jane Beaty, Kathyrn Bernardis, Christine Borisuk, Susan Boyd, Philip P. Caccavale, Ann Carline, Cheryl Cator, Barbara Chertoff, Johnnie Cole, Vicki Contente, Maria Conway, Sue Corrado, Maryanne Crowley, Susan Dammeyer, Ruth Davitt, Jean DeSantis, Marcia Diamantis, Celia Einhorn, Edith Green, Sheila Hackett, Kathleen Hadley, Peter Heaney, Carl Howard, Barbara Jones, Kathy Kelly, Mary Lou Keyes, Laura Kotch, John LaVigne, Shana Leib, Nancy D. Letteney, Dana Licamelli, Cheryl Majerscak, Marianne Marino, Janice Markovic, Frank Massaro, Susan McGrath, Sue Meldonian, Virginia Modla, Elsie Nigohosian, Betsy O'Brochta, Regina Pesce O'Hanlon, Joan Pearlman, Michael Petillo, Beverly Pilchman, Bonnie Prohaska, Bernard Ready, Carol Santa, Mary Ann Savino, Thomas A. Simpson, Julie Smith, Lyn Stampa, Erika Steinbauer, Arleen Swift, Rosemary Taylor, Gerry Wahlers, Cindy Weaver, Janis Young, Leslie Young, Leslie Zackman, Edie Ziegler, and Irv Ziegler.

Contents

CHAPTER 1

Literacy Development: An Overview 3

CHAPTER 4

Moving from Basals to Literature-Based Programs 151

CHAPTER 5

Incorporating Technology into Elementary Reading 223

CHAPTER 6

Extending Materials to Content Area Learning 279

MOVING FORWARD WITH LITERATURE
Basals, Books, and Beyond

CHAPTER

1

LITERACY DEVELOPMENT: AN OVERVIEW

Chapter Overview

THE NATURE OF READING

READING AND WRITING

The Writing-As-Process Movement /
Reading and Writing as Related Processes

RATIONALE FOR INTEGRATING READING AND WRITING

INSTRUCTIONAL IMPLICATIONS

The Primary Years / The Mid-Elementary Grades

THE ROLE OF BASALS, LITERATURE, AND OTHER PRINT

Basal Reading Programs / Literature-Based Programs /
Other Materials from Which Children Learn to Read

THE ADVERTISING EXECUTIVE with an MBA and his college professor wife with a Ph.D. were reading, for the sixth time, their proposed will, which also set up a trust fund.

She: I had some problems with article five. Let me look at my notes. Oh, yes, it begins talking about a "marital trust" but then proceeds to refer to it as a "family trust." Are they the same? And who is the "personal representative," the executor or the trustee?

He: I don't know. We'll have to ask our attorney what it means. The language is confusing. Did you understand the part about the "sole trustee" and the "successor trustee"? Do we name both? Or can the trustees name anyone they want? Let's decide what we want and rewrite that part so it really reflects our wishes. Also, let's go to the library and mall bookstore to see what we can find on wills and trusts.

As they talked over their concerns, this couple were clearly involved in an active search for meaning, using the print, what they knew about language, and their own general knowledge to try to reconstruct what the attorney had written so that they could make sense out of this important document. Although they could read the surface text without difficulty, they were having trouble with the deep structure or underlying meaning. Their prior knowledge of legal terms and legal ways of stringing together language was lacking.

But they were not totally stumped. They had strategies to help them. They knew what they needed to know and would look for some books to clear up legal terms. They would ask people with legal backgrounds to explain parts. Together they talked about the text, making terms more understandable by replacing them with names of people, for example:

She: Oh, now I get it. Even though "personal representative" is singular, it refers to Susan and Don, our co-execs, who could still serve as co-trustees.

Soon a complicated text became comprehensible, and the couple were satisfied that they understood the proposed document and could make decisions about rewriting sections so that their goals would be clearly stated and, hopefully, understood by others.

AS HIS MOM READS Eric Carle's *The Very Hungry Caterpillar* (1969) to him, 4-year-old Duane can hardly wait for her to come to the part when, on Saturday, the hungry caterpillar eats through many everyday foods such as a piece of chocolate cake, an ice-cream cone, a piece of cheese, and a slice of watermelon. These are the pages he reads, reciting the words like a litany as he runs his little finger along under the beautifully illustrated text.

Of course, he calls the sausage a "hot dog" because that term fits his concept of ground meat in a casing tied at both ends, and this information overrules the print information supplied by the word *sausage.* In fact, he doesn't seem to notice *sausage* at all because his reading makes sense. But, when asked to point to the word *watermelon,* he does so accurately, never indicating *slice* or *of.* Although he doesn't yet know all the letters of the alphabet, he knows many words by sight. For example, he knows the word *watermelon* which has a distinctive configuration and is a household favorite. Also, he has seen it in other contexts such as the supermarket vegetable department where he points it out as his mom wheels him through the aisles. After reading, he often gets his crayons and draws "other things for the caterpillar to eat" such as a pancake and a potato chip.

Duane is actively constructing the text. He hasn't merely memorized it. He uses all the information he needs—the pictures, the print, his memory of prior readings, and his knowledge of foods—to read and add to this story. And he understands what the text means because he invariably adds, "He'll feel sick from eating all that stuff!" before his mom reads the next words that say almost the same thing.

The Nature of Reading

Both of these scenarios, one showing how experienced, accomplished adult readers operate and the other showing how a novice child reader negotiates written language, illustrate the nature of reading. *Reading is a purposeful, active, strategic search for meaning in which readers use everything they know to make sense of written language.* Frank Smith (1985) says they use their knowledge of the world, their knowledge of the language, and what they know about the specific topic of the text to help them.

Knowledge of the world, also known by such terms as **prior knowledge, schemata, cognitive framework**, and **nonvisual information**, refers to all the information that readers have stored in their brains, what they've learned from life's experiences. According to Anderson and Pearson (1984) and Mason and the staff at the Center for the Study of Reading (1984), generalized schemata come into play as readers interact with text. In our first scenario, the will-readers had this kind of knowledge, but they lacked specific schemata about legal writing. In the second scenario, Duane showed that he possessed generalized information about common things to eat and specific knowledge about most of the items in Eric Carle's book.

In addition to using this dynamic schematic cue system as they process text, readers also use their knowledge of language and its systems: the **graphophonic, semantic,** and **syntactic cueing** systems. Graphophonic cues are supplied by the letters/spelling patterns and the sounds they represent. Syntax refers to the grammar (word order or structure) of a language. Semantic cues come from our knowledge of word meanings in general and their specific meanings when they are used in connected discourse.

Syntax and semantics together supply us with what is often termed "context clues" (Weaver, 1988).

For example, to figure out the word *inchoate* in the following sentence, readers may find the semantic and syntactic cues most helpful: "We couldn't agree on what to do for the weekend, so our plans remained *inchoate*." The reader senses the unfamiliar word is probably an adjective because of its position in the sentence (syntax). Reasoning from the meanings of the other words and their interrelationships in the sentence (semantics), the reader concludes that since they couldn't agree, their plans must still be "up in the air" or "undecided." Using only the graphophonic cues, the reader could come up with a pronunciation (in–chote) by assuming the "ch" is similar to the sound in "*church*" and "oa" is like the sound in "*coat*." Cunningham (1975–76) calls this word identification through analogy: readers use known words to predict pronunciations of unknown words. Alone, this cue system doesn't get readers to meaning, and, in this case, it doesn't even help them to predict standard pronunciation, which is rather unusual if you haven't heard it (in–kō′–it).

Over the last two decades, a hybrid discipline called **psycholinguistics** (*psycho* from psychology or the study of the mind and *linguistics* from the study of language) has sprung up to help us understand the nature of reading. According to the psycholinguists (Smith, 1985; Weaver, 1988), readers simultaneously use all available information as they process text. There is a constant interplay between visual (print) and nonvisual (what's in the brain) information. The more nonvisual information (generalized and specific schemata and language knowledge) readers possess, the less **visual information** (surface structure of a text represented by the print) they need to understand the **deep structure** or underlying meaning.

Psycholinguists say that reading is making predictions (based on nonvisual information) and confirming or rejecting them based on what comes next and what readers already know. In essence, they predict and confirm their way through text, within the constraints of the visual and memory processing systems. As graphic input (letters, words, chunks of words) brought in by the visual system (eyes) are identified, they are held in **short-term memory (STM)** until more of the text is processed. If subsequent ideas fit in with what is in STM and the reader's schemata, rich chunks of meaning (not necessarily the exact words of the text) are moved into **long-term memory (LTM)**, and readers reconstruct the text for themselves. As these complicated interactions occur, readers are said to be "comprehending the text."

Readers have their own goals for interacting with written language. As suggested by Halliday's functions of language (1975), they read for a myriad of purposes, for example, to gain information, to communicate with someone from afar, to be entertained, to be transported into different worlds, to share thoughts, and to learn how to do something. As we saw in our scenarios, readers actively process text for their own specific goals. The experienced readers want to be sure that the text conveys their exact wishes; they want no ambiguity to foil their plans. Duane is entertained by the caterpillar story and takes delight in being able to demonstrate his control over the text to others.

Reading is also strategic and social. Although a natural propensity to learn language is innate, readers are not born. They need to learn strategies for figuring out text, and they can learn these strategies from being in a literate society. They need plenty of experiences in interacting with print—with feedback from mature readers—to learn to use the language cue systems and their own schemata efficiently and effectively. As they predict and confirm their way through text, readers ask themselves and others, "Does this make sense?" "Does it sound like language?" When it doesn't, mature readers go back and reread to see if they've missed something. They may push ahead to see if more information will help, or they may seek help by finding out meanings of specific words or asking others to help. Using these "fix up" strategies is said to be employing **metacognition** or "thinking about thinking" (Garner, 1987).

The will-readers recognized that they were not sure of what their document meant, but they had strategies to help them. They reread and discussed; they read other sources; they asked experts; they planned to have the author explain in language they could understand. Their search for meaning was conducted in various social situations: their own give and take, conversations with experts, and round table discussions with their attorney.

Duane's strategies were much more simple. He used pictures and configuration to predict, and he wanted his mom to confirm his predictions for him. He wasn't satisfied with a hurried oral reading. He read deliberately and carefully, looking sideways at his mom for her reaction after he read each phrase. This was a warm, social literacy event, bonding mother and child in a very special way.

To summarize, reading is an active, purposeful, strategic search for meaning that is based on one's prior knowledge and that is learned and refined in social contexts. Readers construct their meanings using all sources of information found in the text, themselves, and the context in which they read.

Reading and Writing

Recall that in our scenarios, readers wrote in connection with their reading. The will-readers took notes and rewrote parts of their text. In his research on reading-writing relationships, Tierney (1990) found that readers often "rewrite" a text in their minds, if not overtly, as in our scenario. Duane added to his text through his "writing" (drawing pictures). Reading and writing go together naturally, yet, in most of our schools, they are taught separately: reading through published basal readers and writing through language arts textbooks or workbooks.

Although the idea of teaching reading and writing together has been around for a long time, curriculum makers have only recently begun to emphasize the connection. In fact, if this book were being written a decade ago, we would not even be talking about writing as an integral part of reading instruction; for years, writing was the stepchild of the language arts and received little attention in educational research and practice. As we see it, two factors have precipitated this new thrust of seeing reading and writing as related cognitive and sociolinguistic processes: the writing-as-process movement and the comprehension research emanating from the Center for the Study of Reading (Feeley, 1990).

THE WRITING-AS-PROCESS MOVEMENT

Traditionally, we taught writing by assigning topics, correcting papers mainly for spelling and mechanics, and concentrating on a presentable end product. Process was ignored, and often meaning was lost in the pursuit of perfection in form. From the Bay Area Writing Project in California (Camp, 1982) to research emanating from hundreds of writing centers across the country (now called the National Writing Project), we have learned how writers write and how to teach writing. Moffett (1981a) has called the resulting curriculum changes the most positive development in English education since World War II.

The National Writing Project researchers studied writers in action, describing writing as a **recursive process** of prewriting or planning, drafting, reading, revising, and editing. Making and communicating meaning was at the heart of the process. The

implications for teaching were to take the focus off the product and place it on the process. We learned how to teach writing by having students go through the process: writing frequently on self-selected topics with feedback from teachers and peers and learning about content and mechanics from editing selected pieces.

In the 1980s the process approach was introduced in elementary schools through the work of Donald Graves (1983) and Lucy Calkins (1986). Instead of teaching writing through workbook drills and language arts textbooks, they proposed setting up a workshop atmosphere, similar to one used by artists and sculptors learning their craft.

During **writing workshops**, children write on topics of their own choosing and read their pieces to the teacher or peers to get feedback on whether or not their writing makes sense to others. This is called conferencing. Next, they revise, if necessary, and edit with the teacher's help if the writing is going to be "published." Publishing may mean making a bound book, entering a piece in a class anthology, or merely stapling together pages with appropriate illustrations. As they critically examine their own writing and that of others, children begin to see themselves as authors; they say that they like to write and look forward to writing workshop (Feeley, Wahlers, & Jones, 1990). What a far cry from the days when writing was considered "hard" and something young and old alike "blocked" at doing!

The writing process researchers also refocused our attention on how literacy develops naturally, just like oral language (Calkins, 1986; Graves, 1983; Harste, Woodward, & Burke, 1984). Children learn to speak their home language because they are immersed in language in meaningful situations. Adults don't try to teach a sound or word a day; they just model language, give feedback, and celebrate children's early approximations such as *ba-ba* for *bottle* and *peese* for *please*. Yet when it comes to writing, an extension of oral language, we don't expect children to be able to communicate via written symbols until the latter half of first grade! And then we expect them to begin writing in conventional, adult ways!

Now, because of a vast amount of recent research (Bagban, 1984; Bissex, 1980; Calkins, 1986; Clay, 1975, 1985; Dyson, 1983; Ferriero & Teberosky, 1983; Graves, 1981; Harste, Woodward, & Burke, 1984), we know that children can write much earlier. In fact, writing researchers have learned that children go through stages in producing written language just as they go through oral language stages. Figure 1.1 shows the stages of spelling development based on the work of Gentry (1981, 1987) and Temple, Nathan, Burris, and Temple (1988). We have added examples from our own observations of young children. Young children begin by drawing and scribbling and then move to adding a few letters. While Gentry says that scribbling parallels babbling in oral language development and calls this the precommunicative stage, Temple et al. (1988) call the early writing of random letters the prephonemic stage. Children write letters (**graphemes**) but don't associate them with sounds (**phonemes**).

Through informal exposure to print in their environment and being read to, children begin to internalize the **alphabetic principle** that letters and sounds are related and start to write using only consonants. Temple et al. (1988) call this the early phonemic stage and give the following example: "RCRBKDN" = "Our car broke

PREPHONEMIC OR PRECOMMUNICATIVE

- Begins with scribbling, gradually produces shapes that resemble letters
- Copies words such as names and logos of popular stores and fast food places
- Writes random letters, usually all in upper case, in a string
- Has no letter-sound knowledge

Example

Four-year-old Brian says he is writing "a message." He names the symbols, "t, one, o, a, i," but asks his grandmother what it says.

EARLY PHONEMIC OR SEMI-PHONETIC

- Begins to relate letters to sounds
- Uses mainly prominent consonants
- One or more letters may represent an entire word
- Knows most letters
- May or may not understand left to right sequence of letters

Examples

L L L L L B B
A 5-year-old writes these letters as he sings the first line of the song "La Bamba."

I WT TO A KNIVL
In September a first grader writes, " I went to a carnival."

LATER PHONEMIC OR PHONETIC

- Spells words the way they sound (invented spelling)
- Writes all words in the message; now has concept of a word
- Begins to use vowels, although with variable spellings
- Leaves out unheard nasals (*wet* = *went*) and vowels (*pet* = *paint*)
- Uses letter names (*r* = *our* or *are*; *u* = *you*)

Examples

Sinday i thru up five tiem. i had a lieta ov Gengrel.

"Sunday I threw up five times I had a liter of gingerale," wrote a precocious kindergarten child in her June journal.

i Wet to the Ws Pom BCh in flari
"I went to the West Palm Beach in Florida" was written in the journal of a first grader.

FIGURE 1.1
Stages of spelling development

TRANSITIONAL

- Moves from strictly phonological spelling to more standard forms
- Uses many common words learned from reading and spells them conventionally
- Includes most letters but may reverse some
- Partially understands alternate spellings for some phonemes and morphemes
- Uses vowels in all words and syllables

Example

I mite go to the barn to play with Ameliea. I mite ride the Pony Prinses.

Toward the end of first grade, Mandy plans her afternoon in her journal.

CORRECT OR CONVENTIONAL

- Has internalized most of the rules of the English spelling system
- Has mastered many irregular spellings
- Has learned to spell many commonly used words and writes them automatically

---

FIGURE 1.1
(continued)

down." With the accompanying illustration, the message is perfectly understandable. Forester (1980) compares this writing with the **holophrases** children begin to utter around the age of two.

One of us recently had the opportunity to see her two grandsons demonstrate these comparative oral and written stages. Two-year-old Scott has control of the holo-phrase, "Ah ahnt _____ " ("I want _____ "), fleshing out the pivot phrase ("I want") with a growing open class of words representing objects or actions, for example, "Ah ahnt poo" ("I want to go to the pool") and "Ah ahnt passi" ("I want my pacifier"). Simultaneously, his brother Brian, who just turned five, is labeling pictures with *B* for Brian and Bob (his grandfather) and *S* for Scott and Sarah (his cousin), demonstrating that he is moving from the prephonemic random letter stage to early phonemic writing.

Next children move into the later phonemic stage in which vowels begin to appear along with prominent consonants (Chomsky, 1979; Gentry, 1987; Read, 1986; Temple et al., 1988). They begin to "invent" spellings according to their own phonemic rules, for example, *chran* for *train* and *pan* for *pen*. Soon standard spellings are mixed with invented spellings, and children are said to be in a transitional stage. (See writing samples in Figure 1.1.) Spelling tends to become more standard as children go through school, but invented spellings can be found at all levels. When young writers use mainly standard spelling, they are said to be in the correct or conventional stage.

Children will develop control over written language if they are encouraged to write frequently in a workshop atmosphere in which they draw and write about real events in their own lives and read their work to peers in all-group share time (Calkins, 1986; Graves, 1983; Hansen, 1987; Hansen & Graves, 1983; Newkirk, 1989; Routman, 1991). Because it is a grassroots movement that puts teachers and students in control of their language arts program, teaching writing-as-process has taken root in elementary school classrooms from coast to coast.

READING AND WRITING AS RELATED PROCESSES

As the **constructivist view** of reading comprehension, described above in the section on the nature of reading, was developing at the Center for the Study of Reading, interest finally turned to similarities between what readers (comprehenders) and writers (authors) do with written language. Tierney (1990) says that while reading research was languishing in the early 1980s, writing researchers were flourishing but not applying their process model to reading. He and others began to look at writing research to see if it could contribute to a better understanding of reading comprehension. In a benchmark article, "Toward a Composing Model of Reading," Tierney and Pearson (1984) made a major breakthrough by describing both reading and writing as composing processes, making an analogy between the processes that readers and writers go through as they interact with written language: planning, aligning, drafting, revising, and monitoring.

Purpose-setting and knowledge mobilization occur during the planning phase of both reading and writing. Writers select a topic, gather ideas from their schemata, and think about organizing them according to their goals and audience (Scardamelia & Bereiter, 1986). Similarly, readers look at a title, make a prediction about what the piece will be about and how it will be organized, and then activate schemata needed to help them comprehend for their own purposes.

Tierney and Pearson (1984) use the terms *alignment* and *engagement* to refer to visualizing and forming an opinion. Readers and writers identify with what is in a text and align themselves accordingly. Based on their own prior knowledge and feelings, they take a stance and find themselves either agreeing or taking issue with the ideas in a text.

Just as writers begin to draft out their thoughts, readers tentatively skim a text to get the overall picture, often rereading to fill in details if this is necessary. Readers begin to make meaning for themselves with implicit reader-writer negotiations working in both directions. Readers look for implied as well as surface information; writers consider their readers' background knowledge and anticipate questions.

Knowledge of text structure comes into play here. In writing narratives, authors try to use a predictable story structure with such elements as setting, characters, problem, and solution so that their piece will be easy to follow. Readers who have a well-developed schema for stories will mobilize this information as they re-create the plot for themselves. In reading expository writing, readers who have written report-style pieces will try to predict the author's plan to help them process and organize the information (Raphael & Englert, 1989).

Just as writers revise their work upon rereading it, readers often change their interpretations as they progress through a text, rereading to make sense of the ideas within the context of their own prior knowledge and the developing text-world. Fitzgerald (1989) sees a connection between revising in writing and critical reading, saying that both lead to "dissonance location and resolution" (p. 44). In other words, writers and readers spot parts of a text that don't make sense or conflict with what they know or expect, and they work to resolve these issues.

According to Tierney (1990), research is continuing on reading and writing as similar cognitive and **sociolinguistic** processes. From looking at writing as a way to reinforce and aid the teaching of reading, Tierney and others have turned now to how reading and writing might work together to promote learning.

Rationale for Integrating Reading and Writing

Integrating the teaching of reading and writing has several advantages. First, when considering teaching beginners to read and write, it makes good sense to combine the two processes. Since oral language grows in a language-rich environment, it follows that both reading and writing, which are rooted in oral language, will best grow in a literacy-rich environment. New research in **emergent literacy**[1] (Mason & Allen, 1986; Strickland & Morrow, 1989; Teale & Sulzby, 1986) examines how reading and writing (literacy) emerge in the everyday lives of children from their earliest years. Children who have had many meaningful experiences with print such as being read to often and being encouraged to experiment with writing are more ready for school literacy programs than those who have not had such exposure (Mason & Allen, 1986; Morrow, 1989). Emergent literacy research suggests that learning to write complements learning to read.

In addition to relying on the same oral language base, readers and writers both need to gain control over the conventions of written language. They have to internalize the rules of the graphophonic system, learning letter-sound relationships, spelling, and the organization of written language. They need to learn how to use the other language cue systems, syntax and semantics, to help them make meaning in their dealings with print. Squire (1984) calls reading and writing "two sides of the same process" and suggests they should be taught together.

Also, combining reading and writing focuses on the reader-writer relationship. Shanahan (1990) says that this combination fosters a "communicative stance," and

---

[1]Over the past decade, the phrase "reading readiness" has given way to **"emergent literacy."** While reading readiness was thought of as the necessary level of preparation in such skills as alphabet knowledge, word recognition, and visual discrimination that children should attain to get "ready to read," emergent literacy looks at both reading and writing as they are emerging in the everyday lives of children.

May (1990) says it creates "communication partners." Students gain an understanding of authorship and audience simultaneously, learning that reading is not just getting information and writing is not just composing a product; they internalize the true meaning of literacy, the ability to communicate through print. Fitzgerald (1990) calls reading and writing "mind meeting," in which readers' and writers' sentiments (feelings, emotions), knowledge, and skills interact in a dynamic, developing text world.

Since both reading and writing are basic tools for learning, it would seem to be most efficient to teach them together in realistic contexts requiring the use of authentic text. For example, after students have read and discussed a certain **genre** of literature such as fables, they can begin to try to write in that genre (Strickland & Feeley, 1985). When engaged in the study of a historical era, besides reading texts and trade books, they can learn by writing their own reactions and creating original pieces (newspaper accounts, historical fiction, letter exchanges) that can be shared (Pilchman, 1991). (See Chapter 6 for a full description of Pilchman's initiatives.)

The writing-as-process movement demonstrated that writers develop best in social settings in which they can interact with others as they write (Graves, 1983; Calkins, 1986). Other researchers extended the workshop idea to reading, pointing out that readers naturally want to share ideas with others as they read (Atwell, 1987; Hansen, 1987). Readers and writers both gain when they can discuss interpretations, feelings, and insights; Fitzgerald (1989) suggests that readers who have read the same text should be encouraged to hold group conferences to ask the same questions writers do when they confer about their emerging pieces.

Finally, since reading and writing rely on the same cognitive processes, with both readers and writers constructing meaning from their prior knowledge base, we are really enhancing thinking when we teach the two together. With the recent NAEP findings (Mullis & Jenkins, 1990) still confirming that our students can read and write with *surface understanding* but only a small percentage can *reason effectively* about what they read and write, developing higher level thinking skills through our literacy programs emerges as a high priority in the 1990s.

In summary, since reading and writing are related cognitive and sociolinguistic processes that rely on the same knowledge base, they flourish when taught together in literate communities of learners who support each other in their negotiations with authentic written language in realistic situations.

Instructional Implications

Given the research base and resulting rationale for teaching reading and writing together, we now offer instructional implications for the primary and mid-elementary grades.

THE PRIMARY YEARS

Young children come to school knowing a great deal about language. Researchers such as Brown, 1973; Klima and Bellugi-Klima, 1966; McNeil, 1970; Menyuk, 1969; and Templin, 1987, have found that kindergarteners have a vocabulary of several thousand words and that they have internalized the phonology and most of the basic syntax of their language. Also, they know that language is functional, and they use it for their own purposes.

From the emergent literacy research and the work of the early writing researchers cited previously, we now know that children come to school knowing a great deal about written language. They know how to read environmental print and recognize slogans and advertisements for things such as cereals and fast food restaurants because these trademarks are meaningful and useful to them. They are willing to take risks and "pretend read" storybooks to entertain themselves and others, and they write out signs and commands such as "DN T" ("Don't Touch") to prevent a block corner building from becoming dismantled because they know that others attend to printed messages. Because they see adults and older children using print in their everyday lives, young children are interested in and curious about reading and writing. They ask questions such as "What does that say?" and "What did I write?" (Clay, 1975). They experiment with print in play situations such as selling lemonade, playing restaurant, and forming clubs (Taylor, 1983). Readers and writers in their environment provide the necessary feedback as children test out their hypotheses about written language in natural, social interaction.

As for what primary children write about, Manning, Manning, and Hughes (1987) found that first graders write mainly about themselves, their feelings, and their families, pets, and friends. By studying the journals kept by her second graders over a year, Carline (1991) found that while girls continue to write about personal experiences, including family and friends, boys more often chose to write about secondary experiences and material objects. Third graders begin "to test the waters" of "grown-up" writing by composing fiction.

As for the writings of primary children, Calkins (1986) found that first graders begin by writing "all-about" or attribute books, gradually moving toward narratives in which events are chronologically ordered. As second graders move away from "all-about" pieces, their main revision strategy is adding more information. This leads to "bed to bed" stories which include everything that is remembered with all events being given equal weight. Third graders often seem preoccupied with conventions and correctness, and they enjoy showing what they know, such as using special punctuation marks profusely (Calkins, 1986). Writing can become more focused by grade three, especially when children are encouraged to conference about pieces with teachers and peers and when they have been exposed to good literature.

When it comes to reading, Bussis, Chittenden, Amarel, and Klausner (1985), who studied the reading development of 26 children from kindergarten to grade two, found that all their subjects began school with some knowledge of letter-sound correspondences, a small sight vocabulary, a belief that reading had to make sense, and their own preferred learning styles. Although exposed to diverse reading programs, all had teachers who read to them daily, provided a large selection of trade books with time to read, and encouraged writing frequently. By the end of grade two, these students learned to orchestrate their various knowledge bases (language cue systems and schemata) to construct meaning from text to varying degrees.

As readers, third graders can usually integrate all the cue systems (semantic, syntactic, graphophonic, and schematic) to make meaning for themselves. Cochrane, Cochrane, Scalena, and Buchanan (1984) say that these students like to read orally for others and silently for their own pleasure and information. If they have had wide exposure to many kinds of texts and book reading, they will know the difference between expository and narrative structures and will make use of this information when they read.

In looking at what primary children like to read, we see the same egocentricity found in their writing. They like stories about children their own age and families and animals, but they also enjoy fairy tales, folktales, humor, and modern fantasy (Feeley, 1981). Martinez and Teale (1988) studied kindergarteners' use of a classroom library and found they most frequently selected familiar books with predictable texts, reflecting the above genres. In their work Bussis et al. (1985) also found that young children read nonfiction to meet special interests or school assignments. Every child in their sample elected to read some informational books on such wide-ranging topics as exploring space, making puppets, and caring for animals.

Since they come from a print-rich world in which they are learning to read and write naturally, young children should have primary programs that build on their emerging literacy. The following recommendations for literacy programs in the primary grades are based on our own observations and models suggested by Harste, Woodward, and Burke (1984), Mason and Au (1990), McGee and Richgels (1990), and Schwartz (1988).

A LITERACY-RICH ENVIRONMENT

This means a class library filled with appropriate children's literature; songs, poems, and chants in bold manuscript displayed around the room; language experience stories (group-composed text) and notices or rules on charts for all to read; and prominent reading, listening, and writing centers to invite children to interact with written language. Literacy routines such as reading to children and writing with them should be an integral part of the school day.

HYPOTHESIS TESTING

Children should be given many opportunities to test out their hypotheses about the conventions of written language in a risk-free environment. Smith, Goodman, and Meredith (1976) say that children in the primary years are between the stages Piaget calls "intuitive" and "concrete operations" and need interactive experiences with print. Tumner, Herriman, and Nesdale (1988) found that children's ability to acquire **metalinguistic awareness** (ability to talk about the conventions of print) depends on their operativity, or level of **concrete operational thought**.

Teachers should encourage children to write and accept their invented spellings as being intentional and communicative. Shanahan (1990) says that working through invented spellings helps children to internalize phoneme-grapheme relationships. "Big books" with enlarged print that all can see, which are read together several times before children read them to themselves, are another example of an activity that encourages hypothesis-testing about print conventions (Holdaway, 1979). Language experience activities (Hall, 1981; Stauffer, 1980), in which teachers write down what children dictate and have them read it back, also promote internalization of the forms of written language. Lastly, uninterrupted reading and writing time provides children with opportunities to learn about print at their own pace.

SOCIAL INTERACTION

There should be opportunities for children to interact with each other in social settings as they learn to read and write. The workshop approach (Calkins, 1986; Graves, 1983) described earlier is ideal for encouraging interaction as children share their topics, drafts, and finished pieces with each other and their teacher. Peer conferences and **all-group sharing** time provide real situations for children to become sensitive to the reader-writer relationship; they learn that they must engage their readers and give adequate information if they want to communicate with others via writing. Also, they learn to become good listeners and sympathetic critics of other children's writings; author-audience give-and-take promotes what Shanahan (1990) calls "the communicative stance."

FUNCTIONAL USES

Literacy programs for young children should focus on purposeful, functional uses of written language. Ellermeyer (1988) says such programs should broaden each child's experiential background; as the conceptual base grows, so will the vocabulary for reading and writing, which are tools for getting things done in real life. In the primary grades this often translates into thematic units in which children learn about their world and grow as readers and writers simultaneously. For example, O'Brochta and Weaver (1991) report a theme study for first graders on "Me, Myself, and I." The children learned social studies by interviewing parents and grandparents to find out how life was when they were 6 years old. Places where their family lived or visited were marked on a map of the United States. Their teacher read books such as *Nobody Asked Me If I Wanted a Baby Sister* (Alexander, 1970) and *Alexander and the Terrible, Horrible, No Good, Very Bad Day* (Viorst, 1972). The class then developed charts, recorded by the teacher, on their fears and worries and what makes a good day or a bad day. Children wrote books on "My Family" and "What I Can Do." Class-made big books were developed on topics such as "When I was a baby I _____ , now I _____ ." To learn math, the class made graphs about such things as the number of people in their families, times they go to bed, how much they weigh, and how they come to school. The teacher read books such as *Happy Birthday, Sam* (Hutchins, 1978), *You'll Soon Grow into Them, Titch* (Hutchins, 1983), *Only Six More Days* (Russo, 1988), and *Me and My Family Tree* (Showers, 1978). The theme approach provides for schema forming and reforming as children learn new concepts and clarify existing concepts that are meaningful to them. (See also, "Grade 1: Teaching with Themes" in Chapter 4.)

McGee and Richgels (1990) also recommend author and genre studies so that young children can begin to internalize literary concepts such as author, style, and types of literature. One second grade teacher we know always starts off the year with a study of Tomie De Paola's picture books. Besides learning to appreciate his wonderful illustrations and engaging texts, the children learn about the folktale genre in which he so often chooses to write. In situations like these, reading, writing, and learning develop together in functional settings.

SKILLS IN CONTEXT

Making meaning should be at the center of all language activities: skills should be taught within the context of real reading and writing tasks rather than through isolated workbook and worksheet activities. The latter, such as a page on the phoneme *b* or the suffix *ed,* are not meaningful, realistic uses of written language; they are what Frank Smith (1985) calls "nonsense" and what the authors of *Becoming a Nation of*

Readers (Anderson, Hiebert, Scott, & Wilkinson, 1985) say are too often the main reading and writing tasks primary children are asked to perform every day. It would make much more sense to highlight *b* in a known nursery rhyme such as "Little Boy Blue" and to find verbs ending in *ed* in a big book so that children could see the effect that the past tense marker has on the story.

We know a third grade teacher who does an author study of William Steig. Through his engaging picture books, students learn the important strategy of using context to figure out unknown words. (See "Grade 3: Connecting Reading and Writing" in Chapter 4.) Young children, as well as most of us, learn skills best when they go from the whole to the part and when they deal with them in meaningful text.

MODELING

Through all the shared reading opportunities in a school day, such as reading aloud a piece of literature or reading a big book or poem with the children, teachers should model the prediction-confirmation strategies that mature readers use automatically. Children should be encouraged to predict from the title, illustrations, and developing text; all reasonable predictions can be accepted at the start but only those that are confirmed by the unfolding text are kept. Strategies such as using the context, looking back, pushing on, or looking outside the text for help should be modeled so they can be readily internalized.

Teachers can also model writing throughout the day by such activities as manu-scripting the day's news, group-composed stories, and records of daily routines. When children write in workshop settings, teachers should write with them, sharing journal entries and pieces in progress just as the children do.

When the dynamic, constructive processes of reading and writing are taught to-gether all day long through such activities as those just described, young children will learn to read, write, and think naturally by engaging in these processes by themselves and with others in authentic social contexts.

THE MID-ELEMENTARY GRADES

By the time children reach the mid-elementary grades, they demonstrate growing control over the mechanics of written language. Because third grade writers are preoc-cupied with "getting everything right," they often have trouble with revision. Since their thinking is now what Piaget calls "concrete operational," they put down every-thing they know and often revise by copying over without changes. Lacking a central executive function that allows one to shuttle back and forth between writing, reading, and speaking (Bereiter & Scardamalia, 1982), they find it difficult to make real changes in their pieces in response to their own rereading or questions raised by peers during conferences.

On the other hand, usually from grade four on, children can reread and revise, especially if they are encouraged to conference with others. Soon they are able to "hold their own internal conferences," reflecting Vygotsky's (1962) "zone of proximal learning" theory which posits that what children can do today with others, they can do tomorrow alone. More and more, writing becomes thinking and rethinking.

By grades five and six, children begin to view their writing through the eyes of a reader, going back and forth from writing to reading what they have written. They move away from writing personal narrative and learn to express themselves in a variety of genres and a variety of voices, using their craft of writing to please an audience.

As they move through school, children's ability to comprehend is limited only by their prior knowledge (schema theory) in general and their knowledge of text structures specifically (Mason & Au, 1990). Their rapidly developing schemata help children to make inferences, summarize, remember, add new knowledge, and make decisions about what is important in a text (McNeil, 1987). Children in the mid-elementary grades are active readers who can ask questions as they read rather than read just to answer the questions found in textbooks (Palinscar & Brown, 1984; Singer, 1978; Stauffer, 1975). Besides being active, questioning readers, they are strategic readers. Since metacognition, the ability to think about thinking, begins to develop at this time, they can begin to monitor their understanding of what they read and develop increasingly more sophisticated mental strategies to help them comprehend and learn through text.

As for reading interests, strong sex differences emerge by grade four, with girls choosing fiction (social empathy, fantasy, and mystery-adventure) more than do boys. While they enjoy science fiction, boys show more preference for nonfiction than do girls. Also, boys often choose nonfiction categories such as biography, sports, history, and science (Feeley, 1981; Graham, 1986; Wolfson, Manning & Manning, 1984).

Burgess (1985) found that elementary school children from grade four up selected books by appearance, author, and recommendations of peers, parents, and librarians. Unfortunately, teachers were not viewed as resources for recreational reading. Interestingly, both boys and girls were choosing more nonfiction, especially a technology category that included books about computers. All children in this ChildRead survey reported having at least one favorite book that they had read several times.

With the active, inquisitive, thoughtful, and increasingly more competent language users who are from 8 to 12 years old in mind, we offer the following instructional recommendations based on those of Strickland and Feeley (1991):

WORKSHOP APPROACH

Reading and writing should continue to be taught through a **workshop approach** that supports the social aspect of literacy and encourages attention to the reader-writer relationship (Calkins, 1986; Graves, 1983; Hansen, 1987). The conference aspect, in which others provide the external executive function needed by children still mainly in the concrete operational stage, works well for both reading and writing. Allowing for some choice in selecting books and topics provides for the sex differences that can be noted at this time. And, of course, children need a wide selection of literature from which to choose.

SCHEMA ACTIVATION

Schema activation before reading and writing should be encouraged so that students make good use of their prior knowledge in constructing meaning. Langer (1984) developed a Pre-Reading Plan (PREP) to tap students' text-specific background knowledge before reading and found that the process significantly improved their comprehension. McNeil (1987) suggests that background-generating and organizing activities such as semantic mapping, webbing, and brainstorming can significantly aid both readers and writers.

VOCABULARY IN CONTEXT

Students' vocabulary should be expanded within the context of real reading and writing. Nagy, Anderson, and Herman (1987) found that beginning about third grade, the major determining factor to vocabulary growth is the amount of free reading. Students learn rapidly, at the rate of 3,000 words a year; however, the amount of vocabulary learned depends on the quantity of written language a student is exposed to, the quality of the text, and the student's ability to remember the meanings when encountered again. Nagy, Herman, and Anderson say the most effective way to increase vocabulary is to have students read a great many books of high literary quality, whether fiction or nonfiction.

For developing vocabulary among third and fifth graders, Gipe (1978–79) found that an interactive context method was superior to most other conventional methods such as looking up the definitions of lists of words in a dictionary. In an interactive context method, students read a short passage in which a target word is used in a defining context a few times. After reading the passage, students write a phrase or word from their own experiences that defines the word for them. (See Chapter 2 for an example.)

TEXT STRUCTURE

Teachers should give increasing attention to expanding students' knowledge about text structures. Langer (1986) found that while 8-year-olds understood exposition when reading, they tended to use mainly description/collections, dominated by a title, when they wrote reports. She suggests starting with what they know and then moving on to other rhetorical structures. For example, after writing separate reports on English horseback riding and Western riding, students could compare the two in a new piece.

In fact, we recently encountered a third grade teacher who did just this. First, her students wrote expository reports on endangered animals of their choosing. Then, after reading aloud *Amos and Boris* (Steig, 1971), a narrative about a mouse and a whale who become friends and help each other out of life-threatening situations, she had the students write animal fiction tales about two of the endangered animals they had researched. From the factual information they had collected, they chose two very different animals to create characters who would become friends in a narrative piece. (See "Grade 3: Connecting Reading and Writing" in Chapter 4.)

METACOMPREHENSION STRATEGIES

Students in the mid-elementary grades, who are naturally developing metacognitive abilities, should be encouraged to monitor their attempts at constructing meaning. Paris, Cross, and Lipson (1984) successfully taught third and fifth graders to monitor their reading through a program called Informed Strategies for Learning (ISL). In the ISL program, teachers directly provide information about reading strategies. First students are engaged in activities that lead to the realization that the goal of reading is to construct meaning and to make connections between the text and their prior knowledge. Then students are taught to analyze a task before reading by asking three questions: What kind of reading is this? Why am I reading this? Is it easy or hard to read? They are also taught such strategies as formulating a reading plan, figuring out unknown words from context, paraphrasing, and monitoring their understanding as they progress through the text. Becoming significantly more aware of reading strategies and ways to improve their performance on reading tests, these students learned to plan, evaluate, and regulate their own comprehension.

Stevens, Madden, Slavin, and Farnish (1987) taught third and fourth graders similar metacomprehension activities for reading in a cooperative learning environment. When writing, students used a process or workshop approach with peer and teacher conferences that encouraged the monitoring of emerging pieces. Finding that their program, called Cooperative Integrated Reading and Composition (CIRC), had very real effects on several measures of literacy achievement, Stevens et al. (1987) concluded that a cooperative learning program that was augmented by direct instruction in metacomprehension strategies could significantly increase student achievement in reading and writing.

ACROSS THE CURRICULUM

Since reading and writing are both tools for learning, they should be emphasized across the curriculum to enhance learning in the content areas. Langer (1986) found that students were more able to talk about what strategies they had used and how their knowledge had changed after reading *and* writing than after just reading. She says that writing seems to be useful in helping students gain a real understanding of subject matter.

In *Coming to Know: Writing to Learn in the Intermediate Grades,* Nancie Atwell (1990) shares the experiences of a group of teachers whose students approached reading and writing through many avenues. The students collected information by reading, conducting interviews, and setting up experiments; they reported their findings in a variety of written ways such as novels, biographies, letters, articles, reports, and documentaries. Some teachers used learning logs, notebooks for each subject area in which students did focused writing for no more than 10 minutes a day. Students were encouraged to think in special ways about what they were learning in math, literature, social studies, and science. Atwell says that when reading and writing workshop approaches come to the content areas, the day becomes a "learning workshop" in which reading and writing and world knowledge are learned together.

After offering instructional implications that flow naturally from current research in reading and writing instruction, we now turn to the kinds of literacy materials generally found in schools.

The Role of Basals, Literature, and Other Print

Children in American schools learn to read through a wide variety of materials. By far, the most frequently encountered materials are published basal reading series. Also found are children's books in various formats such as "big books" with accompanying small book copies and libraries of soft and hard bound selections from the world of children's literature. Besides these two readily identifiable staples, there are a host of other printed materials from which children learn to read and write, either directly or indirectly, such as workbooks, kits, newspapers, magazines, content area texts, and computer programs. Let's take a look at these sources to see how they fit in with the dynamic, emerging model of literacy learning that we have been describing in this chapter.

BASAL READING PROGRAMS

Most of us remember learning to read through one of the basal reading programs produced by well-recognized publishers such as Scott-Foresman, Ginn, and Houghton-Mifflin. As students we had a reading textbook (called a reader) and an accompanying workbook with related skill lessons. As we went through the grades, we noticed that the workbooks disappeared and the readers became more like anthologies of fact and fiction pieces; we read the "stories" and wrote answers to the questions at the end of each of them. Other than a bi-monthly composition on a teacher-assigned topic, writing was used mainly to report what we had read and to show what we had learned (Moffett, 1981b). The teacher functioned as Examiner and Grammarian in responding to what we wrote (Daniels, 1990). We need to examine the effectiveness of this mainstay for teaching literacy since the majority of American schools still use basals, more or less as prescribed by the manuals.

WHY ARE BASALS SO POPULAR?

For the most part, basals are popular because many teachers and administrators like them. Teachers who don't fully understand the nature of literacy and literacy learning and don't feel secure about teaching children to read and write like the structure of a ready-made system. Duffy and Roehler (1989) say that teachers like a basal because "It tells them what to do and say, puts materials into students' hands to keep them busy, and provides tests to determine whether progress is being made" (p. 13). If the children don't learn, the blame can be put on the program or the children, not on the teacher who has diligently had them complete all the activities.

Administrators like basals because they appear to provide an organized, sequential curriculum for reading instruction through the grades. (It should be noted that the sequence often differs from publisher to publisher because it is not research-based but rather is decided by the publishers' senior authors and staff; our research that is reported in the next chapter bears this out.) Because of the heavily scripted nature of the manuals, administrators believe that teaching will be uniform among teachers, with beginners performing as well as seasoned instructors. Administrators readily admit to preferring "teacher-proof" materials. Also, the unit and level tests supply them with an on-going evaluation of achievement that they can report to parents. In fact, many school districts use students' performance on basal reader level tests as a major criterion for promotion!

Being able to read the basals and perform on their tests (which often focus mainly on lower level skills which can be easily tested with paper and pencil exercises) is being equated with being literate. All too often nobody asks if children can read books, magazines, newspapers, and other forms of print for a variety of purposes; nobody asks if children enjoy reading from basals or, for that matter, if children like to read at all.

Basals are popular because they make management and accountability easier for both teachers and administrators. But strict reliance on basals may not be what is best for children.

Do Basals Have a Place in Reading Instruction?

After considering some of the utilitarian reasons for using basals, you may ask if they have a place in schools at all. Practically speaking, the answer would have to be a qualified "yes." Basal materials are a fact of life in most schools and can be used in a total reading program as long as teachers are in control and not the authors of the ubiquitous teacher's manuals.

Teachers must be selective in what they offer their students to read. They must not be made to feel that they have to use every selection, with all the accompanying skill pages, in the order presented, or their students will fail. We are reminded of a pre-primer selection in a current basal that refers to a "bulldozer" (which is prominently featured in the pictures) as "it" in an obvious attempt to keep the readability (difficulty level) of the passage low. Children who read this story commented, "Why didn't the page say *bulldozer*? We had to look at the picture to see what *it* was." In this case, *bulldozer*, with its recognizable configuration and the surrounding context would have been easier to read than the placeholder *it*. Stories with stilted language like this are best skipped.

Current basals contain many fine selections from children's literature that can be used for group lessons to develop concepts such as genre, mood, or point of view. Rather than have students read to answer comprehension questions, teachers could have them discuss their interpretations in small groups, becoming an "interpretive community," a group of readers who come together to reach a consensus on meaning (Fish, 1980). In this way students can construct their own "stories" and compare them with those of their peers. During these exchanges teachers can highlight the literary concept to be taught. For instance, if the focus is on a particular genre such as animal fantasy, the teacher can point out significant elements such as animals who talk and behave like people; other important animal fiction titles can be shared and students can be encouraged to read self-selected books in the genre.

This approach is sometimes called "going in and out of the basal" because teachers do just that: they may start with a basal selection for a focus lesson, then have students read from a variety of related tradebooks as suggested above. Thus, the teacher has everyone in the group read the same passage for the focus lesson, but students have a choice after that. Also, the teacher may ask students to choose to read only one of the three or four selections in a particular unit in a basal. Students who chose the same stories can then discuss them in small groups, to be followed by all-class sharing of the unit, which usually has an identifiable theme.

Teachers who find that workbooks have been ordered for them can use the exercises selectively; students should do only those that are related to their specific needs. For example, if a page is on the differences between *their, there,* and *they're,* only children who consistently misspell or use them incorrectly should do the practice page; other students could spend this time doing further reading or writing in response journals.

Teachers can use some workbook pages with all students to prepare them for test-taking. Rather than working alone, students can work collaboratively in pairs or small groups to do selected skill pages as a problem-solving activity. Together they can test hypotheses, come to consensus, and get accustomed to this special genre, "reading test reading" (Reardon, 1990).

If their school system permits, teachers can choose to skip the workbooks, instead using their budget allotments to buy supplements that have durability and wider applicability, for example, big books and laminated poem charts in the primary grades and libraries of trade books in the middle grades. Teachers should be making decisions about what components to order and use and about which suggestions in the manuals make sense for them and their students. To make informed decisions they need to be well versed in the nature of literacy learning and teaching and about how to make practical applications in their own classrooms. This comes through college course work, in-service programs, conferences and workshops, professional reading, and continual experimentation.

Teachers and administrators must think of reading and writing more broadly, not as subjects to be taught via one set of materials, but as related processes to be nurtured in literacy-rich environments where there is choice, interaction, and response. In Chapter 2 we will take a closer look at basals and share our research on the content of seven current basal series.

LITERATURE-BASED PROGRAMS

Teaching reading and writing without published instructional materials such as basals is not new. Several notable trends in the recent past led to less structured, informal approaches. Sylvia Ashton-Warner (1964), a British educator who worked with the Maoris of New Zealand, taught them to read by writing down their most intensely personal words for them to read back. Gradually, these important "key" words were woven into sentences and became their first reading materials.

Other teacher-researchers of that time (Lee & Allen, 1963; Stauffer, 1980; Veatch, Sawicki, Elliott, Barnette, & Blakey, 1973) espoused Ashton-Warner's approach and developed it further into the **Language Experience Approach** (LEA) we know today. LEA works like this: After having engaged in a real experience, such as taking a trip, baking cookies, or welcoming a new turtle to their terrarium, children dictate their own "stories" about the event. Acting as scribe, the teacher writes down what the children say, usually on chart paper; the children then read back the text many times, both as a group and individually. Eventually, these experience stories are duplicated and made into little booklets. In effect, the children compose their first learning-to-read books.

Veatch (1978) proposed moving from LEA stories to easy trade books once children had mastered the basics. In this approach, called "Individualized Reading," children picked their own books from a selection of appropriate picture books and read them at their own pace. Teachers monitored reading by holding individual conferences during which children read orally and told about the content; also, children usually engaged in various language arts activities based on the books read. During this era teachers often combined LEA, individualized reading of literature, and basal readers to offer what was called an eclectic approach.

All this ended rather abruptly as the back-to-basics movement of behavioral objectives that fractured reading into hundreds of subskills took hold in the 1970s; published, prescriptive materials pushed literature into a supplementary role (Feeley, 1975). Children were tested and moved through worksheets and skill books until they reached "mastery level" on a host of discrete, testable skills such as phonics and syllabication rules. There was no time to read books; teachers felt fortunate to be able to engage children in whatever stories and nonfiction passages that the basals offered.

As cited earlier, the writing-as-process movement surfaced during the 1980s and brought teachers and children rather than skills and tests back to the forefront. When teachers found that they could teach writing by establishing writing workshops in which children learned to write by writing frequently and going through the conferencing, revising, and editing process, they soon became disenchanted with their basal programs. Teachers wanted children to become just as excited about reading as they were about writing. The next step for most is to apply the writing process approach to reading; teachers who have been reading children's literature to and with their students in writing workshop now want to use real books in their reading programs.

In the late 1980s California led the way for change when its legislature adopted the California Initiative, establishing a literature-based reading curriculum that is integrated with the teaching of writing, speaking, and listening (Honig, 1988). California schools are now mandated to reduce the use of workbooks and dittos and to increase the use of trade books from a recommended list of children's literature.

Teachers in California and across the nation who have been experimenting with writing workshop are moving toward using trade books exclusively or along with basals so that their students will have reading experiences similar to their writing process experiences, that is, some *choice* in selecting what to read, *conferences* on what they are reading, an emphasis on personal *response,* and a sense of *community* in learning (Hansen, 1987). What is emerging is a literature-based curriculum similar in some ways, yet different, from the **Individualized Reading** of the 1960s.

Today, literature-based reading programs usually begin in the primary grades with children and teacher engaging in shared reading activities (Holdaway, 1979). Together they read big books, poems, songs, and nursery rhymes as the teacher leads and points to the text. Soon beginners can read these familiar, predictable texts by themselves, "almost magically," according to one kindergarten teacher we interviewed. At the same time that they are involved in these shared reading activities, children are encouraged to write personal narratives and responses to their literature experiences, thus learning to read and write simultaneously. While LEA is still a part of the shared reading menu, it is not the major thrust of the beginning reading program.

From shared reading, children move on to reading books, with some self-selection being encouraged. They may start with small book versions of familiar big books and appropriate picture books that supply rich context clues in their illustrations. Besides these individually read books, small groups may read the same book so that they can discuss, compare interpretations, and read orally to one another. They may read books by the same author, for example, Frank Asch, in the primary grades and Roald Dahl in the middle grades. In an author study children compare and contrast characters, themes, and writing style, getting to know one author in-depth. Often students write to authors to learn more about them as people and as practitioners of a craft.

In the mid-elementary grades students continue reading both self-selected and assigned books in small and large groups. They learn about the writer's craft as they discuss such elements as leads, the use of dialogue, and plot development; in turn, they use these new insights as they write in their writing workshops. Besides author studies, they engage in genre studies; for example, in a fourth grade class children read several classical folktales as their teacher read to them a modern folktale, *Fantastic Mr. Fox* (Dahl, 1970). This led naturally to the children's writing folktales, including elements such as animals talking, an obvious villain or hero, repeated phrases, and a series of three events to develop the plot. Through listening to and reading many examples, they had internalized elements of the genre.

Teachers who have begun to use literature as the staple of their reading program tend to focus on literary conventions, for example, point of view and voice. Students ask implicit questions such as, "Who is telling this story and from which point of view?" One fifth grade group heard the old favorite *The Three Little Pigs* told from two very different points of view: the third pig's, told in the traditional way, and the wolf's, told in an amiable, "tough guy's" voice in *The True Story of the Three Little Pigs* (Scieszka, 1989). Then they wrote their own retold tales from varying points of view, for example, *Cinderella* as told by the stepmother or one of her daughters and *The Three Bears* as told by Papa Bear from his point of view. Scieszka has written another retold tale, *The Frog Prince Continued* (1991), which is a parody of some real marriages beset by nagging and bickering. The prince tries to get out of the marriage by becoming a frog again; actually, both turn into frogs and live happily ever after.

In literature-based reading programs, teachers and children grow into a community of learners and view themselves as readers and writers. In his provocative essay *The Scribal Society* (1990), Alan Purves says that for too long schools have been turning out consumers of print that is produced by a diminishing, elite group of scribes. It appears that chidren who are being nurtured in literature-based, process-oriented reading-writing classrooms are being groomed for entrance into the Scribal Society. In Chapters 3 and 4 we will share ways that teachers are integrating literature into their literacy programs.

OTHER MATERIALS FROM WHICH CHILDREN LEARN TO READ

Children in American schools learn to read from many other printed materials found in classrooms besides basal readers and children's literature. Depending on the teacher's or school district's philosophies, workbooks for teaching areas such as phonics, spelling, grammar, and handwriting may be found. Often these are used *in addition to* basals and literature. Again, teachers and administrators who are insecure about literacy learning and teaching tend to rely on more published materials to ensure that skills are emphasized. The quality of these materials varies, and purchasing them should raise serious questions since much of their content can be taught through an integrated language arts approach. Phonics can be learned within the context of reading beginning basals and big books; spelling, grammar, and handwriting can be learned as tools needed by writers working in a workshop setting.

Many types of kits and skill materials devoted to "teaching reading comprehension" are also used in schools. Leveled by color or letters, these materials present short, decontextualized passages that children read and then answer questions about, usually in multiple-choice format. Again, while these sources may be useful in preparing students for taking standardized tests, they are no substitute for reading and responding to real books.

Most schools order newspapers and magazines for their students to read. Newspapers published for children such as *The Weekly Reader* present current, nonfiction content in tabloid form, giving children real-world print to read and discuss. Children's magazines such as *Ranger Rick, Highlights for Children,* and *Cricket* may be seen in school libraries or found circulating among classrooms. Again, these represent examples of authentic reading matter found in real life.

While not necessarily thought of as literacy materials, all textbooks used in the content areas are sources of print from which children learn to read indirectly. When math problems are read and reviewed, children and teachers are practicing a very concentrated type of reading for details and problem solving. When social studies and science books are used for unit work, children are exposed to tight, specialized, factual writing that requires knowledge activation and careful monitoring. Teachers need to know how to use textbooks with their students if they want them to comprehend and learn from these experiences. Also, teachers who decide to take Nancie Atwell's advice and teach the content areas using trade books and many reading and writing activities other than textbooks may choose to augment textbooks with a wide variety of books such as historical fiction, drama, science logs, biography and other nonfiction genres. In Chapter 6 we will show examples of how teachers integrate literature and writing into the content areas.

Computers are now common in the workplace and in schools; they are used mainly as tools and tutors and require much reading of text both on and off screen. As tutors, computers can drill the same skill areas addressed by workbooks but have the advantage of being nonconsumable. As tools, they are unmatched when it comes to writing and the storing and retrieving of data. Even young children can learn to use simple word processing programs and write without the physical effort that goes into paper and pencil construction. Students who master commonly found word processing programs gain great control over their writing. They can revise easily, correcting spelling and punctuation and moving blocks of text around at the stroke of a few keys.

Databases of information on social studies and science topics are available and can be accessed with a few commands. Students and teachers can create databases, for example, a listing of all the trade books in their class library with spaces for readers to enter comments. Classroom uses of the computer as a tool are almost limitless. Children become better readers and writers as they work with written language on and off the screen, especially when they read accompanying materials and write in response to computer-generated experiences. In Chapter 5 we offer many suggestions for how teachers can use technology to promote reading, writing, and learning.

Concluding Remarks

Since both reading and writing are dynamic, active, purposeful, and strategic meaning-making processes that are based on one's world knowledge and fostered in supportive social contexts, it makes sense that they be learned and taught together in rich literacy environments by teachers who are well grounded in theory and practice. Frank Smith (1985) says that children learn to read from people, not from materials. Whether they use basals, literature, or other forms of written language (and more likely a combination of all three) to build this literacy-rich environment, teachers are the key to successful reading and writing programs: teachers who know children, who know children's literature and instructional materials, who know the dynamics of literacy learning and teaching, and who can orchestrate all this knowledge into an exciting, vibrant, literacy program that invites children to want to be lifetime—not sometime—readers and writers and potential members of the Scribal Society.

Questions for Discussion

1. What do we mean when we say that readers use several cue systems when they read?
2. How has the writing-as-process movement affected the teaching of reading and writing?
3. Why does it seem natural that reading and writing be taught together?
4. How can basals and literature be used together in a reading program?
5. How can we get teachers more actively involved in children's literature so that they will use trade books more in their literacy programs?

Application Activities

1. Observe a beginning reader (a 5- or 6-year-old) as you read a favorite picture book together. What parts does the child want to read aloud? What cue systems come into play? What do you want to do naturally when you're finished? Talk about the story? Write or draw in response? Write a report on this literacy event by describing the child, the book, the setting, and answering the questions posed here.
2. Visit a kindergarten or first grade to observe how beginning reading and writing are being taught. Use the recommendations for primary programs offered in this chapter as guidelines to look for when you visit. Compare your findings with the six recommendations and decide whether this teacher is providing a well-balanced program. What suggestions for improvement would you offer?
3. Spend a day in a mid-elementary classroom to observe the breadth of the literacy program. Take notes on what occurs during the reading/language arts period. What books and materials are the children using? What do they do after reading and writing? How are reading and writing activities handled during other periods like social studies and math? Compare your notes with the suggestions offered in this chapter for mid-elementary programs. How does the classroom stand up to these guidelines? What recommendations can you make?
4. Inspect a complete basal reading system for one grade level. Use the teacher's manual and all recommended components such as pupil edition, workbook pages, skill sheets, and supplementary materials to write a plan for using one story with a group of children. How long do you think it will take you? What did you think of the story? What activities did you like best? least? What suggestions would you make for using basals?
5. Pick a piece of children's literature, for example, *Where the Wild Things Are* (Sendak, 1963) for beginners or *Stone Fox* (Gardiner, 1980) for older children, and read it with a group. (If you don't have multiple copies, read the book to them.) Plan some post-reading activities that will be appropriate for the children and the book. What reading and literacy skills are they learning? Report how the session went and share any writing or drawing that results from it. How did you feel about your experience? What recommendations would you offer teachers?

References

Anderson, R. C., Hiebert, E. H., Scott, J. A., & Wilkinson, I. A. G. (1985). *Becoming a nation of readers: The report of the Commission on Reading.* Champaign, IL: The National Academy of Education, The National Institute of Education, The Center for the Study of Reading.

Anderson, R. C., & Pearson, P. D. (1984). A schema theoretic view of basic processes in reading. In P. D. Pearson (Ed.), *Handbook of reading research* (pp. 255–291). New York: Longman.

Ashton-Warner, S. (1964). *Teacher.* New York: Simon & Schuster.

Atwell, N. (1987). *In the middle: Reading, writing, and learning with adolescents.* Portsmouth, NH: Heinemann.

Atwell, N. (1990). *Coming to know: Writing to learn in the intermediate grades.* Portsmouth, NH: Heinemann.

Bagban, M. (1984). *Our daughter learns to read and write: A case study from birth to three.* Newark, DE: International Reading Association.

Bereiter, C., & Scardamalia, M. (1982). From conversation to composition: The role of instruction in a developmental process. In R. Glaser (Ed.), *Advances in instructional psychology* (Vol. 2, pp. 1–64). Hillsdale, NJ: Erlbaum.

Bissex, G. L. (1980). *GYNS at WRK: A child learns to read and write.* Cambridge, MA: Harvard University Press.

Brown, R. (1973). *A first language: The early stages.* Cambridge, MA: Harvard University Press.

Burgess, S. A. (1985). Reading but not literate: The ChildRead survey. *School Library Journal, 31,* 27–30.

Bussis, A. M., Chittenden, E. A., Amarel, M., & Klausner, E. (1985). *Inquiry into meaning: An investigation of learning to read.* Hillsdale, NJ: Erlbaum.

Calkins, L. (1986). *The art of teaching writing.* Portsmouth, NH: Heinemann.

Camp, G. (1982). *Teaching writing: Essays from the Bay Area writing project.* Portsmouth, NH: Heinemann.

Carline, A. (1991). *The effectiveness of daily journals as vehicles for writing assessment.* Unpublished master's project. William Paterson College, Wayne, NJ.

Chomsky, C. (1979). Approaching reading through invented spelling. In L. B. Resnick, & P. A. Weaver (Eds.), *Theory and practice of early reading* (pp. 43–65). Hillsdale, NJ: Erlbaum.

Clay, M. (1975). *What did I write?* Portsmouth, NH: Heinemann.

Clay, M. (1985). *The early detection of reading difficulties.* Portsmouth, NH: Heinemann.

Cochrane, O., Cochrane, D., Scalena, S., & Buchanan, E. (1984). *Reading, writing, and caring.* Katonah, NY: Richard C. Owens.

Cunningham, P. M. (1975–76). Investigating a synthesized theory of mediated word identification. *Reading Research Quarterly, 11,* 127-143.

Daniels, H. (1990). *Young writers and readers reach out: Developing a sense of audience.* In T. Shanahan (Ed.), *Reading and writing together: New perspectives for the classroom* (pp. 99–124). Norwood, MA: Christopher-Gordon.

Duffy, G. G., & Roehler, L. R. (1989). *Improving classroom reading: A decision making approach.* New York: Random House.

Dyson, A. H. (1983). The role of oral language in early writing processes. *Research in the teaching of English, 17* (1), 1–30.

Ellermeyer, D. (1988). A kindergarten reading program to grow on. *The Reading Teacher, 41,* 402–405.

Feeley, J. T. (1975, May). A critical look at reading management systems. *NJEA Review, 48,* 17–18.

Feeley, J. T. (1981). What do our children like to read? *NJEA Review, 54* (8), 26–27.

Feeley, J. T. (April, 1990). *The reading teacher as integrator of reading and writing processes.* Paper presented at International Reading Association Symposium, George Washington University, Washington, DC.

Feeley, J. T., Wahlers, G., & Jones, B. (May, 1990). *Helping parents understand the writing process.* Paper presented at the International Reading Association Convention, Atlanta, GA.

Ferriero, E., & Teberosky, A. (1983). *Writing before schooling.* Portsmouth, NH: Heinemann.

Fish, S. (1980). *Is there a text in this class?* Cambridge: Harvard University Press.

Fitzgerald, J. (1989). Enhancing two related thought processes: Revision in writing and critical thinking. *The Reading Teacher, 43,* 42–48.

Fitzgerald, J. (1990). Reading and writing as "mind meeting." In T. Shanahan (Ed.), *Reading and writing together: New perspectives for the classroom* (pp. 81–97). Norwood, MA: Christopher-Gordon.

Forester, A. D. (1980). Learning to spell by spelling. *Theory into practice, 19,* 186–193.

Garner, R. (1987). *Metacognition and reading comprehension.* Norwood, NJ: Ablex.

Gentry, J. R. (1981). Learning to spell developmentally. *The Reading Teacher, 34,* 378–381.

Gentry, J. R. (1987). *Spel. . . is a four letter word.* Portsmouth, NH: Heinemann.

Gipe, J. P. (1978–1979). Investigating techniques for teaching word meanings. *Reading Research Quarterly, 14,* 624–644.

Graham, S. (1986). Assessing reading preferences: A new approach. *New England Reading Association Journal, 21* (1), 8–11.

Graves, D. H. (1981). *A case study observing the development of primary children's composing, spelling, and motor behaviors during writing process.* Durham, NH: University of New Hampshire. (ERIC Document Reproduction Service No. ED 218-653).

Graves, D. L. (1983). *Writing: Teachers and children at work.* Portsmouth, NH: Heinemann.

Hall, M. A. (1981). *Teaching reading as a language experience.* Columbus, OH: Merrill/Macmillan.

Halliday, M. A. K. (1975). *Explorations in the functions of language.* London: Edward Arnold.

Hansen, J. (1987). *When writers read.* Portsmouth, NH: Heinemann.

Hansen, J., & Graves, D. L. (1983). The author's chair. *Language Arts, 60,* 176–183.

Harste, J. C., Woodward, V. A., & Burke, C. L. (1984). *Language stories and literacy lessons.* Portsmouth, NH: Heinemann.

Holdaway, D. (1979). *The foundations of literacy.* Sydney, Australia: Ashton Scholastic.

Honig, W. (1988). The California reading initiative. *The New Advocate, 1,* 235–240.

Klima, E. S., & Belugi-Klima, U. (1966). Syntactic regularities in the speech of children. In J. Lyons & R. Wales (Eds.), *Psycholinguistic Papers* (pp. 145–156). Edinburgh: Edinburgh University Press.

Langer, J. A. (1984). Examining background knowledge and text comprehension. *Reading Research Quarterly, 19,* 468–481.

Langer, J. A. (1986). *Children reading and writing.* Norwood, NJ: Ablex Publishing.

Lee, D. M., & Allen, R. V. (1963). *Learning to read through experience.* New York: Appleton-Century-Crofts.

Manning, M., Manning, G., & Hughes, J. (1987). Journals in first grade: What children write. *The Reading Teacher, 41,* 311–315.

Martinez, M., & Teale, W. (1988). Reading in a kindergarten classroom library. *The Reading Teacher, 41,* 568–573.

Mason, J. M., & Allen, J. (1986). A review of emergent literacy with implications for research and practice in reading. In E. Rothkopf (Ed.), *Review of research in education* (pp. 3–47). Washington, DC: American Educational Research Association.

Mason, J. M., & Au, K. H. (1990). *Reading instruction for today.* Glenview, IL: Scott, Foresman.

Mason, J. M., & The Staff at Center for the Study of Reading (1984). A schema-theoretic view of the reading process as a basis for comprehension instruction. In G. G. Duffy, L. R. Roehler, & J. Mason (Eds.), *Comprehension instruction: Perspectives and suggestions* (pp. 26–38). New York: Longman.

May, F. B. (1990). *Reading as communication: An interactive approach* (3rd ed.). Columbus, OH: Merrill/Macmillan.

McGee, L. M., & Richgels, D. J. (1990). *Literacy's beginnings: Supporting young readers & writers.* Boston, MA: Allyn & Bacon.

McNeil, J. (1970). *The acquisition of language: The study of developmental psycholinguistics.* New York: Harper & Row.

McNeil, J. D. (1987). *Reading comprehension: New directions for classroom practice.* Glenview, IL: Scott, Foresman.

Menyuk, P. (1969). Syntactic structures in the language of children. *Child Development, 34,* 407–422.

Moffett, J. (1981a). *Active voice: A writing program across the curriculum.* Portsmouth, NH: Heinemann.

Moffett, J. (1981b). *Coming on center: Essays on English education.* Portsmouth, NH: Boynton/Cook.

Morrow, L. M. (1989). New perspectives in early literacy. *The Reading Instruction Journal, 32,* 8–15.

Mullis, I. V. S., & Jenkins, L. B. (1990). *The reading report card 1971–1988: Trends from the nation's report card.* Princeton, NJ: National Assessment of Educational Progress.

Nagy, W. E., Anderson, R. C., & Herman, P. A. (1987). Learning word meanings from context during normal reading. *American Educational Research Journal, 24,* 237–270.

Newkirk, T. (1989). *More than stories: The range of children's writing.* Portsmouth, NH: Heinemann.

O'Brochta, E. P., & Weaver, C. P. (1991). Linking reading and writing through thematic teaching in a first grade. In J. T. Feeley, D. S. Strickland, & S. B. Wepner (Eds.), *Process reading and writing: A literature-based approach* (pp. 7–21). New York: Teachers College Press.

Palinscar, A. M., & Brown, A. (1984). Reciprocal teaching of comprehension. *Cognition and Instruction, 1,* 117–175.

Paris, S. G., Cross, D. R., & Lipson, M. Y. (1984). Informed strategies for learning: A program to improve children's reading awareness and comprehension. *Journal of Educational Psychology, 76,* 239–242.

Pilchman, B. (1991). Extending reading and writing process to the teaching of social studies. In J. T. Feeley, D. S. Strickland, & S. B. Wepner (Eds.), *Process reading and writing: A literature-based approach* (pp. 85–98). New York: Teachers College Press.

Purves, A. C. (1990). *The scribal society.* New York: Longman.

Raphael, T. E., & Englert, C. S. (1989). Integrating writing and reading instruction. In P. N. Winograd, K. K. Wixson, & M. Y. Lipson (Eds.), *Improving basal reading instruction* (pp. 231–255). New York: Teachers College Press.

Read, C. (1986). *Children's creative spelling.* Boston, MA: Routledge & Keagan Paul.

Reardon, S. J. (1990). Putting reading tests in their place. *The New Advocate, 3,* 29–37.

Routman, R. (1991). *Invitations.* Portsmouth, NH: Heinemann.

Scardamelia, M., & Bereiter, C. (1986). Research on written composition. In M. C. Wittrock (Ed.), *Handbook of research on teaching* (pp. 778–803). New York: Macmillan.

Schwartz, J. I. (1988). *Encouraging early literacy: An integrated approach to reading and writing in N–3.* Portsmouth, NH: Heinemann.

Shanahan, T. (1990). Reading and writing together: What does it really mean? In T. Shanahan (Ed.), *Reading and writing together: New perspectives for the classroom* (pp. 2–18). Norwood, MA: Christopher-Gordon.

Singer, H. (1978). Active comprehension. *The Reading Teacher, 31,* 901–908.

Smith, E. B., Goodman, K. S., & Meredith, R. (1976). *Language and thinking in school.* New York: Holt, Rinehart & Winston.

Smith, F. (1985). *Reading without nonsense.* New York: Teachers College Press.

Squire, J. R. (1984). Composing and comprehending: Two sides of same basic process. In J. M. Jensen (Ed.), *Composing and comprehending* (pp. 23–32). Urbana, IL: National Conference on Research in English.

Stauffer, R. (1975). *Directing the reading-thinking process.* New York: Harper & Row.

Stauffer, R. (1980). *The language experience approach to teaching reading.* New York: Harper & Row.

Stevens, R. J., Madden, N. A., Slavin, R. E., & Farnish, A. M. (1987). Cooperative integrated reading and composition. *Reading Research Quarterly, 22,* 433–454.

Strickland, D. S., & Feeley, J. T. (1985). Using children's concept of story to improve reading and writing. In T. L. Harris & E. J. Cooper (Eds.), *Reading, thinking, and concept development* (pp. 163–175). New York: The College Board.

Strickland, D. S., & Feeley, J. T. (1991). The learner develops: Development in the elementary school years. In J. Flood, J. M. Jenson, D. Lapp, & J. R. Squire (Eds.), *Handbook of research on teaching the English language arts* (pp. 286–302). New York: Macmillan.

Strickland, D. S., & Morrow, L. M. (1989). *Emerging literacy: Young children learn to read and write.* Newark, DE: International Reading Association.

Taylor, D. (1983). *Family literacy: Young children learning to read and write.* Portsmouth, NH: Heinemann.

Teale, W., & Sulzby, E. (Eds.) (1986). *Emergent literacy: Writing and reading.* Norwood, NJ: Ablex.

Temple, C. A., Nathan, R. G., Burris, N. A., & Temple, F. (1988). *The beginnings of literacy.* Boston, MA: Allyn & Bacon.

Templin, M. (1987). *Certain language skills in children: Their development and interrelationships.* Minneapolis: University of Minnesota Press.

Tierney, R. (1990). Learning to connect reading and writing: Critical thinking through transactions with one's own subjectivity. In T. Shanahan (Ed.), *Reading and writing together: New perspectives for the classroom* (pp. 131–143). Norwood, MA: Christopher-Gordon.

Tierney, R. J., & Pearson, P. D. (1984). Toward a composing model of reading. In J. M. Jensen (Ed.), *Composing and comprehending* (pp. 33–45). Urbana, IL: National Conference on Research in English.

Tumner, W. E., Herriman, M. L., & Nesdale, A. R. (1988). Metalinguistic abilities and beginning reading. *Reading Research Quarterly, 23,* 134–158.

Veatch, J., Sawicki, F., Elliott, G., Barnette, E., & Blakey, J. (1973). *Key words to reading: The language experience approach begins.* Columbus, OH: Merrill.

Veatch, J. (1978). *Reading in the elementary school.* Katonah, NY: Richard C. Owen.

Vygotsky, L. S. (1962). *Thought and language.* Cambridge, MA: MIT Press.

Weaver, C. (1988). *Reading process and practice: From socio-psycholinguistics to whole language.* Portsmouth, NH: Heinemann.

Wolfson, B. J., Manning, G., & Manning, M. (1984). Revisiting what children say their reading interests are. *Reading World, 24* (2), 4–10.

Trade Books Mentioned

Alexander, M. (1970). *Nobody asked me if I wanted a baby sister.* New York: Dial.

Carle, E. (1969). *The very hungry caterpillar.* New York: Philomel.

Dahl, R. (1970). *Fantastic Mr. Fox.* New York: Knopf.

Gardiner, J. (1980). *Stone fox.* New York: Thomas Crowell.

Hutchins, P. (1978). *Happy birthday, Sam.* New York: Greenwillow.

Hutchins, P. (1983). *You'll soon grow into them, Titch.* New York: Greenwillow.

Russo, M. (1988). *Only six more days.* New York: Greenwillow.

Scieszka, J. (1989). *The true story of the three little pigs*. New York: Viking.

Scieszka, J. (1991). *The frog prince continued*. New York: Viking.

Sendak, M. (1963). *Where the wild things are*. New York: Harper & Row.

Showers, P. (1978). *Me and my family tree*. New York: Crowell.

Steig, W. (1971). *Amos and Boris*. New York: Farrar, Straus & Giroux.

Viorst, J. (1972). *Alexander and the terrible, horrible, no good, very bad day*. New York: Atheneum.

CHAPTER
2

BASALS AND THEIR USE

A FTER TWO YEARS OF substitute teaching Ms. E. finally finds her first full-time job as a first grade teacher. She spends her summer organizing files and preparing materials for her long-awaited magical moment. By the time the first day of school arrives, Ms. E. is bursting with ideas to try with her beginning readers.

During the second hour of her orientation her bubble bursts. Her principal informs here that her reading program is the basal, and nothing else. He tells her that, yes, she has to cover every story in the basal, because it is a Board of Education mandate. When she asks why, he explains that the students might not be exposed to the skills that are needed to pass the standardized test. He then proceeds to tell her that if she wants to enjoy a successful tenure with him, she'd better follow the rules. Four months later Ms. E. is utterly frustrated with her reading program. She feels that she teaches "skills, skills, and more skills" with little or no time for recreational reading and process writing. She feels imprisoned in a system that has little regard for her need to feel free to make choices about what and how she teaches. She has to shelve her once-ambitious ideas until she finds a school district that shares her beliefs in the way reading should be taught.

Why would a budding teacher with fresh ideas about how to teach feel this way after such a short time in the classroom? Many **whole language** proponents would say that it is her forced reliance on the basal that is causing her feelings of disenchantment and helplessness. Others would blame Ms. E. for her inability to assimilate into a basal-driven system. Ms. E.'s problem is not the basal per se, but the political baggage that accompanies its use. For her district the basal is seen as the only viable system for accomplishing its goal: decent scores on a standardized test. As a result, Ms. E. believes that she has been stripped of her professional dignity. Although he has not verbalized it, her principal has nevertheless communicated to Ms. E. that her ideas are not nearly as important as her ability to follow a publishing company's teaching prescription.

Why does Ms. E.'s administrator feel so strongly about the basal? Why does Ms. E. feel otherwise? This chapter addresses these two questions by looking carefully at basals and their uses in the classroom.

What Is a Basal?

A **basal** is a sequential, grade-specific, all-inclusive set of instructional materials for teaching reading in grades kindergarten through eight. Every basal has a reading curriculum in the form of a **scope and sequence** chart. Its scope is the entire reading curriculum of skills that students will encounter as they progress through the basal program; its sequence is the ordering or hierarchy of skills that students are supposed to follow to develop reading proficiency. The instructional mainstay of basals—student texts, workbooks, and skill sheets—support and sustain a basal's scope and sequence. Instructional strategies for using and extending the basal's curriculum and materials are included in a teacher's guide. A dazzling array of supplementary and optional materials such as trade book libraries, teaching charts, management and assessment systems, writing activities, idea banks, audio- and videotapes, filmstrips, computer programs, and posters are provided to enhance the basics of a basal system (Anderson, Hiebert, Scott, & Wilkinson, 1985; Goodman, Shannon, Freeman, & Murphy, 1988).

Evolution of Basals

When was the basal developed? Why was it developed? This section presents a brief history of the basal's evolution. Essentially, the basal was developed during the 1920s with the advent of teachers' manuals. These manuals and their explicit directives and standardized instructions about what and how to teach used "scientific" principles to compensate for teachers' idiosyncratic teaching behaviors. Supposedly cost-effective and psychologically sound, teachers' manuals almost guaranteed that all children would learn to read.

Prior to the birth of basals, materials and practices for reading instruction reflected the philosophical tone of each era. Before the middle of the 18th century, when many Americans did not become literate, students' memorization of Bible verses was the ultimate goal. Goodman, Shannon, Freeman, and Murphy (1988) explain that hornbooks (paddles that contained the alphabet, a list of syllables, and the Lord's Prayer), psalters (books of spelling lessons, lists of syllables and words, and Bible verses), and religious textbooks such as *The New England Primer* were the materials from which children learned to read. A century later, when universal literacy became an American goal, reading was defined as reading aloud. Initially, children learned to read with the spelling method, learning to spell and pronounce lists of words of various lengths before they began to read sentences orally. Most urban schools then shifted from an emphasis on spelling to one of pronunciation, from letter names to their sounds (Goodman et al., 1988).

The *McGuffey Eclectic Readers,* first written by William Holmes McGuffey in 1836, continued the trend in students' oral reading. *McGuffey's Readers* were the earliest schoolbooks to introduce vocabulary gradually, use word repetition, and control sentence length. They firmly established the concept of graded format, using meaningful moral and literary selections. They also popularized the use of illustrations related to the content of the lesson and offered suggestions and aids to teachers in short, manageable lessons. In effect, the features in *McGuffey's Readers* were predecessors to many features that are commonplace in basal systems today (Bohning, 1986; Leu & Kinzer, 1991).

While the early 20th century marked a period of debate about whether to fine-tune traditional methods or adopt a more child-centered, language-based curriculum, the industrialized spirit of the times influenced the push for a more organized, scientific approach to existing methodologies. Consequently, along with a teacher's manual came a comprehensive system of basic books, workbooks, and activities that were sequentially organized. These teacher-proof instructional systems supposedly were designed to compensate for some teachers' lack of professional training in teaching reading. Since children's book publishing was not as developed then as it is today, student texts were the main vehicle for the "content" of reading instruction. Yet, the literary content of these materials continued to change, with real life and fantasy stories accounting for the majority of reading selections.

Seventy years later basals—with their reading selections about everyday life and the rewards of good behavior—continue to be the predominant method for reading instruction (Vacca, Vacca, & Gove, 1991). Although basal systems are substantially different in size, diversity, and content, they nevertheless continue to support the basic reading tenets of the early part of this century (Goodman et al., 1988).

Basal Use in the Classroom

Using basals is the most traditional method of reading instruction in today's schools. Although the figures vary from one report to another, 80 to 90% of the children in the nation learn to read from a basal program (Aaron, 1987; Farr, Tulley, & Powell, 1987; Weaver & Watson, 1989). Because 90% of all instructional decisions are based on the textbooks that are used in the classroom (Barnard & Hetzel, 1989; Muther, 1985), basals strongly influence how reading is taught in American schools and what students read (Anderson et al., 1985).

The basic premise behind a basal is that children must be taught to read. It is said that learning to read without systematic instruction will not help children to develop reading proficiency (Aaron, 1987). Publishing companies and recognized reading researchers work together to blend skill development with reading experiences so that students can move forward in their reading development. Although not often stated in print, basal publishers try to guarantee reading success for every student everywhere if their programs are followed precisely. While proudly proclaiming the academic prowess of their balanced team of authors, basal publishers give the impression that programmatic decisions are scientific truths. Notwithstanding recent attempts at basal bashing, the popularity and importance of basals has not diminished in most American classrooms (McCallum, 1988).

McCallum (1988) explains that a basal's widespread use can be attributed to a "package-deal" mentality. Let's face it. If, for the same price, you had a choice of selecting a vacation plan with a well-developed itinerary and pre-paid meals versus an open-ended, catch-as-catch-can vacation scheme, which would you pick? Although some of you would opt for the latter, most of us would choose the former. It's that same "do it for me" feeling that sells basals to the majority of school systems. Trial and error is fine; however, a blueprint for purported success is even better.

Basals come as a package and are designed to address a wide range of reading-related skills from **decoding** to literary appreciation. In addition to suggesting instructional practices, they provide opportunities for guided practice within the text. They also provide a **management system** for coordinating reading instruction, which is an important feature for teachers who are concerned about meeting the goals set by parents and legislators (McCallum, 1988).

Yet, a basal reading series was never intended to be a complete, self-contained reading program (Aaron, 1987; Bridge, 1989). "The pupil texts of a series do not and cannot include as much reading material as students need" (Aaron, 1987, p. 126). Furthermore, some of the material simply is inappropriate or unnecessary for many students. The problem stems from many teachers' and administrators' myopic vision of reading instruction. Without soul-searching and philosophical forethought, the basal has *become* the curriculum, defining precisely what children will learn and the order in which they will learn it. Skipping a story selection or set of skill exercises is considered detrimental to students' reading development, lest the students not do well in the numbers game of testing. Because the basal is merely a set of materials and strategies for teaching reading, it is not inherently good or bad. Its problem is what it symbolizes to American education. Its abuse and misuse have distorted our ideas about reading education. Yet, because the basal is so prominent in literacy development, we need to understand what parts of it, singly or in combination, support our reading goals.

Components and Characteristics of Basals

Six months before writing this chapter, we wrote to the leading basal companies to request material for examination; we asked for the first grade readers (grade one text that follows the preprimers and primer) and the fourth grade reader, with all supporting material for each level. Rather than depend on other researchers' descriptions of basals, we wanted to examine the basal's components firsthand. More importantly, we wanted to see how basal publishers have handled current demands for better quality material and more strategic instructional techniques. In this section we describe the basic components and characteristics of seven basals we examined: D. C. Heath; Harcourt Brace Jovanovich; Houghton Mifflin; Macmillan; McGraw-Hill; Scott, Foresman; and Silver Burdett & Ginn. All of them have 1989 copyrights. In the next major section we analyze how the content of these various materials reflects our current understanding of reading and writing. Even though basals published after 1989 will change again in content to reflect even more of the recent research, we believe that our analysis will highlight essential basal characteristics.

The first thing we learned is that basals truly differ, especially in the kinds of materials and strategies used to promote reading. Although all basals follow a **Directed Reading Activity (DRA)**, or some minor variation of the same procedure, the flavor of the lessons is different enough to have an impact on the way reading instruction is delivered. The DRA is a lesson framework in which some type of preparatory activity occurs prior to reading, guided reading activities, post-reading activities, and follow-up skill work (Wixson & Peters, 1989). Today's DRAs are not much different from Betts's (1946) original description.

Preparatory activities often include providing relevant background, creating interest, introducing meanings and/or pronunciations for new vocabulary, and establishing purposes for reading. The guided reading activities often include silent reading focused on answering purpose-setting questions, oral reading and responses to questions dealing with short sections of the text, and/or oral rereading to clarify or verify a point. Post-reading activities frequently consist of group discussion and answering general end-of-selection questions. Follow-up activities consist of a variety of skill lessons and practice exercises that may or may not be related to the reading selection. (Wixson & Peters, 1989, p. 22)

Within this framework basal publishers produce 20 or more different kinds of materials for instruction, assessment, and management of their systems. Ways to orchestrate this panoply of basal components are delineated in the teacher's guide. Even though each basal offers a different array of materials, the seven basals we examined have eight components in common: student texts, workbooks, skill practice books, classroom libraries, teacher resource files, word cards, teaching charts, and assessment tests. (See Figure 2.1.) All components are at least identified and usually organized for instruction in the teacher's guide. Let's look at these components.

TEACHER'S GUIDE

The teacher's guide (or teacher's edition) is a manual that contains precise lesson plans for a specific grade level of the basal series. In addition to step-by-step, scripted plans, the guide provides a brief description of the series' authors, program components, philosophy, instructional strategies, and assessment program. Scope and sequence charts, annotated lists of children's books, as well as reinforcement, enrichment, and **cross-curricular** activities round out the guide's overview. (See Figure 2.2 for a few sample pages of D. C. Heath's teacher's guide for the first grade reader. These pages provide teachers with an overview of the lesson and help them to prepare students for the reading selection.)

New and experienced teachers often are overwhelmed by the voluminous amount of information contained in these guides. One of our teacher friends told us that it took her an entire evening to review the introduction and one-half of an annotated lesson plan for one of the newer basals. Dolores Durkin (1990a) stated that the 1989 guides contain many more pages than their predecessors, and she will not bring the manuals to her undergraduate classes because they would be too intimidating to preservice teachers. We found that the 1989 teachers' guides for the first readers contain between 368 and 647 pages, whereas the teachers' guides for fourth grade contain between 672 and 1,571 pages. (See Tables 2.1 [p. 46] and 2.2 [p. 46] for the number of pages contained in each basal's teacher's guide.)

One of us, along with several hand-picked teachers, had the opportunity to revise the language strand of a teacher's guide for a basal series in 1987. At the time publishers were trying to satisfy the interests of California (the most populous state in the United States) and its initiatives for more literature and more writing (Honig, 1988). Only the books of publishers "adopted" by California could be considered for purchase with state funds. Determined to bring a fresh look to the guides, we decided not to look at old guides but rather to brainstorm original ideas for every reading

FIGURE 2.1
Common components in seven basal series

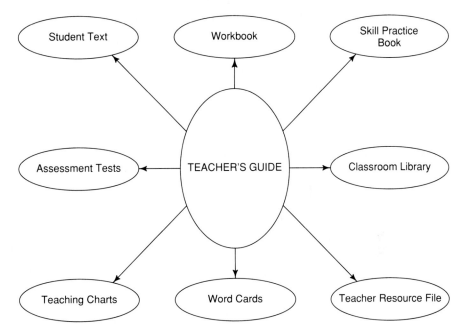

selection. As a team we wrote many ideas for oral and written expression, including interviewing, creating plays, writing memoirs, and drawing cartoons. Our activities could be placed before, during, or after reading the selection, and we dutifully tried to tie them to the scope and sequence charts. The teachers tested all the activities with their students, and we deleted the "bombs" or revised as needed.

Unbeknownst to us, other teachers across the country were working with other professors to write activities for the *same reading selections* for the other strands (for example, vocabulary, comprehension, decoding, literature, extension activities, cross-curricular activities) in the same teacher's guide. Everything then was funneled to a central office where editors compiled and edited the information into one guide. It took this experience of working on a teacher's guide for us to understand why there are so many pieces to "cover" with one selection and why most teachers need a week to do one selection with a group. We share this story to help you to understand that, while all the suggested ideas, activities, and strategies may be excellent, they do not all have to be done for students to learn to read and write.

Durkin (1990a) also found that the teachers' guides she evaluated are so dense with information and scripted material that it is impossible for teachers to digest the material in a brief amount of time. Those who follow these recipe-like guides word-for-word end up becoming drillmasters of skill acquisition rather than nurturers of lifelong literacy. As Heilman, Blair, and Rupley (1990) suggest, it is up to us to determine the feasibility of teacher's guide offerings in light of our own professional wisdom about our students' needs and interests.

You cannot pick up a 1989 teacher's guide without seeing words such as *empowering, emergent literacy, modeling, literature-based, functional situations,* and *cooperative*

44

A. Think Ahead

Building Vocabulary and **Exploring Ideas** emphasize word meanings and ideas important to selection understanding. Use these sections to
▲ determine and expand children's familiarity with words and concepts
▲ stimulate and extend prior knowledge of related background
▲ preview, predict, and purpose-set

BUILDING VOCABULARY

Key Words

TC 1A					
beach	sky	water	orange	pretty	great	carry

Materials   *Key Word cards*

Introduce and read Key Words

Display the Key Words on the Teaching Chart. Provide each child with a set of Key Word cards to use as response cards in the following activities. (See the Key Word card copymasters in the back of this Teacher's Edition.) Give children an opportunity to read the words they know or can figure out. Ask them to explain how they figured out the words. Then point to each word as you read it aloud to ensure that children recognize all the words.

Categorize Key Words

Have children hold up or point to the words and say them as they answer the following questions. As children give their answers, have them arrange the words in groups under the headings: **color words, nice words, lake and ocean words, doing words.**

1. Which word is a color word? (orange)

2. Which two words say something nice about something? (pretty, great)

3. Which three words tell about things you see at a lake or at the ocean? (beach, sky, water)

4. Which word is something you can do? (carry)

Now say the words listed below and have children tell with which words they would go. For example,

▶ With which words would you put sand? (Sand would go with beach, sky, and water.)

Use words such as these: blue, fish, draw, run, nice, yellow. Some children might notice that fish could go in more than one category.

Use Key Words in oral cloze

Read each sentence aloud, saying "blank" where a word has been omitted. Ask children to say the Key Word that completes the sentence and to explain how they knew the answer. After they respond, repeat the sentence, inserting the correct word.

4   Unit 1   MIXING COLORS

LESSON 1

The Picture

Summary

In the animal story "The Picture," a rabbit goes to the beach to paint a picture. Several animals criticize his work and suggest improvements. Finally a bug family admires and compliments the rabbit on his painting. Since the bugs appreciate it so much, the rabbit gives them the painting. As they carry it away, he wonders how they will ever get it into their little house.

Selection Notes

James Marshall is the author and illustrator of "The Picture." The self-taught artist, who also writes as Edward Marshall, has published over 30 books for beginning readers, including his series of books about two hippopotamus friends, George and Martha. *George and Martha* (Houghton, 1972) was an ALA Notable Book and was featured on the *New York Times* Outstanding Books list in 1972.

A. *Think Ahead*	B. *Think While Reading*	C. *Think Back*
Building Vocabulary Introduce Key Words • categorize • oral close	**Comprehension Focus** draw conclusions	**Extending Ideas** Review Comprehension Discuss purpose *Think About It*
Exploring Ideas Recall prior knowledge about the beach Preview and predict selection content Set purposes for reading the selection	**Independent Reading** *The Picture* PE 8–15 **Guided Reading** Check and clarify selection comprehension with storyline and probe questions TE 7–11	Create and Share: paint a picture Explore: discuss art and museums Project Reminder: color mixing chart **Applying Ideas** Drama: act out the story Written language: write a group story Art: make a diorama
		Relating Skills: TE 14–22 TE WB
		T Decoding: vowel digraphs 14 3
		T Decoding: long vowels 16 4
		T Comprehension: elements of fiction 18 5
		T Study Skills: follow directions 20 6
		T Language: speaking and listening 21 –

Materials			
TE 4–6 WB 1 TC 1A	TE 7–11 PE 16	TE 12–22 TC 1B, 1C PE 16 WB 2–6	

Additional Materials: *Part A:* Key Word Cards 1; *Part C:* easel or drawing paper, paints (including tempera paints), brushes, books of famous paintings, plastic spoons, coffee stirrers, paper or muffin tins, stiff paper, string, paper punch, markers, chart paper, crayons, shoe box, construction paper, old wallpaper samples, scissors, paste; *Picture Word Cards:* bite, cake, cry, cube, go, he/she, penny, pie, rose

Skill Pad: Reinforce and Reteach (1–6)   **Creative Assessments:** Attitude/Appreciation, Strategy, Language
Unit Test: administer after Lesson 9   **Assessments** (TE 184–185)
   Language Enrichment Program Lesson 1

The Picture   3

FIGURE 2.2

Sample pages from D. C. Heath's Teacher's Guide

Note. From *Teacher's Guide to Accompany First Grade Reader, My Best Bear Hug* (pp. 3–6), 1989, Lexington, MA: D. C. Heath. Copyright 1989 by D. C. Heath. Reprinted by permission.

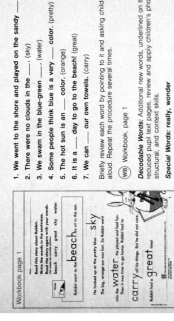

Workbook page 1

Read this story about Rabbit.
Write the words in the sentences.
Read the story again with your words.
(The words are given above.)
beach   carry   great   sky   water

Rabbit went to the **beach** (to sit in the sun.)

He looked up at the pretty blue **sky**

The big, orange sun was hot. So Rabbit went

into the **water** all his things. But he did not care.

carry all his things. But he did not care.

Then it was time to go home. Rabbit had to

Rabbit had a **great** time!

1. We went to the shore and played on the sandy ____. (beach)

2. There were no clouds in the ____. (sky)

3. We swam in the blue-green ____. (water)

4. Some people think blue is a very ____ color. (pretty)

5. The hot sun is an ____ color. (orange)

6. It is a ____ day to go to the beach! (great)

7. We can ____ our own towels. (carry)

Briefly review each word by pointing to it and asking children to read it aloud. Repeat the procedure several times.

(WB) Workbook, page 1

Decodable Words: Additional new words, underlined on the following reduced pupil text pages, review and apply children's phonic, structural, and context skills.

Special Words: **really, wonder**

Write the words **really** and **wonder** on the chalkboard and pronounce them for children. Then give an example of each meaning by saying the following sentences: "I **wonder** if a rabbit can paint." "Do you **really** think a rabbit can do that?" You may wish to encourage children to tell about some of the things that they wonder about and some of the things that they believe are really true.

EXPLORING IDEAS

Tell about experiences at the beach

Ask children if they have ever been to a beach. Encourage them to share their experiences by asking:

1. Where was the beach? (by the ocean, by a lake)

2. Describe some sounds and smells you can remember.

3. What things did you do at the beach?

Preview and predict what the rabbit will do

Now have children open their books to the Table of Contents. Briefly discuss its purpose and have children use it to locate the first selection "The Picture." Read the title aloud and ask children to look at the opening illustration. Tell children that the main character in this story is a rabbit. Then guide them to predict what the story will be about. Ask:

1. Where is the rabbit? (at the beach)

2. What do you think will happen in the story? (The rabbit will paint a picture.)

3. What makes you think so? (the story title, the rabbit is holding an easel)

4. What do you think will happen to the rabbit's picture in this story?

Record some of the children's predictions on chart paper or on the chalkboard and have them check their predictions after reading the story.

Set purposes

Now model for the children how to use their predictions to ask questions about the story to set a purpose for reading. Say:

► **I know from the title that the story is about a picture. I see from the illustrations that the rabbit will paint a picture. Let's read to find out what happens to the rabbit's picture. Here is a question we can be thinking about while we read.**

► **What happens to the rabbit's picture?**

Write the question under the children's predictions so that they can refer to it as they read.

FIGURE 2.2
Continued

45

TABLE 2.1
Number of pages in teacher's guides for first grade in seven basal series

FIRST GRADE BASALS						
*SF	H	MM	HBJ	SBG	HM	MH
Number of Pages 368	451	432	553	455	647	450

*Abbreviations for all tables and figures in this chapter and in the appendix are as follows: SF = Scott, Foresman; H = D. C. Heath; MM = Macmillan; HBJ = Harcourt Brace Jovanovich; SBG = Silver Burdett & Ginn; HM = Houghton Mifflin; MH = McGraw-Hill.

learning. These buzzwords indicate that the basal series are trying to reflect the reading research from the 1980s. In fact, Durkin (1990a) mentioned and we also observed certain trends and emphases: more concerted effort to include literature, consistent reference to language arts, explicit comprehension instruction strategies through modeling, many writing activities focused on the writing process, classroom organization activities that include cooperative learning strategies, ideas for relating content subjects to language arts, and suggestions and materials for different types of learners.

Even with these changes manuals need to be used judiciously so that our teaching practices come from our own thinking, rather than a publisher's preconceived notions. If you use basals ask yourself the following questions as you decide how to use the teacher's guide.

1. What is the focus of each lesson? Is it in line with my curricular objectives?
2. What material does the guide suggest I use during a lesson? What is the purpose of each type of material? Do I need all, some, or any of them?
3. What is the time frame for a lesson plan? Within that time frame what is the ratio of real reading to skill sheet exercises? If too little reading is suggested, what can I do to make sure that my students are engaged in more coherent reading?
4. What pre-reading, during reading, and after-reading activities are suggested? Are they necessary? Do they enhance my instructional goals?
5. Which comprehension questions are important for my students? Which ones are unnecessary?

TABLE 2.2
Number of pages in teacher's guides for fourth grade in seven basal series

FOURTH GRADE BASALS						
SF	H	MM	HBJ	SBG	HM	MH
Number of Pages 832	860	672	918	1517	1035	728

6. What strategies are offered to help my students monitor their comprehension of what they read?
7. Are there suggested reading and writing projects that I can use along with other reading material?
8. How can I streamline the lesson plans so that I am using what is essential for my students?

A book entitled *Improving Basal Reading Instruction* (Winograd, Wixson, & Lipson, 1989) is a good resource of constructive suggestions about ways to use basals as part of a more complete, balanced, and effective program of reading instruction.

STUDENT TEXTS

Student texts are softbound and hardbound books of stories, poems, plays, songs, lessons, and articles. Multiple copies are provided so that groups of students can use them at the same time (May, 1990). The content of today's student texts differs from yesteryear's "Father Knows Best" basal. In addition to including a much better balance of roles, lifestyles, and cultures in the stories (McCallum, 1988; Weaver & Watson, 1989), the basal contains more literature written by noted children's authors (see Figure 2.3 for an example in D. C. Heath's first grade reader of an animal fantasy that is similar to the George and Martha chapter books, written and illustrated by James Marshall).

We still need to examine student texts for their meaningfulness. Bettelheim and Zelan's (1982) clinical studies revealed that children could not remember what they had read in a basal reading selection because it was meaningless to them. Bettelheim and Zelan concluded that, because the reading selections in the basals were devoid of text that was meaningful to students, students were not interested in learning to read.

READABILITY

One reason for bland reading selections may be that basal publishers strictly control **readability** scores for their reading selections and student texts. While basal publishers are beginning to relax their standards for using these readability scores for every single reading selection, these scores strongly influence teachers' and administrators' decisions about what students can read, and when.

Readability tells the reading level of the text, and it is usually derived from formulas based on the number of syllables in a word and the number of words in the sentences. For example, if a book has a readability of 2.1, that book is supposedly appropriate for students whose reading level is at the first month of second grade, as measured by a standardized test. The biggest problem with a readability score is that it does not tell you anything about the content or concept load of the story. For example, "To be, or not to be," the opening statement of Prince Hamlet's famous speech in which he considers suicide as an escape from his troubles, would have a low readability score because it is a short sentence with single-syllable words; yet its meaning is very complex. Furthermore, when sentences are chopped up for lower readability scores, they often are more difficult to understand. For example, "I went to the store. I needed a

The Picture
by James Marshall

One day a rabbit came to the beach.

"Wow," he said. "I must paint a picture of this!"

So he sat down. Soon he had painted the sky and water.

"This is a lot of fun," he said. "I really like my picture."

Just then a dog walked by.

"Oh no," said the dog. "That's not right. The sky is too blue. Put in more white."

The rabbit went on painting. Soon a bird came by.

"No, no, no," said the bird. "The sun is too red. Put in some more yellow. That will make it orange."

"No, thank you," said the rabbit. "I like it my way."

"Very well," said the dog. "It's **your** picture." And she went away.

"No, thank you," said the rabbit. "I like it my way."

"Well, it's **your** picture," said the bird. And she went away.

FIGURE 2.3

Sample story from D. C. Heath's First Grade Student Reader

Note. From *First Grade Reader, Student Text, My Best Bear Hug* (pp. 13–14), 1989, Lexington, MA: D. C. Heath. Copyright 1989 by D. C. Heath. Reprinted by permission.

The rabbit went on painting. Soon a toad came by.

"Oh my," said the toad. "That water isn't right. It's too green. Put in more blue."

"No, thank you," said the rabbit. "I like it my way."

"Very well," said the toad. "It's **your** picture." And away he went.

"Everyone has something to say," said the rabbit.

He went on painting. Just then a family of bugs came by.

"**Now** what?" said the rabbit.

"Wow!" said the father bug. "Will you look at that!"

"What a pretty red!" said the mother bug.

"What great greens and blues!" said the bug kids.

"Do you really think so?" said the rabbit.

"Oh yes!" said the bug family.

"Yes?" said the rabbit. "Well then, it's **your** picture."

FIGURE 2.3
Continued

"May we really have it?" said the father bug.

"We will put it in our house," said the mother bug.

"Wow!" said the bug kids.

Then the bug family picked up the picture to carry it home.

"I wonder how they will get it in their house," thought the rabbit.

loaf of bread" has a lower readability score than "I went to the store because I needed a loaf of bread." However, the former statements require an inference, whereas the latter statement does not, making the first statements slightly more difficult to understand.

VOCABULARY

Another reason for the lack of meaningful text could be the basal's often too-fervent control over the vocabulary load, that is, the number and rate of introducing new words. Basal publishers want to introduce a common core of words early. When Barnard and Hetzel (1989) examined the vocabulary introduced for the first grade basals, they found that 80% of the words in any one series are common to at least one other series; only 20% of the words are unique to a series.

Goodman (1988) believes that, among other things, controlled vocabulary leads to the "basalization" of children's literature. When basal publishers rewrite well-known children's books to fit the basal's formulaic guidelines, the original language can become so stultified that a once artful portrayal of an authentic situation turns into a poorly contrived, synthetic version of the author's message. Goodman cites how one basal publisher changed the title, sentences, and name of one of the major characters in Judy Blume's book *The One in the Middle is the Green Kangaroo* (1981), so that it would fit into basal-imposed constraints. For instance, Blume's version describes the main character's problem of being a middle child: "He felt like the peanut butter part of a sandwich, squeezed between Mike and Ellen." The basal version eliminates this metaphor altogether, giving children the illusion that Blume writes simple, sterile sentences about important issues to children.

CONTENT

A third area of concern is the content of reading selections. Realistic fiction and factual articles are the two most widely used literary forms in basals. Interestingly, in their analysis of basals published between 1977 and 1980, Schmidt, Caul, Byers, and Buchmann (1984) found that basals differ in the kind of material they present:

> Many articles, poems, and stories in these texts expose students to content dealing with (1) subjects such as art and science, (2) enduring social themes, (3) applied knowledge of processes of human functioning, and (4) living and acting rightly. But many basal selections contain no opportunities to learn any or all of these dimensions from text. (p. 159)

Basals still differ in their commitment to different forms of knowing. Yet, basals determine what children will read. In our analysis of current student texts, we found that the quality of literature presented to children varies greatly. We also discovered that some basals are moving away from rigidly controlling the rate at which vocabulary is introduced. We found that only about 10% of the cumulative vocabulary up through the first grade reader was common to all basals.

Basal publishers are trying to broaden their use of literature; in fact, we understand that more nonfiction will be coming in the 1992 editions. Nevertheless, it is important that *you* determine a reading selection's appropriateness and appeal for a given group of students in relation to your curricular and instructional goals (Wixson & Peters, 1989). By scrutinizing the content and language of the student text, you are helping to make a difference in the kind of material to which your students are exposed. We recommend that you consider the following six guidelines before using any reading selection:

1. Check for the reading selection's authenticity. If the reading selection is from a trade book, try to find the book to see if and how the reading selection has been adapted. We have found that, while some reading selections are faithful to the original versions, others have been tampered with in varying degrees. Make sure that the language and message of the author is not too distorted.
2. Read the reading selections beforehand. Analyze each selection for its content, purpose, and message. Is it teaching about a curricular area of study? Does the reading selection provide good information? Does it help students understand something about problem solving, reasoning, initiative, creativity, or humor? Does it help students to understand such human qualities as humility, patience, courage, kindness, honesty, and hope? If the reading selection contains one of these areas, the chances are good that students will learn something from reading the selection. If the reading selection is devoid of all three elements, ask yourself: "Why use it?" Exposing students to empty words results in meaningless messages about the purpose of reading.
3. Look at the way language is used. If it is presented merely to help students acquire a sight vocabulary, rather than to read for meaning, think about skipping that "reading selection" for a more interesting one.
4. Look for more "whole texts" rather than excerpts.
5. Think about how the reading selection fits into the basal's cluster, theme, or unit. If the reading selection's fit is questionable, skip it for reading selections that have stronger connections to the theme.
6. Consider whether the reading selection's message is appropriate for your students' abilities, interests, and needs. Remember that first grade basal stories are written for millions of faceless children around the country whose academic, social, psychological, and economic profiles may differ greatly from those of your students.

WORKBOOKS

Workbooks are softbound books that contain a series of skill-based activities to reinforce what the students have read from the student text. As with student texts and teacher guides, workbooks are part of the "basic" package of any basal system. Two issues arise in using workbooks: (a) their inherent value, and (b) how they are used. Each will be discussed below.

Workbook tasks should be inextricably linked to what students read. They should help students hone their understanding of story elements, analyze how and why characters behave as they do, as well as reinforce and extend vocabulary and comprehension skills. For example, Figure 2.4 presents a workbook page that is related to the reading selection in Figure 2.3. Students use key vocabulary words from the reading

Name _____

Read this story about Rabbit.
Write the words in the sentences.
Read the story again with your words.

| Write |

beach   carry   great   sky   water

Rabbit went to the _____ to sit in the sun.

He looked up at the pretty blue _____ .

The big, orange sun was hot. So Rabbit went

into the _____ . He played and had fun.
Then it was time to go home. Rabbit had to

_____ all his things. But he did not care.

Rabbit had a _____ time!

Have pupils tell what they would like to do at a beach, a lake, or a river.

"The Picture," pages 8–16
Vocabulary: key words   1

© D.C. Heath and Company

FIGURE 2.4
Sample workbook page for First Grade Student Reader
Note. From *Workbook to Accompany First Grade Reader, My Best Bear Hug* (p. 1), 1989, Lexington, MA: D. C. Heath. Copyright 1989 by D. C. Heath. Reprinted by permission.

selection to complete a paragraph about the rabbit's experience at the beach. Students have the opportunity to rethink the rabbit's experience as they use key words in a meaningful context. "Workbooks are the ideal place for the maintenance of the information that students read in their readers" (Osborn, 1984, p. 183).

Workbook activities also should be appropriate for students. Directions should be clear, unambiguous, and easy to follow. Activities should contain content that is relevant and culturally sensitive to students' background. Osborn (1984) shows how some workbook activities include references to words that probably are not part of students' in-school or out-of-school experiences. Equally important is the way students work with language as they complete workbook tasks. Rather than circling, numbering, or "x"ing out items, students should have opportunities to write words and sentences in meaningful contexts, as shown in Figure 2.4.

Workbooks have come to be seen as unnecessary time-fillers because of their often mindless or inappropriate tasks. They often occupy too much precious time that could be spent on real reading. However, they do serve a purpose when used discreetly. As Osborn (1984) suggests, don't use a workbook activity unless it serves an instructional purpose, is written clearly enough so that students understand what to do, is accurate and precise, and helps students to learn something that they do not already know.

Consideration also must be given to *how* workbooks are used. Workbook pages typically are seen as busy work for one group of students to do independently at their seats while the teacher is free to work with another group of students. The problem is not with the organization itself; rather, the problem is the lack of forethought about what "seatwork" the children are really doing. Undoubtedly, if used properly workbooks can provide meaningful practice and serve as important diagnostic tools. In this vein, consider the following questions before assigning workbook activities:

1. Why are my students working on this workbook task?
2. What do I need to do to help my students complete this workbook task?
3. Can my students work independently on this workbook task, or might they profit from working cooperatively? (for example, on phonics activities that require saying and listening for specific sound-symbol correspondences)
4. How much time will my students need to complete this workbook task?
5. Is there something better that my students could be doing with their time?

The idea of workbooks is not as much of a problem as their misguided use in the classroom (Heilman, Blair, & Rupley, 1990). Although students need multiple opportunities to develop their reading abilities, they cannot be overburdened with trivialized components of the reading process. For students to develop as readers, they need more time to read than to complete one-page activity sheets. The workbook really should be considered as a supplement rather than the mainstay of reading instruction. In fact, if workbooks serve no real instructional purpose, they should be left out altogether.

SKILL PRACTICE BOOKS

Skill practice books (also called skill packs or skill books) are intended for additional practice. Students who have difficulty with the skills and activities provided in the workbook pages can use skill packs or skill books to reinforce what they did not assimilate the first time. While workbook exercises often relate to what the students have read in the student text, skill practice books usually do not. For example, Figure

Name _____

Write the word that best fits in each sentence.

beach	**orange**	**sky**
carry	**pretty**	**water**
great		

1. Rob ate an _____ for lunch.

2. Kevin went to the _____ to play
in the sand.

3. Kim will _____ her books
to school.

4. Meg gave her dog _____
to drink.

5. The sun is in the _____ .

6. The water feels _____ on a
hot day.

7. The _____ green dress will look
great on Clara.

"The Picture," pages 8–16
Vocabulary: key words

MY BEST BEAR HUG **1**

FIGURE 2.5
Sample skill practice sheet for First Grade Student Reader
Note. From *Skill Practice Book to Accompany First Grade Reader, My Best Bear Hug* (p. 1), 1989, Lexington, MA: D. C. Heath. Copyright 1989 by D. C. Heath. Reprinted by permission.

2.5 is an example of a skill practice sheet that has students work with the key words from the reading selection in Figure 2.3. Although students are not exactly working with the content of the reading selection, they still are using the key words in sentences. As with workbook pages, students' experiences with skill practice books should be appropriate and meaningful.

Skill practice books compound the skill-based aura of basal programs. Consequently, instruction with basals often reflects an emphasis on skills (Barr & Sadow, 1989) because students end up spending at least twice as much time on skill-based seatwork as they spend on coherent-text reading.

The generic material in skill sheets does not limit their usefulness to basal material. Skill practice books should be considered as "extras" for the basal program and used *only* when students need them for further reinforcement. Alternatively, they can be used along with a trade book program to satisfy your diagnostic needs about students' skills for testing.

CLASSROOM LIBRARIES

Classroom libraries are packages of trade books that supplement the basal reading program. They vary in the number of titles and number of copies that accompany a basal series. While some companies specify when a trade book is appropriate for a unit theme, others merely list the books that are available in their classroom libraries. Moreover, while some companies take their trade book collections seriously and create

accompanying activity cards, others treat their libraries as insignificant components to their series.

These books serve an important purpose in communicating to students the need to read beyond the basal. We recommend that you use the books from these libraries as frequently as the student text or, in many cases, *instead of* the story from the student text. Whenever trade books have been identified for basal-related themes (for example, sharing, fears, or friendship), you can adapt many of the theme-related enrichment ideas to the trade books. (See Figure 2.13 for an example of how this can be planned.)

If you do not already have a classroom library from your basal, you may want to consider purchasing the same trade books from vendors such as Scholastic. Often, books from these vendors are less expensive than the same books from a basal publisher. Or, you can use the list of suggested titles from a basal's classroom library and borrow them from the library.

TEACHER RESOURCE FILE

Every basal system comes with a teacher resource file. Organized by categories, these files or kits include an array of materials for the basal system, for example, reteaching and reinforcement masters, activity masters, parent involvement forms, assessment tests, writing activities, materials for Limited English Proficient, and language arts masters. Varying in durability and aesthetics, these crate-like kits essentially are filing systems for the massive amount of materials that come with any basal. One resource file includes an excellent idea book with overhead transparencies and bulletin board templates that can be used for reading and writing activities not connected with the basal. Although initially overwhelming (it took us days to read through only part of the material), these materials can offer many wonderful ideas that you can incorporate into your reading and writing plans.

WORD CARDS

Word cards contain key vocabulary words and examples of phonics elements to reinforce the skills and activities in each lesson. They are supposed to be used as additional visuals to introduce new words, build sentences, or play vocabulary games. Every basal seems to have a different system for using their word cards. Some companies do not include them in their overall lesson plans; others provide specific directions on which cards to use and what to say for each word. Before deciding whether to use these cards, ask yourself: "How can these cards enhance instruction?" If you cannot find a good reason to use them, spend your money and time on other components.

TEACHING CHARTS

Teaching charts are intended to eliminate board work. Specific directions and a picture of the teaching chart are included in the teacher's guide to help you execute your lesson. Although they do minimize the tedious work of copying information for basal instruction, they highlight the prescriptive complexion of basal instruction. Imagine all students everywhere looking at Chart 3 to prepare themselves for the vocabulary words in an upcoming selection. Just because these charts appear in every basal series, we hope you will challenge their usefulness for your teaching situation before using them.

ASSESSMENT TESTS

Assessment tests represent the publisher's attempt to offer a "scientific" means to evaluate at which reading level students are functioning. They are used to place students into an appropriate basal level and assess how well students are doing at a specific level. There are as few as three different types of tests for one basal system and as many as seven tests for another system. Typically, *placement* tests determine at which level students should begin, *unit* tests determine students' mastery of skills for a unit within a level, and *level* tests determine students' overall progress at a particular grade level. Some basal publishers have developed additional assessment tests such as unit process tests (students' reading comprehension through speaking or writing) and informal reading inventories (individual assessments of students' decoding and comprehension abilities) to provide more qualitative information.

Even though we were able to examine only a few assessment instruments, we noticed that the tests genuinely reflect the program's orientation. When a basal system tries to focus more on comprehension than on skill acquisition, the tests contain more opportunities to assess comprehension, and vice versa. We also found that some of the same skills (for example, multiple meaning words) are tested at the same level and many are not, leading us to believe that a student's success with one basal test does not guarantee success on another basal test, a statewide test, or a nationally standardized test.

This inconsistency is particularly obvious for the vocabulary assessed in end-of-unit or end-of-level tests. The words come from the vocabulary used in the stories, which differs from basal to basal. As for the comprehension portion of these tests, we believe that there is no magical formula used in basal systems. Although questions are sometimes earmarked as main idea, inference, sequence, or cause/effect, students can acquire the skills for the assessment tests without depending on basal materials.

If your school district depends on basal-driven assessment tests, examine the tests carefully before deciding on your instructional plans. If you are concerned about students' acquisition of specific skills, determine what is tested in the basal tests and which portions might be useful to you. Use your own strategies or the basal's suggested strategies to help you develop skills that you might otherwise omit so that your students fare as well as other students on the tests. One teacher, Gerarda Wahlers, whom you will read about in Chapter 3, uses the basal assessment tests as pre- and post-tests for her trade book program. She finds that these tests serve as yardsticks for planning which skills need to be taught during the year.

How Are Seven Popular Basals Similar and Different?

While the previous section discussed common features of all basals, this section looks at how basals differ in content and organizational complexity. Barr and Sadow (1989) found that fourth grade basals differ in organizational complexity but not really in content. In this next section we compare the first grade reader (first hardcover book) and fourth grade reader of each series for four areas: literature, lesson structure, scope and sequence, and metacomprehension development. We analyzed three total lessons—one from the beginning, one from the middle, and one from the end of the book—for each of the seven basals.

LITERATURE IN BASALS

Basal critics are in their glory when given carte blanche to critique the quality of basal literature. Acknowledged by most to be woefully inadequate representations of the English language because of their artificial settings, colorless characters, and contrived sentence structure, basals receive few accolades in the literary department. In response to these criticisms, basal publishers have begun to emphasize the "real" literature that students read in the newest editions of the basals. Current basals make fancy claims such as "Looking for Great Literature? Follow these signs" and "A Sparkling Variety of Great Literature." Because we believe so strongly in using material that whets students' appetites for reading at a young age, we read or skimmed all the reading selections in the first and fourth grade readers for each series to see what "literature" students are reading.

We looked at three factors: the number of reading selections in each student text, the development and quality of the literature, and the genres used. In looking at the quality of literature, we considered whether the story was created specifically for the basal with all its readability accoutrements or whether the story was reprinted with permission from an original source. We also noted whether the story was written in its original form or whether the story had been adapted to fit a basal formula. Our general feeling is that including original, unexcerpted literature from trade books written by highly acclaimed authors should be the aim of every basal publisher, because students' continued literacy development depends on their interest in reading books, not basals.

Figure 2.6 shows what we found for first grade. Not one basal company has more trade book originals than basal-created stories. In other words, most of the stories in the basals have been written or adapted to control for vocabulary and sentence length. However, our findings are not as bleak as you would expect. D. C. Heath and McGraw-Hill have made a concerted effort to include stories from original sources without any adaptations. (When we had a specific trade book available, we actually compared our published version with the basal version to check for any changes in the language.) Forty-two percent of D. C. Heath's stories are original; 37% of McGraw-Hill's stories are original. Furthermore, Harcourt Brace Jovanovich (HBJ), Houghton Mifflin, and McGraw-Hill happen to have at least half or more of their stories originating from outside sources, albeit with minimal or moderate adaptations.

FIGURE 2.6
Sources of literature for first grade in seven basal series

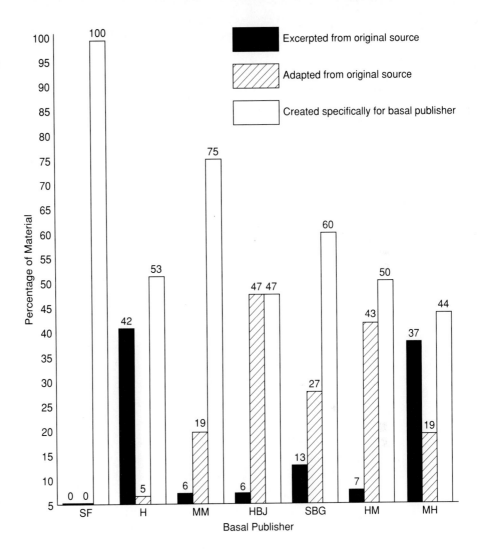

Some of the adaptations do slight authors of their "real" writing voices. In any case, more than half of the basal companies are using materials from real books.

Figure 2.7 indicates an overall higher percentage of original source literature (real text) for fourth grade than for first grade. Over 80% of the stories for all the fourth grade readers come from outside sources. D. C. Heath and Silver Burdett & Ginn contain the highest percentage of original text (no modifications whatsoever) with 71% and 67%, respectively. HBJ and Houghton Mifflin happen to have approximately half of their stories adapted from outside sources. There is a marked difference between the first and fourth readers for literature created for the basals. Whereas most of the stories for first grade are not from original sources, most of the stories for the fourth grade are.

FIGURE 2.7
Sources of
literature for
fourth grade in
seven basal series

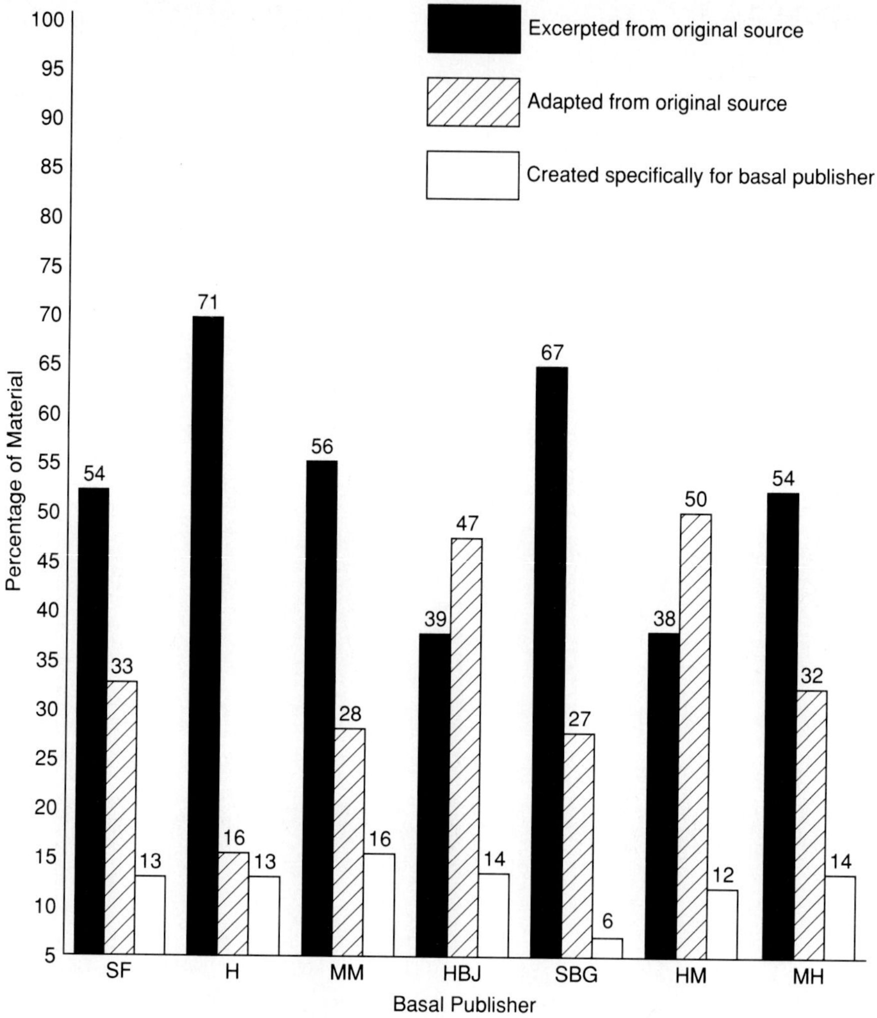

We also noticed that even basal-created stories have some redeeming features. First of all, many of them communicate an important message to young children. Secondly, many of them are written by well-known children's authors or are well-known fables and folktales that have been rewritten. For instance, we noticed that James Marshall, noted author and illustrator for the George and Martha books about two hippopotamus friends, has written three delightful stories for three basal series (D. C. Heath, Silver Burdett & Ginn, and Houghton Mifflin). We also saw that folktales such as *Stone Soup* and *The Three Wishes* are retold by notable storytellers and authors.

Genre differences between basals are not as obvious as the authenticity of the stories. Most basals provide a balance of realistic fiction, fantasy, informational pieces, and folktales. Mysteries, fables, fairy tales, and biographies appear a bit more sporadically.

Generally speaking, there are major differences among publishers in the literature they include in their student texts. Some basals include literature in its original form; others still seem compelled to subscribe to a "basalesque" genre, especially at the first grade level.

What is obvious to us from this small sampling, and we hope to you, is that basals differ markedly in the kinds of materials they deliver to our students. Right now all we can do is discover which basals serve our purposes best and hope that other basals will follow similar paths. For the future we need to demand that more and better pieces of authentic children's literature be included. We also need to convince basal publishers that including a few whole books might be far better than featuring excerpts from many books. As Sam Sebesta, professor of education at the University of Washington in Seattle, points out, "An excerpt of a really strong novel is unlikely to carry the force of the whole work."

LESSON STRUCTURE

Our analysis of each basal's lesson structure is based on the format and treatment of skillwork for six lessons, three first grade and three fourth grade taken from the beginning, middle, and end of the books. Although a Directed Reading Activity (DRA) format forms the framework, a great deal of content and activity variability exists within this basic structure.

LESSON FORMAT

Table 2.3 shows approximate headings and subheadings to guide teaching. Basal lessons contain from two to four main headings; however, a three-step framework appears in a majority of the guides. Step 1 typically includes some type of preparatory work for reading. Six of the seven basals use this stage primarily to introduce decoding and vocabulary skills. Only D. C. Heath uses this first step to actually prepare students to read the student text by exploring students' ideas and predictions about the selection. In Step 2 five of the seven publishers prepare students to read the selection by exploring prior knowledge, previewing and predicting, and setting purposes for reading. Within Step 2, questions are available to guide students through reading. Step 3 extends students' reading with a variety of decoding, vocabulary, comprehension, and study skill activities. This step also is used for enrichment, maintenance, and cross-curricular activities.

Although the basals follow similar paths of preparation, during-reading guidance, and follow-up, they communicate different messages through their guidelines and activities, particularly during and after reading. Three differences in during-reading guidelines are immediately obvious: (a) D. C. Heath and McGraw-Hill are the only two basals that actually encourage students' independent reading of the student text,

TABLE 2.3

Approximate lesson headings and subheadings in seven basal series

SF	H	MM	HBJ

1. Teach Vocabulary
2. Read Selection
  a. Prior Knowledge
  b. Purpose
  c. Promote Comprehension
3. Respond to Literature
	1. Think Ahead
	  a. Build Vocabulary
	  b. Explore Ideas Prior Knowledge Preview/Predict Purpose
	2. Think While Reading
	3. Think Back
	  a. Extend Ideas
	  b. Apply Ideas
	  c. Relate Skills
		1. Prepare for Reading
		  a. Key Skills
		  b. Vocabulary/Concepts
		2. Read for Comprehension
		  a. Background
		  b. Purpose
		  c. Read/Discuss
		  d. Guide & Apply
		  e. Think & Talk
		3. Teach Reading Skills
			1. Prepare for Reading
			2. Read and Respond
			  a. Prior Knowledge
			  b. Purpose/Predict
			  c. Direct & Model Reading Process
			  d. Respond to Selection
			3. Continue Essential Skills and Strategies

SBG	HM	MH	

1. Introduce Skill
2. Vocabulary
3. Guide Comprehension
  a. Build Background
  b. Purpose for Reading
  c. Guide Reading
  d. Ideas for Selection Follow-up
  e. Language Arts Connections
4. Extend Skills
	1. Prepare Skill
	  a. Decoding
	  b. Vocabulary & Concepts
	2. Read
	  a. Prepare
	  b. Vocabulary/Skill/Background
	  c. Think & Predict
	  d. Purpose
	  e. Guide Reading
	  f. Story Wrap-up
		1. Introduce Skills
		2. Introduce and Read Selection
		  a. Prior Knowledge
		  b. Vocabulary
		  c. Set Purpose
		  d. Guide Reading
		3. Respond, Extend, and Reread
		4. Apply Skills	

and only McGraw-Hill states ways to guide students to read independently or semi-independently. (b) HBJ and Houghton Mifflin are the only two basals that state a purpose for which students read before each page of text. The rest simply ask questions afterwards about what was read. (c) Scott, Foresman provides one question for every one or two pages of text; the other basals contain three to eight questions for a similar number of pages. This latter option seems to interrogate students about their reading more than encourage them to read for their own purposes.

After-reading activities also differ. Macmillan, HBJ, and Silver Burdett & Ginn reinforce skills before getting into cross-curricular enrichment activities; D. C. Heath, Houghton Mifflin, and McGraw-Hill include activities and projects before skills. Scott, Foresman does not really include after-reading extensions.

While we were impressed with the creativity in some of the more comprehensive lesson formats, we often became so dizzy from too many options (and we know firsthand how so many options get into one lesson) that we couldn't help but wonder how other teachers could do it all without jeopardizing students' opportunities for real reading. This thought also triggered another concern: the ratio of coherent reading to skillwork.

SKILLWORK

We define **coherent reading** as continuous reading from the student text. We define **skillwork** as paper-and-pencil tasks in workbooks and skill practice books. There is also the possibility of other written responses (for example, journal writing) that is not included in the following analysis. Figure 2.8 (first grade) and 2.9 (fourth grade) show the percentage of pages devoted to coherent reading versus skillwork. Scott, Foresman and Houghton Mifflin are eliminated from this comparison because they did not submit skill practice books for examination.

On the first grade level, only Macmillan has more pages devoted to reading coherent text (58%) than to doing skillwork (42%). The rest have more pages devoted to skillwork than to coherent reading, with HBJ devoting less than 35% to reading.

On the fourth grade level, 51 to 55% of the pages in D. C. Heath, Macmillan, and HBJ are devoted to coherent reading. Silver Burdett & Ginn and McGraw-Hill have students working more with skillwork than with coherent reading.

In general, first grade students read 7 to 9 pages in the student text and complete an average of 11 pages of skillwork per story. Fourth grade students read 8 to 15 pages in the student text and complete an average of 8 pages of skillwork per story. However, these graphs do not record the actual *time* spent reading versus the total amount of time needed to complete worksheets. While the number of pages of text may be comparable to the pages of skillwork, there is actually a disproportionate amount of time spent on skillwork if all the pages are completed. For example, according to a friend of ours who is a fourth grade teacher and uses the basal regularly, students generally complete the text reading in one sitting, yet need 2 to 3 days to complete the skill sheets for the same lesson.

Another significant issue is the way in which basals treat the skillwork that is offered. All seven basals include in their scope and sequence charts four major skill areas: decoding, vocabulary, comprehension, and **study skills.** With this information in mind, we asked ourselves two questions: (a) Which skills are emphasized in the skillwork? and (b) Is the skillwork related to what students are reading? In other words, do the workbook and skillbook pages have something related to the essence of the

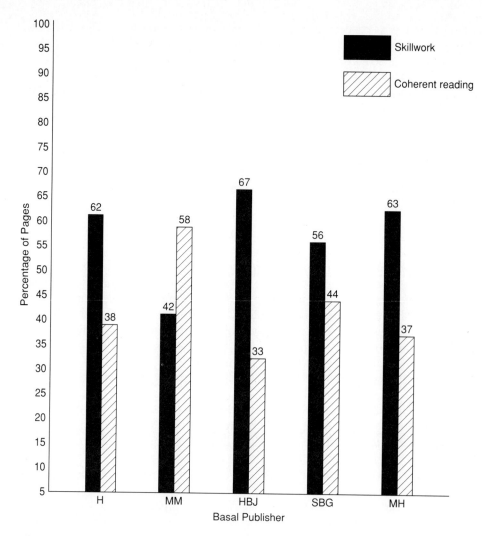

FIGURE 2.8
Pages devoted to student reading and skill sheets for first grade in five basal series

story? For example, just because the word *dog* is used on a skill page does not necessarily mean it is related to the basal's story about a dog. The skill sheet could be used in any other context.

To answer these two questions, we examined 214 skill sheets (116 workbook pages and 98 skill book pages) for first grade and 167 skill sheets (100 workbook pages and 67 skill book pages) for fourth grade for the three sample lessons at each grade level.

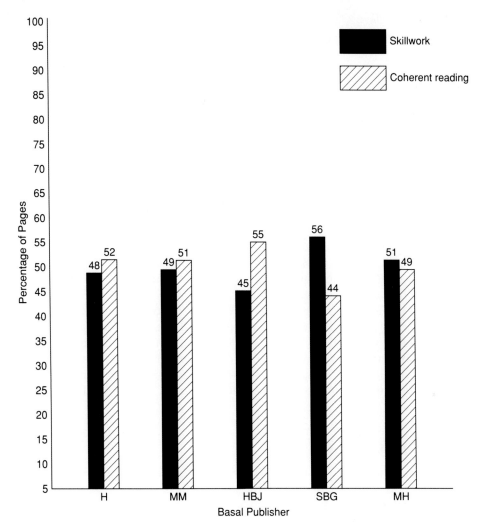

FIGURE 2.9
Pages devoted to student reading and skill sheets for fourth grade in five basal series

The following summarizes what we found. (See Appendix A for a detailed analysis of our findings.)

First Grade

- *Type of skillwork:* Decoding prevails as the skill activity of choice for the first grade lessons. Comprehension, vocabulary, and study skills follow as second, third, and fourth choices, respectively.

- *Content of skillwork:* Seventy-two percent of all the skillwork is unrelated to what students are reading.

Fourth Grade

- *Type of skillwork:* Comprehension prevails as the skill activity of choice for the fourth grade lessons. Vocabulary is the second most concentrated area. Study skills, decoding, and writing follow as third, fourth, and fifth choices, respectively.
- *Content of skillwork:* Fifty-seven percent of all the skillwork is unrelated to what students are reading.

In summary, a disproportionate amount of skillwork is required, especially when compared to the amount of required reading. First grade students complete more than one skill sheet for every page of text they read in the student text. Fourth grade students complete a skill sheet page for every one to two pages they read in the student text. Moreover, only about one-fourth and two-fifths of the skillwork for first grade and fourth grade, respectively, reflect what the students are reading; the rest of the skillwork could be done for any reading material from a trade book or a basal without any difficulty whatsoever.

Although this analysis merely reflects three lessons for two grade-level basals, it is obvious that most basals overload us with skillwork. Some basals make an occasional effort to connect their skillwork to the student texts in meaningful ways; most do not. It behooves us to analyze what we have by asking: How many skill sheets are offered? What is the focus of each skill sheet? Is the skill sheet activity a meaningful one? Is it related to what my students are reading? Finally, Why would I use the skill sheets offered?

SCOPE AND SEQUENCE

Since most skill sheets relate to the basal's scope and sequence, it is important to look at the skills addressed. How similar are the skills across basals? Where do differences lie? In our analysis, we looked at all the skills listed in each series for the first and fourth grade readers. While we summarize our findings herein, a more detailed analysis is included in Appendix A.

First Grade

- *Number of Skills:* The number of skills listed in each basal's scope and sequence varies widely, from a high of 98 to a low of 30.
- *Type of Skills:* Decoding/phonics and comprehension have the largest number of skills.

Fourth Grade

- *Number of Skills:* The number of skills listed in each basal's scope and sequence also varies widely at grade four, from a high of 130 to a low of 37.
- *Type of Skills:* Comprehension and study skills have the largest number of skills.

Are there differences in the skills that the basals address? The following four sections highlight what we found. Tables and explanations are available in Appendix A. (Detailed tables of each basal's skill coverage are available in Wepner et al., 1991.)

DECODING AND PHONICS

Chances are that any first grade basal you select covers basic decoding and phonics skills, for example, recognizing and using consonants, consonant clusters, and short and long vowels. Even Houghton Mifflin, which glosses over its coverage of decoding skills in its scope and sequence chart, addresses many of the same skills as its basal counterparts. You simply need to dig into the teacher's guide to find out when and where the skills appear.

While most basals include similar decoding and phonics skills, the publishers are not really connecting these skills to what students are reading. This finding supports Durkin's (1990a) sentiments that decoding and phonics instruction is usually not well-coordinated with the stories. She believes that the anti-phonics movement (see Kantrowitz, 1990) has created ambivalence among basal publishers about the role of phonics in early reading. Recently, though, Adams (1990) stated:

> Research indicates that the most critical factor beneath fluent word reading is the ability to recognize letters, spelling patterns, and whole words, effortlessly, automatically, and visually. Moreover the goal of all reading instruction—comprehension—depends critically on this ability. (p. 14)

Adams believes that activities requiring children to attend to the individual letters of words, their sequencing, and their phonological translations should be included in any beginning reading program. Since basal publishers cannot deny the inclusion of decoding and phonics skills in basals, authors of these systems should, at the very least, coordinate phonics instruction with the rest of their reading program so that they can be dealt with in context, especially since phonics can be an important tool for helping students to tackle new words (Yopp & Yopp, 1991). If you are inclined to have a strong phonics program, your best bet is to look for systems that try to teach phonics in context and relate instruction to students' reading.

VOCABULARY

Although most basals do cover basic vocabulary skills (for example, word meaning, synonyms/antonyms, multiple meanings/homographs, and classification), they seem to differ markedly in their treatment of this skill area.

Since vocabulary is so basic to students' development as readers (Nagy, 1988), it is important to assess how your basal handles vocabulary for its skillwork and classroom activities. While our analysis of skillwork (refer to Figures A.1 and A.2 in the appendix) indicates that most vocabulary skill sheets are connected to what students are reading, every publisher handles vocabulary skillwork differently. If you find that your basal treats vocabulary unsatisfactorily, supplement this area with non-basal vocabulary activities that extend naturally from the reading selection (for example, using words from stories read aloud, content studies, and self-selected books).

As mentioned in Chapter 1, Gipe's (1978–1979) *interactive context method* for teaching word meaning helps students to comprehend new words as they work with sentences in familiar contexts. Students read a three-sentence passage that contains simple sentence structures and common words. Each sentence uses the target word in defining context. Students respond in writing after reading the sentences and give a word or phrase from their own experience that defines the new word. For example:

1. People thought that she was *aloof* because she was shy.
2. Someone who is *aloof* does not talk to people much.
3. An *aloof* person is someone who does not seem interested.

Describe how an *aloof* person would be at a party.

COMPREHENSION

The comprehension skills of main ideas/details, sequence, comparison/contrast, and cause/effect appear in all seven basals for both grade levels. However, many other comprehension skill are not addressed consistently, if at all, across the basals.

As with vocabulary, look at how the basal supports comprehension. While comprehension skill sheets cover the skills listed in the scope and sequence, more of them are unrelated than related to what students are reading. Yet, oral comprehension questions during and after reading not only cover the skills in the scope and sequence but also deal with the content of the student text. Because comprehension is fundamental to reading, the number of comprehension activities is not nearly as important as the quality of activities used. Rather than barrage students with questions about the text, we are better off encouraging group discussion about the content of the text so that our students can reach their own conclusions about what the text means (Fish, 1980; Temple, 1990). Any of the metacomprehension strategies discussed in the upcoming "Metacomprehension Development" section also facilitate students' comprehension. Focus on the strategies that your basal is using and supplement with others so that your students are actively attempting to understand what they read. An excellent resource for helping students to focus on the meaning of what they read is *Responses to Literature, Grades K–8* (Macon, Bewell, & Vogt, 1991).

STUDY SKILLS

As expected, many more study skills are consistently addressed across basals for fourth grade than for first grade. Such basic study skills as following directions, identifying parts of a book, and knowing alphabetical order appear in first grade, whereas more complex skills such as using graphic aids and working with test-taking strategies appear in fourth grade. Generally, though, study skill coverage varies so much from basal to basal that other guides and materials should be used to support what is important for your grade level. One book that contains helpful suggestions for teaching study skills is *Study Skills Handbook: A Guide for All Teachers* (Graham & Robinson, 1984).

In summary, most skills are represented unevenly across basals for both first and fourth grades. Decoding and phonics is the only area where more than half of the skills are consistently addressed in grade one. Study skills is the only area where more than half of the skills are addressed in grade four.

This analysis indicates that basals differ in *content* focus in important areas for reading development. Some basals are more skill oriented than others. Following one basal's scope and sequence chart probably will produce a different "reading" curriculum than following another's. Dole and Osborn (1989) suggest the same notion from their work with basal selection committees.

We acknowledge that scope and sequence is only one indicator of how a skill is addressed. Some basals may cover scope and sequence skills cursorily; others may address the same skill in depth yet fail to identify it as such in their scope and sequence chart. Because basals vary considerably in their purported curriculum, it is unwise to adopt a basal's scope and sequence as your curriculum. Instead, your curriculum should serve as the fulcrum for balancing basals with other materials. As you determine how much weight to give the basal, look for how scope and sequence skills are integrated into students' reading and writing activities. Is skill development connected to students' reading? Are the skills taught in a meaningful context? If not, your basal may not be accomplishing what you want to accomplish with your students.

METACOMPREHENSION DEVELOPMENT

There is an evolving view that comprehension is a holistic and unitary process that is affected by the teacher, the learner, the context, the purposes for reading, and the materials to be read. The subskills approach to analyzing comprehension (for example, learning about sequence in texts by practicing sequence exercises) seems less important than an approach that promotes more holistic strategies (for example, using summarizing to help students cope better with the ideas in a given text). Recently, our role in advancing students' reading comprehension is seen as far more important than the reams of skill sheets used in the past. Moreover, students play an important role in directing their own learning (Robinson, Faraone, Hittleman, & Unruh, 1990).

As discussed in Chapter 1, readers need opportunities to reflect on, monitor, and evaluate their understanding as they read. When they are, for example, **generating questions** about what they read, summarizing, paraphrasing, retelling, or **thinking aloud**, they are actively engaged in monitoring their comprehension. As teachers, we need to help our students read strategically so that they are aware of what they know and need to learn.

Unfortunately, as Schmitt and Baumann (1990) found, we do very little during guided reading of basal selections to help our students become independent readers. While we activate background and pose purpose-setting questions prior to reading the selections, we do not do enough to help our students to read strategically and achieve independence. Most of the questions we ask are verbatim or close paraphrases of questions from the teacher's guide. Schmitt and Baumann believe that more metacomprehension-promoting directives need to be included in basals so that we are more likely to help our students develop as strategic readers.

To analyze what the basals currently are doing to help promote students' reading independence, we looked at the same three sample lessons for first and fourth grades for six **metacomprehension** strategies: *generating questions* (creating one's own questions about an upcoming reading selection), *summarizing* (condensing information from the reading selection), *paraphrasing* (restating a statement or paragraph), *retelling* (reporting the essence of the reading selection), *predicting and verifying* (forming hypotheses before reading and confirming or changing hypotheses after reading), and *thinking aloud* (verbally expressing thoughts as one reads the selection). These six strategies reflect the metacomprehension strategies discussed by Schmitt and Baumann.

Table 2.4 indicates the degree to which first grade basals foster students' strategic reading.

1. Only Scott, Foresman and Macmillan prompt the teacher to have students *generate* their own *questions* about what they think the reading selection will be about.
2. All basals encourage students to *summarize* every few pages during reading or summarize the essence of the reading selection after reading. (Interestingly, not all basals include this comprehension skill in their scope and sequence charts.) Unlike most basals, Silver Burdett & Ginn informs teachers when they are helping students to read strategically, a nice feature of its guided comprehension section.
3. HBJ and McGraw-Hill encourage students to *paraphrase,* or tell in their own words, what a character said in a reading selection.

TABLE 2.4

Metacomprehension strategies in first grade in seven basal series

METACOMPREHENSION STRATEGY	BASAL PUBLISHER						
	SF	H	MM	HBJ	SBG	HM	MH
1. Generating Questions	√		√				
2. Summarizing	√	√	√	√	√	√	√
3. Paraphrasing				√			√
4. Retelling	√	√	√	√	√	√	√
5. Predicting and Verifying	√	√	√	√	√	√	√
6. Thinking Aloud	√	√	√	√	√	√	√

4. All basals have students *retell* a reading selection. Most of the basals suggest using props or drama as students retell a reading selection.
5. All basals encourage students to *predict* what they will read about and *verify* their predictions. Whereas six of the seven basals have students verify their predictions after reading the entire story, HBJ has students predict and verify after every page or two of text.
6. All basals foster students' *thinking aloud* with questions such as "How do you know?" or "What did you do to answer the question?"

Table 2.5 shows the fourth grade basals' metacomprehension practices.

1. All basals, except HBJ and Houghton Mifflin, prompt teachers to have students *generate* their own *questions*.
2. All basals, except D. C. Heath, have students *summarize*. Silver Burdett & Ginn continues to inform teachers when they are helping students to read strategically.
3. Houghton Mifflin encourages *paraphrasing*.
4. All but Silver Burdett & Ginn have students *retell*.
5. All basals encourage students to *predict* and *verify*.
6. All but D. C. Heath encourage students to *think aloud*.

Overall, the basals are making strides to help students become strategic readers. However, as with the other areas analyzed, some basals are stronger than others in their efforts. Even if we do not use a story from the student text, we should look at the ways in which the guidelines encourage students to become more active in monitoring their comprehension. We should apply these strategies—and more—to other reading material as well.

TABLE 2.5
Metacomprehension strategies in fourth grade in seven basal series

METACOMPREHENSION STRATEGY	BASAL PUBLISHER						
	SF	H	MM	HBJ	SBG	HM	MH
1. Generating Questions	✓	✓	✓		✓		✓
2. Summarizing	✓		✓	✓	✓	✓	✓
3. Parapharsing						✓	
4. Retelling	✓	✓	✓	✓		✓	✓
5. Predicting and Verifying	✓	✓	✓	✓	✓	✓	✓
6. Thinking Aloud	✓		✓	✓	✓	✓	✓

The following five broad questions, used in our comparison of seven popular basal series, may serve as a guide for you to set up criteria for selecting and using basals for your own teaching:

1. To what extent do the basals use authentic, unexcerpted literature in their student texts?
2. How do the teacher's guides structure their lessons?
3. What is the focus of the basals' skillwork and how does it relate to what students are reading?
4. What are the contents of the scope and sequence charts, and how do they compare with your district's reading curriculum guide?
5. What do the basals do to develop metacomprehension strategies?

Two resources that also can help you with the selection and use of basal reading programs are *A Guide to Selecting Basal Reading Programs* (n.d.), a series of booklets that are produced by the Center for the Study of Reading at the University of Illinois at Urbana-Champaign, and *Selecting A Basal Reading Program: Making the Right Choice* (Barnard & Hetzel, 1989).

Basals in the Regular Classroom

For every point made in favor of basal use in the classroom, there is a counterpoint made against its use. Those who support basals say that the newer basals have a higher percentage of quality literature, provide ideas for building background, include co-operative and shared learning experiences, teach children to set purposes and make predictions, and make writing an integral part of the reading program (Heymsfeld, 1989; Squire, 1989). Those who oppose the basal believe that these programs operate on the principle of moving from part to whole in a controlled, sequential, and hier-archical way that is the antithesis of natural language development. They also see the basals as perpetuating the habit of isolated skill instruction that is too far removed from normal everyday reading (Mickelson, 1989; Snowball, 1989).

Some teachers see the basal as a way to remove the guesswork, and they rely heavily on its suggestions; others want to throw it out and spend their money on class sets of trade books. In a 1987 survey of teachers, Turner (1988) found that, while 56% of her 339 respondents are not required to strictly follow a basal reading program, 85% still use it. Similarly, when we interviewed classroom teachers for this book, we found that 78% of our teachers are using basals in some way. Although 47% of these teachers see themselves as moving away from the basal in favor of trade books, 31% see themselves as primarily basal users. Most of them commented that they used the basal because of school or district expectations. Yet, for every weakness noted, there was a strength mentioned. Those who felt the most satisfied with their basal-oriented program had taken the initiative to adapt the basal in some way so that students' desire to read was not secondary to acquiring a set of skills.

TABLE 2.6
Pros and cons for using basals

PROS	CONS
Is organized and sequenced	Tries to cover too much material
Covers skills	Does not always coordinate with what students are reading
Uses experts in the field as authors and consultants	Does not provide enough coordination among the authors and consultants
Features wide variety of literature	Does not always include literature that is authentic or well-written
Uses excerpts from good literature	Uses too many excerpts and not enough "whole texts"
Includes preplanned lessons that encompass reading and skillwork	Lessons encourage too little reading and too much skillwork
Includes activities for all children	Difficult and time-consuming to coordinate all activities
Provides sense of security for new teachers who don't have to develop lessons	Provides little incentive for teachers to be creative
Provides numerous ideas, many of which are great	Takes up too much time
Focuses on comprehension	Does not emphasize enough development of higher level thinking skills
Encourages writing	Does not provide enough writing in response to reading

In view of what teachers have shared with us and what we have discovered from our own analysis, we offer some of our own impressions of the pros and cons of using basals in the regular classroom in Table 2.6. We look upon the "con" statements as opportunities to take the initiative in deciding which basal activities should and should not be used. And, the teachers you are going to read about are doing just that. Unlike Ms. E. in our opening vignette, they are figuring out their own ways to use the basal to their advantage. Although these teachers still feel pressure to make sure that their students are skilled enough to pass the basals' unit and level tests, they feel more and more confident to branch away from the voluminous directives in basal guides.

The next two sections share how six teachers use basal systems daily and weekly. Not every grade level is represented; however, the information shared can apply across grade levels. We hope that, if you are using a basal system, you can glean organizational and instructional ideas from teachers who were kind enough to paint their picture of reality for us.

A TYPICAL DAY

Even though first grade teacher Edith Greene (you will read more about her in the technology chapter), is supposed to use all parts of the basal, she has decided to skip most of the workbook activities and some of the reading selections to make room for **Sustained Silent Reading** (SSR) and poetry. She not only has reorganized the order of skills taught and created her own teaching charts, but she also has developed her own comprehension questions for the reading selections and poems that she does use. To help her students comprehend the text better, she models how to generate questions. She also uses story grammar questions for narratives (for example, What problem occurs? How does the main character feel about the problem? What does the main character decide to do about the problem? What happens? What are the consequences?) and structured questions for nonfiction (for example, What do I know? What do I want to learn? What did I learn?).

Every morning for 15 minutes her students read silently from a book or magazine. All students have a basket of books and magazines on their desk which they can change before SSR. She allows her less able students to pick a partner to read with them if they are interested in a book that is too difficult.

Before the class breaks into three reading groups, Edith conducts a whole class lesson on a decoding skill (for example, adding *ing*). She then works with each group individually so that she can help them transfer their skill learning into practice. (Curiously, not one of her groups is using the student text prescribed. Her above average group is using a second grade text, and her average and below average groups are using another basal series altogether which she purchased with her own money.) Rather than review the vocabulary at length beforehand, and because she wants her students to learn to use context, she develops vocabulary as it comes up. She also discusses the story's theme, based on students' real-life experiences.

Meanwhile, those students engaged in seatwork are writing their own poems, copying a favorite poem into their poetry books, or researching and writing about the reading selections from the basals. As Edith sees it, only 10% of her time is spent on skill sheets; 90% is spent on discussion and related reading and writing activities. For example, her students write in journals daily, write to their pen pals, and create their own Big Books as part of her effort to help her students recognize their own desires to read and write.

Because second grade teacher Barbara Jones feels less confident about skipping reading selections in the basal, lest her students miss a concept that will be tested, she has devised ways to make students' basal reading more enjoyable. She often has her students conduct her reading groups. Each child is responsible for asking questions of the group about a page of text read. And, rather than belabor lessons with follow-up skill sheets, she makes sure that she does some type of cross-curricular activity. For example, with the Gingerbread Man story, she has the children make gingerbread cookies to reinforce mathematics concepts and students' skills in following directions. Since she knows that thinking and sharing are more important than isolated skillwork, she also spends one-third more time reading and discussing the reading selections than on the skill sheets.

Fourth grade teacher Mary Lou Keyes also covers almost every reading selection in the basal, yet with a twist. Inasmuch as she is committed to getting students to write, she has students write a letter to her in their journals about every reading selection instead of doing the post-reading exercises suggested in the teacher's guide. It could be a summary, an analysis of character traits, a response to the goals of the story, or a few comments about the author's point of view. She also has her students engage in paired reading so that the daily, three-group, round-robin reading syndrome is avoided.

Since all fourth grade students in Mary Lou's building switch for reading, she has the "average" readers. To help these students sustain themselves with print and extend their reading of a particular genre beyond her basal's reading selections, Mary Lou uses a whole book occasionally. For example, she uses Roald Dahl's (1970) *Fantastic Mr. Fox* to help her students learn about the folktale genre. For this study they leave the basals for awhile and read the book as a class since each student has a copy. Again, she has her students write their responses to her so that they continue to get comfortable with the idea of communicating in writing.

As you can see, these three teachers are making important decisions about the materials and methods they use within their basal program.

A TYPICAL WEEK

Second grade teacher Ann Carline is required to use her entire basal system. To accomplish this, she has devised a weekly system for covering one reading selection each week. (See Figure 2.10 for a sample of Ann's weekly plan.) Because she knows that tapping prior knowledge is important, she uses mapping to introduce each selection. And because she modifies the teacher's guide suggestions to make post-reading activities more personal to her students, she has her students illustrate their favorite part of the story, write letters to characters from the stories, compare stories within the basal, and compare authors' trade books to the stories in the basal.

Although her district mandates that students experience every facet of the basal, the district still provides for a "Literature in the Classroom" program so that students have opportunities to read trade books. You may be asking yourself: "When does Ms. Carline possibly have time for this?" In addition to Ann's scheduled reading time, she and the other teachers in her building have **DEAR** (Drop Everything And Read) three times a week. Undoubtedly, Ann feels pressure to cover everything and she would rather spend less time on skill sheets. However, she works hard to get in those "extra" activities—such as writing in response to reading selections—because she knows they make a difference in helping students to experience pleasurable reading experiences.

MONDAY	Introduce skills. Use charts and boardwork. Use workbook as teaching tool. Students complete Skill Practice Book on their own.
TUESDAY	Introduce selection vocabulary. Use charts with words in sentences. Do mapping to introduce the basal selection. Students do map individually and then we do one together on board. Do workbook together. Students complete Skill Practice Book.
WEDNESDAY	Guided Silent Reading of selection. Discussion. Review skills and concepts. Review any problem areas from Skill Practice Book.
THURSDAY	Review story. Do comprehension check from Student Test together and students complete comprehension pages in workbook and Skill Practice Book on their own.
FRIDAY	Students complete any unfinished work from the week. Some Vocabulary and Writing activities may be assigned. Students having problems receive small group or individual help (may be paired with bright student for peer-teaching). Some time allowed for computer and/or independent reading.

FIGURE 2.10
Weekly plan
Note. From "Weekly Plan" by Ann Carline, 1991. Copyright 1991 by Ann Carline. Reprinted by permission.

Fourth grade teacher Christine Borisuk uses the same amount of basal materials as Ann; however, she feels she has more leverage to determine what she does with the material. Her students do not read every reading selection. Instead, because she wants to give her students some choice in what they read, she has her students vote on which reading selections they want to read. And she does not use the teacher's guide religiously. She skims it to see which skills need to be taught and searches for extension or enrichment activities that might fit into her plans. She also creates her own comprehension activities culled from her professional reading so that her students are involved in a great deal of supplemental reading, researching, discussing, and writing before and after reading basal selections. Students keep response notebooks where their pre-reading and post-reading activities are kept. Sometimes students' writing is discussed, while sometimes it is graded; other times, the students just respond to selections, and Christine writes back to each student.

Although she does not always finish the student text, she gets comfort in knowing that her students see reading as interacting with a variety of texts rather than as an unrelenting series of workbook pages. Every day her students read a minimum of 15 minutes in the classroom and 15 minutes at home. She also has her students write in response notebooks before and after reading basal selections. Although she bemoans the fact that she is more skillbound than she likes, she manages to create a weekly schedule that gets her students really reading and writing. Figure 2.11 highlights how Christine organizes her groupwork and seatwork. In addition to the seatwork listed for this weekly plan, she has students do research, content area reading/writing, and a host of other language activities. Frequently, the students take workbooks home for homework so that the other activities can be used for seatwork.

Christine does not think the basal is as much a problem as the teachers who use them. She feels that teachers complain about boring or inane reading selections, yet continue to use them year after year. As far as she is concerned, the basal is merely a guide for finding ways to create meaningful reading experiences for students.

BEYOND THE TYPICAL WEEK

Sixth grade teacher Thomas A. Simpson feels as if he is enlivening his basal-driven diet with his team-taught penpal letter writing project. Amid his story-skillwork-more skillwork weekly routine, he has his at-risk students write letters to athletes at

	GROUPWORK	SEATWORK
MONDAY	Vocabulary activities Possible skillwork with charts or workbooks	Workbook for vocabulary Pre-reading writing activity or reading activity Free reading
TUESDAY	Pre-reading discussion or activities	Workbook for skills Read story (sometimes she reads to them or they read in small groups) Response notebooks Free reading
WEDNESDAY	Discuss story (sometimes she and her students write group summaries or responses)	Post reading writing activity Free reading
THURSDAY	Skillwork or pre-reading activity for Friday's work	Skill tests Free reading
FRIDAY	Literature, Junior Great Books, Creative writing. Students take Skills Unit Tests when it's time.	

FIGURE 2.11

Weekly teaching and seatwork plan

Note. From "Weekly Teaching Plan" by Christine Borisuk, 1991. Copyright 1991 by Christine Borisuk. Reprinted by permission.

the University of Georgia. He and his teammate, language arts teacher Taylor Mc-Kenna, organized this program with a university professor, Michele Simpson, who is involved with some of the athletes through the Educational Opportunity Fund (EOF) program.

Beginning in October, Thomas' students write letters to their penpals twice a month; they also receive a letter from their penpals twice a month. This continues until the middle of January when the sixth graders visit the University of Georgia to have lunch with their penpals.

Because so many of Thomas' sixth grade students are reading below grade level and often are placed in a fourth grade basal, he developed this project to see if there would be a difference in students' reading-writing patterns and attitudes. He has been pleasantly surprised in both areas. Because his students keep folders about their penpals, including press releases, newspaper articles, and statistics about the games, students read much more voluntarily. Inasmuch as the athletes give the sixth graders free autographed paperbacks, the sixth graders read them voraciously.

Thomas' students also write an autobiography based on the theme "heros" by following this format: the first paragraph contains autobiographical data about who they are; the second paragraph contains thoughts about their hopes and dreams; the third paragraph contains information about someone in their life who is a real hero to them. Even though the basal is still the mainstay of his reading program, Thomas finds that this type of mentorship project motivates his students to want to stay in school and learn to read and write.

A YEARLONG PLAN

As our teachers have indicated, their ultimate goal, besides teaching students the mechanics of reading, is to instill in them a desire to read and write. Even within the confines of a system, they have been able to incorporate their own ideas into their daily and weekly plans so that their students have more opportunities to practice with coherent text for real purposes. Some still are not satisfied with what they are doing. They want to use newer techniques, even if their districts are not interested in them. They want to use more trade books and writing to accomplish their goals. In other words, they want to use the basal as just one tool in their overall reading program.

Part of their anxiety stems from their lack of confidence in using less prescriptive materials for helping students to acquire skills. Since basal systems do not have magical formulas for their instructional schemas, anyone of us can create our own visionary yearlong plans for successfully accomplishing the same objectives. Toward this end, we provide a five-step guide to help you bridge the gap between internal satisfaction and external pressure.

1. Create a chart or grid to help you develop a yearlong plan. (See Figure 2.12 for an example of a form that you could use for each theme/cluster/unit developed throughout the year.) List all the skills you need students to acquire for the year.

	THEME/CLUSTER/UNIT:	
	Basal Story (BS)/Book (B)	Activities/Project
SKILLS		
Decoding		
Comprehension		
Vocabulary		
Study Skills		
Literature		

FIGURE 2.12
Form for yearlong plan

Use your basal's scope and sequence, district or school's curriculum guide, and standardized tests to help you identify necessary skills to directly teach. Although we did not list the skills that you would address in a year in Figure 2.12, we listed the four areas (decoding, comprehension, vocabulary, and study skills) that are consistently included in basal scope and sequence charts plus a fifth area, literature, that is often included.

2. On the same chart, write down the themes, clusters or units of study that are important for your grade level. Figure 2.13 indicates an example of how you could adapt D. C. Heath's first grade cluster of "New Friends and Old" to "Friendship."

3. Under each theme, write down any appropriate basal stories and trade books. Use students' reactions to stories to determine whether they should be used or not. If you are a first-time teacher, read through the basal to determine if (a) the stories are appealing and (b) they fit into a theme, cluster, or unit. Use the teacher's guide and your library media specialist for suggestions about trade books. Figure 2.13 indicates how you could work with one basal reading selection, *The Mixed-Up Lunch* by Bernard Wiseman, and one trade book, *Frog and Toad Are Friends* by Arnold Lobel (1970). You would actually substitute one of the basal reading selections for a trade book that happens to be included in D. C. Heath's suggested list of readings for this cluster.

4. See which skill and strategies are being developed in the basal for a particular reading selection. Assess whether these skills are important for your students. Think of ways to develop the same skills and strategies (for example, predicting outcomes) with your trade book. Generate a list of extension activities and cross-

	THEME/CLUSTER/UNIT: FRIENDSHIP	
	Basal Story (BS)/Book (B)	Activities/Projects
	The Mixed-Up Lunch (BS) by Bernard Wiseman *Frog and Toad Are Friends* (B) by Arnold Lobel	Workbook Pages: Contractions and Multiple Meanings Letter to Penpal Friendship Big Book
SKILLS		
Decoding contractions	× (basal and book)	× (workbook)
Comprehension predict outcome	× (basal and book through predicting/verifying and generating questions)	
Vocabulary		
multiple meanings antonyms	× (basal)	× (workbook)
Study Skills follow directions		× (Letter to Penpal Friendship Big Book)
Literature realistic fiction	× (basal and book)	

FIGURE 2.13
Example of one set of books and activities for yearlong plan

curricular projects that can develop the same skills. Write down these activities next to your reading material. Figure 2.13 indicates how specific skills and strategies are connected to reading and writing activities. Some of the activities can come from the basal's teacher's guide, including appropriate workbook pages, some can be modified, and some can be created or come from other resources. (Many resources that teachers are using successfully are identified in subsequent chapters.)

5. Look back at your list of skills and check any additional skills that are addressed with your plans. Although not indicated in Figure 2.13, you may find that as you work with your plan, you cover additional skills. For example, while students read "The Story" from *Frog and Toad Are Friends,* you may have students dramatize

Toad's sequence of events for trying to think of a story to tell his sick friend, Frog, thereby, helping students with the literal comprehension skill of sequencing. While not indicated at first, some skills will be covered as you work with a book.

Although you may find yourself using most of the stories in the basal or, possibly, none at all, this type of yearlong planning helps you to feel in control of your reading program. Rather than subscribing to the mythical wisdom of publishers who know nothing about your students, you are using your own professional judgment to determine what happens in your classroom.

Concerns and Considerations About Basal Use

Barnard and Hetzel (1989) believe that reliance on commercial materials stems from three beliefs held by teachers and administrators: (a) materials are based on "scientific truths" about the latest research; (b) children *will* learn to read if the materials are followed precisely; and (c) administrators expect teachers to dutifully follow commercial material prescriptions.

This latter concern hits home with a third grade teacher we know. Before a new basal program was implemented in her district, she had started a writing workshop and a literature-based reading program in her classroom. She felt quite comfortable making the transition after working with a consultant to her school district. Before the next academic year began, she was told by her administrator, as the other teachers were, that she had to use most of the components from a new basal program that had been purchased for the district. She found that her entire morning, from 9:00 to 11:30, had to be devoted to her basal to use everything prescribed. Needless to say, because she had no time for anything else—including the writing workshop and literature-based reading—she was frustrated.

Others feel that there is still a significant gap between how reading appears to be learned and how it is taught and assessed by today's basal reading systems. In fact, Weaver and Watson (1989) identify four major concerns about basal reading series:

1. Skill organization is based more on the logistics for developing a sequential system than on a sound understanding of how children learn to read.
2. Even though there is overwhelming evidence that extensive reading and writing are crucial for literacy development, only a slight amount of time is spent actually reading.
3. Students are not encouraged to think.
4. "Going through the paces" is more important than taking responsibility for one's own teaching or learning.

These concerns reflect what educators have come to accept. As we suggest in Chapter 5 (see the section entitled "Technology, Basals, and Trade Books: Where We Are and What We Can Do"), the bottom line for publishers is sales. If they find that we are not accepting what they have to offer, they will change to get our business. As we

1. The basal reading selection that I am considering is
   a. authentic, meaningful literature from a trade book.
   b. excerpted with minor adaptations so that its authenticity is still intact.
   c. written for the basal, yet it conveys a meaningful message with natural-sounding language.
   d. poorly adapted and excerpted from a trade book.
   e. written for the basal with a meaningless message and contrived language.
   If you select *d* or *e,* find a more suitable reading selection that communicates a similar message and/or addresses the basal's cluster or theme.
2. Based on my reading time frame and the basal's lesson plans, my students will have the opportunity to read and write
   a. daily.
   b. four times a week.
   c. three times a week.
   d. two times a week.
   e. once a week.
   If you select *b* through *e,* begin to reduce the skillwork by: (a) determining whether the skill is important for your students' success, and if it is, (b) assessing what your students already know in order to avoid duplicative skill exercises, (c) searching for other sections in the basal that address the same skill, (d) selecting the "best" of the skillwork and paper-and-pencil tasks to use for needed skills, and (e) developing needed skills through other content area learning activities. Subsequently, find additional reading material to supplement the basal selection so that your students are exposed daily to coherent text.
3. Writing is treated as an
   a. integral part of students' reading development.
   b. obvious afterthought.
   If you select *b,* analyze where writing can be woven into your lesson. Use the activities provided, search for others, or create your own.
4. Metacomprehension strategies are
   a. used frequently to guide reading
   b. used sporadically to guide reading.
   c. used rarely to guide reading.
   If you select *b* or *c,* analyze which strategies (for example, retelling and generating questions) are used and create others to fill in the gaps.
5. My basal's scope and sequence
   a. supports most of my objectives for my students' literacy development.
   b. supports some of my objectives for my students' literacy development.
   c. supports none of my objectives for my students' literacy development.
   If you select *b,* determine which of your objectives are not supported and supplement with additional activities and materials. If you select *c,* consider alternative basal systems or, better yet, other literature-based programs.

FIGURE 2.14
Five-question basal exercise

saw in our comparison of the seven basal series, some changes already are taking place, and many more are coming. Some companies are cutting back on skillwork or making an effort to provide skill sheets that connect meaningfully to students' reading. More authentic text from trade books, with little or no adaptation, is appearing; let's hope that complete books will appear, rather than excerpts. Metacomprehension strategies and higher level reading and writing activities are increasing. Activities and projects are less skill-driven and more conceptually oriented. Furthermore, caveats for using paper-and-pencil activities as optional—rather than required—tasks are appearing at ever-increasing rates.

Nevertheless, because basals still attempt to be all things to all people, their overriding goal of providing children with daily opportunities to read and write coherent text is lost in the maze of piecemeal activities. Readers and writers are not born; they are developed over time. Practice creates prowess. Experience with one or two stories a week is just too meager a diet for reading development, especially when each reading selection is sandwiched between a dozen or more skill sheets. Yet, if balanced with other reading material and activities, basals offer guidelines, activities, and reading selections that can make our jobs easier, particularly if you can tap into the strengths of your own basal system. At all times, though, you must exert your own professional judgment about the "whys" and "hows" of using basals. Figure 2.14 provides a simple exercise for you to use as you decide what is best for your students.

Concluding Remarks

We acknowledge that basals matter in American classrooms. We also appreciate basals' contributions as comprehensive support systems for reading instruction. Yet, we have reservations about the role that basals play in determining what happens to instruction. Durkin (1990b) believes that our dependence on basals has fostered more attention to "covering material" than to selecting both important and suitable instructional objectives. Many of the teachers we interviewed about their reading goals responded tongue-in-cheek about "getting through the basal" before offering ideas about "developing confident readers" and "helping students to want to read." Ironically, the essence of their instructional focus is the basal. One teacher, in fact, revealed the degree of basal-dependence in her school: "I have the low group. Our group went past the average group in the basal. The average group teacher said, 'You can't do that. We're supposed to be higher than you.'"

We need to look seriously at the educational opportunities basals do or do not offer. We need to question the publishers' instructional prescriptions before inflicting on our students dull dosages of reading and skill activities. If we find that we do not like what is prescribed, we should look elsewhere for antidotes without fear of reprimand from administrators or concern about students' performance on **standardized tests**. What we now know about reading and writing will eventually be reflected in standardized tests (see entire issues of *Language Arts* (Dillon, 1990) and *The Reading*

Instruction Journal (Margolis, 1990) that are devoted to assessment) so that test-driven administrators will feel free to encourage meaning-centered, literature-based curricula.

We also need to view the basal as only one part of the total school program. We recognize that many teachers are still in situations that are similar to that of Ms. E.; yet, many options are available for reorganizing and consolidating what is offered so that there is room to experiment with other resources. Although our six teachers in this chapter are not as precariously situated as Ms. E., they still have had to create palatable conditions for satisfying their classroom needs.

As Socrates once said, the key to finding the meaning of life is to "know thyself." If you know what is important to you when it comes to helping your students develop as readers and writers, you will know what to do and use. If you know that you are creating that spark in your students' eyes, you will undoubtedly know that you are moving your students forward in their literacy development.

Questions for Discussion

1. Respond *yes* or *no* to this statement. Basals should be the predominant mode of instruction in K–6 classrooms. Explain your answer.
2. Consider the nine major components of a basal system that are discussed in this chapter. Which components do you think are important for your reading program? Give a reason for each one of your selections.
3. Look back at the section "Comparison of Seven Basal Series." Do any of the basal series satisfy your teaching needs? If so, which ones? If not, why?
4. If you were in a position to assist other teachers, what advice would you give them about using basals in the classroom?
5. What changes would you like to see in basal development and basal use? Why?

Application Activities

1. Look at a current basal for the grade level you teach or intend to teach. Read through the reading selections and rate each one with one of the following votes: ****Two thumbs up! ***Worth reading! **Has some potential! *I wouldn't waste my time! Count up the number of reading selections in each category. What happened?
2. Look back at Question #1 for the reading selections that you rated * and **. (If none had fewer than three stars, select seven stories that were somewhat borderline.) Identify under which cluster, theme, or thematic unit the story is included. Find one theme-related trade book to substitute for every reading selection rated

below three stars. Record the book's title, author, copyright date, publisher, place of publication, grade level and/or interest level, and summary to share with others.

3. For every trade book you identified in Question #2, create a Directed Reading Activity plan for reading the trade book with questions and activities for strategic reading. Record your plans to share with others.

4. Review a lesson in a current basal at the grade level you teach or intend to teach. List the skills that are covered through skill sheets. Create two to three activities that you could use in lieu of the skill sheets. Write down these activities to share with others.

5. Survey 10 teachers and two to four administrators (some in a traditional environment and some in a nontraditional environment) with the following questions:

a. In 10 years basals will continue to be the most prevalent material for reading instruction. _____ Yes _____ Maybe _____ No

b. In 10 years nationally standardized tests will determine students' reading placement. _____ Yes _____ Maybe _____ No

c. In 10 years nationally standardized tests will reflect basal instruction. _____ Yes _____ Maybe _____ No

d. In 10 years students will need to read basals to pass nationally standardized tests. _____ Yes _____ Maybe _____ No

e. In 10 years students will need to have more experience reading a variety of non-basal materials to pass standardized tests. _____ Yes _____ Maybe _____ No

f. In 10 years trade books will supplant basals. _____ Yes _____ Maybe _____ No

Compare your teachers' responses to your administrators' responses. What did you find? Why do you think you found these results? What would you like to do with your findings? How will you do it?

References

Aaron, I. E. (1987). Enriching the basal reading program with literature. In B. E. Cullinan (Ed.), *Children's literature in the reading program* (pp. 126–138). Newark, DE: International Reading Association.

Adams, M. J. (1990). *Beginning to read: Thinking and learning about print—A summary*. Urbana: Champaign, IL: Center for the Study of Reading.

Anderson, R. C., Hiebert, E. H., Scott, J. A., & Wilkinson, I. A. G. (1985). *Becoming a nation of readers: The report of the Commission on Reading*. Champaign, IL: The National Academy of Education, The National Institute of Education, The Center for the Study of Reading.

Barnard, D. P., & Hetzel, R. W. (1989). *Selecting a basal reading program*. Lancaster, PA: Technomic.

Barr, R., & Sadow, M. W. (1989). Influence of basal programs on fourth-grade reading instruction. *Reading Research Quarterly, 24*, 44–71.

Bettelheim, B., & Zelan, K. (1982). *On learning to read*. New York: Knopf.

Betts, E. A. (1946). *Foundations of reading instruction*. New York: American Book.

Bohning, G. (1986). The *McGuffey Eclectic Readers: 1836–1986. The Reading Teacher, 40,* 263–269.

Bridge, C. A. (1989). Beyond the basal in beginning reading. In P. N. Winograd, K. K. Wixson, and M. Y. Lipson (Eds.), *Improving basal reading instruction* (pp. 177–209). New York: Teachers College Press.

Center for the Study of Reading. *A guide to selecting basal reading programs.* Urbana, IL: Author.

Dillon, D. (Ed.). (1990). Entire issue. *Language Arts, 67* (3).

Dole, J. A., & Osborn, J. (1989). Evaluation, selection, and use of reading materials. In S. B. Wepner, J. T. Feeley, & D. S. Strickland (Eds.), *The administration and supervision of reading programs* (pp. 109–130). New York: Teachers College Press.

Durkin, D. (1990a, May). *Are the new basal reader programs any better than their predecessors?* Paper presented at the Tenth Conference on Reading Research, Cosponsored by the International Reading Association and The Center for the Study of Reading at the University of Illinois, Atlanta, GA.

Durkin, D. (1990b). Matching classroom instruction with reading abilities: An unmet need. *RASE: Remedial and Special Education, 11* (3), 23–28.

Farr, R., Tulley, M. A., & Powell, D. (1987). The evaluation and selection of basal readers. *The Elementary School Journal, 87* (3), 268.

Fish, S. (1980). *Is there a text in this class?* Cambridge: Harvard University Press.

Gipe, J. P. (1978–1979). Investigating techniques for teaching word meanings. *Reading Research Quarterly, 14,* 624–644.

Goodman, K. S. (1988). Look what they've done to Judy Blume!: The "basalization" of children's literature. *The New Advocate, 1* (1), 29–41.

Goodman, K. S., Shannon P., Freeman, Y. S., & Murphy, S. (1988). *Report card on basal readers.* Katonah, NY: Richard C. Owen.

Graham, K. G., & Robinson, H. A. (1984). *Study skills handbook: A guide for all teachers.* Newark, DE: International Reading Association.

Heilman, A. W., Blair, T. R., & Rupley, W. H. (1990). *Principles and practices of teaching reading* (7th ed.). Columbus, OH: Merrill.

Heymsfeld, C. R. (1989, August/September). Point/Counterpoint: The value of basal readers. *Reading Today,* p. 1.

Honig, W. (1988). The California reading initiative. *The New Advocate, 1,* 235–240.

Kantrowitz, B. (1990, Fall/Winter). The reading wars. *Newsweek,* pp. 8–9, 12, 14.

Leu, D. J., & Kinzer, C. K. (1991). *Effective reading instruction, K–8* (2nd ed.). New York: Macmillan.

Macon, J. M., Bewell, D., & Vogt, M. E. (1991). *Response to literature, grades K–8.* Newark, DE: International Reading Association.

Margolis, H. (Ed.). (1990). Entire issue. *The Reading Instruction Journal, 33* (3).

May, F. B. (1990). *Reading as communication: An interactive approach* (3rd ed.). Columbus, OH: Merrill.

McCallum, R. D. (1988). Don't throw the basals out with the bath water. *The Reading Teacher, 42,* 204–208.

Mickelson, N. (1989, August/September). Point/Counterpoint: The value of basal readers. *Reading Today,* p. 18.

Muther, C. (1985). What every textbook evaluator should know. *Educational Leadership, 42* (7), 5.

Nagy, W. E. (1988). *Teaching vocabulary to improve reading comprehension.* Newark, DE: ERIC Clearinghouse on Reading and Communication Skills, National Council of Teachers of English, and International Reading Association.

Osborn, J. (1984). Workbooks that accompany basal reading programs. In G. G. Duffy, L. Roehler, & J. Mason (Eds.), *Comprehension instruction: Perspectives and suggestions* (pp. 163–186). New York: Longman.

Robinson, H. A., Faraone, V., Hittleman, D. R., & Unruh, E. (1990). *Reading comprehension instruction 1873–1987.* Newark, DE: International Reading Association.

Schmidt, W. H., Caul, J., Byers, J. L., & Buchmann, M. (1984). Content of basal text selections: Implications for comprehension instruction. In G. G. Duffy, L. Roehler, & J. Mason (Eds.), *Comprehension instruction: Perspectives and suggestions* (pp. 144–162). New York: Longman.

Schmitt, M. C., & Baumann, J. F. (1990). Meta-comprehension during basal reader instruction: Do teachers promote it? *Reading Research and Instruction, 29* (3), 1–13.

Snowball, D. (1989, August/September). Point/counterpoint: The value of basal readers. *Reading Today,* p. 18.

Squire, J. R. (1989, August/September). Point/counterpoint: The value of basal readers. *Reading Today,* p. 19.

Temple, C. (1990). How literary theory expands our expectations of children's reading and writing. In T. Shanahan (Ed.), *Reading and writing together: New perspectives in the classroom* (pp. 23–56). Norwood, MA: Christopher-Gordon.

Turner, R. R. (1988, April). How the basals stack up. *Learning 88,* pp. 62–64.

Vacca, J. A. L., Vacca, R. T., & Gove, M. K. (1991). *Reading and learning to read* (2nd ed.). New York: HarperCollins.

Weaver, C., & Watson, D. (1989). *Report on basal readers.* Urbana, IL: National Council of Teachers of English Commission on Reading.

Wepner, S. B., Hudak-Huelbig, E., Keyes, M. L., McLane, A., & Stellingwerf, E. (1991). *Analysis of first and fourth grade components of seven basal systems.* Submitted for publication.

Winograd, P. N., Wixson, K. K., & Lipson, M. Y. (Eds.). (1989). *Improving basal reading instruction.* New York: Teachers College Press.

Wixson, K. K., & Peters, C. W. (1989). Teaching the basal selection. In P. N. Winograd, K. K. Wixson, & M. Y. Lipson (Eds.), *Improving basal reading instruction* (pp. 21–61). New York: Teachers College Press.

Yopp, R., & Yopp, H. (1991). Ten best ideas for reading teachers. In E. Fry (Ed.), *Ten best ideas for reading teachers* (pp. 132–134). Menlo Park, CA: Addison-Wesley.

Trade Books Mentioned

Blume, J. (1981). *The one in the middle is the green kangaroo.* New York: Dell.

Dahl, R. (1970). *Fantastic Mr. Fox.* New York: Knopf.

Lobel, A. (1970). *Frog and Toad are friends.* New York: Harper & Row.

Basal Publishers' Addresses

D. C. Heath and Company
Dept. 6242
125 Spring Street
Lexington, MA 02173

Harcourt Brace Jovanovich
School Department
Orlando, FL 32887

Houghton Mifflin Company
One Beacon Street
Boston, MA 02108

Macmillan
866 Third Avenue
New York, NY 10022

McGraw-Hill School Division
1200 Northwest 63rd Street
Oklahoma City, OK 73116-5712

Scott, Foresman and Company
1900 East Lake Avenue
Glenview, IL 60025

Silver Burdett & Ginn
250 James Street
Morristown, NJ 07960

CHAPTER
3

CONNECTING BASALS AND LITERATURE

Chapter Overview

RATIONALE FOR CREATING CONNECTIONS BETWEEN BASALS AND TRADE BOOKS

VIEWS OF LITERACY INSTRUCTION

EXAMPLES OF TEACHER CONNECTIONS

PRIMARY (K–3) / ELEMENTARY (4–6) / READING SPECIALIST

ESSENTIAL ELEMENTS FOR CREATING CONNECTIONS BETWEEN BASALS AND TRADE BOOKS

RESOURCES / ACTIVITIES / SCHEDULE / SKILLS AND ASSESSMENT

GUIDELINES FOR MOVING TOWARD TRADE BOOKS FOR LITERACY DEVELOPMENT

WHAT TO THINK ABOUT / WHAT TO DO

M R. E. HAS BEEN TEACHING first grade for 14 years, and he's quite good at it. Parents send him letters periodically, thanking him for giving their children a glorious beginning to their academic careers. His colleagues and administrators have tremendous respect for his ability to put his creative talents to work in the classroom. He is the kind of teacher to whom parents gravitate because of his sensitivity, sense of humor, and dedication.

Four years ago, Mr. E. began a master's degree in reading. As a first grade teacher he wanted to learn as much as he could about strategies and techniques for helping beginning readers. He was not prepared for what he discovered during his first semester. His professors were criticizing the heart of his reading program: basals. As they were advocating the wisdom of **process-oriented, literature-based classrooms**, he was worrying about getting through all the skills that accompanied the basal. Sure he read trade books to his class, and sure he read to his students from the first day of school, but Mr. E. was a devout basal user. His students' scores on the district's standardized test were his obsession; his students' mastery of skills was the key to their success.

At first Mr. E. rationalized his behavior by claiming that his professors were too removed from the real pressures of schooling to fully understand what he was up against. Then, as Mr. E. began to experiment with some of the suggestions from his graduate courses, he discovered how much fun he and his students were having. He also realized that he didn't have to abandon the basal; he just had to organize his time differently. Although he stumbled a great deal during that first year because of his decade-long dependence on a basal system, he learned how to branch out so that his students could enjoy trade books in his classroom the way they were enjoying them at home.

Mr. E. is not unique in his hesitation to move away from a system that works. After all, why should any teacher jeopardize a sterling reputation in the community for what is considered to be a loosely conceived notion about reading instruction? And Mr. E.'s apprehension about students' performance on standardized tests is well-founded, particularly since his instructional rating among his peers and administrators is based on his students' percentile scores. What really helped Mr. E. begin to change was realizing that his students weren't learning about the joys of reading from him. Their daily reading experiences came only from his basal. And because of his obsession with skills, workbook pages and skill sheets consumed his students' independent work time. Mr. E. wanted more for his students and himself.

Why should more teachers do what Mr. E. is doing? How should teachers wean themselves away from the crutch of a packaged system? These are the two main questions addressed in this chapter as you read what others are discovering about creating connections between basals and trade books.

Rationale for Creating Connections Between Basals and Trade Books

Most talent is developed through repeated practice. Certainly, some of us are predisposed to a certain prowess, but if we are interested in any kind of noteworthy achievement, we need to rehearse over and over. And somewhere deep in our psyche we need to know that there will be psychological dividends for our "stick-to-it-iveness."

Take us, for example. We laugh at our inability to throw a football because somewhere in our early years we learned that it was inconsequential to our development to become team-quality football players. Although we may or may not have had a special talent for this sport, we did not have enough opportunities to test our athletic inclinations. On the other hand, we are proud of our ability to sink our analytical teeth into the printed page. In our early stages of development we had role models—parents, grandparents, and teachers—who read for their own enjoyment. They, in turn, communicated to us that our reading excursions were acceptable and necessary for our own development as literate adults. Our role models praised us every time we went that extra mile to read and write independently. We knew we could count on someone to steer us to books of interest and ask us, with all sincerity, whether we enjoyed what we read. We also knew that our awkward prose or contrived poems would not be criticized as much for form as they would be applauded for effort and creativity. We learned early on that our reading and writing adventures elicited appreciation from important people in our lives. Our natural proclivity towards reading and writing, if any, was far less important than our drive to practice that which was reinforced in our environment.

For children to develop as readers and writers, they need to know that their efforts are not in vain. Even though children develop at different rates and to varying levels of proficiency, they need to know that adult role models encourage and appreciate any strides they make. However, as with the evolution of any talent, children need time and opportunity to develop literacy. They need to hear good models of written language so they can create their own links between what they read and what writers write (Butler & Turbill, 1984; Cullinan, 1987). They need to internalize the idea that reading and writing are as purposeful, functional, and meaningful as listening and speaking, so that they are inspired to keep developing. And they need to think of themselves as readers and writers so that they read like writers and write for other readers.

Readers and writers of all ages engage in similar development: they know how to recognize how a message is conveyed and how language is used to convey the message; they look to other authors as models for advancing their own skills; and they apply what they learn in a variety of printed contexts. Yet, these skills do not develop overnight; rather, they are nurtured through constant practice over an extended period of time.

The concept of providing daily opportunities in the classroom for children to improve their reading and writing is certainly not revolutionary. Yet, it has tempered our overzealous responses to the various systems that compartmentalize reading into a series of subskills. Reading and writing have become so materials-driven (Otto, 1991) that some teachers worry more about getting through the programs than thinking about the real purpose of their teaching. We have spent too much time focused on worksheet lessons that fragment our language and fail to demonstrate to children the relationship between subskills and reading or writing (Shannon, 1989). As a result, we have left ourselves and our students too little time to practice the "whole" of reading and writing.

What message are we giving our children, then, when we spend three-fifths of their reading time doing skill sheets? Heller (1991) shares what one child felt as he said to his teacher: "Whew. I don't know what I just did, but I'm through with all my five papers (worksheets) for today. Now may I please read?" (p. 65). Yet, at the same time, in a nearby school, third grade teachers are asking their principal: "How can we afford the time to do trade books when there's so much material to cover in the basal?"

Moving away from an overdependence on something secure requires a great deal of courage and self-examination. It involves taking stock of our views toward literacy instruction in relation to the materials and strategies used.

VIEWS OF LITERACY INSTRUCTION

Although reading and writing are no longer viewed as just a series of *skills* that make up the whole, or as products that are tested and retested, many of our instructional materials and strategies still perpetuate these views. Basal systems, which control how vocabulary is introduced and are based on the skills delineated in scope and sequence charts, still limit the "whole" of reading to no more than the sum of its parts. Those who believe that children must know the sounds of the alphabet before they can read coherent text view reading as a unitary skill made up of numerous subskills. They view writing in the same way, with correct sentence construction preceding creative paragraph development.

Users of materials that subscribe to such a *products* view believe that tests of students' ability to comprehend text or to write correctly are the ultimate goals of skill instruction. A familiar refrain for assessing the product of reading is: "Read the story and answer the comprehension questions" (Heller, 1991, p. 6). Passing scores on basal assessment tests and standardized reading and language arts tests tell us that our students have acquired the products of reading and writing. Those who use pre-packaged comprehension questions and Warriner-type composition handbooks as their sole guides for judging students' ability to read and write believe that the result is far more important than the processes used along the way.

Even though it is easier to base reading instruction on a skills approach and a products view of testing, these views do not reflect real reading and writing. They do not help us consider all the other factors that affect a student's interaction with text: background knowledge about a topic, understanding of text structure, and interest in a topic. These views do not encourage the creation of readers and writers; they merely strive to mold reading and writing behaviors.

In contrast, the more recent constructivist *process* view of reading and writing (see Chapter 1 for further information) sees readers and writers as active participants in constructing meaning for themselves. This view accounts for students' background knowledge of concepts, events, and ideas as critical variables for interacting with text, while creating conditions for helping students to improve their comprehension.

A personal exchange that one of us had illustrates the need to know what others bring to any form of communicative exchange. The conversation went like this:

S: I found out that I have a corrupted disk. I tried every way I could to open it up, but to no avail. I called Seattle for help, and I found out that there's a special program that I can use that might save me from hours of agony. When I called our technician friend, So-and-So, she told me to come in next week for an evaluation to see whether my disk could be recovered. Her fees are high, though. Do you think I can find someone who is less expensive for the same service?

L: How can So-and-So help you with your back problem?

S: Back problem?

L: You said you had a corrupted disk.

S: Oh, my! I was talking about my computer disk. That's the term used when you can't open files that are on the disk.

L: Ah! Now, I see why you wanted to use So-and-So. Don't use her! I would definitely look for someone less expensive.

As much as we think that we are on the same wavelength as others, we often are not. In the preceding example, L had just been talking about medical insurance coverage for chiropractors. Memories of this conversation spilled over into her conversation about the disk. Once she heard the word *disk,* she associated everything heard to back problems.

Now, how would the three literacy views affect our interpretations of students' learning patterns? Someone with a *skills* view would believe that L needs work with vocabulary and comprehension skills, including multiple-meaning words, word referents, and main idea. Someone with a *products* view would believe that L's comprehension was simply unacceptable for any grade-level reader. Someone with a *process* view would search for reasons for L's misunderstanding through questioning. In the end, one with the process view would appreciate that L was neither skill deficient nor slow to comprehend, but rather full of personal knowledge from a different vantage point.

However sound the process view may be, its widespread use in classrooms nationwide is probably a long way off. It's much easier to follow someone else's prescription for reading and writing instruction. It's also safer to use scores from a test to label students as above average, average, or below average.

Two kindergarten teachers come to mind immediately. One teacher has been teaching the same way for 28 years, and her students leave her classroom "ready" for first grade. She spends the entire year teaching the letters and sounds of the alphabet with the activities that accompany her basal system. Her students' writing experiences are nothing more than practicing how alphabet letters should be written. The students who come to her class already reading are put into linguistic readers that contain rhyming word-sentences devoid of any meaning. This teacher is quite comfortable with her program and would never consider altering it. She firmly believes that this is how reading should be taught, and she isn't interested in new instructional views. She thinks of herself as an expert teacher, and she garners respect throughout the community for her well-organized program.

The other teacher, Elsie Nigohosian, has been teaching for about seven years. (You will read more about her program in the next section.) Elsie wants her students to think of themselves as readers and writers from the first day. She still covers the letters of the alphabet; however, she is creating her own program as we write this book. Every week she discovers something new about herself as a teacher and her students as learners. And while she's excited by what she is doing, she is not totally comfortable with it all. Her reinforcement does not come from a test score or from her administrator's praise, but rather from what she sees her students doing. Even though parents respect her for her innovative ideas and dedication, they nevertheless are a little apprehensive about this shift in routine. Elsie still does not think of herself as an expert teacher; she knows it will take a few years before she feels comfortable with her self-created program.

Although teaching in different districts, both teachers have students whose parents spend time reading to them. Which teacher, though, is perpetuating the "warm fuzzies" of reading and writing that began at home? Which set of students will develop the confidence to use their own trial-and-error techniques to continue along their road toward literacy?

Although not an easy road to travel (as you will see when we describe teachers who are taking this risk), the benefits of the process view of reading and writing to students are immeasurable. As with learning to talk, children learn to read and write by being immersed in meaningful, purposeful, and functional language (Cambourne, 1984). They need exposure to literature and all other written materials so that they understand what written language is all about (Butler & Turbill, 1984). Students' classroom environments need to be forums for learning literacy skills in a meaningful context.

Examples of Teacher Connections

To show what can be done, we will share how 10 teachers—five primary, four elementary, and one reading specialist—are connecting basals and trade books in their reading program. While some have practically eliminated most components of the basal in favor of a trade book emphasis, others are steeped more deeply in a basal system.

When we interviewed and/or observed these teachers, we noticed the pride with which they described their self-created programs. Even in adverse environments, these teachers have had the courage to move beyond security to establish a lively, ever-changing reading program. As you read what these teachers have created for their students and themselves, think of how you might use their ideas in your classroom.

PRIMARY (K–3)

KINDERGARTEN: CROSS-CURRICULAR PLANNING WEBS WITH LETTERBOOKS

Elsie Nigohosian, a full-day kindergarten teacher, truly is breaking new ground in her school district. She alone has developed an integrated language arts plan that incorporates her district's basal into unit-based, process-oriented, cross-curricular plans. What we saw and what we are about to describe did not happen overnight. Elsie has been struggling to change for the last few years. Although always a believer in "whole language," she didn't begin to apply her views until she started to take graduate courses, attend conferences, and read professional books and journals. Until that time, she believed that her administrators' concerns with budgets, standardized tests, and scope and sequence charts had to be hers. Once she heard what others were doing, she decided to take a risk within her own teaching.

Elsie established five goals for herself as she planned her program:

1. Develop critical thinking skills.
2. Develop process skills.
3. Develop problem-solving skills.
4. Integrate the curriculum.
5. Elaborate on ideas throughout the curriculum.

She uses a different alphabet letter from her district's basal's letterbooks as the basis for her cross-curricular weekly plans (see Figure 3.1). Her administrator's willingness to let her schedule her own school day has been a major coup, since it enables her to integrate the curriculum by providing large blocks of time for thematic units. Within her weekly plan Elsie creates a web of content area activities that are related to her letterbook (see Figure 3.2). She uses *R is for Rainbow: Developing Young Children's Thinking Skills Through the Alphabet* (Anselmo, Rollins, & Schuckman, 1986) to help develop her web. Every piece of literature connects with her letter of the week and content area activities. For instance, during her language arts work time, she reads aloud *Where the Wild Things Are* by Maurice Sendak (1963). Before she even reads the book, though, she provides background information about Maurice Sendak. With help from two professional resources, *An Author a Month (for pennies)* (McElmeel, 1988) and *Bookpeople: A First Album* (McElmeel, 1990), she is able to present her authors as real people who write about things they know and care about. She incorporates comprehension questions and strategies as she reads: prediction and verifying, retelling, making comparisons to other books that the author has written, drawing conclusions, and reacting to the content of the book. She also has her students chorally respond to her questions, so that the students who are not developmentally ready still feel part of the group.

Students then create their own *Where the Wild Things Are* book about themselves (see Figure 3.3, p. 98) in varying sizes: small books, big books, or big, big books. For creative dramatics, which takes place during "Theme Work" time in Elsie's weekly plan, students act out the book with stick puppets that they previously created during their art time. Her ideas for this book come from one of her resources, *Creative Connections: Literature and the Reading Program, Grades 1–3* (Olsen, 1987).

MONDAY	TUESDAY	WEDNESDAY	THURSDAY	FRIDAY
Arrival Class Meeting	Arrival Class Meeting	Arrival Class Meeting	Arrival Class Meeting	Arrival Class Meeting
Language Arts Work Time • Listening • Speaking • Reading • Writing	Language Arts Work Time • Listening • Speaking • Reading • Writing	Language Arts Work Time • Listening • Speaking • Reading • Writing	Language Arts Work Time • Listening • Speaking • Reading • Writing	Language Arts Work Time • Listening • Speaking • Reading • Writing
Art	Centers	Centers	Centers	Computer Art
Large-motor Activities	Large-motor Activities	Large-motor Activities	Large-motor Activities	Large-motor Activities
Library	Music	Music	Language Arts	Language Arts
L	U	N	C	H
Story Quiet time	Story Quiet time	Story Quiet time	Story Quiet time	Story Quiet time
Theme work	P.E.	P.E.	Health	Theme work
Math Science	Theme work	Theme work	Theme work	Math Science Social Studies
Social Studies	Math Science Social Studies	Math Science Social Studies	Math Science Social Studies	Circle Time
Centers	Centers	Centers	Centers	Centers
Snack/Play	Snack/Play	Snack/Play	Snack/Play	Snack/Play

FIGURE 3.1

Kindergarten weekly schedule

Note. From "Kindergarten Weekly Schedule," 1991. Copyright 1991 by Elsie Nigohosian. Reprinted by permission.

Elsie also uses nursery rhymes and poems for students to chant and re-create during her language arts period. When we visited her classroom, her students were chanting:

Wee Willie Winkie runs through the town
Upstairs and downstairs in his nightgown
Rapping at the window, crying through the lock,

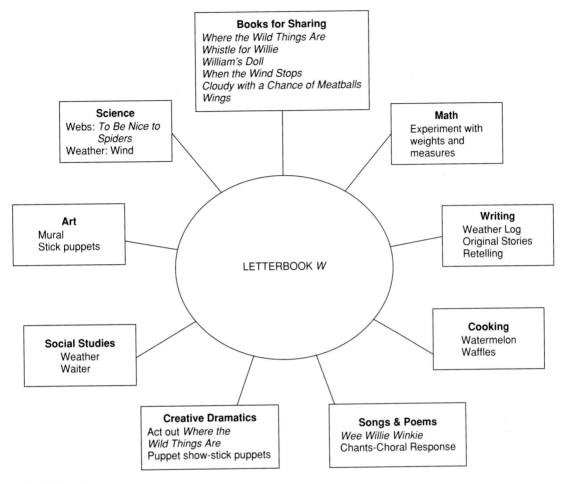

FIGURE 3.2

Kindergarten planning web

Note. From "Kindergarten Planning Web," 1991. Copyright 1991 by Elsie Nigohosian. Reprinted by permission.

"Are the children in their beds, for now it's eight o'clock?" (de Angeli, 1954, p. 11)

After they repeated the chant together two times, they created a mural of pictures of the nursery rhyme. The mural idea for *Wee Willie Winkie* comes from *And What Else?* (Massam & Kulik, 1986). This book contains a colorful photo display of how over 70 activities can be used for literacy learning.

Her "W" ideas for science, social studies, and mathematics are equally exciting. Her science project of creating webs with yarn begins with her reading of an abridged version of E. B. White's (1952) *Charlotte's Web* from *The Weekly Reader,* Columbus,

This is me in the sailboat.
The wild things are chasing me.   Page 1

This is me being chased to
my boat.   Page 2

FIGURE 3.3

An example of a student's book, *Where the Wild Things Are* (Sendak, 1963)

Note. From original student writing, 1991. Copyright 1991 by Christopher Shadek. Reprinted by permission.

This is me back in my sailboat
going home to eat.   Page 3

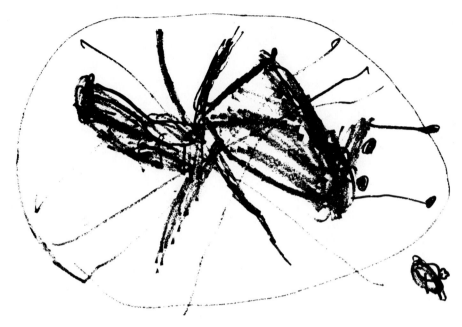

FIGURE 3.4
An example of student's illustrated booklet of *Charlotte's Web* (White, 1952)
Note. From original student drawing, 1991. Copyright 1991 by Jason Silverstein. Reprinted by permission.

Ohio. Students also illustrate their own versions of the book (see Figure 3.4). She also uses the topic of weather for science, social studies, and writing. In science, students talk about wind before flying kites outside. Students also keep science logs to illustrate and record what they discover. In social studies, students forecast the weather each day. They use their writing logs to graph the weather for a week.

The last thing that Elsie does during the week is the basal's letterbook. Although she refuses to incorporate the array of subskill activities contained in these books, she does use some of the suggested art and literary projects. Because Elsie recognizes some of her students do not need to focus on the letters of the alphabet from the letterbook, she provides time for these students to read and write independently. She creates separate writing folders for these students, *a la* Graves (1983). On the inside front cover students brainstorm "Things to Write About." After they write each story, they record on the outside front cover "Titles of Stories I Have Written" (see Figure 3.5).

First and foremost in Elsie's mind is the need to help her students see that reading is a communicative exchange with an author. She also believes that she must help her parents, administrators, and colleagues view reading and writing as processes that happen across the curriculum. As part of her educative role, she sends home weekly

I CAN CLIM

I CAN CLIM CAN
YOU TOO CAN
YOU RUN TOO
I CAN RUN TOO
CAN YOU ROLE
I CAN TOO
CAN YOU DO WTE
EVR I DO.

Titles of Stories I
Have Written

1. I CAN CLIM
2. MOMS R GOOD
3. I CAN SWEM.
4. IN P'OTR RYCO.
5. MY BABY SETR

FIGURE 3.5

An example of student's process writing folder

Note. From original student writing, 1991. Copyright 1991 by Jessica Miller. Reprinted by permission.

newsletters to explain what her kindergarten children have been doing throughout the week (see Figure 3.6). Prior to sending home a newsletter, she gives it to her principal to review, so that he also knows what is happening in her classroom.

Although Elsie sometimes questions whether her uphill battle of creating instructional changes within a conservative system is worth the effort, she quickly snaps out of her self-doubting persona when, like magic, her children demonstrate to her that they love what they are doing and understand what reading and writing are all about (see Figure 3.7).

GRADE 1: THEMATIC UNITS AND AUTHOR STUDIES

First grade teacher Regina Pesce O'Hanlon decided a few years ago that, while the student texts of the basals had a place in her classroom, the workbooks did not. Every book or basal selection that her students read—and they read plenty—is related to a thematic unit or an author study. In the beginning of the year Regina combines the basal with the Dr. Seuss books, *The Ear Book, The Eye Book, The Nose Book,* and *The Foot Book* (all 1968) to help her students learn about parts of the body and color words. She finds that the controlled vocabulary and repetition of words help students experience immediate success. Many of her students who are just beginning to recognize words in print can follow along through memorization. She also uses this basal-trade book combination as a springboard for students' creation of books about themselves and their own body parts.

During the second month of school students read Mercer Mayer books; again, because of their repetitive patterns. (See listing of six Mercer Mayer books that her students read in "Trade Books Mentioned" at the end of this chapter.) She continues her author studies with Robert McCloskey's books, *Make Way for Ducklings* (1941), *Lentil* (1940), and *Blueberries for Sal* (1963); and Frank Asch's books, *Happy Birthday, Moon* (1982), *Mooncake* (1983), and *Moongame* (1989). In between, she has students read books related to seasons such as *The Snowy Day* by Ezra Jack Keats (1962), *Mousekin's Golden House* by Edna Miller (1964), and *It's Groundhog Day* by Steven Kroll (1987). She also ties in her science unit on seeds with nonfiction books such as *The Reason for a Flower* by Ruth Heller (1983) and *Corn is Maize: The Gift of Indians* by Aliki (1976). Toward the end of the year her first grade students work with chapter books such as Judy Blume's (1971) *Freckle Juice* and Arnold Lobel's *Frog and Toad Are Friends* (1970), *Frog and Toad Together* (1972), *Frog and Toad All Year* (1976), and *Days with Frog and Toad* (1970).

Her grouping procedures change as the year progresses. In the beginning, when all students are reading the basal, Dr. Seuss, and Mercer Mayer, she always groups students randomly to help them with socialization. By the end of the year she leans more toward ability grouping so that she can assign different books to each group. While her more advanced students are reading *Freckle Juice,* her less able readers are reading *Frog and Toad Are Friends* because of its controlled vocabulary.

Each day during her three-group reading session she follows a similar procedure. She starts by reading aloud a basal selection or book to them. Because students have a copy of every trade book assigned, some of her students join in as she reads aloud.

BOARD OF EDUCATION
Laurence Shadek
President
Susan Penn
Vice President
Heather Donohue
Janet Adler
Barbara Vitale

Mathew R. Glowski, Ed.D.
Chief School Administrator
Dorothy A. Welch, M.A.
Business Administrator/
Board Secretary
Michele A. Slaff, M.A.
Assistant Principal

KINDERGARTEN NEWSLETTER

May 5, 1989

Dear Parents,

This week in Reading, your child participated in many listening, speaking, reading and writing activities which were webbed around the Letterbook W. Stories and poems that were shared this week included Where the Wild Things Are, Whistle for Willie, William's Doll, Cloudy With a Chance of Meatballs, Charlotte's Web, Wee Willie Winkie, When the Wind Stops, among others. Your child participated in activities which included listening for the sound of the letter W in context and retelling stories orally and through the use of story maps. Special attention was paid to the order and sequence of events. In addition, original art projects were completed as an extension of the literature shared.

In Writing, your child continued making entries in his/her journal using invented spelling. After the shared reading of William's Doll, many of the children wrote about things they enjoy doing for fun. In response to Where the Wild Things Are, your child made stick puppets and wrote and performed original stories about their own "wild things." Some children wrote and gave their own "weather forecast" after hearing the story Cloudy with a Chance of Meatballs. After chanting and singing the poem Wee Willie Winkie, the children created a class mural sequencing the events. The housekeeping corner was transformed into a restaurant as the children took turns being waiters, chefs, and customers. Much writing occurred as waiters took orders which they then read to the chef.

In Science and Math, your child ate watermelon, estimated how many seeds his/her piece had, classified the seeds by shape and color, and graphed who had the most seeds. Many of us planted our seeds and are anxiously awaiting to see what happens. We are logging this information in our Science Journals.

Much measuring and observing took place as we made waffles. We paid special attention to the importance of organizing the materials and ingredients, and sequencing the procedures correctly. The recipe was recorded on a class chart for all to read. The best part was eating them!

In response to Whistle for Willie and When the Wind Stops, we had great fun trying to whistle. The kites we made and tried to fly outside were an exercise in perseverance and determination!

In Social Studies/Green Circle, your child had the opportunity to discuss the concept of Loyalty and why being loyal was an important quality for a friend to have. Wilbur and Charlotte in the story Charlotte's Web were used as an example. The children

brainstormed many ideas and then decided that the most important one was that you need to be loyal to a friend when it might not be the popular thing to do. The children enjoyed role-playing various situations demonstrating loyalty and/or the lack of it.

Thank you for your cooperation and have a nice weekend.

Sincerely,

Elsie Nigohosian

Elsie Nigohosian

FIGURE 3.6
Sample of weekly letter to parents
Note. From "Weekly Letter to Parents," 1989. Copyright 1989 by Elsie Nigohosian. Reprinted by permission.

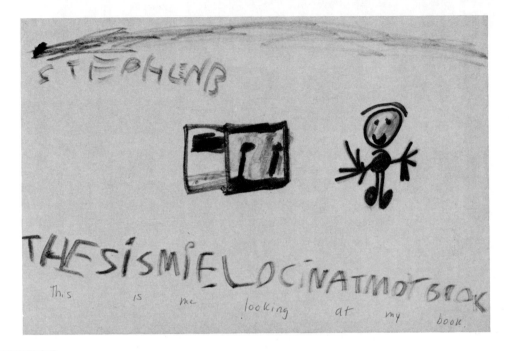

FIGURE 3.7
An example of student's booklet about reading
Note. From original student writing, 1991. Copyright 1991 by Stephen Berkeley. Reprinted by permission.

The next day she has the students take turns and read to her. They often tape-record their reading so they can hear how they sound. During the third day she and her students discuss the book or basal selection so that they can respond in writing in their response logs. Her students generally identify their favorite parts of the selection or book, highlighting major characters and events.

As part of her commitment to help students develop as readers, she has created a "Reading is Dino-mite" program for her students. Every night students take home a trade book to read to their parents or siblings. Along with a book goes a "Reading is Dino-mite" form (see Figure 3.8) that a parent signs after a student has read the book fluently to a family member. Because Regina wants her students to read books appropriate for their developmental levels, she spends the first part of the year helping them select books. She reads the following poem to them as an introduction to her mini-unit on book selection:

Book Search
Since I can't tell a book by its cover,
A page or two helps me discover;
Do I like what I see?
Can I read easily?
Or should I go search for another? (Hajdusiewicz, 1990, p. 200)

READING IS DINO-MITE

Date	Title	Author	Parent's or Guardian's Signature

FIGURE 3.8

Student-parent form for *Reading is Dino-Mite* program

Note. From "Reading Is Dino-Mite Program," 1991. Copyright 1991 by Regina Pesce O'Hanlon. Reprinted by permission.

Her "Reading is Dino-Mite" program is an offshoot of a "Reading Incentive Program" that she and another first grade teacher developed to encourage reading as well as to help with math skills. Essentially, students follow a similar pattern of reading at home each night. A major difference between the two programs is the teachers' chart work with column addition and subsequent rewards for reaching a goal. Here's how their "Reading Incentive Program" works:

1. Both teachers create picture charts in their classrooms with the ones, tens, and hundreds columns. They use cut-out eggs to symbolize the number of books read by the class as a whole.
2. Every time a student completes a book, they add an egg to the chart.
3. As the ones column in the chart is completed, all the eggs are removed and one egg is put in the tens column to represent that ten books were read. A similar procedure is followed for the tens column.
4. When students have read 100 books, which is represented by one egg in the hundreds column, the class celebrates with a popcorn party as they watch a literature-based video.

Regina told us that one year her class read over 1,000 books. They ended up having a popcorn party about once a month. Both teachers use students' reading choices to help them select books which, by the way, are categorized by level (based on children's responses) and kept in a closet between the two classrooms. They order multiple copies of popular books so that as many students as possible can read their first choices. Regina finds that using students as her guide for selecting books and basal selections has made a remarkable difference in everyone's attitude toward reading.

GRADE 1: BASALS AND BIG BOOKS

Another first grade teacher, Michael Petillo, has a basal-trade book schema that is different from Regina Pesce O'Hanlon's. Whereas Regina views the basal as just one of many cogs in her array of reading materials, Michael Petillo uses the basal as the hub of reading instruction. However, because of his desire to use trade books more and more, he has managed to harmonize his district's mandates for basal instruction with his philosophical commitment to real reading experiences. One way that he supplements basal instruction is by using the real-book versions of abridged or edited selections in the basals. He also keeps eliminating skill sheets by assessing the skills that students need by other means. While he uses the basal's charts, student reader, and activity book, he uses only those selections that he finds appropriate for his students. He also has created a yearlong, seasonal-related Language Experience Approach (LEA) program that he uses instead of the myriad activities in the teacher's guide (see Figure 3.9 for highlights of his LEA plan).

Big books characterize Michael's whole-class, trade book connection. Every other week he devotes a few days to a big book such as *Chicken Soup with Rice* (Sendak, 1962), *The Three Billy Goats Gruff* folktale (Galdone, 1973), *Noisy Nora* (Wells, 1973), *Shhhhh, It's a Secret!* (Myers, 1973), and *Caps for Sale* (Slobodkina, 1947). As

SEPTEMBER	OCTOBER	NOVEMBER	DECEMBER	JANUARY
Write daily dictated stories on large chart paper to plan the day. Discuss special events, weather, special classes, lunch, etc. For "Fire Prevention Week," arrange for the town fire department to visit school with a fire truck. Make a class chart of fire safety rules. Children will take home large, cutout firepeople with the rules written on the raincoat.	Play an album of thriller sounds. Students write about and draw pictures of what the sounds make them think of. Paint over their drawings with diluted, purple tempera paint to give students that "eerie" feeling. Have children write a story telling what they will be for Halloween. Have them draw themselves in costume in the upper part of the paper.	Have children write story on large cornucopia to tell what they are thankful for on Thanksgiving. Share the story at the feast. Have children share a sentence to show someone is speaking. Use elbow macaroni to help students understand how to use quotation marks.	Make a large "Holiday Pictionary" of the words that the children use throughout the month. Have children make pictures for each word. Have children write a story about what it would be like to live in a gingerbread house that they create in class.	Have children create a "Words to Keep Us Warm" bulletin board with their stories about warm weather words. Read story about Martin Luther King. Have students write story about a dream that they would like to see come true.

FEBRUARY	MARCH	APRIL	MAY	JUNE
Discuss and write a class chart on people who wear uniforms. Invite anyone who wears a uniform to speak to the class. Visit the post office in town. Write a class story about the visit.	Children create ladybugs from small paper plates. They then write a class story about what it would be like to be a ladybug. Have children write about different hats from home that they bring to class.	Have children act out a play that they rewrite that is based on Mother Goose's nursery rhymes. Have children create a chart that shows the importance of trees. Add a collage of pictures of anything made from trees.	Have children create a bouquet of daisies. On each petal have children write reasons why their mothers are important to them. Have children create a booklet describing their favorite things.	Have students create a list of chores that they can do to help their father around the house. Have students write a story about why they are proud to live in America.

FIGURE 3.9
Highlights of a month-by-month language experience approach plan
Note. From "Month-by-Month Language Experience Approach Plan," 1991. Copyright 1991 by Michael Petillo. Reprinted by permission.

he reads a book aloud to his students, they follow along in their smaller versions. Students then listen to a tape of the book before engaging in some type of creative activity. Three activities that Michael's students find particularly appealing are highlighted below:

1. After students read *Chicken Soup with Rice,* they form student groups by season and create their own bowl-shaped books that are color-coded for the months of their season.
2. After students read *The Three Billy Goats Gruff,* they create a puppet show with the scenery from the book.
3. After students read *Shhhhh, It's a Secret!,* they write down their own secrets and put them together in a class-created "secret" book.

Michael has been so enthused by his students' responses to his trade book activities that he is purchasing additional sets of trade books for his class from grant money. Although he still feels compelled to cover all the skills from the basal so that his students fare as well as the other students in the district's testing program, he feels pleased with the progress he has been making in reaching out for other materials.

GRADE 2: THREE TRADE BOOK CONFIGURATIONS WITH BASALS

Second grade teacher Maryanne Crowley uses her basal's student readers, workbooks, and teacher's guide by choice. She chooses those selections that lend themselves to content area learning or contain natural-sounding language with real-life characters. She also uses the teacher's guide to identify which skills to teach sequentially and to glean suggestions for enrichment activities.

Each of her three reading groups follows the same weekly pattern:

- *Monday:* Enrichment activities to stimulate students' thinking about a story, including character introductions, vocabulary review, and prediction strategies.
- *Tuesday:* Read part of a story aloud and confirm predictions. Teach a skill.
- *Wednesday:* Review skill, continue reading, and make predictions. Reread for higher level thinking skills. Children ask each other questions about the story.
- *Thursday/Friday:* Writing enrichment activities about the story and group share.

Because Maryanne appreciates children's needs to understand and work with story grammar (for example, the story's setting, initiating event, goal, reaction, outcome, and resolution), she finds that her basal system contributes greatly to her cause.

However, even with her basal focus, she continues to blend trade books into her reading program in three ways:

1. She uses one book with the entire class (all students have the same book) every month. Some of the books she uses, which were chosen in conjunction with her librarian and reading specialist, are *Amelia Bedelia* (Parrish, 1963), *Magic Fish* (Littledale, 1985), *Owl at Home* (Lobel, 1975), *Why Mosquitoes Buzz in People's Ears* (Aardema, 1975), *Sylvester and the Magic Pebble* (Steig, 1969), *Velveteen Rabbit* (Williams, 1975), *The Story of Ferdinand* (Leaf, 1936), *Where the Wild Things Are* (Sendak, 1963), and *The Talking Eggs* (San Souci, 1989).

She spends the first day doing her "story buildup" in which she talks about the author, provides an overview, reviews difficult vocabulary, and has students brainstorm their thoughts about the book. She uses the next couple of days for reading and rereading the book silently and orally. She then has students work with the book's story grammar. Concurrently, small groups or individual students have the opportunity to visit centers that she created for her book of the month. Here is an example of some of the center activities that students engage in for *Why Mosquitoes Buzz in People's Ears:*

- Paint your favorite animal in water color. Outline water color in black.
- Make a stick puppet of your favorite animal, using a pattern provided or an original one. (Once stick puppets are created, students pair off into groups to create a skit.)
- Write a paragraph describing characteristics of a selected character, and tell why you chose him. (On the day after students write their paragraphs they have a conference with Maryanne about their paragraphs, recopy them, and attach them to their water color drawings.)
- Work with a partner to read a fable to each other.
- Work with three or four other children to paint a large mural of the scene depicted on the chalkboard.
- Look at the sun's position and its facial expressions throughout the story. Draw various sun faces and write a sentence or two about the expressions.

2. She has small-group, trade book reading along with the basal. Periodically she has one of her three groups put aside the basal for a week to read from a trade book. She uses the same instructional plan—minus the learning centers—with her small groups that she uses with the whole class.

3. She has independent daily reading of a trade book with students reporting to their small groups as well as to the entire class. She has 10 book baskets organized by genre all around her classroom so that students have a wide variety of books from which to select.

Maryanne frequently does author studies; for example, she will read many of Tomie de Paola's books, provide time for children to read some of his books, and involve students in writing projects about a favorite de Paola book. She also selects a specific genre, for example, fairy tales or folktales, and reads many examples of the genre so students feel comfortable writing their own.

Just as Michael Petillo does, Maryanne focuses a great deal on Language Experience Approach activities; in fact, she uses this technique as a vehicle for moving into the writing process. She then uses her daily process-writing time for students to respond to what they are reading in their trade books or basals. Although she feels rushed at times, she believes that her approach to combining the use of the basal and trade books is "turning her students into readers who are aware of literacy all around them."

GRADE 3: EVERY OTHER DAY WITH TRADE BOOKS

Cheryl Cator, a third grade teacher in an inner-city school, has a different system for combining basals and trade books in her classroom. Every Monday, Wednesday, and

Friday she uses a basal; every Tuesday and Thursday she uses a trade book. She uses her 80 minutes each day to read two to three basal selections and two trade books each week. Even though she has to cover every selection and skill in the basal for the district's testing program, she does so rapidly so that she still has time to work with trade books on a regular basis.

When Cheryl works with the basal, she follows the suggestions in the teacher's guide for pre-reading instruction and skill development. However, rather than working with three groups daily, she works with only one group each day. While she works with a small group of randomly selected students, the rest of her class reads the same story silently and records in response logs the following information: title, author, date, opinion, and special words.

When Cheryl works with trade books, she first reads a book aloud. She then has all her students read aloud together the same book before responding in their reading logs with the aforementioned information. Every Friday she collects students' reading logs and responds to them. Some of the books that she selected for her students to use are *Frog and Toad Are Friends* (Lobel, 1970), *Miss Nelson is Missing* (Allard, 1977), *Tikki Tikki Tembo* (Mosel, 1968), *Ming Lo Moves the Mountain* (Lobel, 1982), and *The Adventures of Ali Baba Bernstein* (Hurwitz, 1985).

After students complete their trade book reading, they have choices about reading-related projects. They might, for example, make story characters out of clay, create

paperbag puppets, design posters to advertise or retell the book, or read the book to a kindergarten or first grade student.

Although Cheryl knows that it is much easier to use a basal and she often feels that she is "ready to pull out her hair" in trying to organize the trade book facet of her reading program, she knows that she could never go back to being a basal purist. Once her students experience the "good feeling" of having read an interesting trade book in its entirety, they complain to her about being bored with the basal selections. And she cannot afford the risk of losing her students' interest in reading. Because she teaches students whose parents are plagued with illiteracy, she believes that, if nothing else, she must help her students to experience the value of reading in their everyday lives.

SUMMARY

The five primary teachers we have discussed here have created different configurations of their basals and trade books that work for them. While two teachers, Elsie Nigohosian and Regina Pesce O'Hanlon, minimize basal usage, the other three teachers, Michael Petillo, Maryanne Crowley, and Cheryl Cator, use basals as their primary instructional source. However, all have reshaped their instructional plans—including scheduling, grouping practices, and activities—to include trade books.

ELEMENTARY (4–6)

GRADE 4: TRADE BOOKS FOR READING, BASALS FOR TESTING SKILLS

Fourth grade teacher Gerry Wahlers uses the basal for pre- and post-testing only. She tests her students to learn what skills from the basal they do not know, instructs them accordingly, and tests them again. Gerry's move away from basals began about three years ago when she discovered that her above-average group was not doing any recreational reading. She started by having students vote on which selections they would like to read, so that they would begin to see reading as enjoyable. As time progressed she decided that her basal use would consist only of selected enrichment activities and skill-based "jargon" so that her students would be prepared for their swing back to basal-based reading experiences in fifth grade.

Gerry uses trade books in two ways. First, students have a book of their choice that they read in school daily and at home five times a week for 20 minutes. Second, all students read the same trade book in class as part of their shared book reading experience. She assigns such trade books as *Fantastic Mr. Fox* (Dahl, 1970), *Anastasia Krupnik* (Lowry, 1979), *Bridge to Terabithia* (Paterson, 1977), and *Where the Red Fern Grows* (Rawls, 1961).

In the beginning of the year, when her students have an "I hate reading" attitude, she uses lighthearted fiction to whet their appetites for the idea of reading. By the time her students read *Bridge to Terabithia,* they are ready for a more serious analysis of a book's characters and theme. She chooses the first three books for her entire class to read during shared reading; however, she allows her students to vote on which one of two other book choices to read thereafter. Once students embrace the idea of reading fiction, she moves into nonfiction and poetry with *Joyful Noise, Poems for Two Voices* (Fleischman, 1988).

During each of her 40-minute reading periods, she devotes the first 10 minutes to reading, discussing, and rereading a poem. She then moves into a **mini-lesson** or discussion about the trade book that her class is reading. She uses this time to encourage students to share their reactions to what they are reading; yet, she also plans ahead to focus on certain issues (for example, a book's theme or certain literary elements). Students then read an assigned portion of the trade book, read their self-selected books, or write in their response logs. She adapted Nancie Atwell's (1987) letter-writing requirements in which students must write one letter to her and one letter to a friend each week. Students also use their response logs to record their predictions before reading a new chapter. (See Kathy Kelly in Chapter 4 for a more lengthy description of "literature letters.")

As students read or write about their book, Gerry meets with those students who did not do well on a specific skill in the basal pretest. She also holds conferences with students to discuss the words that they have discovered during the week's readings. She assesses students' growth in reading and writing from their response logs, their ability to discuss a book critically, and their individual portfolios. Her portfolios include basal tests, lists of words discovered during reading, a weekly contract that incorporates independent reading responsibilities at home, and the letters mentioned above.

When we asked Gerry if she was satisfied with her reading program, she was quick to say that she wasn't. She explained that her time period for reading was not long enough to connect writing with reading. But she also was realistic enough to appreciate that every day she is learning something new in her transition. She is certain of one thing: her students are beginning to enjoy reading enough to want to go back for more.

GRADE 4: ONE APPROACH TO PHASING OUT BASALS

Another fourth grade teacher, Rosemary Taylor, also has begun to branch away from the basal crutch. Even though she knows it is easier to use the basal for time management and communication ("It tells the world what I'm doing!"), she knows in her heart that the selections are too boring and the skills too piecemeal to make readers out of her students. As she sees it, her yearlong, five-day basal routine—teach a skill, read selection aloud, reinforce the skill, test the skill, start over—is gradually being phased out. Although she continues to follow this pattern for the first marking period, she begins to combine trade book reading and basal reading during the second marking period and thereafter. She uses only selected stories from the basal's student text so that she has time for such trade books as *Soup* (Peck, 1974), *Dear Mr. Henshaw* (Cleary, 1983), *Joyful Noise, Poems for Two Voices* (Fleischman, 1988) (see how Rosemary combines this book of poetry with technology in Chapter 5), *The Lion, the Witch, and the Wardrobe* (Lewis, 1950), and *The Cabin Faced West* (Fritz, 1958).

When Rosemary uses a trade book, she has her students do the following:

1. Think of a time, place, or event from your own lives that is related to the book.

2. Study the book, including the front and back covers. Predict what you think will happen.
3. Read the first chapter with me.
4. Write a summary of the first chapter in your reading logs.
5. Work with your group (randomly arranged) of four on the rug and listen to each other's summaries.
6. Check your predictions against your original ideas. Discuss vocabulary sheet. (Rosemary types up a list of vocabulary words for each student.)
7. Read independently.

As students read independently, they know to do one of Mrs. Taylor's activities in their reading logs (see Figure 3.10 for her list). By the end of any book that students read, they know that they will have had to work with each of the activities. At the end of the book, students engage in some type of enrichment activity such as "Write a letter to the President of the United States and explain what the main character discovered that everyone should know."

Contrary to Gerry Wahlers, Rosemary does not collect students' reading logs until they are finished reading the book, and she does grade their logs for their report cards. Curiously, even though students do much more work when they work with a trade book, they have told her that they prefer reading from trade books rather than from a basal reader. She feels that this testimonial is enough to keep her reshaping her reading program into her image of how reading should be taught.

GRADE 5: BASALS FIRST, TRADE BOOKS SECOND EVERY DAY

Fifth grade teacher Mary Ann Savino uses the basal more than our two fourth grade teachers. Although she chooses to use all basal components with her students, she uses only those basal selections that are interesting and focus on critical skill areas. Her format for working with the basal is similar to the framework prescribed in her teacher's guide: background and vocabulary introduction, silent reading followed by written questions, discussion, and follow-up activities.

Even though she uses her basal every day, she also uses trade books daily for independent or small-group reading. Her self-selected trade books focus on themes comparable to basal selections. Some of the trade books she uses are: *From the Mixed-Up Files of Mrs. Basil E. Frankweiler* (Konigsburg, 1967), *Abel's Island* (Steig, 1976), and *The Terrible Wave* (Dahstedt & Robinson, 1989). She follows a similar format with trade books, using students' oral and written responses to assess students' understanding of the book.

GRADE 6: TRADE BOOKS WITH READING WORKSHOP

Sixth grade teacher Ruth Davitt uses the basal only when a selection coordinates with her self-developed thematic/skill units. She uses Nancie Atwell's (1987) **Reading Workshop** framework for her lesson plan structure in which she conducts a mini lesson about what they are reading, has students read independently, and respond orally and in writing to what they read. She selects trade books to which her students

FIGURE 3.10
Activities and
guidelines for
reading logs

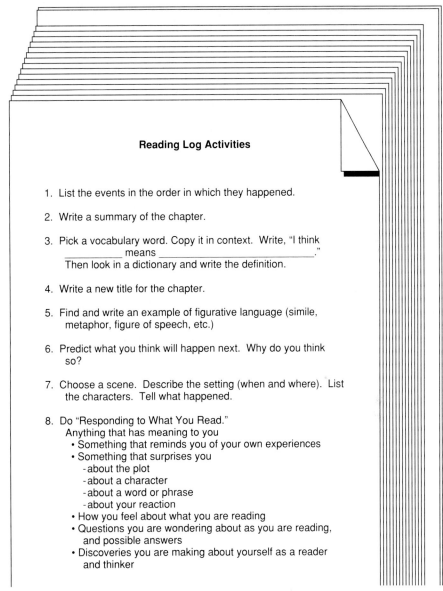

Reading Log Activities

1. List the events in the order in which they happened.

2. Write a summary of the chapter.

3. Pick a vocabulary word. Copy it in context. Write, "I think
   _____ means _____."
   Then look in a dictionary and write the definition.

4. Write a new title for the chapter.

5. Find and write an example of figurative language (simile,
   metaphor, figure of speech, etc.)

6. Predict what you think will happen next. Why do you think
   so?

7. Choose a scene. Describe the setting (when and where). List
   the characters. Tell what happened.

8. Do "Responding to What You Read."
   Anything that has meaning to you
   • Something that reminds you of your own experiences
   • Something that surprises you
     - about the plot
     - about a character
     - about a word or phrase
     - about your reaction
   • How you feel about what you are reading
   • Questions you are wondering about as you are reading,
     and possible answers
   • Discoveries you are making about yourself as a reader
     and thinker

Note. From "Guidelines for Readings Logs," 1991. Copyright 1991 by Rosemary Taylor. Reprinted by permission.

can relate from book reviews and other sixth grade teachers' recommendations. Some of the books she uses are *Sixth Grade Can Really Kill You* (DeClements, 1985), *The Pinballs* (Byars, 1977), *Tuck Everlasting* (Babbitt, 1975), and *Kidnapping Mr. Tubbs* (Schellie, 1978).

When students read a trade book, she uses no other reading material to distract their attention. She assesses students' comprehension through discussion, mapping activities, and responses to directed reading activities. She also finds that projects such as book cubes, mobiles, pictorial time lines, and student-created tests add another dimension to students' involvement with a book.

SUMMARY

As with the primary teachers, the four elementary teachers vary in the frequency with which they use basals and trade books. Whereas Gerry Wahlers and Ruth Davitt have eliminated most basal components, Mary Ann Savino still relies heavily on her total basal program. Rosemary Taylor, on the other hand, is still searching for her ideal instructional niche. However, these elementary teachers pride themselves in knowing that they have been successful so far in finding alternatives to more traditional approaches.

READING SPECIALIST

Kathleen Hadley is a remedial reading teacher for students in grades three through five. As she puts it, "Although the teachers in my building have an image of me doing true remedial work, I see myself as a literature-based person." She uses books such as *Charlotte's Web* (White, 1952), *James and the Giant Peach* (Dahl, 1961), *The Secret Garden* (Burnett, 1962), *Ramona the Pest* (Cleary, 1968), and *Otherwise Known as Sheila the Great* (Blume, 1972), either because they are used in the regular classroom or because her students have asked to read them.

She also uses *The Baby-sitters Club* by Ann Martin (1979–present) and the *Encyclopedia Brown* series by Donald Sobol (1986 to present). Even though some might question Ms. Hadley's choice of *The Baby-sitters Club* series because of its debatable literary quality, Kathleen, along with Mackey (1990), believe that this series excites otherwise unmotivated readers about the pleasures of reading. It just so happens that, according to Violet Harris (1991), Ann Martin is one of a few authors who successfully captures the culture of nonwhite members of our society through some of the characters in her baby-sitter's club series. And, as Kathleen does, we firmly believe in using whatever it takes to get children to want to read.

That's not to say that Kathleen does not teach with the basal. But she uses only those selections in the basal that will pique students' interest to read further. Kathleen strongly believes that if you can find basal selections and books to which these students can relate, they will be that much more interested in reading. Although she depends more on trade books than on basal selections as literary sources, she finds that the more engaging selections provide "quick reads" during class time.

Kathleen does not ignore skills either. She analyzes her district's testing program in relation to her students' profile of skill and strategy needs. As she works with a basal selection or trade book, she weaves needed skills and strategies (for example, making inferences about the main idea). She also uses skill books from the basal system and other commercial sources to reinforce students' skill development.

She has established the following weekly plan for her students:

- *Monday:* Skill book
- *Tuesday:* Trade book

- *Wednesday:* Basal selection
- *Thursday:* Discussion of stories and/or television scripts read
- *Friday:* Extension of Thursday with vocabulary games

Within this framework Kathleen's class time is quite flexible. She describes her class as a "beehive" where students are doing different things at different times. For instance, during trade book reading some students may be listening to a tape while others are reading along with her. Typically, only three students are reading the same book.

The luxury of small class size (six students per class) allows for such diversity. Kathleen has daily conferences with individual students or small groups of students. This conference time informs Kathleen of students' progress on their respective reading tasks. As students retell, discuss, and question what they read, she is able to determine students' ability to grasp the author's message. She uses conference time, as well as her trade book reading time, to shed light on confusing parts of a book.

Once students finish a book they pursue some type of cooperative learning project that involves research and writing. For example, after reading *The Secret Garden* (Burnett, 1962), students decided to do research on health concerns.

The television script portion of her program emanates from the CBS Television Reading Program. (Address is Educational and Community Services Department, CBS/Broadcast Group, 51 West 52nd Street, New York, NY 10019.) This program provides a teacher's guide and script for TV programs. Within the teacher's guide are the following components: synopsis of the TV program, description of the cast of characters, suggestions for studying the script, background information about the story, vocabulary and language activities, and comprehension activities about the plot, characters, setting, theme, and literary devices (for example, simile, alliteration, and foreshadowing).

TABLE 3.1
Basal-book continuum of 10 teachers

	MORE WORK WITH BASAL	IN THE MIDDLE	MORE WORK WITH TRADE BOOK
Nigohosian			X
Pesce O'Hanlon			X
Petillo	X		
Crowley	X		
Cator	X		
Wahlers			X
Taylor		X	
Savino	X		
Davitt			X
Hadley		X	

FIGURE 3.11

Matrix of 10 teachers' basal-book initiatives

	BASAL COMPONENT	OTHER LITERATURE	READING STRATEGIES	WRITING STRATEGIES	LITERATURE-RELATED ACTIVITIES	CLASS ORGANIZATION	PARENT COMMUNICATION/ INVOLVEMENT
NIGOHOSIAN (KINDER-GARTEN)	Letterbook-basis of cross-curricular plans	Fiction and nonfiction books related to letter from letterbook Nursery rhymes Poems	Read alouds to whole class Choral response to comprehension questions from read-alouds Chanting	Content-based writing logs Stories in writing folders Student-created books	Creative dramatics with student-created props Murals Book-related illustrations Arts and crafts (e.g., web with yarn)	Whole class Spontaneous small groups Individual activities	Weekly newsletter to parents
PESCE O'HANLON (FIRST)	Student Reader—related to theme or author	Multiple copies of fiction and nonfiction books related to thematic unit or author study	Read alouds to small group Small-group discussions Classroom library	Student-created books Response logs	Tape-recording of students and reading	Three small groups—randomly and by ability	At-home reading program with incentives
PETILLO (FIRST)	Student Reader—selected stories Workbook Charts	Books for basal selections Big books Multiple copies of small versions of big books	Read-alouds to whole class	Student-created books	Yearlong LEA plan Listening to tapes on book Puppet shows Class-created books	Whole class and small groups by ability	

CROWLEY (SECOND)	Student Reader—selected for content area applications and realistic portrayal Workbook Teacher's Guide—for skill-work and enrichment	Single and multiple copies of different genres and specific authors Classroom library with 10 book baskets	Pre-reading activities Story grammar Student reporting Independent reading Read-alouds to whole class Semantic mapping Genre-attribute analysis	Book-related stories Reactions to books Student's writing of specific genre Reading logs	Vocabulary development LEA	Small groups by ability Activity centers for small groups or individuals Whole class
CATOR (THIRD)	Student Reader Workbook Skill sheets Teacher's Guide—for pre-reading instruction and skill development	Multiple copies of fiction and nonfiction	Basal-based pre-reading instruction Read-alouds to whole class	Reading logs Book-related projects (clay characters, puppets, posters, student-created books)		Small groups, randomly selected; works with one a day Whole class
WAHLERS (FOURTH)	Assessment Tests Teacher's Guide for enrichment	Student selected books Multiple copies of fiction, nonfiction, and poetry	Independent reading Shared reading Whole-class discussion Conferencing Assessment portfolios	Reading logs Letter writing	Poetry reading	Whole class Individual Weekly contracts At-home reading program

FIGURE 3.11
(continued)

	BASAL COMPONENT	OTHER LITERATURE	READING STRATEGIES	WRITING STRATEGIES	LITERATURE-RELATED ACTIVITIES	CLASS ORGANIZATION	PARENT COMMUNICATION/ INVOLVEMENT
TAYLOR (FOURTH)	Student Reader—selected stories Workbook Skill sheets	Multiple copies of fiction, nonfiction, and poetry	Prediction-Verification Independent reading Teacher-student read-alouds	Chapter summaries Specific reading log activities	Vocabulary development Book-related enrichment activities	Small groups by ability Randomly selected groups	
SAVINO (FIFTH)	Student Reader—selected for interest and critical skill areas Workbook Skill sheets Teacher's Guide—for instructional framework	Multiple copies of fiction and nonfiction	Pre-reading activities Oral response to questions Discussion	Written response to questions		Small groups by ability Individual	
DAVITT (SIXTH)	Student Reader—selected for thematic/skill units	Multiple copies of fiction	Mini-lesson Discussion Mapping Oral response		Book-related projects—book cubes, mobiles, pictorial time lines, student-created tests	Whole class	
HADLEY (READING SPECIALIST)	Student Reader—selected for interest Skill sheets	Multiple copies of fiction, including series books	Questions Discussion Conferencing		Listening tape Television scripts	Individual Cooperative learning groups	Television program

When we interviewed Kathleen, she had just completed the TV script for *The Secret Garden* to reinforce students' trade book reading. Once students read the script in class, they watched the program at home. They discussed in class what they saw and completed some of the vocabulary activities from the guide. Subsequently, Kathleen sent home a packet of comprehension activities for her students to do with their parents.

Although Kathleen's support for her program comes mostly from herself, she feels that her students must be *motivated* to read. Sure, they have to pass the district's test program, but she truly believes that success on a test one year does not guarantee subsequent reading success. On the other hand, if she can open up her students' eyes to the joys of reading, she feels that her students' pursuit of reading will translate naturally into passing test scores.

Take a look at Table 3.1 (p. 115) to see where each of our 10 teachers (Elsie Nigohosian, Regina Pesce O'Hanlon, Michael Petillo, Maryanne Crowley, Cheryl Cator, Gerry Wahlers, Rosemary Taylor, Mary Ann Savino, Ruth Davitt, and Kathleen Hadley) fall on a basal-book continuum. Now look at the matrix in Figure 3.11 for highlights of the kinds of activities and strategies that each teacher uses to combine basals and other literature. As we hope we have communicated in our descriptions of their work, each teacher has found his or her niche for combining both basals and trade books comfortably. And, while some teachers spend more time with basals than with trade books, they still have created a rich array of self-created, literature-based activities that challenge children to think through writing, discussion, and projects.

Essential Elements for Creating Connections Between Basals and Trade Books

As the teachers in the previous section demonstrated, formulaic guidelines for moving away from the basal would themselves interfere with the idea of tailoring materials and strategies to individual classroom situations. In fact, Zarrillo (1989) found from his analysis of 23 teachers' interpretations of literature-based reading that teachers' interpretations are quite different. We applaud this acceptance of diversity since all teachers encounter different conditions for connecting trade books and basals.

Any shift in instructional focus can be quite liberating. Although it can be initially frightening to let go of a proven organizational system for instruction, those anxious moments are soon replaced with extended periods of self-satisfaction when witnessing children's surprising excitement over an activity that was once considered unappealing—reading. Yet, in our encounters with teachers across grade levels, we are often told "I want to use more literature but. . ." or asked "Where do I begin?" Although each teacher must mix and match materials and strategies so that they are tailored to the particular students, the particular classroom, the particular school, and the particular community at large, four essential elements should always be considered: resources, activities, schedule, and skills and assessment (see Figure 3.12). Facets of each element will be described in the pages that follow.

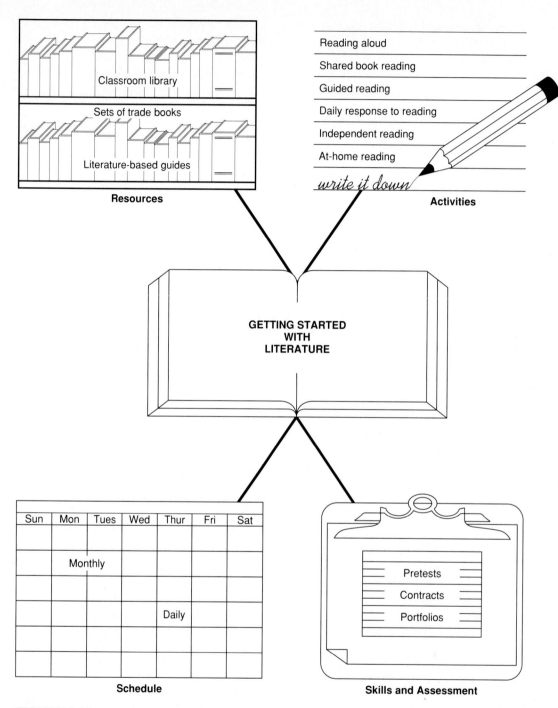

Resources

Classroom library

Sets of trade books

Literature-based guides

Activities

Reading aloud

Shared book reading

Guided reading

Daily response to reading

Independent reading

At-home reading

write it down

**GETTING STARTED
WITH
LITERATURE**

Schedule

Sun	Mon	Tues	Wed	Thur	Fri	Sat
	Monthly					
			Daily			

Skills and Assessment

Pretests

Contracts

Portfolios

FIGURE 3.12
Getting started with literature: Four areas to consider

RESOURCES

Recently, in an article written for the Education Life section of *The New York Times*, Richard Anderson, Director at the Center for the Study of Reading, was quoted as saying, "There are schools without libraries, schools with bad libraries, and schools reluctant to let books circulate for fear of losing them" (Cohen, 1991). Cheryl Majerscak, a second grade teacher in an inner-city district, knows all-too-well about poorly stocked schoolwide libraries. To integrate trade books into her classroom reading program, she realized that she had to create her own classroom library. She used the ideas from her professional reading (Morrow, 1982, 1989; Morrow & Weinstein, 1982) to help her decide how to set up her library corner, so that it would be visually and physically accessible and contain varied types and levels of children's literature. She did the following:

- color-coded all books according to category; for example, all animal stories are coded with yellow tape.
- arranged her library with rugs and pillows for floor reading, divided tables for private reading, and arranged tables to have supplies for team projects. Her supplies include crayons, markers, pastels, paint, paper, yarn, and glue.
- organized a listening table with a tape recorder so that students could listen to taped stories or tape stories or thoughts of their own.
- created a bulletin board entitled "Our Best Book," which contains photographs of her students and herself with their favorite book of the month.

Classroom Library

Cheryl took an important step in providing resources for her children through her classroom library, the first of three important resources to consider. Classroom libraries also should include magazines, student-published books, newspapers, pamphlets, brochures, poetry, atlases, almanacs, and dictionaries so that students have access to a world of different print sources. If, unlike Cheryl, you are blessed with a good school library, think of borrowing books for a certain period of time to begin to build your classroom library. If funds are scarce, consider soliciting donations from parents and local businesses and loans from homes to supplement your collection (O'Halloran, 1987).

Sets of Trade Books

A second important resource that makes the transition between basals and trade books easier is the accumulation of class or group sets of trade books. Search for books that are recognized for their excellence—for example, Caldecott or Newbery Award winners; state book award winners (e.g., Illinois has the Rebecca Caudill Award for the book that children vote as their favorite [Fuhler, 1990]); and the International Reading Association's annual, annotated listing of "Children's Choices," which is published in the October issues of *The Reading Teacher*. Sources such as the National Council of Teachers of English's *Adventuring with Books* (Jett-Simpson, 1989), *The Horn Book* (published by The Horn Book Inc. in Boston, Massachusetts), and *The School Library*

Journal (published by the American Library Association in Chicago, Illinois) will provide guidance for books. Fuhler also recommends *EYE OPENERS!* (Kobrin, 1988) to help with the selection of nonfiction books.

While accumulating class or group sets, look for books of different genres (for example, realistic fiction, animal stories, historical fiction, fairy tales, fables, science fiction, poetry, and nonfiction), so that students can begin to understand forms and patterns of genre writing. Also consider books written by the same author, so that students can study a particular author's style of writing. Most importantly, though, get to know the books so that you can match them with your children's interests (Nathan & Temple, 1990). Depending on the instructional activities (see next section), books can be selected by teachers, students or both (Hiebert & Colt, 1989).

LITERATURE-BASED GUIDES

A third resource that makes these first strides easier is the acquisition of **literature-based guides** that can be used along with trade books. These guides typically provide creative ideas for using trade books comprehensively. However, as with the teacher's guide in the basals, they should be used more as suggestions than marching orders. Many commercially prepared activity packets are available (see "Commercially Published Literature Guides" at the end of this chapter for names and addresses of some of these). Schools and districts also are creating guides for their own selected pieces of literature. For example, Philip Caccavale, Supervisor of Reading, has spent the last three summers working with his teachers to create literature-based guides for books that they selected jointly for each grade level.

Teachers also have begun to create their own literature-based guides that they share with other grade level teachers. Arleen Swift, a fourth grade teacher in a rather affluent district, found that the only way that she felt comfortable with her district's mandate to use literature was to create guides for each book selected. Although initially apprehensive about this new challenge, she soon learned that she could achieve her goal for developing thinking readers by using the kinds of activities that she created in her literature-based plans.

ACTIVITIES

We will describe six activities that can help you combine your use of basals with trade books: reading aloud, shared book reading, guided reading, **daily response to reading, independent reading**, and at-home reading. Each of these activities contributes to a total literature-based reading program; yet, each can be used independent of the others within a modified basal environment.

READING ALOUD

Reading aloud to students is an integral part of a literature-based reading program. "The word-by-word readers meet the fluent readers on common ground when a teacher reads to a class" (Fuhler, 1990, p. 314). Reading aloud also helps students to build their own sense of story and improve linguistic development as they develop a love of reading on their own. Through modeling, the teacher helps children to develop their retelling, thinking, and reasoning skills.

According to Regie Routman (1991), reading aloud is regarded as the single most influential factor in young children's success with learning to read. Often, though, it is a neglected aspect of language programs. Ross and Fletcher (1989) found that, when they used a questionnaire to assess rural, inner-city, and suburban children's exposure to literature, students indicated that only 34% of their teachers read aloud daily to them and 18% never read to them at all. Since reading aloud is the easiest component to incorporate into any instructional program at any grade level, and because it promotes story enjoyment and literature appreciation, it should be part of the host of language activities. Any type of material—fiction and nonfiction books, short stories, poems, excerpts or articles—can be read aloud to promote listening skills, stimulate discussion, introduce a concept, or encourage further reading.

SHARED BOOK READING

Shared Book Reading is a relaxed, social activity in which students see the text, observe an expert—usually the teacher—reading it with fluency and expression, and are invited to read along (Routman, 1991). Developed by Don Holdaway (1979) to support his developmental model of language, shared book reading enables learners to observe and participate with competent readers to feel secure enough to practice reading independently.

Although typically associated with beginning reading in the primary grades, shared book reading is appropriate for learners of all ages. Big books, regular-sized books, favorite rhymes, songs, poems, chants, and stories can be read and reread to demonstrate that reading is a pleasurable and meaningful experience.

In addition to creating a bond between the reader and listeners, a shared book reading experience allows children to participate in reading while honing their thinking skills through questioning and discussion. Consider using the following steps as you create your own shared book experiences (Butler & Turbill, 1984; Haile, 1987):

1. Find a story that is appealing and suitable for your students. Stories should help children to understand each other, familiar events, interesting situations, and feelings. Think about the story line, the way illustrations support and enhance the text, and the way language is used. Be certain that all children are able to see the text and illustrations by using big books, multiple copies of small books, or overhead transparencies.
2. Before introducing the story, discuss any concepts or background information necessary for understanding the story.
3. As you introduce the story, discuss the cover, title, author, and illustrations. Encourage students to predict what the story is about. After reading parts of the story dramatically, invite students to retell the story in their own words and verify their predictions. When you come to words, phrases, or ideas that should be emphasized, make sure that children understand how they contribute to the meaning of the story. When illustrations are available, help students to see how they complement the story. Help students to connect the story to their own lives by asking

if events similar to those in the story ever happened in their own lives, if they ever felt like anyone in the story felt, or if they knew anyone like the characters in the story.

4. Read the story again to encourage increased participation. Students might repeat familiar refrains, mimic the motions of the characters, or guess the next word. Beginning readers also benefit from this rereading by becoming more aware of the conventions of print (for example, words, spaces, left to right, top to bottom, and one-to-one correspondence between written and spoken word), sight vocabulary, and phonics applications. Encourage students of all ages to predict and think critically about the story. If children are inclined to dramatize a part of the story, allow them—encourage them—to do so.

5. Plan some type of after-reading response activity similar to Elsie Nigohosian's mural of *Wee Willie Winkie*. Encourage students to keep a response log. Tape-record your reading so that students can listen to it at a later time at the listening center.

6. Generate students' interest in reading the same book independently and doing follow-up work about the book.

GUIDED READING

Guided reading is an in-depth examination of a book with a small group of children. Whereas shared book reading really requires some type of literature other than the basal, guided reading does not. As seen from Chapter 2, guided reading exists in every teacher's guide; however, skills typically drive instruction. In fact, Wixson and Peters (1989) suggest ways in which to modify guided reading procedures for basal selections so that students focus more on the *strategies* needed to read specific selections and the *content* that they are reading. These same strategies can be applied before, during, and after reading with your group or class set of trade books.

For example, *before reading,* students need to think about the type of text they will read, the purposes for which it might be read, and the strategies needed for reading. As Wixson and Peters note, focusing on information and activities that activate or build the meaning of key concepts is much more important than decoding difficult or phonetically regular words. Show students how to preview the text, hypothesize about the content, and generate questions so that they are prepared for reading the text. This is also a golden opportunity for using creative ideas to introduce a story. For instance, Tompkins (1990) shares how a fourth grade teacher in Fresno, California, uses students' brainstorming and subsequent clusters about their favorite games to introduce Chris Van Allsburg's *Jumanji* (1981), a book about a jungle adventure game.

Students need to integrate important information *during* their *reading* of a book so that they are aware of a text's major ideas, its text type (for example, fable or fairy tale) and its organizational features (for example, listing ideas chronologically). Vocabulary and comprehension skills should be developed within the story's context. In addition to helping students understand how words are used to convey meaning, they need to understand why characters behave as they do, and why certain events are occurring in the story. Students' discussion of characters and events helps them to reflect on their initial hypotheses and generate more questions to answer during subsequent readings.

Let's look at how students can integrate information from the book, *Silver* (Whelan, 1988), a "Children's Choice for 1989." Set in Alaska, *Silver* is about 9-year-old Rachel who convinces her dad to give her the runt of his litter of racing dogs so that she can train her dog (named Silver) to become a potential lead sled-racer.

As students read this book, they can use a semantic map to identify what they learn about Alaska: its characteristics, special places, special events and activities, and what it's like to live there. They also can develop their vocabulary of Alaskan terms (for example, *Iditarod, mushers, parkas,* and *chute*) as they read about Rachel's experiences. Students' understanding of Rachel's needs for nurturing a racing dog can come through their oral or written response to aspects of Rachel's life: being an only child, being isolated from her neighbors, and coping with Alaska's climate. Students can compare what they know about Rachel with their own lives to get greater insights into Rachel's character. They then can use this information to predict how she reacts to each of the events in the story.

After reading, students need time to verify or reject hypotheses and summarize to assess how well they understood what they read. These strategies, along with the other metacomprehension strategies used during guided reading, help students to understand how to read strategically to comprehend better (Paris, Cross, & Lipson, 1984; Schmitt, 1990; Schmitt & Baumann, 1986). One technique—story grammar—helps students to synthesize what they read by reflecting on the book's text structure. With *Silver,* students can analyze how the story events are used to show how Rachel reaches her goals. Figure 3.13 contains ideas from a reproducible for recording students' responses to such questions as: Who is the main character of the story? Where does your story take place? How does the story begin? What is Rachel's goal? What does Rachel do to reach her goal? What happens as a result of Rachel's attempts? How does the book end?

Additionally, students benefit from engaging in projects related to their books. Projects replace traditional seatwork and workbook assignments. Students can work individually, in small groups, or as a whole class with projects. Many of the 26 project ideas listed in Figure 3.14 come from a variety of teachers and sources (Butler & Turbill, 1984; Jernigan (personal communication, September 20, 1990); Laughlin & Watt, 1986; Majerscak, 1990; May, 1986; Spellman, 1980; Tompkins, 1990).

DAILY RESPONSE TO READING

Children need daily opportunities to write in reading logs or other journals about what they read. Students who write about what they read are better able to understand text (Petrosky, 1982). Students can use open-ended response journals in which they write letters to the teacher to tell what they are reading and why they are reading it. They can use a Dual Entry Diary (DED) in which they record what they read and respond to it on the same page. Barone (1990) has students draw a vertical line down the middle of a journal page. The left side contains a description of what students

FIGURE 3.13
Story grammar
format for the
book, *Silver*
(Whelan, 1988)

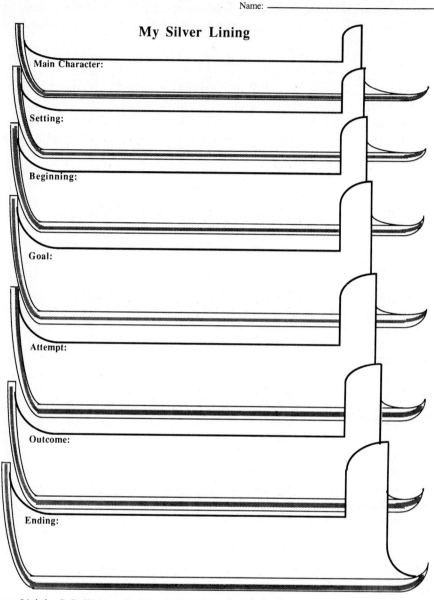

Name: _____

My Silver Lining

Main Character:

Setting:

Beginning:

Goal:

Attempt:

Outcome:

Ending:

Note. From *Literature Lesson Links* by S. B. Wepner, K. Layton, & J. Beaty, 1991, Gainesville, FL:
Teacher Support Software. Copyright 1991 by Teacher Support Software. Reprinted by permission.

read; the right side contains a reaction to the same piece of text read. For instance, with Cynthia Voigt's (1982) Newbery Medal book, *Dicey's Song,* students could use the form in Figure 3.15 as an example of DED for describing or reacting to their reading.

Advertisement for book
Bag-A-Book (decorate brown bag to reflect content of book)
Comic strip about the story
Dramatized commercial to encourage others to read the book
Edible book report (make food that ties into book)
Five-senses poem about a story
Gallery of characters
Holiday habits of characters
Interview of someone who assumes role of character
Jigsaw of book's highlights
Kaleidoscope of events in the story
Living biographies (dress up as characters)
Model of story setting
Novel news
Overhead transparency with oral report
Present for the main character in the book
Questions everyone can answer after reading the book
Retell the story into a "scroll television"
Sequel to book
Time line of events
U-shaped openings (letter *u* is used as framework for drawing or writing about book)
Vertical poems (character from book written vertically)
Write about a character you would like to have as a friend
X-ray vision of the main character's future (sunglasses used as students predict)
You be the judge (moot court simulation judging character's actions in the book)
Zany caricatures of the characters

FIGURE 3.14
The ABCs of book projects

Alternatively, students can respond to prompts. Tompkins (1990) tells how Ms. Chavez uses the following prompts when students need them:

1. What do you think will happen next in the story? Why?
2. What puzzles you about the story?
3. Which character are you most like? Why?
4. What does this story remind you of? Why?
5. How does this story make you feel? Why?
6. What would you change about the story, if you could?

Kelly (1990) found that, regardless of ability, all students are successful in responding to literature when guided by prompts.

Understand, though, that what works for one teacher may not work for another. Some teachers prefer having students use response logs as references for small- or large-group discussions; others use them as forums for written student dialogues *a la*

FIGURE 3.15
Application of dual
entry diary for
Dicey's Song
(Voigt, 1982)

Name: _____

Description of What Was Read	Reaction to What Was Read
Date: _____ Chapter: _____	
Date: _____ Chapter: _____	

Note. From *Literature Lesson Links* by S. B. Wepner, K. Layton, & J. Beaty, 1991, Gainesville, FL: Teacher Support Software. Copyright 1991 by Teacher Support Software. Reprinted by permission.

Atwell (1987). And, as we indicated before, some teachers find that formats to follow or questions to answer offer students guidance while others don't want to impose any type of structure at all on students. The handling of **response logs** also varies. Some teachers read and respond to them or grade them for students' insights. Other teachers don't even collect them since they use students' reference to logs during small-group discussions to determine how students are thinking. Since there is no one right way to use response logs, how they are used and handled depends on what satisfies you and your students.

Whenever feasible, children's responses to reading also should take on additional forms that are written for publication. Such activities as an all-school loudspeaker radio show, school newspaper entry, classroom anthology, news flashes that go home, bulletin board displays, school hall displays, stories turned into play form and acted out, letters to editors, and letters to published authors encourage students to use their ideas about their reading in creative formats (Nathan & Temple, 1990).

Once students develop the habit of responding to what they read, their initial one-line "it was good" statements turn into surprisingly insightful analyses.

INDEPENDENT READING

Of utmost importance is the opportunity for children to read books independently for pleasure. No matter what you call it—Uninterrupted Sustained Silent Reading (USSR), Sustained Silent Reading (SSR), Drop Everything And Read (DEAR), or Super Quiet Uninterrupted Reading Time (SQUIRT)—children should read without interruption for a specified period of time. Critical to this component is students' ability to self-select what they want to read, so that they have a personal interest in their reading and their resulting achievements (Fuhler, 1990). The element of choice also frees students from always being members of the low group, since all students are on equal footing during this time.

Even though poor readers are less capable than good readers at selecting literature that is relevant to their interests and reading levels, they eventually develop better selection abilities through practice. Word-of-mouth comments and recommendations from students, teachers, parents, and librarians help children, particularly those with undeveloped selection skills, to choose "quality" literature that entertains, informs, and uses language in ways that captivate the reader (O'Halloran, 1987). A discussion of book selection techniques early in the program also helps students to choose books they are likely to enjoy and read with success (Berglund & Johns, 1983; Graham, 1987).

Equally important to student selection of reading material is the handling of this time for independent reading. McCracken and McCracken (1979) suggest that, for starters, a timer is set for 2 to 3 minutes, with the time increased each day as long as each child sustains his or her reading. They believe that kindergarten classes should be able to work to 10 minutes, first grades should be able to read for 10 to 20 minutes, and second and third grade classes should be able to sustain themselves for 30 minutes, if they had SSR in kindergarten and first grade. While the amount of time set aside for independent reading is negotiable, the teacher's status as role model in reading for enjoyment is not. It is critical for students to see teachers reading for their own enjoyment so that they, in turn, internalize the value of lifelong practice.

Of course, independent reading is easier said than done. One of our teacher friends constantly talks about the contrast between the philosophical premise of independent reading and the frustrating realities of its implementation. Her special education students cannot sustain their interest long enough to read a book for recreational purposes. Their reading is so labored that they put more energy into disrupting the class than into attending to the printed page. Teachers in similar situations need to make sure that material is available that appeals to these students' interest. Comics, magazines, and picture books should be tolerated to get students in the habit of reading something—anything—for a specified period of time. Furthermore, students need to begin this practice with shorter time frames, so that they feel immediate success. If troublesome students still interfere with other students' reading, O'Halloran (1987) recommends finding ways to convince the disruptive students of the value of this opportunity. For example, on a number of occasions she has stopped independent reading and begun a grammar lesson, one of the least attractive components of the curriculum for her students. Eventually, peer pressure stopped the problem.

Moreover, while some view independent reading as free reading where students are not required to do anything other than read the book, others view this activity as the core of their literature-based program. "Unfamiliar vocabulary and questions about authors' techniques and points of view become the basis for instruction. Ideas gained from independent reading are shared and challenged in small and large group discussions" (Hiebert & Colt, 1989, p. 18). Response journals and projects emanate from students' daily independent reading.

How you use this activity depends on your classroom needs. If you find that you are using guided reading for other literature so that students are acquiring critical reading strategies, you may choose to use this activity as a recreational event for reading additional material. However, if you want to combine guided reading with independent reading, you may choose to use this activity as a springboard to your guided reading procedures. However independent reading is used, it should be considered a high priority within any instructional configuration.

AT-HOME READING

Establishing an **at-home reading** program serves two important purposes. First and foremost, it involves parents in children's reading development which, as research indicates, inevitably helps to produce better readers in the classroom (Allen & Freitag, 1988; Brown, 1990; Fredericks & Rasinski, 1987; Henderson, 1988; Rich, 1985; Smith, 1988). Secondly, it helps to minimize *aliteracy*—the rejection of books by children and young adults who know how to read but choose not to—by helping students see that reading is something that just doesn't happen only in school. Cohen

(1991) shares that many bright young adults don't read, probably because there were no role models in their homes who encouraged them to read as children.

Even with the nation's attention directed to children's recreational reading development, schools still need to provide direction and encouragement so that parents know what to do (Au & Mason, 1989; Fredericks, 1989). One school-home partnership for encouraging parents to read along with their children is Project CAPER (Children And Parents Enjoy Reading), a program implemented in East Brunswick School District, East Brunswick, New Jersey, an affluent suburban school district characterized by families with adequate literacy skills. Interestingly, after the first year of the project, students' attitudes toward themselves as readers improved significantly.

In Project CAPER, volunteer parent-child teams read together daily. Time was set aside each day for pleasure reading, with parents and children reading any type of acceptable reading material which is enjoyable and informational (for example, books, magazines, newspapers, poetry, and manuals). Teachers involved in the project distributed a color-coded, double-sided monthly Reading Record that students and parents completed. On one side students recorded daily the amount of time spent reading and the title or type of material read; they also recorded the total time spent reading each week and the hours and minutes spent reading per month. Parents did the same on the reverse side of the same form (see Figure 3.16). When students turned in their Reading Record each month, they received the same form in a different color and a small token (e.g., a paper bookmark) for their efforts (Wepner & Caccavale, 1991).

Although this type of at-home reading project may not work for you, certain important elements, as Regina Pesce O'Hanlon also discovered, are important to keep in mind.

1. Set up some type of monitoring system, so that students know that you are keeping abreast of their reading efforts at home.
2. Make sure that some type of communication is sent to parents, so that they know their role in your program.
3. Provide guidelines for parents: time frame for daily reading, expectations for students' performance, and type of parental monitoring and assistance expected.
4. Try to expand students' reading experiences.

As part of her at-home reading program, Joan Pearlman presents her fifth grade students with 11 categories of books for their book-a-month reports, so that they are exposed to a variety of genres (see Figure 3.17). Students can select any book of interest; however, they must read a different book for each category so that they are expanding their horizons. Among her many projects is a Holiday Book Report for a main character in a book. (See Figure 3.18, p. 134, for the directions she shares with students.) One of us watched two children work indefatigably on this project. The students' ideas about the characters kept evolving as they thought of more and more ways to use decorations to depict the characters' thoughts and feelings.

PARENT READING RECORD

Please fill in daily the amount of time spent reading and the title or type of material read.

Sunday	Monday	Tuesday	Wednesday	Thursday	Friday	Saturday
						1
2	3	4	5	6	7	8
9	10	11	12	13	14	15
16	17	18	19	20	21	22
23	24	25	26	27	28	29
30						

Total time spent reading this week _____.

Total time spent reading this week _____.

Total time spent reading this week _____.

Total time spent reading this week _____.

Total time spent reading this week _____.

I read for a total of _____ hours and _____ minutes this month.

Name _____
(please print)

_____
Signature

FIGURE 3.16

CAPER monthly progress report

Note. From "Project CAPER (Children And Parents Enjoy Reading): A Case Study" by S.B. Wepner and P. Caccavale, 1991, *Reading Horizons, 31,* pp. 228–237. Copyright 1991 by *Reading Horizons.* Adapted by permission.

132

CATEGORIES

_____ Mystery-fiction

_____ Realistic fiction

_____ Historical fiction

_____ Humor-fiction or nonfiction

_____ Biography or autobiography-nonfiction (Do not use until notified.)
Biographical fiction

_____ Science fiction

_____ Myths and legends-fiction

_____ Sports-fiction or nonfiction

_____ Adventure-fiction or nonfiction

_____ Animal-fiction or nonfiction

_____ Fantasy-fiction

There are 11 categories of books listed here. During the year you will be required to read approximately one book each month outside of class. You will be choosing books from the different categories above, and I must approve each book that you read for a book report.

Sometimes you will be doing only a book review on a 5″ × 8″ index card. At other times you will be doing a major book report and you will receive detailed instructions at least three weeks prior to its due date. Most major book reports must be accompanied by a book review.

PLEASE NOTE: Keep this sheet in your notebook. You will need to refer to it frequently.

FIGURE 3.17
Students' checklist for at-home reading
Note. From "Checklist for At-Home Reading," 1991. Copyright 1991 by Joan Pearlman. Reprinted by permission.

HOLIDAY BOOK REPORT

1. Choose a book and have it approved. Make sure that you choose your book from a category you have not used already.

2. Read the book.

3. You will be making a present for the main character in the book. If there are more than two main characters, choose one of them. Get to "know" your character while you are reading your book—likes, dislikes, favorite foods, etc.

4. Decide what would be a good present for your main character. For example, Claudia was the main character in *From the Mixed-Up Files of Mrs. Basil E. Frankweiler.* You learned that she wanted to feel special and different. You also learned that she wanted to visit Mrs. Frankweiler after her adventure was over. What kind of present do you think she would like to receive? Money? A railroad pass? A famous statue? Clean clothes?

5. After you decide, gather material to MAKE the present. You may not buy the present. It must be something that you make—a picture, something sewn, something painted, something made of clay, etc. USE YOUR IMAGINATION!

6. Find a box that is large enough for your gift. Put your present inside the box.

7. Wrap the present. Use a solid color paper because you will be decorating the paper. (*Hint:* freezer wrap works perfectly)

8. Decorate the wrapping paper. You may either draw or paste on pictures that have something to do with your book. For example, Claudia's paper could be decorated with a picture of a bus, a train, a fountain, a statue, the train station, a laundromat, books from the library, or Michelangelo's stone mason mark. Remember that a box has six sides and you should be decorating all of them.

9. Make a card for your gift. Fold a piece of solid paper in half. On the front write your main character's name (for example, "To Claudia").

    On the inside write a short note explaining why you are giving your gift. Why is it a perfect gift for the character? Sign your name. On the back of the card, write the title of the book, the author, and the category.

FIGURE 3.18

Directions for holiday book report

Note. From "Directions for Holiday Book Report," 1991. Copyright 1991 by Joan Pearlman. Reprinted by permission.

SCHEDULE

Before a schedule can be created, thought must be given to the kind of instructional configuration desired. Consider the following questions: What role do I want my basal to play? What basal materials do I need to use? What role do I want trade books to play? How often and in which ways should I use trade books? If we think back to some of our teachers from the previous pages, we find that their decisions about how they wanted to combine basals and trade books determined their schedules.

On the one hand, there is Elsie Nigohosian (kindergarten), Regina Pesce O'Hanlon (first grade), Gerry Wahlers (fourth grade), and Ruth Davitt (sixth trade) who decided that the basal would be just one small component of the literature-based program. Whereas Elsie Nigohosian used the basal's letterbook, Regina Pesce O'Hanlon used the student reader. Gerry Wahlers decided that the only basal material worth salvaging were the tests (refer back to Figure 3.11). Elsie Nigohosian, Regina Pesce O'Hanlon, and Gerry Wahlers created all-day, half-day, and 45-minute schedules, respectively, to incorporate the four in-school activities (shared book reading, guided reading, daily response to reading, and independent reading) into their everyday plans.

On the other hand, Michael Petillo (first grade), Maryanne Crowley (second grade), Cheryl Cator (third grade), Rosemary Taylor (fourth grade), and Mary Ann Savino (fifth grade) see their basals as more important components to their reading programs. They use basals and trade books side-by-side: they use parts of the teacher's guide suggested Directed Reading Activity to guide instruction with the basal; and they use the four aforementioned in-school activities to create their own instructional patterns with trade books. They also vary the frequency with which they use trade books with the entire class; from twice a week to once every other month. Because they are easing away slowly from basal dependence, they are experiencing instructional dichotomies in the way they handle basals and trade books. They do, though, foresee how their differing instructional techniques will fuse into one overriding pattern as they continue to incorporate more trade books into their reading program.

Because this transition is so evolutionary, begin by creating monthly schedules that incorporate your trade book and basal reading plans. Include the book titles and basal stories, along with coordinated activities and projects. Skills and strategies can also be included (see Figure 3.19). Eventually, after experimenting with your monthly schedules, you will find how easy it is to create a yearlong plan that includes both trade books and basals or leans more heavily toward trade books.

In setting up a daily schedule think of ways to incorporate reading aloud, shared book reading, guided reading, daily response to reading, and independent reading. This allows for a combination of teacher-led instruction, teacher- and student-led interaction through small group discussion, and independent application (Hiebert & Colt, 1989).

Nathan and Temple (1990) suggest following a format for reading similar to one established for process writing. For example, the following can be accomplished in a 45-minute period. Begin a period with 5 minutes of sustained silent reading in which everyone, including the teacher, is reading. For the next 10 minutes the teacher moves around the room to visit individuals who are having problems or need encouragement with their reading. All students continue reading while the teacher circulates. During the next 20 minutes, invite five or six students who are reading the same book to come to the circle and discuss it. For the last 10 minutes, invite one student to come forward and share with the whole class a book he or she is reading. Alternatively, you could begin the period with a mini-lesson on reading and end the period with a checkup to see how students are able to employ the lesson in their reading that day.

RESOURCES/ACTIVITIES			SKILLS/ STRATEGIES
Trade Book	Genre/Theme/ Author	Activities/Projects	Comprehension
Anastasia On Her Own	Realistic fiction/ Acceptance: working mother/Lois Lowry	Dialogue journal between teacher and parents	Note details Comparison-contrast Draw conclusions Categorize Evaluate and make judgments Summarize
		Gallery of Characters: portrait of Anastasia and her family	
		Sequel to the book	Literary Elements
			Character's traits, motives, and feelings
			Plot-resolution
Basal Stories	Genre/Theme/ Author	Activities/Projects	Setting Theme
On My Own	Realistic fiction/ Acceptance: working mother/ Susan Shreve	Response journal about each of main characters' reactions to their situations	Author's purpose and point of view
			Comprehension Strategies
		Comparison-contrast chart of main characters in each story	Purposes for reading Schema development Semantic mapping
The Medicine Bag	Realistic fiction/ Acceptance: family members/ Virginia Driving Hawk Sneve	Cooperative activity: Create magazine about families	Vocabulary
			Content area vocabulary Context clues Synonyms

FIGURE 3.19
Sample of monthly schedule

If you happen to have more time for reading or you are able to combine your reading/language arts period, you could flesh out Nathan and Temple's (1990) suggestions and create a schedule similar (see Table 3.2) to the one created by a teacher friend of ours in her self-created literature program for her inner-city, second grade children. She uses this plan three days a week when she works with trade books, and

TABLE 3.2
Example of a
schedule used by
second grade
teacher

COMPONENT	TIME ALLOTTED (1 hour 55 minutes)
Mini-lesson Focuses on one strategy related to reading and writing.	5 minutes
Paired Reading Stronger reader works with reader who needs reinforcement. Readers take turns reading to each other from same book.	15 minutes
Small-Group Share Students work with other students who read the same book, respond to book independently through drawing or writing, or participate in teacher-led small group discussion.	15 minutes
Whole-Group Share Students share their written or illustrated responses to book.	10 minutes
Writing Workshop Students write and conference with teacher. Students spend last 10 minutes sharing their pieces. This facet of program occurs daily.	45 minutes
Read-Aloud Program Teacher reads aloud as students listen and try to predict what will happen next in the story.	15 minutes
Sustained Silent Reading Students read books borrowed from the public library or the classroom library.	10 minutes

she uses the basal's teacher's guide plans two days a week when she works with basals. She does, however, have writing workshop five days a week, as indicated in Table 3.2.

Kerin (1987) has arranged her schedule around four daily options for her randomly selected groups of 8- and 9-year-olds: listening post (children listen to commercially prepared tape-recording of story and complete follow-up activity); book promotions (children read story and write advertisement about the book, describing main events and characters); silent reading (children choose book and read it quietly); and group work with the teacher (children work on reading strategies such as predicting outcomes and retelling). As students cycle through each area, Kerin has time to work with all of her four groups daily.

It is also important to allot time in your schedule for conferencing. Children need opportunities to confer on a one-to-one or small-group basis. They also need guidance from the teacher about what they read and write (Butler & Turbill, 1984). Conferencing helps children to develop their critical and creative thinking as they relate reading to their personal experiences (O'Halloran, 1987). In addition to allowing teachers to listen to students respond to their books, conferencing provides a perfect opportunity to assess how well students can read and comprehend the text. Anecdotal records—pertaining to the books being read, the reading strategies used, and insights students have—should be kept after each conference to keep a running record of students' progress. Conferences should be scheduled whenever other students are engaged in meaningful activities, so that discipline does not become an issue.

Both resources and activities must be considered in establishing your classroom schedule. With time, both will shift in emphasis. The more students use trade books the more you will find yourself substituting books for basal selections. The more you experiment with reading aloud, shared book reading, guided reading, daily response to reading, and independent reading, the more inclined you will be to schedule these activities into all your plans.

SKILLS AND ASSESSMENT

Never think for one minute that moving away from basals means that you are ignoring students' skill proficiency; nor are you jeopardizing students' successes on standardized tests. Tunnell and Jacobs (1989) share the many studies conducted with all types of students that indicate "stunning" levels of success on standardized tests for students involved with literature-based programs. A teacher friend of ours, who wishes to remain anonymous, and whose instructional schedule we presented in this chapter, found that her students scored significantly better on both a standardized test (*Gates-MacGinitie Reading Tests*) and an attitudinal survey (*Elementary Reading Attitude Survey* [McKenna & Kear, 1990]) after working with her self-created literature program three days a week.

When basals are emphasized less, the strategies and context in which skills are addressed often differ. Think about it a moment. Say, for example, you want students to understand what an analogy is and how authors use analogies in their writing. Is it better to give them x number of skill sheet pages on analogies that do not relate to any cohesive text or introduce and reinforce the concept of analogies through an author's writing? A few skill sheets could be used to help students identify analogous relationships, but a more credible assessment of students' understanding comes from their ability to identify analogies as they read.

Skills per se, especially those listed in basal scope and sequence charts that support students' comprehension of text, are not as much of a concern as the way in which skills are treated. Helping students to, for instance, draw conclusions about what they are reading should be part and parcel of our instructional repertoire. Yet, students don't need to be bombarded with an exhausting array of drawing conclusions skill sheets that relate questionably to what they are reading. Needed skills should be addressed in the context of students' reading. For example, Tompkins (1990) talks about how fourth grade teacher Ms. Chavez ties in frequently confused verbs (e.g., *lie/lay*, *sits/sets*) during her students' guided reading of Chris Van Allsburg's books (see Trade Books Mentioned at the end of this chapter for a listing of the books she uses). Ms. Chavez provides four pairs of verbs and has students break into small groups to prepare fill-in-the-blank sentences on charts to share with their classmates. One group of students prepared such sentences as:

- The children saw a board game *laying/lying* on the ground in the park.
- The boy *sits/sets* down in a comfortable seat on the Polar Express.
- There was a mysterious force *raising/rising* the window.
- "*Leave/let* me sail my ship again," said the man with a limp.

Of course, the question of "which skills?" always comes to mind. While we can't specify the skills that your students need in the context of your teaching situation, we can only suggest that you use your district's reading curriculum guidelines as a first step in determining the skills to address. Take it upon yourself, though, to think of ways to work with these skills so that they are incorporated meaningfully into the texts you use.

Even if you understand that skills are not forfeited with the diminished role of basals, the fear of abandoning a secure structure is still real for many of us. For instance, Eldredge (1991) communicates a concern that beginning readers will not master the word recognition skills necessary for effective comprehension. To maintain the integrity of a literature-based reading program, yet satisfy an expressed need to help students acquire prerequisite decoding skills, he developed a modified "whole language" program for first grade children. Along with reading and responding to children's literature, students engaged in 10 to 15 minutes of daily, systematic phonics instruction. He found that students involved in his program made greater achievement gains in phonics, vocabulary, reading comprehension, and total reading achievement than comparable first grade students involved only in a basal program. While students engaged in recreational and functional reading and writing activities for most of their classroom time, they spent a small portion of each day with phonics activities that differed from the basal's phonics program. They also were taught to use their phonics skills *only* when the use of the context didn't work for them.

Even though Eldredge (1991) created his own sequence of skill activities, ready-made basal tests and selected skill sheets can help to satisfy concerns about students' skill acquisition. As you read earlier, one of our fourth grade teachers, Gerry Wahlers, discovered that pretesting with basal tests helps her to key in on weak spots and skip mastered skills so that students spend more time reading and less time with skillwork. Four or five pretests can be administered once a month. If students achieve 80% accuracy, students can spend their reading period reading, rather than working on skills. Skill and strategy development then can occur during guided reading or conferencing. Students' progress can be analyzed through a chart in which students' names are placed on the left side and the names of skills and strategies are placed across the top of the chart (Taylor & Frye, 1988).

Another way to help assess students' progress is to create assignment sheets or contracts for students, so that they know what they will be responsible for doing. Such sheets could include one or two assignments for one book, many assignments for one book, or a series of assignments for many books. Some of the assignments could be a retelling, a description of the story with illustrations, a letter to someone about the book, an open-ended, student-created project for a book, a poem, or a literary hunt for similes and metaphors. Alternatively, a generic weekly language contract can be devised so that students engage in silent reading, reading to an adult, listening to an adult read to them, at-home reading, conferencing with the teacher, responding in a reading journal, completing specified writing and publishing activities, and learning new vocabulary words (Kerin, 1987).

One thing is certain. Multiple pieces of data provide a more comprehensive profile of children's growth through literature than any one piece of information. While it is best for you to decide the best assessment methods, the following might be used:

1. checklists for reading behaviors. Existing lists of literacy skills and strategies can guide you in creating your own checklist. Marie Clay's (1985) "Concepts of Print" test can help in identifying students' early literacy behaviors. This checklist assesses students' knowledge of book handling, directionality, and letter and word knowledge. Karen Wood's (1988) Group Comprehension Matrix can help to assess students' comprehension behaviors during small-group book discussions. Indicators such as "makes predictions about story," "can retell selection using own words," and "determines word meanings through context" focus on the strategies students use to understand what they read. However, checklists created by others should be only starting points for developing one that meets your needs. Paradis, Chatton, Boswell, Smith, and Yovich (1991) share how three different grade-level teachers, who started with Wood's comprehension matrix, soon realized that, for different reasons, it didn't work for them. The matrix had to be tailored to their grade level and instructional styles. How checklists are used also differs from class to class. Paradis et al. (1991) report how each of the teachers also discovered that their methods for identifying students' comprehension strategies differed significantly. While one teacher felt comfortable tape-recording a book discussion to address her checklist of comprehension indicators, another teacher didn't. Each teacher had to create a system for using checklists that felt comfortable for her.
2. grades for book talks or in-depth book projects.
3. anecdotal records of important reading behaviors acquired and noted through individual conferences and observations. These records also can include students' oral reading and oral and/or written retellings of any text read.
4. interviews and surveys of students' attitudes, strategies, and preferences toward reading. Routman (1991) finds that she learns much more about a student from one-to-one interviews than from written surveys because students tend to respond more freely to oral questions. She says that you can get through an entire class in two weeks if you spend 5 to 10 minutes with several students each day.
5. norm-referenced and criterion-referenced standardized tests.
6. informal tests that are graphed at various intervals to show students' progress with the same text or with different texts.
7. graph or chart of children's voluntary reading habits, including the number and types of books read and the time spent reading each day.
8. samples of students' writing over time.
9. students' self-assessment of their progress. Flood and Lapp (1989) explain that students can assess themselves through written reports, grades, or responses to such questions as: "How well do you think you do in reading? What do you do when you try to read a hard word?" (See Sue Boyd and Kathy Kelly in Chapter 4 for ways they use self-assessment.)

Any of this information can be included in a large folder or **portfolio**, a selection of a representative, ongoing, and changing collection of work samples, to give a complete picture of a student's progress (Flood & Lapp, 1989; Fuhler, 1990; Routman, 1991). Portfolios help to communicate progress to both children and parents. Of course, as Routman states, the collection itself is not as significant as what the collection represents with respect to insights about students' learning. She, in fact, believes that we should look at a portfolio as an approach to evaluation in which students are involved in appraising and selecting representative work samples to include. She suggests beginning with students' writing samples. What's important is not the portfolio per se, but rather the notion that, for assessment to be meaningful, multiple pieces of data should be used judiciously so that an accurate profile of students' progress with reading and writing strategies emerges.

So much to think about: *what* to use, *how* to use it, *what* and *how* to *assess* what's used. And every classroom has a unique blend of internal and external conditions that affect decision-making about creating an environment for literacy development. As you grapple with "What do I do first?" use the following questions in the order provided as guidelines for how to move away from using only basals in your reading program.

1. What resources do I want to use with my students?
2. Which activities should I incorporate with these resources?
3. How can I create a workable schedule that works for me?
4. Which skills do I want to emphasize?
5. How will I assess students' development?

Use the ideas contained in this chapter to help you create your own satisfying learning environment. Use the guidelines that follow to reinforce your hunches about what you are doing.

Guidelines for Moving Toward Trade Books for Literacy Development

This last section provides 10 general guidelines to consider as you contemplate a shift away from using only commercially produced, skill-driven systems in favor of teacher-created, process-oriented plans. Although it is much harder to create an instructional plan than it is to implement someone else's, especially one that works in the public eye, it is far more satisfying to know that you have taken back the control that rightfully belongs to you as a professional.

WHAT TO THINK ABOUT

1. Decide what you want to accomplish with your children. As we stated in Chapter 2, many teachers who are wedded to the basal don't really consider their own goals for their students, since "getting through the basal" is the only viable goal in sight.

Carefully select which basal materials to use, omitting anything that is inappropriate for your students. Ask yourself what you want your students to read and how you want them to react to what they read.

2. Weigh the benefits of the activities that you currently use. Try to eliminate those that do not provide time for students to practice their reading and writing. Think of alternative ways for students to experience reading and writing as processes: for reading—predict beforehand, read for a purpose, verify predictions, and respond in engaging ways; for writing—rehearsal, draft ideas, revise ideas, and publish in creative ways (Butler & Turbill, 1984).

3. Consider how to portray yourself as a role model. Children need to know that their teachers are readers and writers themselves, so that they share similar ideas and emotions about what it is like to read and write. Joan Pearlman, our fifth grade teacher who uses the Holiday Book Report, is an avid reader of children's books. She tries to read a book a night so that she can discuss intelligently any book that her students select for their reading. Her students know she reads, and, of course, marvel at her vast knowledge about books. She knows that her students need to know that she truly practices what she preaches about the need to read.

4. Think about the tenor of your school and your district, and don't despair if your district believes strongly in the basal. Cheryl Cator, our third grade teacher, figured out a way to combine both within the strictures and structures of her skill-driven system. Although she would prefer to have a less harried schedule, she is managing to accomplish what she wants to do. And while Mr. E. in our opening vignette continues to equivocate about his shift in allegiance away from his district's basal focus, he knows from his students' unabashed excitement for reading that he is doing right by them.

WHAT TO DO

1. Work carefully with your librarian, reading specialist, or other professionals knowledgeable about children's literature. Use what you know about students' interests and abilities to help you select material aligned with your goals for students' literacy development.

2. Start small and don't expect things to happen overnight. As Maxine Murphy from Conifer Grove School in Auckland, New Zealand (Butler & Turbill, 1984) states, it takes 4 to 6 weeks to establish new routines in her class. Start by setting aside time for both reading aloud and independent reading.

3. Scale down the amount of skills that students practice. Frew (1990), in his effort to move away from basals, pared down his skill instruction from 75% to 25% of the time. Teach skills in the context of children's reading and writing activities.

4. Regard the basal manual as a source of suggestions to be used along with other literature-based guides.

5. Create a balance between instructional time and independent reading so that students feel ownership for what they are doing, yet feel secure in knowing that they are being guided to become more strategic readers.

6. Communicate with parents so that they are aware of your goals and procedures, and guide them so that they know how to reinforce at home what you are doing

in the classroom. Help them to understand the impact of their own role modeling on their children's literacy development.

Concluding Remarks

This entire chapter boils down to this: decide for yourself what reading is. McGarry (1989), in a candid portrayal of her own transitions, confessed to herself that what she was doing in her fifth grade classroom was boring. Carol Davis, a first grade teacher from Hannibal, Missouri, reflected similar sentiments about her banal basal teaching in an article in *Newsweek* (Kantrowitz, 1990). Both discovered the need to do something more than use smelly stickers to get their students to read isolated word lists and tedious paragraphs about humdrum topics.

McGarry (1989) reflects how she had to take a hard look at herself as a reader and writer, only to discover the need for a communicative interplay and interpersonal relationship between the two. As soon as she realized the dichotomy between what she was doing as a language user and what she was instructing her students to do, she began to change. Never before had she questioned why she was doing what she was doing or considered its effects on her students. She and teachers everywhere are beginning to question why they have anchored themselves so long in systems that do not get their students yearning to do what the systems purport to do. These same teachers are recognizing the urgency of finding literature that inspires students to read voluntarily. Although not prepared to abandon the basal and its accompanying skill sheets altogether, they are scouting out resources and strategies that help them to *teach* literacy the way they *live* literacy.

B. F. Skinner once said, "We shouldn't teach great books; we should teach a love of reading." Those inclined to move toward a literature-based approach are quickly learning that teaching with and about a book is not nearly as important as teaching through books. Only after students have many encounters with authors' imaginatively artful styles for communicating through print will they appreciate the emotional and intellectual value of books. The Mr. E.'s of the teaching world are realizing none too soon that passing from one grade to the next with a respectable standardized test score runs a distant second to leaving a grade with memories of reading a few "good" books.

Questions for Discussion

1. Do you think that teachers should make every effort to blend both trade books and basals into their teaching? If yes, why? If no, why not?
2. Look back at the section entitled "Examples of Teacher Connections." Identify 3 to 5 ideas, techniques, or procedures that you could incorporate into your teaching situation.
3. What types of resources would be most important to you in establishing your own literature-based reading program?

4. Why do students need experience with reading aloud, shared book reading, guided reading, daily response to reading, independent reading, and at-home reading?
5. What is your goal for students' literacy development? Why?

Application Activities

1. Identify a theme, author, or genre that you would like your students to explore. Find five related books that you could use in your teaching situation.
2. Select a book from the activity in item #1. Create a literature-based plan that includes creative and challenging pre-reading, during-reading, and after-reading activities.
3. Use the chart below to determine whether your literature-based plan includes each of the activities. If your plan does not, determine why and how you can incorporate each activity into your plan.

	YES	NO
Reading Aloud		
Shared Book Reading		
Guided Reading		
Daily Response to Reading		
Independent Reading		
At-Home Reading		

4. Try your literature-based plan with a group of students. What worked? What did not work? What would you like to change about your plan?
5. Create a monthly plan for combining basals and trade books. Within your plan, indicate: (a) which components and activities of the basal you will use; (b) when and how you will use these components; (c) which trade book(s) you will use; (d) which literature-based activities you will use; and (e) the amount of time you will devote to basals and trade books.

References

Allen, J. M., & Freitag, K. K. (1988). Parents and students as cooperative learners: A workshop for parents. *The Reading Teacher, 41,* 922–925.

Anselmo, S., Rollins, P., & Schuckman, R. (1986). *R is for rainbow: Developing young children's thinking skills through the alphabet.* Menlo Park, CA: Addison-Wesley.

Atwell, N. (1987). *In the middle: Writing, reading, and learning with adolescents.* Portsmouth, NH: Heinemann.

Au, K. H., & Mason, J. M. (1989). Elementary reading programs. In S. B. Wepner, J. T. Feeley, &

D. S. Strickland (Eds.), *The administration and supervision of reading programs* (pp. 60–75). New York: Teachers College Press.

Barone, D. (1990). The written responses of young children: Beyond comprehension to story understanding. *The New Advocate, 3* (1), 49–56.

Berglund, R. L., & Johns, J. L. (1983). A primer on uninterrupted sustained silent reading. *The Reading Teacher, 36,* 534–539.

Brown, J. (1990). The home/school connection: Parent involvement. *The Missouri Reader, 15* (1), 19–21.

Butler, A., & Turbill, J. (1984). *Towards a reading-writing classroom.* Portsmouth, NH: Heinemann.

Cambourne, B. (1984). Language, learning and literacy. In A. Butler & J. Turbill (Eds.), *Towards a reading-writing classroom* (pp. 5–10). Portsmouth, NH: Heinemann.

Clay, M. M. (1985). *The early detection of reading difficulties* (3rd ed.). Portsmouth, NH: Heinemann.

Cohen, R. (1991, January 6). The lost book generation. *The New York Times,* Education Life Section 4A, pp. 34–35.

Cullinan, B. E. (Ed.). (1987). *Children's literature in the reading program.* Newark, DE: International Reading Association.

de Angeli, M. (1954). *Book of nursery and Mother Goose rhymes.* New York: Doubleday.

Eldredge, L. (1991). An experiment with a modified whole language approach in first grade classrooms. *Reading Research and Instruction, 30* (3), 21–38.

Flood, J., & Lapp, D. (1989). Reporting reading progress: A comparison portfolio for parents. *The Reading Teacher, 42,* 508–514.

Fredericks, A. D. (1989). Community outreach. In S. B. Wepner, J. T. Feeley, & D. S. Strickland (Eds.), *The administration and supervision of reading programs* (pp. 177–190). New York: Teachers College Press.

Fredericks, A. D., & Rasinski, T. (1987). Five good ideas for sharing the reading experience. *The Reading Teacher, 40,* 923–924.

Frew, A. W. (1990). Four steps toward literature-based reading. *The Reading Teacher, 34,* 98–102.

Fuhler, C. J. (1990). Let's move toward literature-based reading instruction. *The Reading Teacher, 43,* 312–315.

Graham, K. (1987). Converting to a literature-based program. In J. Hancock & S. Hill (Eds.), *Literature-based reading programs at work* (pp. 42–52). Portsmouth, NH: Heinemann.

Graves, D. H. (1983). *Writing: Teachers & children at work.* Portsmouth, NH: Heinemann.

Haile, I. (1987). *Integrated language arts.* Unpublished manuscript.

Hajdusiewicz, B. B. (1990). *Poetry works!* Cleveland, OH: Modern Curriculum Press.

Harris, V. (1991, May). *Multicultural children's literature.* Paper presented at the 11th Conference on Reading Research (CORR11), cosponsored by the International Reading Association and the Center for the Study of Reading at the University of Illinois, Las Vegas, NV.

Heller, M. F. (1991). *Reading-writing connections: From theory to practice.* White Plains, NY: Longman.

Henderson, A. T. (1988). Parents are a school's best friends. *Phi Delta Kappan, 40,* 148–153.

Hiebert, E. H., & Colt, J. (1989). Patterns of literature-based reading instruction. *The Reading Teacher, 43,* 14–20.

Holdaway, D. (1979). *The foundations of literacy.* New York: Ashton Scholastic.

Jett-Simpson, M. (Ed.). (1989). *Adventuring with books.* Urbana, IL: National Council of Teachers of English.

Kantrowitz, B. (1990, Fall/Winter). The reading wars. *Newsweek,* pp. 8–9, 12, 14.

Kelly, P. R. (1990). Guiding young students' response to literature. *The Reading Teacher, 43,* 464–470.

Kerin, H. (1987). Developing a program over a year. In J. Hancock & S. Hill (Eds.), *Literature-based reading programs at work* (pp. 13–22). Portsmouth, NH: Heinemann.

Kobrin, B. (1988). *EYE OPENERS!* New York: Penguin Books.

Laughlin, M. K., & Watt, L. S. (1986). *Developing learning skills through children's literature: An idea book for K–5 classrooms and libraries.* Phoenix: Oryx Press.

Mackey, M. (1990). Filling the gaps: *The Baby-Sitters Club,* the series book, and the learning reader. *Language Arts, 67,* 484–489.

Majerscak, C. (1990). *Integrating trade books into the classroom reading program: A basic approach.* Unpublished manuscript. William Paterson College, Wayne, NJ.

Massam, J., & Kulik, A. (1986). *And what else?* Mt. Eden, Auckland, New Zealand: Shortland Publications Limited.

May, F. B. (1986). *Reading as communication: An interactive approach* (2nd ed.). Columbus, OH: Merrill.

McCracken, M., & McCracken, R. (1979). *Reading, writing, and language: A practical guide for primary teachers.* Winnipeg, Canada: Peguis Publishers Ltd.

McElmeel, S. L. (1988). *An author a month (for pennies).* Englewood, CO: Libraries Unlimited.

McElmeel, S. L. (1990). *Bookpeople: A first album.* Englewood, CO: Teacher Ideas Press.

McGarry, S. (1989). *A question of playing jacks and a matter of scrambled eggs: A personal change in the teaching of reading.* Unpublished manuscript. William Paterson College, Wayne, NJ.

McKenna, M. C., & Kear, D. J. (1990). Measuring attitude toward reading: A new tool for teachers. *The Reading Teacher, 43,* 626–639.

Morrow, L. M. (1982). Relationships between literature programs, library corner designs and children's use of literature. *Journal of Educational Research, 75,* 339–344.

Morrow, L. M. (1989). *Literacy development in the early years.* Englewood Cliffs, NJ: Prentice-Hall.

Morrow, L. M., & Weinstein, C. S. (1982). Increasing children's use of literature through program and physical design changes. *Elementary School Journal, 83,* 131–137.

Nathan, R., & Temple, C. (1990). Classroom environments for reading and writing together. In T. Shanahan (Ed.), *Reading and writing together: New perspectives for the classroom* (pp. 173–200). Norwood, MA: Christopher-Gordon.

O'Halloran, S. (1987). An experienced teacher tells how. In J. Hancock & S. Hill (Eds.), *Literature-based reading programs at work* (pp. 3–12). Portsmouth, NH: Heinemann.

Olsen, M. L. (1987). *Creative connections: Literature and the reading program, grades 1–3.* Littleton, CO: Libraries Unlimited.

Otto, W. (1991). Foreword. In M. F. Heller (Au.), *Reading-writing connections: From theory to practice* (pp. ix–x). White Plains, NY: Longman.

Paradis, E. E., Chatton, B., Boswell, A., Smith, M., & Yovich, S. (1991). Accountability: Assessing comprehension during literature discussion. *The Reading Teacher, 45,* 8–17.

Paris, S. G., Cross, D. R., & Lipson, M. Y. (1984). Informed strategies for learning: A program to improve children's reading awareness and comprehension. *Journal of Educational Psychology, 76,* 1239–1252.

Petrosky, A. R. (1982). From story to essay: Reading and writing. *College composition and communication, 33* (1), 19–36.

Rich, D. (1985). *The forgotten factor in school success—the family: A policymaker's guide.* Washington, DC: The Home and School Institute.

Ross, E. P., & Fletcher, R. K. (1989). Responses to children's literature by environment, grade level, and sex. *The Reading Instruction Journal, 32* (2), 22–28.

Routman, R. (1991). *Invitations: Changing as teachers and learners K–12.* Portsmouth, NH: Heinemann Educational Books.

Schmitt, M. C. (1990). A questionnaire to measure children's awareness of strategic reading processes. *The Reading Teacher, 43,* 454–461.

Schmitt, M. C., & Baumann, J. F. (1986). How to incorporate comprehension monitoring strategies into basal reader instruction. *The Reading Teacher, 40,* 28–31.

Shannon, P. (1989). *Broken promises*. Granby, MA: Bergin & Garvey.

Smith, C. B. (1988). The expanding role of parents. *The Reading Teacher, 42,* 68–69.

Spellman, L. (1980). *Book report backpack*. Santa Barbara, CA: The Learning Works.

Taylor, B. M., & Frye, B. J. (1988). Pretesting: Minimize time spent on skill work for intermediate readers. *The Reading Teacher, 42,* 100–104.

Tompkins, G. E. (1990). The literature connection: How one teacher puts reading and writing together. In T. Shanahan (Ed.), *Reading and writing together: New perspectives for the classroom* (pp. 201–223). Norwood, MA: Christopher-Gordon.

Tunnell, M. O., & Jacobs, J. S. (1989). Using "real" books: Research findings on literature based reading instruction. *The Reading Teacher, 42,* 470–477.

Wepner, S. B., & Caccavale, P. (1991). Project CAPER (Children *And* Parents Enjoy Reading): A Case Study. *Reading Horizons, 31* (3), 228–237.

Wixson, K. K., & Peters, C. W. (1989). Teaching the basal selection. In P. N. Winograd, K. K. Wixson, & M. Y. Lipson (Eds.), *Improving basal reading instruction* (pp. 21–61). New York: Teachers College Press.

Wood, K. D. (1988). Techniques for assessing students' potential for learning. *The Reading Teacher, 41,* 440–447.

Zarrillo, J. (1989). Teachers' interpretations of literature-based reading. *The Reading Teacher, 43,* 22–28.

Trade Books Mentioned

Aardema, V. (1975). *Why mosquitoes buzz in people's ears*. New York: Dial.

Aliki (1976). *Corn is maize: The gift of Indians*. New York: Crowell.

Allard, H. (1977). *Miss Nelson is missing*. Boston: Houghton Mifflin.

Asch, F. (1982). *Happy birthday, Moon*. New York: Scholastic.

Asch, F. (1983). *Mooncake*. New York: Scholastic.

Asch, F. (1989). *Moongame*. New York: Scholastic.

Babbitt, N. (1975). *Tuck everlasting*. New York: Farrar, Straus & Giroux.

Barrett, J., & Barrett, R. (1978). *Cloudy with a chance of meatballs*. New York: Scholastic.

Blume, J. (1971). *Freckle juice*. New York: Dell.

Blume, J. (1972). *Otherwise known as Sheila the Great*. New York: Dell.

Burnett, F. H. (1962). *The secret garden*. New York: Harper & Row.

Byars, B. (1977). *The pinballs*. New York: Scholastic.

Cleary, B. (1968). *Ramona the pest*. New York: Morrow.

Cleary, B. (1983). *Dear Mr. Henshaw*. New York: Morrow.

Dahl, R. (1961). *James and the giant peach*. New York: Knopf.

Dahl, R. (1970). *Fantastic Mr. Fox*. New York: Knopf.

Dahstedt, M., & Robinson, C. (1989). *The terrible wave*. Boston: Houghton Mifflin.

DeClements, B. (1985). *Sixth grade can really kill you*. New York: Scholastic.

Fleischman, P. (1988). *Joyful noise, poems for two voices*. New York: Harper & Row.

Fritz, J. (1958). *The cabin faced west*. New York: Putnam.

Galdone, P. (1973). *The three billy goats gruff*. New York: Seabury.

Graham, M. B. (1967). *To be nice to spiders*. New York: Harper & Row.

Heller, R. (1983). *The reason for a flower*. New York: Scholastic.

Hurwitz, J. (1985). *The adventures of Ali Baba Bernstein*. New York: Scholastic.

Keats, E. J. (1962). *The snowy day.* New York: Viking.

Keats, E. J. (1964). *Whistle for Willie.* New York: Viking.

Kennedy, M. (1980). *Wings.* New York: Scholastic.

Konigsburg, E. L. (1967). *From the mixed-up files of Mrs. Basil E. Frankweiler.* New York: Atheneum.

Kroll, S. (1987). *It's Groundhog Day.* New York: Scholastic.

Leaf, M. (1936). *The story of Ferdinand.* New York: Viking.

Lewis, C. S. (1950). *The lion, the witch, and the wardrobe.* New York: Macmillan.

Littledale, F. (1985). *Magic Fish* (retold). New York: Scholastic.

Lobel, A. (1970). *Days with Frog and Toad.* New York: Harper & Row.

Lobel, A. (1970). *Frog and Toad are friends.* New York: Harper & Row.

Lobel, A. (1972). *Frog and Toad together.* New York: Harper & Row.

Lobel, A. (1975). *Owl at home.* New York: Harper & Row.

Lobel, A. (1976). *Frog and Toad all year.* New York: Harper & Row.

Lobel A. (1982). *Ming Lo moves the mountain.* New York: Scholastic.

Lowry, L. (1979). *Anastasia Krupnik.* Boston: Houghton Mifflin.

Martin, A. M. (1986–present). *The baby-sitters club.* Series. New York: Scholastic.

Mayer, M. (1975). *Just for you.* Racine, WI: Western.

Mayer, M. (1977). *Just me and my dad.* Racine, WI: Western.

Mayer, M. (1983). *I was so mad.* Racine, WI: Western.

Mayer, M. (1985). *Just grandpa and me.* Racine, WI: Western.

Mayer, M. (1986). *Just me and my little sister.* Racine, WI: Western.

Mayer, M. (1989). *This is my friend.* Racine, WI: Western.

McCloskey, R. (1940). *Lentil.* New York: Viking.

McCloskey, R. (1941). *Make way for ducklings.* New York: Viking.

McCloskey, R. (1963). *Blueberries for Sal.* New York: Viking.

Miller, E. (1964). *Mousekin's golden house.* New York: Simon & Schuster.

Mosel, A. (1968). *Tikki Tikki Tembo.* New York: Holt, Rinehart & Winston.

Myers, B. (1973). *Shhhhh, it's a secret!* New York: Holt, Rinehart & Winston.

Parrish, P. (1963). *Amelia Bedelia.* New York: Harper & Row.

Paterson, K. (1977). *Bridge to Terabithia.* New York: Harper & Row.

Peck, R. N. (1974). *Soup.* New York: Knopf.

Rawls, W. (1961). *Where the red fern grows.* New York: Doubleday.

San Souci, R. D. (1989). *The talking eggs.* New York: Scholastic.

Schellie, D. (1978). *Kidnapping Mr. Tubbs.* Boston: Houghton Mifflin.

Sendak, M. (1962). *Chicken soup with rice.* New York: Harper & Row.

Sendak, M. (1963). *Where the wild things are.* New York: Harper & Row.

Seuss, Dr. (1968). *The Ear Book.* New York: Random House.

Seuss, Dr. (1968). *The Eye Book.* New York: Random House.

Seuss, Dr. (1968). *The Foot Book.* New York: Random House.

Seuss, Dr. (1968). *The Nose Book.* New York: Random House.

Slobodkina, E. (1947). *Caps for sale*. Reading, MA: Addison-Wesley.

Sobol, D. J. (1986–present). *Encyclopedia Brown*. Series. New York: Scholastic/Four Winds.

Steig, W. (1969). *Sylvester and the magic pebble*. New York: E. P. Dutton.

Steig, W. (1976). *Abel's island*. New York: Farrar, Straus & Giroux.

Van Allsburg, C. (1979). *The garden of Abdul Gasazi*. Boston: Houghton Mifflin.

Van Allsburg, C. (1981). *Jumanji*. Boston: Houghton Mifflin.

Van Allsburg, C. (1982). *Ben's dream*. Boston: Houghton Mifflin.

Van Allsburg, C. (1983). *The wreck of the Zephyr*. Boston: Houghton Mifflin.

Van Allsburg, C. (1984). *The mysteries of Harris Burdick*. Boston: Houghton Mifflin.

Van Allsburg, C. (1985). *The polar express*. Boston: Houghton Mifflin.

Van Allsburg, C. (1986). *The stranger*. Boston: Houghton Mifflin.

Van Allsburg, C. (1987). *The z was zapped*. Boston: Houghton Mifflin.

Van Allsburg, C. (1988). *Two bad ants*. Boston: Houghton Mifflin.

Voigt, C. (1982). *Dicey's song*. New York: Ballantine Books.

Wells, R. (1973). *Noisy Nora*. New York: Dial.

Whelan, G. (1988). *Silver*. New York: Random House.

White, E. B. (1952). *Charlotte's web*. New York: Harper & Row.

Williams, M. (1975). *Velveteen Rabbit*. New York: Atvon.

Zolotow, C. (1962). *When the wind stops*. New York: Abeland-Schuman.

Zolotow, C. (1972). *William's doll*. New York: Harper & Row.

Commercially Published Literature Guides

Book Lures: Literature-Based Reading Guides
Book Lures, Inc.
PO Box 0455
O'Fallon, MO 63366
1-800-444-9450

Enhancing Literature Series
Creative Teaching Press
PO Box 6017
Cypress, CA 90630
1-800-444-4CTP

HPK Teacher Guides
H. P. Kopplemann
Paperback Book Service
PO Box 145 Dept RT-1
Hartford, CT 06141-0145
1-800-243-7724

Literature Lesson Links
Teacher Support Software
1035 Northwest 57th Street
Gainesville, FL 32605
1-800-228-2871

Novel Ties
Learning Links
2300 Marcus Avenue
New Hyde Park
New York, NY 11042

Novel Units
PO Box 1461-Dept. RT
Palatine, IL 60078
1-708-541-8573

Step Into Literature
Literature for Lifelong Learning
112 Harvard Ave., Suite 241
Claremont, CA 91711

Story Strategies
Econo-Clad Books
PO Box 1777
Topeka, KS 66601
1-800-255-3502

CHAPTER
4

MOVING FROM BASALS TO LITERATURE-BASED PROGRAMS

Chapter Overview

RATIONALE FOR LITERATURE-BASED READING PROGRAMS

EXAMPLES OF TEACHERS IN
LITERATURE-BASED PROGRAMS

EARLY ELEMENTARY (K–1) / MID-ELEMENTARY (2–4) /
UPPER-ELEMENTARY (5–6)

COMMON FEATURES OF A LITERATURE-ONLY APPROACH

READING ALOUD / SHARED BOOK READING / READING WORKSHOP /
WRITING WORKSHOP / MINI-LESSONS / PORTFOLIO ASSESSMENT

WHAT THE RESEARCH SAYS

MOVING TOWARD A LITERATURE-BASED PROGRAM

GETTING STARTED / MOVING FORWARD

A HUSH FELL OVER the 20 fourth graders gathered on the rug for the all-class share session that followed their silent reading time. Three or four were going to share favorite parts of books they had chosen to read for their realistic fiction genre study. A few "insiders" had just persuaded the group to let Jamie go first. "His is soooo good," they promised.

Jamie started. First he recapped the events that led up to his favorite part of *Stone Fox* (Gardiner, 1980). A boy named little Willy has to win a dog sled race to raise $500 to pay the taxes on the house in which he lives with his ailing and aged grandfather. He and his dog Searchlight are up against stiff competition, the Indian called Stone Fox and his five fast and sleek Samoyeds who have never lost a race. But little Willy and his dog had an edge in that they knew every inch of the race route and had prepared well by practicing the run over and over again. In fact, they were ahead and very close to the finish line when the unexpected happened. Jamie read:

> Searchlight forged ahead. But Stone Fox was gaining!
> "Go, Searchlight! Go!" little Willy cried out.
> Searchlight gave it everything she had.
> She was a hundred feet from the finish line when her heart burst. She died instantly.
> There was no suffering. (p. 77)

After reading this, Jamie, who had tears in his eyes, stopped to ask the others if they wanted him to go on. Some were dabbing at their eyes while several were crying openly. They seemed to sense that Jamie was "inside" the character of little Willy. They were truly in this "text world" together. Of course, they wanted more.

Jamie told how Stone Fox stopped and confirmed that Searchlight was dead. He read Willy's words, "You did real good, girl. You just rest now. Just rest" (p. 80). He told how the story ends with Stone Fox drawing a line in the snow and threatening to shoot anyone who crosses to the finish line except, of course, little Willy, who slowly walks across carrying the fallen Searchlight.

The children were caught up in a universe of human feelings—love, courage, loss, hollow victory. They were no longer in a classroom in a northeastern suburb; they were with the boy, his dog, and Stone Fox on that snowy road that runs through a small town in rural Idaho.

A READING RESPONSE GROUP of third and fourth graders was discussing the central issue of Natalie Babbitt's haunting fantasy *Tuck Everlasting* (1975). Did Winnie Foster do the right thing in not drinking water from the magic spring that would have allowed her to live forever?

Half the group argued that she should have drunk the water and joined the Tucks in their immortality. Then Winnie could have married Jesse, the youngest Tuck, who was smitten by her. She could have lived to see all the great inventions of the 20th century like computers, videos, and space shuttles.

The rest of the group thought that Winnie had made the right decision not to drink from the spring and to live out her life naturally. They had perceived from the actions and conversations of the Tucks that living forever wasn't so great. Seeing so many generations pass and knowing that they would never pass made the Tucks tired, numb, and unhappy—changeless wanderers who roamed the ever-changing landscape. This group definitely thought that going through life's stages and passing on when it was time was the better choice. But, they had to admit that, like the others in this response group, they were sad when they learned of Winnie's decision via the words on the tombstone in the town cemetery (p. 138):

> In Loving Memory
> Winifred Foster Jackson
> Dear Wife
> Dear Mother
> 1870–1948

D URING READING TIME in Mrs. H.'s second grade in a Harlem school, Jody and four friends chose to read *Cloudy with a Chance of Meatballs* (Barrett, 1978). While all had copies and began by taking turns reading, gradually Jody became the main reader. This was the group's choice: "Jody reads out loud so good. She makes the story more interesting." Soon, Jody became the teacher, stopping at intervals to ask questions ("What's gonna happen next?") and get reactions ("Would you eat stale stuff in the refrigerator?") just as Mrs. H. does when she reads aloud to the class (which she does often).

It's obvious that Jody loves to read and does so whenever possible. Now in third grade, Jody returns to Mrs. H.'s room every day at lunchtime to read to any children who will listen. Mrs. H. calls her "my teaching assistant."

N INE-YEAR-OLD SHERRIE'S SCHOOL READING PROGRAM is centered around literature, and its effects can be readily seen in her love of reading. Reading is such a part of her life that she takes a book with her wherever she goes. Once she was observed reading as her hair was being cut at a local salon. When the stylist asked her to bend forward to toss her long hair in front of her, Sherrie complied but continued to read *The Class President* (Hurwitz, 1990). Even in this "upside down" position, she had to find out if the class election would come out as she predicted!

Rationale for Literature-Based Reading Programs

In calling for "literature as the content of reading," Charlotte Huck (1977) presents a cogent rationale for using real books rather than basals for teaching literacy. Describing the narrative as "the most common and effective form" of ordering our lives, she says that children (and adults, too) need stories to learn how to deal with the whole gamut of human emotions.

Because literature is concerned with feelings, it helps children develop compassion and empathy. Witness the reactions of the fourth graders above to little Willy, Searchlight, and Stone Fox. They were at once suffering with little Willy, feeling the loss of Searchlight, and learning to appreciate Stone Fox. Through the story they were experiencing humanity.

Besides human compassion, Huck says that literature can develop the imagination. In their minds, children can travel to different times and places, real and unreal, just as the children did who read *Tuck Everlasting*. As they read, they moved from the rural 1880s of Winnie's youth to a more familiar suburban scene of the 1940s. Being immortal was an idea they could consider in their own minds and discuss in an in-depth "what if" fashion. By juxtaposing the reality of everyday living with the fantasy of never dying, they were stretching their imaginations and growing in understanding.

As the greatest value of using literature in the reading program, both Huck, Hepler, and Hickman (1987) and Cullinan (1987, 1989) cite the joy that children can experience from becoming "hooked on books" like Sherrie and Jody in the vignettes. Klein, Peterson, and Simington (1991) call literature a powerful, motivating force for engaging children in reading. Leu and Kinzer (1991) concur, pointing out that the more interested children become in books, the more time they will invest in reading, both inside and outside of school. And, since children learn to read by reading (Smith, 1985), committed readers like Sherrie and Jody will become even better readers.

To these personal values that literature can bring to readers, May (1990) adds the aesthetic experiences provided by fine children's books. Who cannot be enchanted by the haunting illustrations and tale found in Chris Van Allsburg's *The Polar Express* (1985) or by the bright, bold colors and engaging language in the surprise alphabet book *Chicka Chicka Boom Boom* by Bill Martin, Jr. and John Archambault (1989)? May reminds us that "some of the best writing and graphic art today is found between the covers of a children's book" (p. 290).

Besides these personal values, Huck et al. (1987) say that literature offers many educational rewards. For example, children who have been exposed to a great deal of story reading at home and who are introduced to reading and writing through books experience a rapid growth in their oral language development. One of us has a 4-year-old grandson who tells stories in elaborated syntax, introduced by "Once upon a time. . . ." We observed a 5-year-old sharing her fairy tale done in a kindergarten writing workshop. From her paper of drawings and beginning letters she read, "Once there lived a princess named Chrissie (her name) and her cat in a palace in the woods." Both of these young children are using literary language very naturally because it has become a part of them.

And this effect on language carries over to the elementary school. Working with children from ages 5 to 10, Carol Chomsky (1972) found that those children who had more exposure to the staples of children's literature were at higher linguistic stages in language development than those children with less exposure.

In literature-based classrooms one usually finds a strong writing component as children move from reading stories to writing their own in writing workshops. The carryover is obvious, as children emulate the authors they are reading. In Kathy Kelly's fourth grade, which we will describe later in this chapter, we overheard one student sharing her emerging text with a partner, "Someone dies in my story. You know, sort of like in Judy Blume's (1981) *Tiger Eyes*." After reading *Why Mosquitoes Buzz in People's Ears* (Aardema, 1975), fifth graders in an inner-city school began writing "pourquoi" tales about their favorite animals. They had borrowed the pattern and were matching wits with the folktale tellers of the world as they tried to explain natural phenomena via the antics of everyday animals in a modern setting.

Along with ideas for content children pick up the syntax and style of what they read. Eckoff (1983) compared the writing of first graders who were exposed only to "primerese" basals with the writing of children exposed to books written in a more natural literary style. While the basal group wrote simple, stilted sentences, one to a line, the other group wrote more complex sentences, spread naturally across the lines of a page. The quality of their exposure to print had definitely affected their written language pieces. Studying the writing of children in phonics, skills, and literature-based programs, De Ford (1981) also found a relationship between what children read and how they write. Whereas the literature group wrote a wide variety of stories, poems, and informational pieces, the skills groups produced a limited range of repetitious, drill-like texts. De Ford also found that the literature group was better at retelling stories than both skills groups.

This brings us to another educational advantage of literature-as-content: it develops children's concept of story, thus aiding comprehension of narrative. Children like Jamie, Jody, and Sherrie in our vignettes, who read good literature regularly, learn to think along *with* an author, anticipating character and plot development. They expect to find a problem to be solved and predict ways the main character will work things out. Also, they write with a sense of story, introducing characters and placing them in a definite setting with a goal to be reached.

We saw this demonstrated in Mrs. H.'s second grade from our opening vignette (Strickland & Hiebert, 1990). After the children had picked out the story grammar elements from Ann Grifalconi's *Darkness and the Butterfly* (1987), an African tale Mrs. H. had read to them, they wrote together their own story about Rudee, an African child who always had bad dreams. One boy proposed a reason and a solution: since the Dream Man gives out good dreams early in the night, Rudee, who goes to bed very late, gets only bad dreams. The solution was obvious: if Rudee goes to bed early, she may have some good dreams. The reading-writing connection was made explicit in this case, and it shows how children immersed in stories can begin to gain control over story structure (Strickland & Feeley, 1985).

Lastly, children can gain a wealth of vicarious experiences and build their lifetime meaning vocabularies through books. Reading historical fiction such as *Johnny Tremain* (Forbes, 1946) and *My Brother Sam Is Dead* (Collier & Collier, 1974), both set in revolutionary times, puts children into another era and lets them learn life lessons along with history. Jean Fritz's biographies of colonial heroes teach much about real people and their times. Words such as *democracy, loyalty,* and *representation* are not just empty terms but take on real meaning when encountered again and again in good literature.

In addition to learning about people and history, children learn vicariously about places through books. One of us remembers taking her young children to Boston for the first time. As we walked through the Boston Commons, the children said they were sure that they had been there before and began pointing out various sights such as the little walk bridges, gazebos, and paddle boats. Then we remembered why everything seemed so familiar. We had read *Make Way for Ducklings* (McCloskey, 1941) over and over a few years back, and this real experience was just like reliving the book. At once they began looking for the Mallard family and were sure they had spotted them!

Literature can enrich every facet of living and learning, helping children develop insights about other people and themselves, helping develop the imagination and a love for reading, and offering a wealth of aesthetic experiences. Besides being a very real source of vicarious learning and vocabulary growth, exposure to literature positively affects children's development in oral language, written language, and concept of story. Let us turn now to examples of teachers who are using literature as the mainstay of their reading-writing programs.

Examples of Teachers in Literature-Based Programs

Aware of the advantages of learning to read and write through authentic, unabridged or edited literature, many teachers have moved completely away from using basals and are making literature "the content" of their literacy programs. To give you some ideas about how these programs work, we visited a sampling of these teachers who have developed their own models for teaching reading and writing through children's books. We will describe four early elementary, three mid-elementary, and three upper-elementary classrooms. One outstanding feature we noticed in all these classrooms is the joyous spirit: these teachers and children love to read and write. They welcomed us into their classrooms and generously shared with us so that we could share with you.

EARLY ELEMENTARY (K–1)

KINDERGARTEN: BIG AND SMALL BOOKS

Janice Markovic, who has been teaching kindergarten for two years, uses literature exclusively to teach the content of her district's kindergarten curriculum. Janice has developed her expertise by taking summer courses on process writing and enrolling in a master's program in reading that focuses on a process-oriented, literature-based approach. All these experiences have reinforced her commitment to introduce her 5-year-olds to the world of print through her own literature selections and activities rather than through published programs and worksheets.

To implement her program Janice has collected over **40 big books** from publishers such as The Wright Group, Rigby, and Scholastic (see Publishers of Big Books and Other Enlarged Texts at the end of this chapter) and hundreds of small books, many with accompanying audiocassettes. She keeps up with new titles by reading the professional literature, networking with other teachers, and attending conferences. For most of her big books, Janice has 4 to 6 small copies so that children can try to read them by themselves after shared reading with the big book. Some of her favorites are *A House Is a House for Me* (Hoberman, 1978), *Oh No!* (Cairns, 1988), and *Mrs. Wishy Washy* (Cowley, 1980).

Janice centers her program around social studies (the family), science (the seasons), and literature (folktales) topics. She then selects books that will develop the topic. She may use a book for one to three weeks, depending on the length of the book, how many activities can be planned around it, and how interested the children are in it. Figure 4.1 shows a typical cycle from introducing a book on day one, through many rereadings, to a final response activity on day five.

To illustrate how a big book can serve as a centerpiece for a topic that crosses content areas, Janice tells how she uses *The Snowy Day* (Keats, 1962). Besides reading and discussing the story several times, the children make snow cones and learn how matter can change from solids to liquids to gases (science). For art, they trace each other on large paper (as do the children in the story), make shoe tracks in paint, and arrange collages à la Ezra Jack Keats.

We visited on the day Janice was finishing up with the big book *Noisy Nora* (Wells, 1973) as part of her family theme. The group reads along with her in animated fashion. Then, they go through the book to find rhyming words (*Kate-wait; door-floor*) and unusual vocabulary words (e.g., *monumental*). Next, as the group reads the story aloud, children act out the story from behind stick puppets of the characters. Char-

DAY 1	Look at the cover, title, and pictures and predict; discuss author and illustrator. Read to children to confirm predictions.
DAY 2	Reread while tracking print; encourage children to relate story to their lives and read along.
DAY 3	Reread as children read along or just do refrains or repeated sections.
DAY 4	Reread with some movement, e.g., act out, use stick puppets, or flannel board figures. Introduce small copies in book nook.
DAY 5	Reread with any favorite activities from other days. Children respond to book by writing or drawing (favorite part, character, picture, etc.).

FIGURE 4.1
A typical week with a big book
Note. From "A Typical Week with a Big Book," 1991. Copyright 1991 by Janice Markovic. Reprinted by permission.

acters are also used to teach math number concepts. The children draw pictures of their favorite characters, and Janice arranges them on a bar graph. With six votes, the main character Kate wins, hands down!

Another activity, used during centers time, encourages the children to order sentence strips of a repeated refrain in a pocket chart. To help the children along, a chart of the refrain is placed near the pocket chart (see Figure 4.2). We noticed two children reading the strips and matching them to the chart before slotting them in the pockets. This paired reading activity, which provides real practice reading in context, is child-initiated during free choice time.

Janice describes her goals for her kindergarten literacy program as follows: Children should learn to

- love reading and enjoy books,
- understand that written language has meaning and that we read for a purpose,
- recognize the conventions of print (letters, words, left to right, some punctuation),
- identify the rudimentary elements of a story (characters, beginnings, endings) and be able to retell,

FIGURE 4.2

Example of refrain cut into strips to be reassembled in pocket chart

Note. From classroom idea, 1991. Copyright 1991 by Janice Markovic. Reprinted by permission.

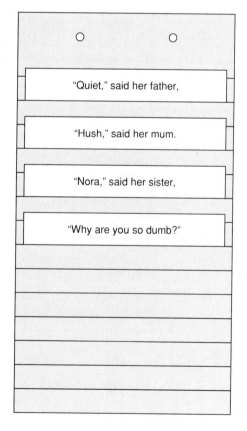

"Quiet," said her father,

"Hush," said her mum.

"Nora," said her sister,

"Why are you so dumb?"

- predict and confirm as they go through a story, and
- enjoy rhyme and rhythm as they share poetry and patterned language.

The teachers who get her children in first grade say that she is successful in achieving her goals. Accordingly, her principal, curriculum director, and parents support her completely. Her principal allows her to spend her materials money on books rather than on workbooks and basal readiness materials. Parents participate in her at-home reading program. One very popular activity is "buddy bear" reading. Each night, a different child takes home a teddy bear with a bookbag strapped to his back. The child selects books to go in the bag from among those they have read in school. They read or "pretend read" the books to the bear and/or parents; parents report that this reading time becomes very special to all.

Research also supports what Janice is doing. Combs (1987), who studied the effect of modeling the reading process with enlarged texts (which Janice does all day long), described the increase in attentiveness that leads to more time in "pretend reading" as one of the most positive results. Another important finding of Combs's study was that, although all the kindergarteners in her sample showed significant increases in retelling abilities, those in the below average group made the most gains and doubled their recall of story elements.

Besides books, Janice uses poetry, songs, and language experience stories in her **"immersion literacy"** program. She loves teaching with literature and couldn't imagine using a readiness approach that teaches letters and sounds in isolation. She is fortunate that her district endorses her nontraditional approach and supports her efforts.

GRADE 1: TEACHING WITH THEMES

In their first grade classrooms in Barrington Elementary School in Upper Arlington, Ohio, Betsy O'Brochta and Cindy Weaver (1991) use children's books thematically to teach reading, writing, and the first grade curriculum. At the beginning of the year children study themselves, the family, and the community; at mid-year, they study dinosaurs, the sea, and foods; toward the end of the year they are ready for folktales, animals, and magic.

Betsy and Cindy try to integrate each content area into a thematic unit. Figure 4.3 shows a planning web for a beginning unit that they call "Me, Myself, and I." Children engage in shared reading and writing activities in a large group (language experience charts, big books), read self-selected books in small groups, write in journals, and generate their own first books in writing workshop. Note that the content comes from the trade books and the children themselves.

The theme opens with the reading of *Will I Have a Friend?* (Cohen, 1967). The children then draw self portraits and write about themselves (invented spellings were the norm). These first pieces provide our teachers with diagnostic information on the children's levels of writing and drawing. On the same day, the children do their first graph, "How did you come to school today?" They sit in a circle with their teacher and place their name cards next to the four choices on a large chart: "I walked," "I rode my bike," "I took the bus," "I came by car." The graph literally appears before

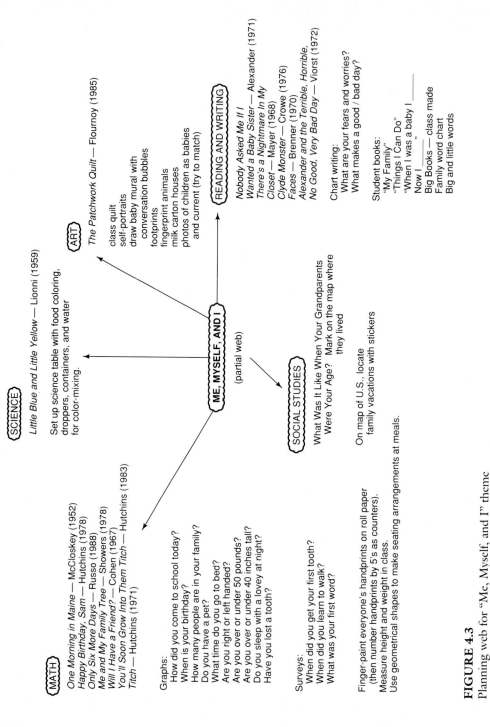

SCIENCE

Little Blue and Little Yellow — Lionni (1959)

Set up science table with food coloring, droppers, containers, and water for color-mixing.

ART

The Patchwork Quilt — Flournoy (1985)

class quilt
self-portraits
draw baby mural with
    conversation bubbles
footprints
fingerprint animals
milk carton houses
photos of children as babies
    and current (try to match)

READING AND WRITING

*Nobody Asked Me If I
Wanted a Baby Sister* — Alexander (1971)
*There's a Nightmare In My
Closet* — Mayer (1968)
Clyde Monster — Crowe (1976)
Faces — Brenner (1970)
*Alexander and the Terrible, Horrible,
No Good, Very Bad Day* — Viorst (1972)

Chart writing:
    What are your fears and worries?
    What makes a good / bad day?

Student books:
    "My Family"
    "Things I Can Do"
    "When I was a baby I _____
        Now I _____"
    Big Books — class made
    Family word chart
    Big and little words

ME, MYSELF, AND I

(partial web)

SOCIAL STUDIES

What Was It Like When Your Grandparents
Were Your Age? Mark on the map where
                    they lived

On map of U.S., locate
    family vacations with stickers

MATH

One Morning in Maine — McCloskey (1952)
Happy Birthday, Sam — Hutchins (1978)
Only Six More Days — Russo (1988)
Me and My Family Tree — Showers (1978)
Will I Have a Friend? — Cohen (1967)
You'll Soon Grow Into Them Titch — Hutchins (1983)
Titch — Hutchins (1971)

Graphs:
    How did you come to school today?
    When is your birthday?
    How many people are in your family?
    Do you have a pet?
    What time do you go to bed?
    Are you right or left handed?
    Are you over or under 50 pounds?
    Are you over or under 40 inches tall?
    Do you sleep with a lovey at night?
    Have you lost a tooth?

Surveys:
    When did you get your first tooth?
    When did you learn to walk?
    What was your first word?

Finger-paint everyone's handprints on roll paper
    (then number handprints by 5's as counters).
Measure height and weight in class.
Use geometrical shapes to make seating arrangements at meals.

FIGURE 4.3

Planning web for "Me, Myself, and I" theme

Note. Reprinted by permission of the publisher from Feeley, Joan T., Strickland, Dorothy S., and Wepner, Shelley B., PROCESS READING AND WRITING: A LITERATURE-BASED AP-PROACH. Figure from Chapter 1. (New York: Teachers College Press, Copyright 1991 by Teachers College, Columbia University. All rights reserved.)

them! Other graphs such as those listed in the planning unit seen in Figure 4.3 are developed similarly.

At least two theme-related books are shared each day, followed by small-group reading and writing activities such as those listed in Figure 4.3. One very successful book extension is centered around *The Patchwork Quilt* (Flournoy, 1985). The book's message is that a quilt can tell about the people who made it. Using fabric crayons

---

8:30–8:40
  Buddy reading (lunch count, etc)

8:40–9:00
  Group meeting
  Calendar activities
  Read-alouds and/or literacy lessons (poetry, big books, pocket chart, information fiction)

9:00–9:45
  Quiet work time (theme work, journals, writing folders, conferencing, handwriting, letter writing, publishing books, small-group skills lessons, spelling patterns, illustrating published books)

9:45–10:00 RECESS

10:00–10:30
  Continue work time

10:30–10:45
  Share writing, books, discoveries, items related to theme

10:45–11:15
  SSR (Sustained Silent Reading), individual reading conferences

11:15–12:15 LUNCH

12:15–12:30
  Group meeting, read-aloud

12:30–1:30
  Work time, theme work (art projects, math activities, science experiments, science journals, writing, literature extensions, individual projects)

1:30–1:45 RECESS

1:45–2:45
  Math

FIGURE 4.4
Typical first grade schedule once literature-based instruction has been established later in the year
Note. From "Class Schedule," 1991. Copyright 1991 by Cynthia Weaver and Elizabeth O'Brochta. Reprinted by permission.

the children design blocks of fabric about things they enjoy doing. Afterwards a parent sews the blocks together and recruits a small group of mothers to stuff and tie it. The class quilt is then hung in the room to tell the stories of the class members.

By mid-year blocks of time are devoted to the theme under study. Figure 4.4 shows how reading, writing, and sharing permeate the school day as these first graders become literate while learning about math, social studies, science, literature, and the arts. These teachers can work in this way because their school is a parent-choice alternative school. The "informal education" philosophy under which these teachers work calls for such tenets as an integrated curriculum; a holistic approach to reading, writing, and oral language development; child choice and decision-making in learning; and attention to aesthetic experiences. Administrators and teachers in this school share this philosophy; parents who choose it, "buy into" this philosophy for their children's education. This unifying force makes for a harmonious educational community.

Draw and tell about
  A character
  A favorite part
  Why you liked or didn't like the story
  What the story reminded you of

Write a letter to
  A character
  The author
  The illustrator

Retell the story
  First,
  Next,
  Then,
  Finally,

Rewrite or add to the story
  Continue the pattern
  Tell another event
  Change the characters, setting, or ending

Plan to act out the story with others

Write a play

Make puppets

FIGURE 4.5

Suggestions for ways students might respond to a book

Note. From "Ways to Respond to a Book," 1991. Copyright 1991 by Sheila Hackett. Reprinted by permission.

GRADE 1: LEARNING TO SPELL THROUGH READING AND WRITING

In her first grade class Sheila Hackett has evolved from using basals for three years, to using basals plus trade books for one year, to using trade books only. Now in her second year of a literature-based, reading-writing classroom, she finds that her children enjoy learning through trade books, and she enjoys teaching with them more than with basals. In fact, she couldn't go back!

Her primary source for materials has been The Wright Group collection of big books with accompanying small versions, but in the past two years she has also been including books from other publishers such as those listed in our resource section. In the beginning of the year Sheila introduces one big book per week, and the class works with that title every day. They read and reread the story and do different follow-up activities such as retellings, discussions of **story grammar** elements, and responses that involve art, drama, or writing. (Figure 4.5 shows a chart offering suggestions for response.) Children are invited to read the big or small book by themselves, to a partner or parent, and, after responding in one or more ways, to the teacher. Figure 4.6 shows how Sheila tracks her students through their reading.

Children select their own books (often books first read with the class) for daily silent reading time. Three times a week Sheila meets with small groups to discuss their books and have them read orally to her. On the other days she reads with individual students, recording her observations and their progress. These sessions and the chil-

---

READING/WRITING WORKSHOP

Name: _____ Date: _____

Title: _____

Author: _____

1. Read to myself _____

2. Read to _____

3. Read to and discuss with a small group _____

   _____

4. Respond (write/draw/act out) _____

5. Meet with Ms. Hackett _____

FIGURE 4.6
Sample record of reading activities
Note. From "Record of Reading Activities," 1991. Copyright 1991 by Sheila Hackett. Reprinted by permission.

dren's written logs and responses to literature supply her with assessment information to help her plan skill lessons and report to parents and administrators.

Sheila used to worry about skills (especially phonics and spelling) and started to use *Language Arts Phonics* (Botel & Seaver, 1985) when she began to abandon the basal. This program introduces letters and sounds through chants and poems, keeping the letter-sound elements embedded in meaningful context. But this year she finds that she doesn't even need this program. She has been teaching phonics through nursery rhymes, poems, the children's writing, and the trade books themselves.

Since she had no formal spelling program, Sheila was concerned about how her students were developing as spellers. For her graduate research project, Sheila looked at the growth of young children's control over spelling by analyzing her students' daily journal entries for one year (Hackett, 1990). She compared the children's spelling development by using the stages developed by Gentry (1982): pre-communicative, semi-phonetic, phonetic, transitional, correct. As seen in Table 4.1, three children who were pre-communicative and two who were semi-phonetic in the fall moved up to the phonetic stage by spring. Nine children identified as phonetic spellers in the fall were classified as transitional by spring, with three of these able to spell conventionally (correct stage) some of the time. By the end of the school year most children could spell most common words in standard or near-standard form and other words

TABLE 4.1
Children's writing samples categorized by month

STUDENTS	PRE-COMMUNICATIVE Random Letters to Represent Sounds, Copy Familiar Words	SEMI-PHONETIC Letters Used to Represent Sounds	PHONETIC All Words Represented, Spell the Way It Sounds	TRANSITIONAL Almost Correct Reverse Letter Positions	CORRECT Standard Spelling
Elliot	Sept.–Oct.	Nov.–Feb.	Mar.–Apr.		
Jarrett	Sept.–Oct.	Nov.–Feb.	Mar.–Apr.		
Ryuji	Sept.–Oct.	Nov.	Dec.–Apr.		
Melissa		Sept.–Oct.	Nov.–Apr.		
Jennifer		Sept.–Nov.	Dec.–Feb.	*Mar.–Apr.	
Renee			Sept.–Oct.	Nov.–Jan.	*Jan.–Apr.
Kyung Tae			Sept.–Oct.	*Nov.–Jan.	*Jan.–Apr.
April			Sept.–Oct.	Nov.–Mar.	*Apr.
Arielle			Sept.–Feb.	*Mar.–Apr.	
Christa			Sept.–Mar.	*Apr.	
Dong Hyun			Sept.–Dec.	Jan.–Apr.	
Jeffrey			Sept.–Feb.	Mar.–Apr.	
Kaleena			Sept.–Feb.	*Mar.–Apr.	
Karen			Sept.–Feb.	Mar.–Apr.	

*Approaching, in between stages.
Note. From "Children's Writing Samples," 1990. Copyright 1990 by Sheila Hackett. Reprinted by permission.

Stages in Spelling Development by Gentry (1982)

in invented spellings that were readily decipherable in the context supplied by drawings. Sheila concluded that she didn't need a formal program because first graders immersed in meaningful print from such sources as big books, trade books, and poetry/story charts—and encouraged to write frequently—would develop their spelling abilities naturally. She recommends that teachers closely observe young children's early writing since there can be such a range (from those who know no letter-sound relationships to those who can spell phonetically) and plan individual and small-group sessions on spelling strategies rather than to have a formal spelling program in which all children learn the same words at the same time and rate.

Sheila sees her students as actively involved, highly motivated, emerging readers and writers. She sees herself as an enthusiastic, highly motivated teacher who loves teaching within a literature framework. She intends to keep the momentum going!

GRADE 1: FOCUS ON PORTFOLIO ASSESSMENT

Sue Meldonian is a first grade teacher in a suburban school that encourages whole language. Having been a basal teacher for over 10 years, Sue started using only trade books just this year. On the day we visited in early September Sue began her morning by having her children add a few items to their weekly newspaper, an oaktag chart on which she writes as children dictate in language experience fashion. Next they read together several chants and poems that are on charts attached to hangers with clothespins. A favorite is "Who stole the cookies from the cookie jar?" Children delight in naming the next culprit who has to lead the reading of the chart, pointing to each word.

After the chanting a new big book is introduced. Sue reads aloud *I Like the Rain* (Belanger, 1988) as the children follow along, predicting the weather and seasons that the author describes. Then, as Sue points to the words, they sing the text a few times, accompanied by a cassette tape. All this shared reading takes place in a comfortable corner rug area. Sue closes this segment by showing the children the beginnings of a class book, appropriately entitled, "I Like _____ ." She asks them to write about one thing that they like and tells them their pieces will all be placed in a class big book that will be "authored, illustrated, and published by Miss Meldonian's First Grade Class."

The children then go to their desks and begin writing. An obvious cooperative spirit prevails as children help each other with spelling and composing. As they finish, Sue writes their message on an "I like" sheet as the children read from their drafts, and she asks them to illustrate their page with magic markers. The class big book is ready for parents to read at a Back-to-School night to occur later that week.

Sue uses The Wright Group Story Box Level 1 and Sunshine Series 2 to 5 (big books and sets of small books), along with similar materials from Scholastic and Rigby (addresses supplied at the end of the chapter). As opportunities arise she teaches skills during mini-lessons that are planned around shared reading. She allows her first graders to select their own books to read during silent reading time; the children also read to each other, the teacher, and parents. Children retell stories to each other and write their reactions in journals. Figures 4.7 and 4.8 show typical

FIGURE 4.7
First grade student's response to *Skyfire* (Asch, 1984)
Note. From original student drawing, 1991. Copyright 1991 by Faisal Rahman. Reprinted by permission.

responses. Reacting to *Skyfire* (Asch, 1984), a story telling how bear explains a rainbow that ends in a pot of golden honey, an Indian child, whose first language was not English, wrote about his favorite part (Figure 4.7). Figure 4.8 shows a response written by Philip, a Chinese-American boy, to several books, including *Gilberto and the Wind* (Ets, 1963), read during a spring unit on "The Wind." He obviously learned much from his exposure to good books.

By mid-October of her first year of whole language teaching, Sue noticed that her students were able to read the basal preprimers that were still in her room. She thought to herself, "I'd just be finishing the readiness materials by now and starting to prepare the children to read those preprimers by teaching sight words. After six weeks of immersion reading and writing, they can read them by themselves!"

Although she knows her students are learning to read and write naturally, Sue is concerned about how to demonstrate growth and is experimenting with a portfolio approach. When parents come for conferences, she reviews with them their children's

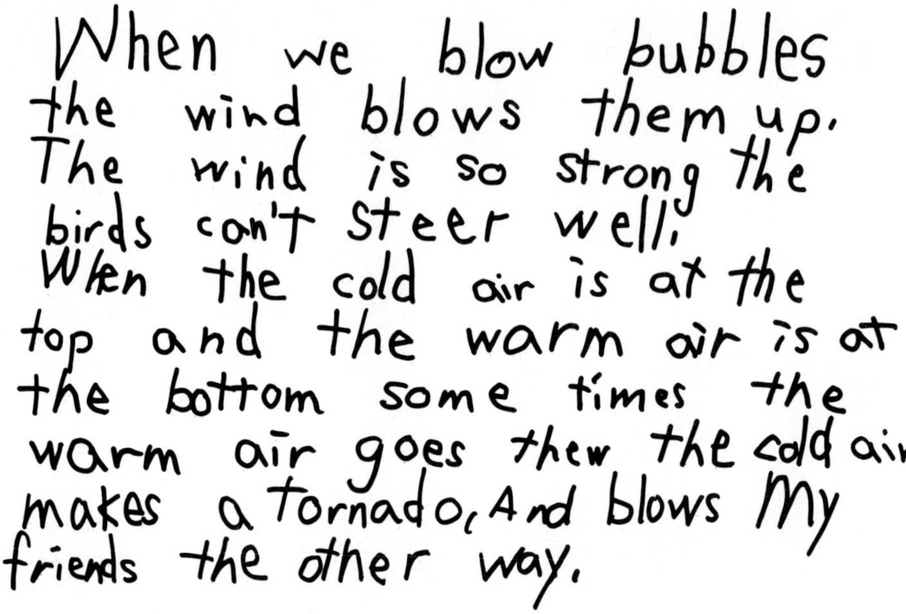

When we blow bubbles
the wind blows them up.
The wind is so strong the
birds can't steer well.
When the cold air is at the
top and the warm air is at
the bottom some times the
warm air goes thew the cold air
makes a tornado, And blows My
friends the other way.

FIGURE 4.8

First grade student's response to *Gilberto and the Wind* (Ets, 1963)

Note. From original student writing, 1991. Copyright 1991 by Philip Hum. Reprinted by permission.

portfolios. These contain reading logs, writing samples, audiotapes of children reading selections from trade books, checklists, and her own anecdotal notes.

The reading logs are 5 × 8 cards on which Sue lists the titles of books the children choose to read on their own. During individual conferences they read parts orally and discuss their reactions as she records her observations. As the children begin reading more and more she enlists parents to help out with the record-keeping. The children learn graphing when they keep line graphs showing how many books they read each month and the total for the year. Figure 4.9 shows an example of the graph used to chart independent reading.

Through their daily journals and selected, dated writing samples, Sue shows how the children are gaining control over skill areas such as spelling, punctuation, and sentence structure. The children help her select pieces for their portfolio. Figure 4.10 shows samples of April's writing. In September she wrote only one sentence, using mainly capital letters, and included a picture to add information. In June she wrote several sentences, used upper and lower case letters, began every sentence with a capital, spelled many words conventionally, and used complex sentence structure. She also told her story without pictures and included humor in it ("I thought it was food so I swallowed it" and "I had to take a gummy shower").

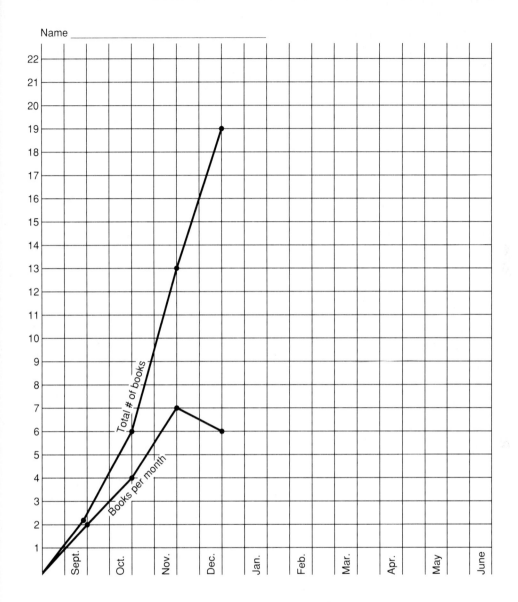

Name _____

FIGURE 4.9
Reading log graph used to record students' independent readings
Note. From "Reading Log Graph," 1991. Copyright 1991 by Sue Meldonian. Reprinted by permission.

I LOVE MY PET

The frst Time
I had gum
I thot it
was food so
I sad it.
I blow a
big bobol
it was so
big it popt
on my face
and inmy hair.
I hat to tack
a gummy
showoer.

April's September
writing sample for assessment
of progress.

April's June
writing sample for
assessment of progress.

FIGURE 4.10
First grade student's writing samples showing progress from September through June
Note. From original student writing, 1991. Copyright 1991 by April Rivera. Reprinted by permission.

   To help assess her children's oral reading, Sue tapes them reading a familiar story on two occasions, three to four months apart. Without practicing the story between tapings, the children reread the same story so Sue can make comparisons. Besides having the parents listen to the two cassettes, Sue also has the children evaluate their own oral reading. They either write or tape their own impressions.

Sue keeps anecdotal records on such items as children's attitudes toward reading and writing through the year; who they read with; what kinds of books they choose; when they seem to be aware of a certain phonics rule or word recognition strategy; and how well they seem to retell and respond to books. She also uses checklists that come with the Story Box program, for example, one that tracks children's concepts about print (whether they can recognize letters, words, and punctuation marks) and one that helps to categorize their spelling development from scribble writing, to writing with consonants, to consonants and vowels, and finally to standard form.

For her master's degree project Sue decided to evaluate the components of her portfolios. She collected survey and interview data from parents, teachers, administrators, and the children themselves (Meldonian, 1991). The parents, teachers, and administrators found that the most valuable components were those the children produced themselves: reading logs, audiocassettes, journals, and other writing samples. The teachers also valued the checklists very highly. On the other hand, the children most preferred the components they shared with their peers: reading logs, writing samples, and journals.

Based on her findings Sue has concluded that her portfolio assessment is recognized and valued by parents, administrators, other teachers, and, most important of all, by her students. She noted a definite improvement in self-esteem among this group of children who became active participants in their own evaluations.

SUMMARY

These four teachers of young children are using many shared reading experiences, encouraging writing, and relying on literature to introduce their students to the world of written language. Ever reflective about their teaching/learning environments, they are experimenting with current educational ideas such as thematic teaching (Janice, Cindy, and Betsy) and assessment through demonstrated competencies (Sheila and Sue).

MID-ELEMENTARY (2–4)

GRADE 2: A CIRCULATING CLASS LIBRARY

As a second grade teacher from upstate New York who had used only a basal approach to teaching reading, Sue Boyd first became aware of literature-based reading when she began teaching in New Jersey. She started her journey into literature by conferring with a mentor in a neighboring school district and reading books from the Heinemann catalog. (Heinemann is a publisher that specializes in resources for "whole language" and literature-based literacy programs; their address can be found at the end of this chapter.)

Sue's reading program revolves around her growing "circulating class library" of sets of books (at least 5 of each title) in a variety of genres. In the mystery section can be found titles such as *Encyclopedia Brown and the Case of the Midnight Visitor* (Sobol, 1977), *Bunnicula* (Howe and Howe, 1979), and *Cam Jensen and the Mystery of the*

Dinosaur Bones (Adler, 1981). Among the books with an "A" for adventure on their spines are *Troll Country* (Marshall, 1980) and *The Island of the Skog* (Kellogg, 1973). Beverly Cleary's *Socks* (1973) is an example of the animal titles, and *Squanto, Friend of the Pilgrims* (Bulla, 1971) can be found in nonfiction. In a section marked "classics" are all-time favorites such as *Ira Sleeps Over* (Waber, 1972) and *Miss Nelson Is Missing* (Marshall, 1977). Sue's reading groups are made up of the children reading the same book. At first she picks the books and the groups, but gradually, the children select the titles and group themselves.

On the day we observed, the children were reading nonfiction. When it is time for Sustained Silent Reading (SSR), the children gather their "group" books and other things they want to read, for example, a new library display book, *Knights of the Kitchen Table* (Scieszka, 1991), and go to the school reading room. This is an empty, carpeted room that classes can sign up to use for SSR. For about 25 minutes the children read quietly, sitting on bean bag chairs, rockers, or the floor. A sampling of the titles we noted were animal/sea life books such as *Corky the Seal* (Irvine, 1987), *I Wonder if I'll See a Whale* (Weller, 1991), *Bear* (Schoenherr, 1991), and *Wolves* (Andrews, 1990), in addition to books about children from other cultures such as *Pueblo Storyteller* (Hoyt-Goldsmith, 1991), a photo story of a young Indian girl who lives with grandparents near Santa Fe, New Mexico, and *Rehema's Journey* (Margolies, 1990), a story about a child who takes her first trip away from home. When the children return to their room, for another 20 minutes they discuss their books with partners, fill out "pair share" forms (see Figure 4.11), and share with their groups. In effect, they are operating in "**literature circles**" of readers who had read the same book and come together to talk about it (Harste, Short, & Burke, 1988).

Sue involves her students in their own evaluations. We observed as together they filled out a form called "My Own Report Card" (see Figure 4.12). As Sue reads and explains each item, the children mark the response that they feel best describes their position on a three-point continuum from "Always" to "Not Yet." We noticed that

---

Name: _____

1. Tell your partner why you selected your group books.

2. Tell what you have learned so far from these books.

3. If you were to write a nonfiction book, what would you write about?

4. Share with your partner some of your favorite parts.

5. Your partner is to write comments here.

Partner's Signature: _____

FIGURE 4.11

Pair share form

Note. From "Pair Share" Form, 1991. Copyright 1991 by Susan Boyd. Reprinted by permission.

FIGURE 4.12
Sample of second
grader's self-report
Note. From "My
Own Report Card,"
1991. Copyright
1991 by Susan
Boyd. Reprinted by
permission.

My own report card

READING	ALWAYS	SOMETIMES	NOT YET
Contributes to group discussions	————	————	————
Actively participates when books are read out loud	————	————	————
Can sustain silent reading	————	————	————
Reads many different genres	————	————	————
Actively participates in written and oral responses	————	————	————
Writes effective responses to literature	————	————	————
Gets involved with the characters they are reading about	————	————	————
Makes predictions while reading	————	————	————
Uses appropriate comprehension strategies to develop meaning	————	————	————
Actively participates during text sets	————	————	————

GOALS: _____
_____

WRITING	ALWAYS	SOMETIMES	NOT YET
Chooses topics with confidence	————	————	————
Produces meaningful writing	————	————	————
Revises work when appropriate	————	————	————
Edits when appropriate	————	————	————
Actively participates in writing conferences	————	————	————
Shares own writing	————	————	————
Uses different writing techniques that have been discussed	————	————	————

GOALS: _____
_____

the children are surprisingly honest in their responses and make discriminating choices. Sue uses these self-reports along with the children's response logs and a sampling of their "pair share" sheets to assess their growth as readers. Just as in Sue Meldonian's class, these checklists and samples are kept in individual portfolios to be shared with parents at "report card" time.

Besides her circulating class library, Sue has "text sets" of books she uses to develop content area topics such as "Native Americans" and "Black History." (Figure 4.13 lists some titles in these sets.) Harste, Short, and Burke (1988) and Heine (1991) describe a text set as two or more books related in some way, either by theme (friendship), topic (colonial America), or author (Van Allsburg). Sue uses her sets in classwork with whole-group, small-group, and independent activities centering around the learning of specific information. The starred titles in Figure 4.13 are books Sue uses as information sources for herself and as read-alouds. The other titles are easy enough for children to read on their own. Children's books, both fiction and nonfiction, are the resources from which Sue's students read, write, and learn.

FIGURE 4.13

Examples of two third grade text sets

*Read-alouds and teacher resources

Note. From "Third Grade Text Sets," 1991. Copyright 1991 by Susan Boyd. Reprinted by permission.

NATIVE AMERICANS

Pueblo Boy: Growing Up in Two Worlds. Marsha Keegan. Cobble Hill Books, 1991.

Dancing Drum. Terri Cohlori. Watermill Press, 1990.

**The Lenapes.* Robert S. Grumet. Chelsea House, 1989.

The Chippewa. Alice Osinski. Children's Press, 1987.

BLACK HISTORY

The Black Snowman. Phil Mendez. Scholastic, 1989.

**James Weldon Johnson.* Patricia and Fred McKissack. Children's Press, 1990.

**Journey to Jo'burg: A South African Story.* Beverley Naidoo. Lippincott, 1986.

**Marching to Freedom: The Story of Martin Luther King.* Joyce Milton. Dell, 1987.

Nettie's Trip South. Ann Turner. Scholastic, 1987.

GRADE 3: CONNECTING READING AND WRITING

Sue Corrado, a third grade teacher in the same school as Sue Meldonian, began using a trade book approach this year. After two years of using a basal, she grew tired of the "cookbook" approach and the "written down" literature selections. Exposed to current research and trends through her graduate courses and professional reading, she was ready to embrace literature-based reading when she arrived in a new school in which the administration encouraged a "whole language" reading-writing program.

Sue begins by having the whole class read the same book, relying on titles available in class sets. Fortunately, she has found sets of some real winners such as *Little House in the Big Woods* (Wilder, 1932), *Charlotte's Web* (White, 1952), *Superfudge* (Blume, 1980), and *Ramona, the Brave* (Cleary, 1981). First, the children make predictions about the story and then read to verify them, writing reactions in their reading journals. At specified stopping points, they hold class discussions to compare their reactions. When a book is finished, they may extend their study of it through art, drama, and writing activities or research into topics that surface during reading. For example, after reading *Charlotte's Web,* the children do research projects on animals. Using Ogle's (1986) **K-W-L** model, they list information and questions about animals chosen for study under three headings: What do I *Know*? What do I *Want* to know? What have I *Learned*? In this way they organized and added to their existing knowledge on animals. (See Chapter 6 for a more complete description of K-W-L.)

Sue also does author studies in which all the children read books by the same author. On the day we visited her class, she was launching a study on William Steig. She begins by reading aloud his animal fantasy about two unlikely friends, a mouse and a whale, *Amos & Boris* (Steig, 1971). Since a skill focus is to learn to use context to identify unknown words, she tells the children that Steig uses many interesting words but that they shouldn't have to run to the dictionary because they can probably decipher the meanings by reading the surrounding text. At several places during the read-aloud, Sue stops to see if the children can guess the meanings of unusual words, modeling what experienced readers do.

After the read-aloud Sue uses some passages from the book to further demonstrate the context strategy. Displaying the excerpts on an overhead so that all can read together and conjecture about the meanings of target words, she specifically uses the shared reading concept. Continuing the focus on context, Sue next displays some passages with blanks (cloze procedure) to show the children how they can use the meaning (semantics) and structure (syntax) to predict the missing words. There is a lively discussion about whether or not suggested fill-ins fit the slots both semantically and syntactically.

Another skill focus for the day is a compare/contrast strategy, used to study the main characters. Again using the overhead, Sue asks the children to help her list ways in which Amos and Boris are alike (compare) and different (contrast). Together they develop a Venn diagram (see Figure 4.14) that clearly shows the areas of overlap and the differences between the two friends.

FIGURE 4.14

Venn diagram showing how Amos and Boris are alike and different

Note. From Venn diagram developed in third grade class, 1991. Copyright 1991 by Susan Corrado. Reprinted by permission.

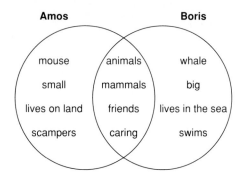

This exercise leads to a writing workshop activity in which the children prepare to write fictional animal stories modeled on *Amos & Boris*. They were planning to take two animals they had researched under the K-W-L project and make them friends who help each other. Sue shows the children how they can make up compare/contrast diagrams for their animals just as the class has done for the mouse and the whale; then they can begin to involve their characters in some likely (or unlikely) escapades. The prewriting activity ends with Sue modeling again with a class-generated sample of how a tale might begin, "Once there lived a woodpecker and a mountain lion in a forest in New Jersey. . . ." The reading-writing connection is made!

GRADE 4: AN ADAPTATION OF THE ATWELL MODEL

Fourth grade teacher Kathy Kelly has been using only trade books for her reading program for two years. Like Sue Boyd, she started by having three groups read from multiple copies of the same title, but she began to feel that she was teaching the reading more than the reader. After reading Nancie Atwell (1987), she decided to adapt Atwell's reading workshop in which students are invited to read from a wide variety of books and respond to their reading through letters written to the teacher or other students. On any given day one can find 15 or so books being read in her reading workshop, ranging from *The Babysitters' Club* series (Martin, 1980s) to *The Prince and the Pauper* (Twain, 1881/1983).

In the beginning of the year Kathy introduces her students to her reading workshop. They must always be reading at least one book which they can get from the class collection, school library, or town library. They will read every day for 30 to 40 minutes during reading workshop and at home for at least 30 minutes, with the at-home reading monitored by a parent (see Figure 4.15).

As they read, they are expected to talk about their books by writing letters to the teacher and classmates in ringed notebooks, called dialogue journals. They may write ideas, feelings, experiences, and questions that come to them as they read. Kathy promises to write back (hence the dialogue) and encourages them to write back to peers who address letters to them. They must write at least two letters a week, and at least one of the letters must go to Kathy. If a letter is written to her, it goes in a mailbox on her desk; if it is for a student, it goes directly to him/her and should be answered within 24 hours. As children finish letters to Kathy or other students, they tack a little book next to their names on a wall chart (see Figure 4.16).

MONDAY

TITLE: _____

AUTHOR: _____

DATE: _____

TIME STARTED: _____ PAGES READ: _____

TIME FINISHED: _____ PARENT'S SIGNATURE: _____

TUESDAY

TITLE: _____

AUTHOR: _____

DATE: _____

TIME STARTED: _____ PAGES READ: _____

TIME FINISHED: _____ PARENT'S SIGNATURE: _____

FIGURE 4.15

Sample home reading log

Note. From "Home Reading Log," 1991. Copyright 1991 by Kathleen Kelly. Reprinted by permission.

All letters must be dated; titles of books must be written properly (capitals for main words and underlined) and authors noted. Also, titles must be entered in a reading log that is taped in the back of the notebook (see Figure 4.17). Kathy tells the children that the notebook will serve "as a record of the thinking, learning, and reading we did together," and will provide one fourth of their grade in reading.

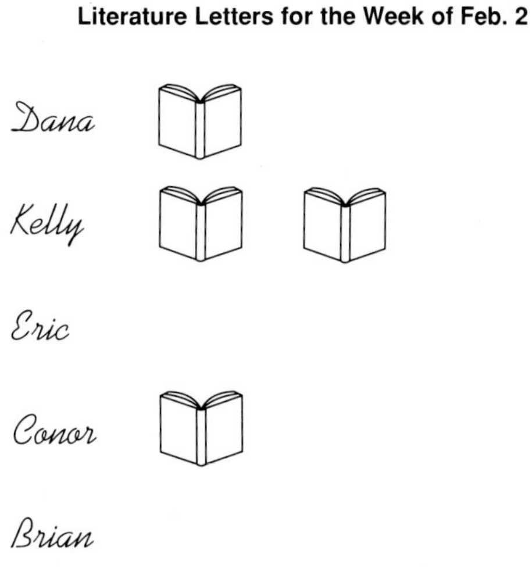

FIGURE 4.16

Sample chart to track fourth grade students' responses to reading

Note. From "Literature Letters," 1991. Copyright 1991 by Kathleen Kelly. Reprinted by permission.

Literature Letters for the Week of Feb. 2

Dana

Kelly

Eric

Conor

Brian

DATE STARTED	TITLE & AUTHOR	DATE FINISHED OR ABANDONED (WHY?)	RATING (1 to 5) (5 is highest)

FIGURE 4.17
Sample reading log
Note. From "Sample Reading Log," 1991. Copyright 1991 by Kathleen Kelly. Reprinted by permission.

For the rest of their quarterly grades, Kathy considers how well students do on district tests, how many books they've read, and how well they have done on one self-selected goal for that quarter. She also consults her observational notes on how well they use their in-class reading time. Her district has a bank of criterion-referenced tests on traditional reading skills such as using the context (word identification/vocabulary), making inferences (comprehension), and understanding figurative language (literature). Most of her students do very well on these tests; for those who don't, she plans small-group or individual lessons on the specific area needed. For the entire class, Kathy keeps a record book of test scores and day-to-day observational notes on reading attitudes and behaviors. Figure 4.18 shows the kind of information Kathy can glean from her record book.

SOME THOUGHTS ON THE PROGRESS OF A FEW OF MY STUDENTS:

*AZIZ

Sept. and Oct. were spent reading exclusively from the *Hardy Boys* mystery series; sub-literature with a formula plot, easy vocabulary. Recent readings include *The Diary of Ann Frank,* read at my suggestion *Number the Stars* (winner of 1990 Newbery medal); a gift from parents *On My Honor,* an award-winning novel, realistic fiction. These books demonstrate much growth (even though they are not tests). They represent 3 different genres, complex plot, and up to 9–10th grade vocab.

*KELLY

Came to me as an excellent reader last year. Enjoyed reading such books as *The Wizard of Oz.* This year after seeing *Les Miserables* on Broadway, Kelly read *The Scarlet Pimpernel* at my suggestion; it also has the French Revolution as background, but is from point of view of the elite. She completed an author study on Steinbeck. Readings include *The Grapes of Wrath, The Pearl,* and *Of Mice and Men,* a biography of Steinbeck, and selections from a book of letters. Presently reading books of Mark Twain. Most of these books range from 10–12th grade reading level.

*JILL

Came to me far below grade level last year. Strongly disliked reading. I was forced to procure extremely easy novels with large print and pictures, as well as books of poetry by Silverstein. Jill miscued constantly and comprehended minimally. The end of last year and the beginning of this year were spent reading exclusively from the *Babysitters Club* series. Jill began to respond to coaching and shifted her attention to Louis Sacher, an author of funny, easy, award-winning books. She recently read *Up a Road Slowly* by Irene Hunt—6th grade reading level, small print, no pictures. She selected it from our classroom library, after a book-talk, by herself. Jill's mother recently thanked me for Jill's dramatic growth. Her mother said she now reads every night & asks to be taken to the bookstore.

*ERIC

Began the year reading exclusively in genre of biography—large print, 3–4th grade level. He has since expanded to such genres as historical fiction—*A Light in the Forest,* 6th grade level; sports fiction—*The Contender* by Robert Lipsyte, 7–8th grade level. He also read *One Fat Summer* by Lipsyte. He followed up on another author mentioned on the jacket of a Lipsyte book. Also read *On My Honor* after a book-talk.

FIGURE 4.18

Excerpts from anecdotal records on student's progress

Note. From "Anecdotal Records," 1991. Copyright 1991 by Kathleen Kelly. Reprinted by permission.

Toward the end of a quarter Kathy holds an evaluation conference with each child. They discuss some question about reading in general such as "What does someone have to do to be a good reader?" (See Figure 4.19). Then they talk about one book in particular, the favorite for that marking period. Lastly, they talk about the student's self-selected goal for that quarter and what they might work on for the next. Some typical goals may be to use SSR time better, to select a new genre (if the student had been reading mainly one kind of book), and to include in their letters more about *how* authors write rather than *what* they write.

The basic structure of the day-to-day reading workshop goes like this. First, Kathy presents a mini-lesson on some aspect of literature, reading, or learning to read. For example, she may teach a strategy such as predicting from a title or a literary concept such as metaphor, or she may give a talk on an author or a book. This is followed by a 15 to 20 minute period of SSR, in which Kathy reads with the children. For another 15 to 20 minutes she circulates for one-to-one conferences. Kathy uses these conferences to assess how students are progressing, do on-the-spot teaching, and collect observational notes. The workshop ends with a whole-class share time in which children talk about their reading experiences.

On the day we visited, Kathy's mini-lesson was a book talk on *Old Yeller* (Gipson, 1956) because she had just received five copies of it and wanted to introduce it to the children. After talking about the setting and main characters, she begins reading a portion aloud so that the children will get a feel for the author's style. When she comes upon an unfamiliar word, she models how to use context clues to figure it out. All this takes place in a corner of the room, with children gathered around informally on chairs or on the floor.

EVALUATION CONFERENCE NOTES

NAME: _____ QUARTER: _____

DATE: _____ GRADE: _____

1. What does someone have to do to be a good reader?

2. What's the best book you read this quarter and what makes it best?

TITLE: _____

AUTHOR: _____

3. What do you want to do as a reader during the next quarter?

FIGURE 4.19
Sample form for an evaluation conference
Note. From "Evaluation Conference Notes," 1991. Copyright 1991 by Kathleen Kelly. Reprinted by permission.

Next, the children go to their desks, take out their self-selected books, and begin SSR, with Kathy reading S.E. Hinton's *The Outsiders* (1967). After 10 to 15 minutes, she begins to zigzag around the room with her notebook, stopping to hear someone softly read a passage aloud, to discuss some child's progress, or to ask about how a plot was developing.

We circle around to sample what the children are reading on this particular day in the middle of the school year. Two boys are reading Matt Christopher sports stories; two others are reading Robert Lipsyte's *The Summerboy* (1982) and *The Contender* (1967). Two girls have chosen Judy Blume stories, *Tiger Eyes* (1981) and *Blubber* (1974), while another is glued to Paula Danziger's *Everyone Else's Parents Said Yes* (1989). While mysteries such as Hahn's *The Doll in the Garden* (1989) and Avi's *Windcatcher* (1991) are understandably popular, it surprises us to find Kelly, described as a superior reader in Figure 4.18, reading *The Hunchback of Notre Dame* (Hugo, 1831/1965). We stop to ask her about the book. She confides that it is not easy reading (she is more than half way through) but that she knows a lot about France and has recently seen *Les Miserables*. She is aware that all this background knowledge is helping her to understand *Hunchback*.

When SSR and individual conferences end, the class gathers in a circle to share ideas or read aloud from their books. Dana retells her favorite part from the Paula Danziger book. While Brian reads from *Mystery Coach* (Christopher, 1973) and Conor shares a humorous excerpt from *Doctor Doolittle: A Treasury* (Lofting, 1967), Anthony engages everyone with an animated rendition of a selection from *The Prince and the Pauper* (Twain, 1881/1983). He points out that he has just learned from the small print on the back of the title page that the book was originally published in

1881. At the close, Kathy encourages the children to add any books they may want to read to the "Future Books" lists in their notebooks.

The transition from reading to writing workshop was easy. From a chart on the wall entitled "Realistic Fiction" we learned that the class had just completed a focused study of this genre. Kathy had read aloud a few picture books such as *Song and Dance Man* (Ackerman, 1988), *Crow Boy* (Yashima, 1955), and *The Snowy Day* (Keats, 1962) to illustrate story elements such as characters, problem, and theme. (See Figure 4.20 for the chart that guided their discussions.) Now the children are ready to write their own pieces of realistic fiction, and Kathy suggests they begin by brainstorming about their stories with a partner.

We sit with one group. Brian tells his story, which is about three boys who meet in a pile-up during the preliminaries for a bike race; they become friends, with two of the boys helping the one who was most hurt in the crash. The badly hurt boy goes on to win the race. Laura's story sounds like a continuation of *Tiger Eyes* (Blume, 1981) that she has been reading. Susan will write about two lost children who finally get home by finding help in a New Jersey phone book. Just as the children keep records of their reading, they also keep track of and rate their writing pieces. See Figure 4.21 for their "First Quarter Writing Inventory."

After this rehearsal the children spend half an hour writing. While some start on the pieces they have just discussed with partners, others put their notes away in folders and start on works in progress. Several boys get their disks plus the Bank Street Writer start-up disk and quietly begin typing final drafts of finished pieces on the four computers in the back of the room. The room is abuzz with writers at work.

REALISTIC FICTION			
	SONG AND DANCE MAN	CROW BOY	THE SNOWY DAY
Setting			
Characters			
Problem			
Theme			
Titles			
Leads			
Endings			
Climax			

FIGURE 4.20
Chart to guide discussion of story elements in works of realistic fiction
Note. From "Realistic Fiction Chart," 1991. Copyright 1991 by Kathleen Kelly. Reprinted by permission.

NAME: _____

DATE: _____

FIRST QUARTER WRITING INVENTORY

STORY	WHAT HAPPENED TO IT	(1 to 5) RATING (5 is highest)

1. _____

2. _____

3. _____

4. _____

5. _____

6. _____

7. _____

8. _____

COMMENTS: _____

_____

FIGURE 4.21
Form for helping fourth graders track and evaluate their writing
Note. From "Writing Inventory," 1991. Copyright 1991 by Kathleen Kelly. Reprinted by permission.

Dear Miss Kelly,

    Thank you for sharing your book with me. I found it to be quite enlightening & very interesting. I understand better now this philosophy of Reading & Writing much better. It appears to be more logical and much more enjoyable than the standard method of "teaching" reading. I agree, the approach of teaching the reader rather than reading is wonderful. Wouldn't it be wonderful if we could apply this freedom of reading method to other courses in our lives?

    Thanks again!

Rosemarie Caterina

FIGURE 4.22

Letter from parent

Note. From parent letter to Kathleen Kelly. Copyright 1991 by Rosemarie Caterina. Reprinted by permission.

Kathy says that she tries to make her reading-writing classroom reflect the three basics that writing process advocate Mary Ellen Giacobbe talks about: time, owner-ship, and response. Her students have *time* to read and write daily, select their own books and topics (*ownership*), and *respond* by "literary talk" with other literate people.

Kathy explains her program to parents in September and at every conference when she reviews the logs, journals, and check sheets with them. Sometimes she shares a book from her professional library with an interested parent. One parent showed her new understanding in a letter (see Figure 4.22) after reading Atwell's *In the Middle* (1987).

Although not all the teachers in the building use only trade books, the principal encourages an emphasis on literature and supports Kathy's efforts. Her district brought in a consultant to work with teachers who wanted help in moving into lit-erature-based programs. But, as with most districts that are seeking alternatives to basals and language arts texts to reach reading and writing, Kathy's district does not force change. It must be the teacher's choice, and Kathy made the choice.

SUMMARY

These three teachers of children in the mid-elementary grades all use a wide variety of literary genres, both fiction and nonfiction, to help their students develop further as readers and writers. Skills are taught as mini-lessons within reading and writing workshops. Sue Corrado taught both reading and writing strategies through shared reading of transparencies. Note the emergence of "literature circles" (Harste, Short, & Burke, 1988) as Sue Boyd's students discussed a specific book in groups and Kathy Kelly's students chatted together about their self-selected titles. As seen with the teachers of beginning readers, attention to assessment continues to focus on self-evaluation, checklists, anecdotal notes, and dated products.

UPPER-ELEMENTARY (5–6)

GRADE 5: LITERATURE AS THE CONTENT OF THE READING CURRICULUM

Beverly Pilchman has been teaching reading and writing through literature for over a decade. Caught up in the writing process movement in the early 1980s, she has adopted and adapted a workshop approach in her self-contained fifth grade classroom. Every day students spend their mornings reading trade books and writing a variety of pieces, sharing in small and large groups, while learning many skills and important information about themselves in the process.

The morning we visited, the class was winding up work on a class novel, *From the Mixed-Up Files of Mrs. Basil E. Frankweiler* (Konigsburg, 1967), which is about two children who run away from their Connecticut home and hide in the Metropolitan Museum of Art. Inadvertently, they stumble on important information about a Michelangelo sculpture, "Angel." On this morning, with just the last chapter to go, the children are wrestling with some unanswered questions such as, "What would their parents do when the children return home?" and "Will the Met find out the truth about the sculpture?"

The class reads the last chapter in book-in-hand fashion, with students reading parts around a narrator who sits poised on a high stool in their midst. When finished, they write in reading logs for 5 to 7 minutes in response to the final surprising pages. Figure 4.23 shows Bev's wall chart that guides her students to write about discoveries, characters, connections, images, and questions they may have about the book. Some

---

RESPONDING TO READING IN YOUR LOG

Record anything that has special meaning for you such as

*discoveries that you are making about yourself as a reader
(For example, ask for clarification about words and passages you find confusing; comment on the author's use of language.)

*connections you make to your own experiences
(For example, agree or disagree with the author's ideas by giving reasons and offering solutions.)

*questions you think about as you read and possible answers

*pictures you see in your mind as you read

*characters you would like to be
(For example, take on a role and write from that point of view.)

FIGURE 4.23
Chart to guide fifth grade log responses
Note. From "Chart to Guide Log Responses," 1991. Copyright 1991 by Beverly Pilchman. Reprinted by permission.

write fairly direct reactions such as, "I liked the ending because everything seemed to turn out all right." Others write questions they still have, for example, "Will the children inherit the sketch of Angel?" Others write letters to Claudia, Jamie, or Mrs. Basil E. Frankweiler.

Then the class breaks into groups of four or five students to share their logs. One group that we join immediately asks, "Who will be notetaker?" Confidant Adrian turns to a clean page in his log and volunteers to record the questions and discoveries shared. What evolves are "grand conversations" about a piece of literature as students actively discuss a book without teacher guidance (Eeds & Wells, 1989). Maggie starts off with a question, "If the children ever get the valuable Michelangelo sketch of Angel, will they sell it?" The others think that a story answering that question would make a good sequel to the book. Sam notices the large amount of narration in the last chapter; he also adds that his favorite part is when the museum guards find the violin case and the trumpet case, both filled with dirty underwear. Everyone agrees that is a funny part. While Steven wonders aloud about what he would have done with Angel and the sketch if he were Mrs. Frankweiler, Adrian looks up from his notes to confess that he finished the book at home because he couldn't wait to find out the ending!

Finally, the class assembles in the rug area, and recorders share summaries of what went on in the small groups. This promotes further in-depth discussion, and it is obvious that they are all looking forward to their class trip to the Metropolitan Museum the next week, armed with maps so that they can locate spots that Claudia and Jamie had described in the book. The consensus seems to be that some of their questions can be answered only within their own minds. In fact, that's what happened in the writing workshop that followed.

Two writing assignments completed by all the children were to compose a letter that Claudia might have written to her mom and dad explaining why she and Jamie had run away (see Figure 4.24) and to write a conversation for some of the characters in the book. Bev explains that since *The Mixed-Up Files* has so much dialogue, she uses it to explicitly teach the mechanics of written conversation (see Figure 4.25).

During the writing share time, Dan asks for help with his dialogue between the children and their parents after the children had returned home. (Without realizing it, he has answered one of the questions raised in the final book discussion!) He has Mom saying that as punishment Claudia "couldn't play with her toys for a week." The group responds that this isn't a realistic punishment for such a "crime" in today's world. Some suggestions that they give are that Claudia could be "grounded," couldn't watch TV for a week, and could be made to "do extra chores around the house."

This exchange comes at the end of a writing workshop that began right after the all-group share about *The Mixed-Up Files*. Bev starts the writing workshop with a mini-lesson on finding interesting verbs in excerpts from *Brave Irene* (Steig, 1986). After the children work in pairs to underline verbs, Bev pools their findings by circling the verbs they offer on an overhead projector for all to see. As they write during workshop, they try to use appropriate descriptive verbs.

FIGURE 4.24
Fifth grade
student's letter
after assuming the
identity of the
character Claudia
in *From the
Mixed-Up Files of
Mrs. Basil E.
Frankweiler*
(Konigsburg,
1967)
Note. From original
student writing,
1991. Copyright
1991 by Samuel
DiLiberto. Re-
printed by permis-
sion.

> 122 Concord lane
> Greenwich Connecticut 0683
> Jan. 7, 1991
>
> Dear Mom and Dad,
>   I ran away because I've
> always dreamed about going to a
> place where it is comfortable an in-
> door place, and a preferably beautiful
> place that's why I am going to give
> you some clues to where I am. It is
> very big and it has a lot of things
> on the wall. Also, it is not in this
> state. I am telling you so you
> dont call the F.B.I, because they'll
> probaly never find us anyway. I took
> Jamie because he is rich, he has
> a transistor radio, and he's good for
> a laugh now and then. One more
> thing, I dont like doing everyone
> elses chores.
>   Your ex daughter,
>   Claudia

Next, a 15-minute period of silent writing follows, with Bev circulating with her clipboard sheet, "Status of the Class" (see Figure 4.26). On it she records what the children are writing, in what stage of the writing process they are working, and what instructional plans she has for them. This type of tracking leads to on-the-spot instructional decision-making and provides a basis for ongoing assessment.

FIGURE 4.25
Fifth grade student's invented conversation between book characters

Note. From original student writing, 1991. Copyright 1991 by Jessie Pearson. Reprinted by permission.

CONVERSATION **By Jessie Pearson**

```
            "See you in a while,"whispered Jamie.
"Yea,"Claudia replied. Jamie went to the men's room and Claudia
went to the ladie's room. Once everyone was gone they both came
out of hiding. "Claud,how about we go hide in the mummy cases
tonight? When we go back to school we can tell all the kids
that we was mummies for a night!"Jamie exclamed
"You can't speak English!"Claudia was getting agitated.
"I talk good English!"Jamie yelled. (You see,Saxonberg Claudia
is a straight-A student,and Jamie...Well...He's...Oh...I don't
want to say what he is.)
            "Anyway,"Claudia exploded,"I have already planned
our stay at the museum and we will go where I say so. We will
sleep in the bed tonight."Claudia said bossily.
            "What kind'a hiding place is that?" Jamie was getting
angry.
            "A comfortable place. Somewhere that we can be
happy."
            "Oh boloney Claude. You're no fun!"
            "Shall we go?"
            "Just don't push me off!"Jamie snorted. Claudia
and Jamie walked to the third floor  and walked into a gorgeous
room. It had furniture from medieval  times. "Jamie,"Claudia
gasped."Look at all this,it's...it's beautiful!"
            "I guess so."
            "Oh,what do you know anyway."
            "Let's go to the bed. Shall we,Lady Claudia?"
            "Yes Sir James." They both jumped into bed.
            "Maybe it won't be as bad as I thought. It's sort'a
nice sleeping in a comfortable spot."
            "Yea,"Claudia said dreamily.
            "Good night Claude."
            "Good night." There was a slight pause.
            "Jamie?"
            "Yes?"
            "I'm sorry if I always correct your grammar...I
mean I can't help it."
            "I know Claude. It's alright."
```

If some children need a conference, they go to the rug area with a partner. For example, Lani reads her "war poem" to Sarit to get an initial response. Lani wrote "A Better Tomorrow, A Better Today" during the height of Operation Desert Storm and it shows her deep feelings (see Figure 4.27). Judson, who is an expert on medieval times, reads his story about the making of a page to Matt who is entranced with its unfolding. A wizard will make the young page into a knight of evil through the help of a magic necklace. And so the writing workshop goes, culminating in the all-group share.

Bev explained her overall reading program. Over the school year she covers four or five class novels, working with the students as we had observed that day. She selects books that are good stories but that can be used to focus on literary or language skills. For example, in September the class read *Midnight Fox* (Byars, 1968) and noted especially how the author uses adjectives. When they read *The Sign of the Beaver* (Speare, 1983), they look for "superb verbs and adverbs." For a class booklet, each student

STATUS OF THE CLASS: WEEK OF 2/20

DATE	STUDENT	STATUS
2/20	Judson	Almost finished with historical fiction piece about a boy becoming a page in the Middle Ages. Shared with Matt today. Will ask if he plans revisions.
2/20	Lani	Has revised her war poem and read it to Sarit. Plan to edit it with her.
2/20	Dan	His conversation piece shows he seems to understand direct discourse; needs help in handling paragraphs and tags. Will work with him and Sam tomorrow, editing their pieces with them.

FIGURE 4.26

A typical status-of-the-class log
Note. From "Status-of-the-Class" log, 1991. Copyright 1991 by Beverly Pilchman. Reprinted by permission.

A BETTER TOMORROW, A BETTER TODAY

I've been thinking,
of a better world,
No guns, no bombs,
no grenades hurled
People say a better tomorrow,
But, I say a better *TODAY!*
I've been thinking
of a better place,
No starving people,
not a trace
People say a better tomorrow,
But I say a better *TODAY!*
I've been thinking,
People say,
the world *will* get better,
someday.
People say a better tomorrow,
But I say a better *TODAY!*

By Lani Waters
Tuscan School
Fifth grade

FIGURE 4.27

Sample fifth grade student's writing
Note. From original student writing, 1991. Copyright 1991 by Lani Waters. Reprinted by permission.

locates sentences and highlights verbs and adverbs that they can illustrate with vivid pictures, for example,

> "**Halfheartedly** he <u>cleaned</u> them and **built up** the fire and <u>roasted</u> them."

Because she knows that the Comprehensive Tests of Basic Skills used in her district have items on similes and metaphors, Bev teaches these skills through her class novels. For example, as they read *The Mixed-Up Files,* the children note similes and add them to their class chart. Some examples are, "Her heart sounded like their electric percolator brewing the morning's coffee" (p. 21); "Ideas drift like clouds in an undecided breeze" (p. 85); "Homesickness is like sucking your thumb" (p. 86). Instead of working through isolated workbook pages on similes, the children are developing this literary concept as they read a piece of well written literature.

Students also complete one or two author studies, that is, read several books by one author such as Betsy Byars or Natalie Babbitt to see how an author develops a predictable style. Bev also does two major units a year in which she combines reading and writing around a theme. Called "Living with Prejudice and Injustice," one is about the Holocaust, and the other is the American Revolution unit that will be described in Chapter 6 on the content areas. In these units the students read a variety of genres such as historical fiction, realistic fiction, and nonfiction to learn American and world history.

In addition to the in-depth study of specific authors and themes, Bev has a read-at-home program in which children read a self-selected book for half an hour a day and write a response in a journal that she checks once a week. Right after lunch they have SSR time that is strictly observed; Bev and the children always have something to read, and they look forward to this quiet time at the start of each afternoon.

Completely supported by her administration and parents, Bev's program is highly regarded. Frequently asked to lead in-service sessions locally and to present at state and national conferences, Bev is considered a master teacher who uses literature as the content of her reading curriculum.

GRADE 5: LITERATURE RESPONSE GROUPS

Fifth grade teacher Jean DeSantis first used only trade books in her reading program back in the 1960s. She abandoned the approach and returned to the basal through the 1970s and 1980s because that seemed to be the route the administrators encouraged in those back-to-basics days. In the 1980s she became involved in the writing process movement and began using writing workshop. Moving back to a literature-based reading program that would complement her writing workshop in the 1990s was a natural step.

Jean favors literature response groups, small groups that read and discuss the same book. She has access to over 70 sets of paperbacks covering all genres. Her response groups differ from Bev's in that Jean is an integral part of each group, focusing students' discussions indirectly through guide sheets she has developed. On the Monday we visited, three groups were just starting their books; that day they met to discuss their impressions of the opening chapters. As the rest of the class reads silently, the first group gathers in the rug area with their copies of *The Wolves of Willoughby Chase* (Aiken, 1962). After identifying the characters and guessing the meanings of some unusual words they have marked with self-stick removable notes (for example, *crenelated* and *impetuosity*), they set a goal to read three more chapters by the time they meet again on Wednesday. Everyone promises to be ready to ask one good interpretive question about the story.

FIGURE 4.28
Form used by fifth grade students in literature response groups

Note. From original student writing, 1991. Copyright 1991 by Daniel Marcus. Reprinted by permission.

Name Daniel Marcus   Date 3/4/91

Reading

I have finished reading chapter one of Hawk Hill_____, pages 1 to 24.

I have _reread_ the chapter and

So far it seems: Ben has a special bond with animals.

or I noticed:
I'm puzzled by:
Ben has a lot of freedom. He can go anywhere.

I have post-its on these words:

The setting seems to be: some miles away from Lake Winnipeg.

I have met the following characters:

Character	Phrase About them
Ben	likes animals
Mrs. MacDonald	caring
Mr. MacDonald	superior
Mr. Burton	sneaky

I found this language interesting: (Quote)
"The word had slipped out unconsciously and MacDonald was immediately contrite. p16

At same time I am independently reading Dogsong

Next, the group reading *Incident at Hawk's Hill* (Eckert, 1971) comes together. They discuss the setting, a large farm in rural Canada, and the main character, young Ben. One boy thinks it is strange that Ben talks to the animals, but Peter says that isn't unusual on farms. Another boy jumps in with, "Piggybacking on Peter's idea, maybe Ben talks to animals because he's lonely." Jean tells us that, guided by the principles of cooperative learning, early in the year she models good discussion techniques and then withdraws somewhat to encourage a natural exchange. Her strategies certainly appear to be working. Figure 4.28 shows a form used to help students keep track of their reading; this one was done by Daniel in the *Hawk's Hill* group. All filed their forms in folders and agreed to read two more chapters for Wednesday.

The third group, composed of nine girls, was reading *Bridge to Terabithia* (Paterson, 1977). The first thing they want to talk about is the main character, Jessie, who they agree is the "favored child" in a family of five. The girls talk openly about who are the favorites in their own families; it is evident they are making real connections with their own lives. Like the fifth graders described by Eeds and Wells (1989), students and teacher engage in "grand conversations" about the meanings they are constructing.

The reading workshop for that day ends with Jean reading from Jean Craighead George's *One Day on the Alpine Tundra* (1984). The information in this well-written piece of nonfiction fits nicely into the present class study of the ecosystems; Jean points out the author's special techniques for writing descriptions that promote visualization. Content and craft converge.

Jean believes students increase their vocabularies from rich reading and learning experiences. To focus on meanings in specific contexts, she has the children select special words from their books and content area study and write them on cards; on the back, they give the date they encountered them, source, definition, and a sentence (see Figure 4.29 for a sample). The children play games with the word cards, teaching each other in small groups. At intervals, Jean gives tests on selected groups of words, and these grades are used along with other samples of their reading growth such as logs, ranking sheets, and literature letters.

In addition to the group novels they read in class, Jean's students also read self-selected books at home and record their responses in reading logs. Figure 4.30 shows

---

OSPREY

Osprey, noun. A large hawk that feeds on fish.

Sentence: The *osprey* flew down to the water and ate a fish that it caught in its bill.

From: Macrosystems Film

Name: *Dana*   Card: #4

FIGURE 4.29
Sample fifth grade vocabulary card for word *Osprey*
Note. From "Sample Vocabulary Card," 1991. Copyright 1991 by Jean DeSantis. Reprinted by permission.

Chris Basilo   2-26-91

<u>Hatchet</u>

Dear Mrs. "D",
Over the vacation I finished <u>Hatchet</u> by Gary Paulson. I enjoyed <u>Hatchet</u> very much but, I didn't like that Brian didn't use all of the things he could of on his journey. I enjoyed the ending of <u>Hatchet</u> but, I really don't perticulary like the adventure style of this book. For example, I don't like the kind of book when someone goes on a journey for a treasure or a person, then survives and finds the person or treasure. Another thing was that I perdicted many things but almost all of them were wrong. Like I perdicted that the piolit would complete the journey with Brian and he didn't. Thank you for welcoming and explaining <u>Hatchet</u> to me. I wouldn't mind reading another Paulson book for our next book.

<u>Author's Tape</u>
Today I listened to Gary Paulson's tape. I learned many things about him. For example, I learned that Gary didn't have many friends in school, and that he had good grades through grammer school but in High School he got "D's. I also learned that he didn't want to be a writer until he was 26 years old, and that he meditates every morning for 30 min. I liked his tape very much.

FIGURE 4.30
Sample fifth grade reading response log
Note. From original student writing, 1991. Copyright 1991 by Chris Basilo. Reprinted by permission.

one of Chris's entries for a book by Gary Paulsen (*Hatchet*, 1987). Notice that he refers to listening to a tape by Paulsen from which he learned much about the author. Jean has a listening library of tapes about writers popular with middle graders. These are available through Dell's Trumpet Book Club and Scholastic's Arrow Book Club.

Name *Melissa M.*   Date 1/4/91

Reading - Ranking 1-5 (One is highest). Books read in class in group.

Let the Circle Be Unbroken - Taylor   One-eyed Cat -
Roll of Thunder, Hear My Cry - Taylor   Stone Fox . R. Gardiner
Book of Three (Black C.) - L. Alexander   Sugar Bee - R. Micklish
The Great Gilly Hopkins - K. Paterson   Hatchet - G. Paulson
The Year of the Boar + J.R - B.B. Lord.   Shirley Temple. C Fiori
Jackie Robinson . Davidson

Please list your top five here. Write the book title.
1. Book of Three
2. The Year of The Boar + J.R.
3. The Great Gilly Hopkins
4. Roll of Thunder, Hear My Cry
5. Let The Circle Be Unbroken

Now, please do another ranking list which includes any of the above, any read orally by Mrs. "D", or any read independently.
1. The Fellowship of The Ring
2. The Island of The Blue Dolphins
3. Book of Three
4. Camp Sunnyside Friends
5. Pen Pals

Also, please explain your reason for deciding not to continue with Let The Circle Be Unbroken at this time. You are entitled to your decision but it would help me in my teaching to know why. Don't use other people's reasons. I really want yours.

FIGURE 4.31
Sample fifth grade survey response
Note. From student's survey response, 1991. Copyright 1991 by Melissa Mia. Reprinted by permission.

At the end of every marking period, Jean has the children rank the books she has read to them or that they have read in class groups or independently. Figure 4.31 shows Melissa's survey for the mid-year. Note the range of titles she had read. Also note that Jean asked the children to explain why some of them had decided to dis-

Daniel
2/5/91

I decided not to continue for a few reasons. One is that I didn't like the plot. I like books with action and this didn't have enough for me. I dislike books that are serious. I like humorous books. I also like books about the future or the Middle Ages. This book is in the time period that I like least. The characters' lives are just kind of boring. If the bull started flying and rain came up from the ground, then I might have liked the book. All in all, it just wasn't my kind of book.

FIGURE 4.32
Fifth grader's reason for abandoning a book
Note. From original student writing, 1991. Copyright 1991 by Daniel Marcus. Reprinted by permission.

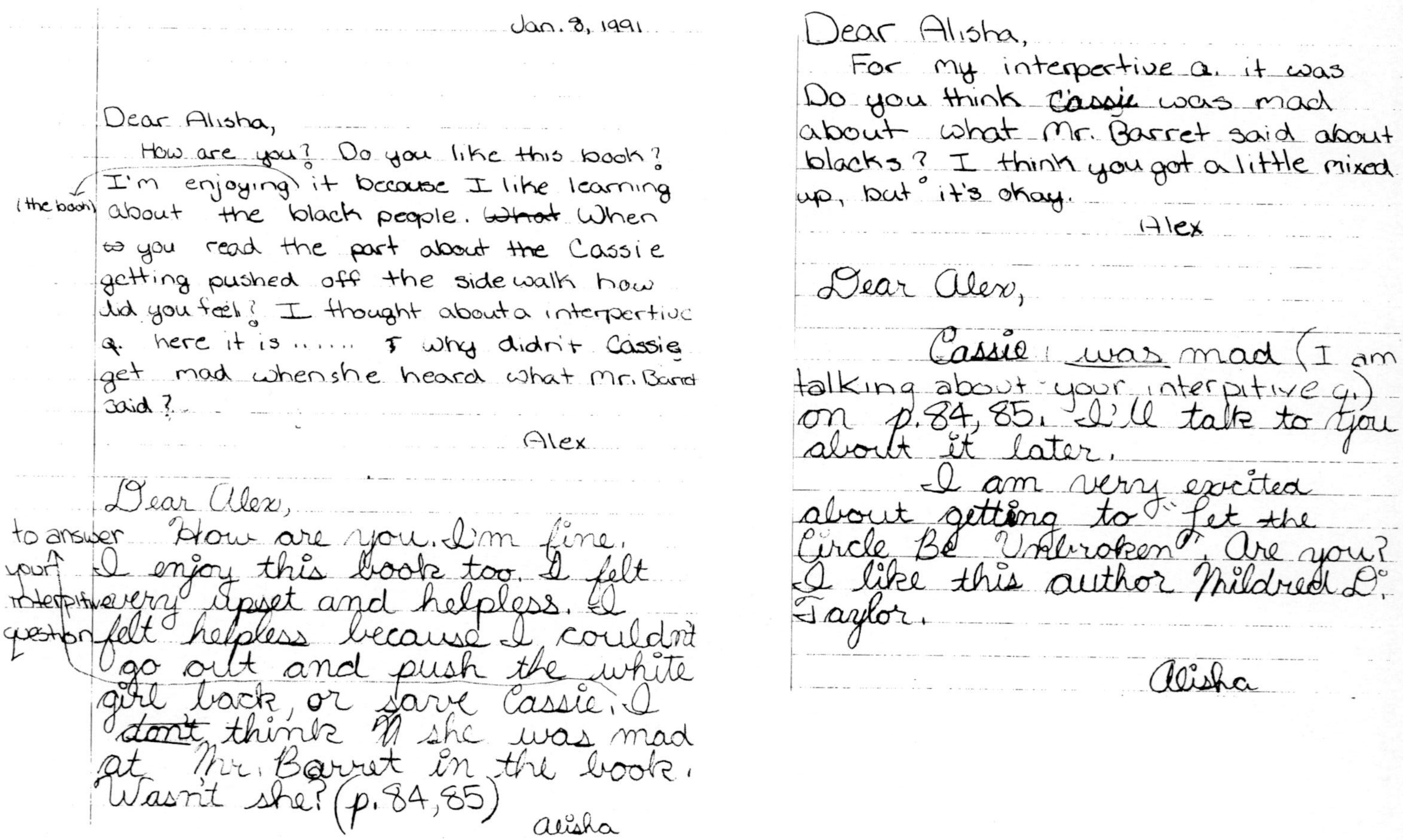

Jan. 3, 1991.

Dear Alisha,

How are you? Do you like this book? I'm enjoying it because I like learning about the black people. ~~What~~ When you read the part about the Cassie getting pushed off the side walk how did you feel? I thought about a interpretive q here it is..... & why didn't Cassie get mad when she heard what Mr. Barri said?

Alex

(the book)

Dear Alex,

to answer your How are you. I'm fine. I enjoy this book too. I felt interpretive just and helpless. I really felt helpless because I couldn't go out and push the white girl back or park Cassie. I don't think she was mad at Mr. Barret in the book. Wasn't she? (p. 84, 85)

Alisha

Dear Alisha,

For my interpretive q. it was Do you think Cassie was mad about what Mr. Barret said about blacks? I think you got a little mixed up, but it's okay.

Alex

Dear Alex,

Cassie was mad about your interpretive q. on p. 84, 85. I'll talk to you about it later.

I am very excited about getting to Let the Circle Be Unbroken? Are you? I like this author Mildred D. Taylor.

Alisha

FIGURE 4.33

Fifth grade letter exchange over *Roll of Thunder, Hear My Cry* (Taylor, 1976)

Note. From original student writing, 1991. Copyright 1991 by Alisha Bjerregaard and Alex Tucker. Reprinted by permission.

continue reading *Let the Circle Be Unbroken* (Taylor, 1981). Daniel gave solid reasons for his decision (see Figure 4.32).

Children who are reading the same book are encouraged to write letters to each other as they go along. Figure 4.33 shows an exchange between Alisha and Alex as they read *Roll of Thunder, Hear My Cry* (Taylor, 1976). Notice their reference to "interpretive questions." Jean models higher level questions in their literature groups and encourages the children to pose questions to their group that require interpretation and not mere regurgitation. She has developed a set of guidelines for children to use when preparing discussion questions for their group meetings (see Figure 4.34).

Jean and some colleagues in her system meet regularly to share what they are doing with literature-based reading. Currently, they are developing a model to describe their theme-based, reading-writing-through-literature program. Figure 4.35 illustrates how such a program might be planned. Note that they start with picture books in September to teach specific literature and language lessons, proceed through playing with language (poetry), appreciating others (Black history), reaching out (environmental issues), and end up getting it together with fun, drama, memoirs (looking backward), and goals (looking forward). Several genres (picture books, poetry, fiction, and non-fiction) and many ways to respond to literature and learning (writing, discussing, drama, choral reading, puppetry, and art) are included in this emerging paradigm. Jean says that she could never go back to basals again: "What I am doing is energizing, potent, palpably alive and growing, and a joy to anticipate each day."

GRADE 6: A PROCESS-ORIENTED PHILOSOPHY

Like Beverly Pilchman and Jean DeSantis, sixth grade teacher Marianne Marino has been experimenting with reading-writing workshops for over a decade. Believing that children need exposure to a large collection of good books, time to read and write

---

CHARACTERISTICS OF GOOD QUESTIONS

You should have your own doubts about the answer to your question.

You are reasonably certain that your question is answerable from the text.

Your question should be specifically suited to the reading. If it could be asked of another book it is *too* general.

Your question should be clear to everyone. Everyone should not need to spend energy figuring out your question. Their energy should go into the answer.

You should care about your question.

Your questions should cause everyone to think deeply about the author's meaning.

FIGURE 4.34
Guidelines for questions
Note. From "Guidelines for Questions," 1991. Copyright 1991 by Jean DeSantis, Reprinted by permission.

FIGURE 4.35
Literature model,
1990–1991

Note. From "Literature Model," 1990–91. Copyright 1990 by Jean DeSantis. Reprinted by permission.

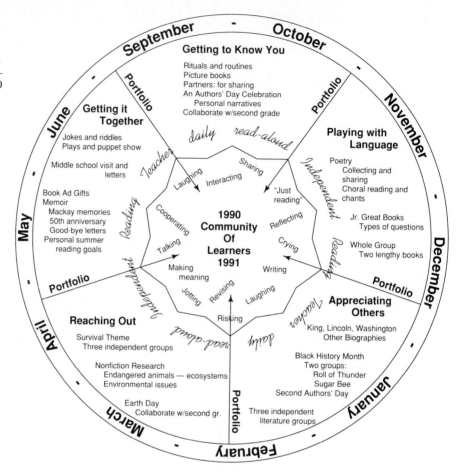

about books of their own selection, and opportunities to talk about books in a literate community, she invites her students to explore literature with her from the very first day of school (Marino, 1991).

Beginning with 15 books in the late 1970s, Marianne now has a class library of thousands of books: class sets, small-group sets, and a great variety of single titles. Examples of authors found in this growing collection include Lois Lowry, Katherine Paterson, and Ellen Conford, all favored by the girls; C.S. Lewis, Lloyd Alexander, H.G. Wells, and Gary Paulsen for the boys; and authors like William Sleator, Rosa Guy, Robert Cormier, Roald Dahl, and Paul Zindel, sought by all students. In addition to using district money that would have been spent on basals, Marianne has applied for grant money over the years to purchase these books. Several grants came from Lucy Calkins' Writing Project at Teachers College, Columbia, and a sizable grant came from the governor of New Jersey. She is always on the lookout for funding sources and claims many are available.

Her reading workshop follows a predictable pattern. Students read their chosen books for about half an hour. During that time Marianne circulates, much like Kathy Kelly, and confers reader to reader with several children. Because the desks are arranged in groups of 4 to 6 students, other children who had previously read a book often join in the discussion. Each day she visits all groups, directing her attention to at least one or two readers in each group.

The class then spends about 10 minutes writing. Because Marianne believes that children need to reflect on their reading in a personal way, she has them keep response journals. Also, the journal entries give the students a jumping-off point to begin their small-group discussions that follow.

Marianne's small response groups resemble Bev Pilchman's "literature circles" (Harste, Short, & Burke, 1988) in that the students run the groups themselves; they differ in that most of the time each student is reading a different book. One group, made up of one boy and two girls, has just started reading new books, so the focus quickly turns to "leads," or how the authors begin their stories to "pull in" the reader. An Asian girl who has begun *The Star Fisher* (Yep, 1991) says that the beginning reminded her of an old Chinese legend; she sensed that the main character, Joan Lee, would probably be caught between new and old cultures. Another girl notes that the new Katherine Paterson novel, *Lyddie* (1991), opens with the sad picture of a fatherless family in Vermont in the 1800s; she feels a sense of foreboding for young Lyddie. The boy in the group shares that a flashback of a shipwreck introduces 11-year-old Tony, the main character in *Windcatcher* (Avi, 1991). This young reader knows there is a "good read" in store for him. The discussion, which lasts about 10 minutes, is on a very high level, with students going back and forth in their books to document their observations.

Next the class assembles on the carpet in the reading corner to share what went on in the small groups. Marianne acts as facilitator, asking each group to report informally; often the focus from one group becomes the focus for the large group. Two topics emerge on this day—leads and flashbacks. Since most readers seem to relate more to the "leads" focus, this becomes the major topic for the day. Marianne believes that both group sessions are important because they help students to confirm or question what they have written in their journals and they supply opportunities for dynamic interaction between readers, texts, and other readers.

Marianne brings closure to the group session by directing the children's attention to a new bulletin board she is setting up about the author, Ezra Jack Keats. In the Writer's Center, she has gathered several books, pictures, and articles about Keats, and carries over the "lead" focus by reading aloud the beginning pages of *The Snowy Day* (1962).

In addition to author studies, Marianne plans five genre studies for the year. In September she begins with realistic fiction because that's where children can make the best connections with their own lives. Then she does folklore, poetry, and historical fiction, ending up the year with the short story because the students will be moving on to the junior high the next year where literature study usually begins with the short story.

And her students are well prepared for junior high English. One of us, who was serving as a consultant to Marianne's school district, was observing a literature session in a seventh grade English class. As the class broke into groups to discuss a piece of literature under study, it became obvious that one of the groups was being expertly guided by one boy. When asked how he had become so skillful, he confided that he had come from Mrs. Marino's sixth grade, "We really learned how to read, write, and talk about books with Mrs. Marino. You can always tell which guys were in her class."

Since her classes are self-contained and heterogeneously grouped, Marianne always has a wide range of readers. She doesn't consider this a problem because students select their own books within the genre or author under study. By reading aloud, often beginning with picture books that can be read and discussed within one litera-ture session, she models for the chidren how to select books. If students pick up books that are too difficult or beyond their experience, they soon discontinue reading and look for something else. Her children are mostly guided by the recommendations of peers, or they get to know authors and search for other books by them, or they get into a specific genre like science fiction and read only that type for a while. She feels that children will develop the ability to make appropriate choices if there is a large collection of books, a program that focuses on authors and genres, and a teacher who models the literature experience regularly.

Figure 4.36 shows all the components of Marianne's reading workshop. Some of the components that we haven't yet described are dialogue journals and mini-lessons. Similar to Kathy Kelly's class, children are encouraged to write letters to each other and to her in a dialogue journal; she responds to each child at least once a week. Often at the beginning or end of a reading workshop, Marianne will present a short, direct mini-lesson on some reading-writing skill such as webbing main and subordi-nate ideas, recognizing subplots, or interpreting a title. Her model shows how all components revolve around the teacher as facilitator.

One question that other teachers often ask Marianne is, "How do your students do on standardized tests?" She readily answers that they do very well, with children at all levels showing considerable growth. One year her principal wondered if a lit-erature approach would work with her sixth graders whose test scores were not as high as those of previous classes. She assured him that they would grow as readers and writers in her usual program; and they did, scoring at the top of all the sixth grades in the district at the end of the year.

Under the terms of the New Jersey governor's grant, her program was evaluated with an instrument used in the National Assessment of Educational Progress in 1979–80, and the results were compared with those of the national sample. While the 13-year-olds in the national sample mainly summarized after reading, Marianne's sixth graders were described as "critical readers and thinkers who are no longer satisfied with just understanding the story but want to dig deeper, . . . responding to what and how the author writes and at the same time making the reading-writing connec-tion" (see evaluation by Queenan in Marino, 1986).

Although Marianne has been teaching in this manner for over a decade, she is quick to tell observers that she is never satisfied. Although she is generally pleased with her results, she is always trying to improve, to add "a new twist." She describes her lit-

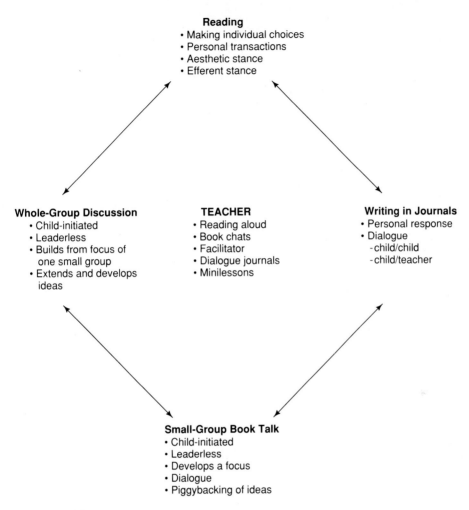

FIGURE 4.36

Components of reading workshop for sixth grade students

Note. From "Components of Reading Workshop," 1991. Copyright 1991 by Marianne Marino. Reprinted by permission.

erature-based, process-oriented teaching as a philosophy, a way of looking at how readers and writers develop in a literature-rich environment, rather than as a method of teaching.

SUMMARY

The fifth and sixth grade teachers in this section all model many literary behaviors for their students. They read with them and to them, show them how to talk about books, and encourage personal response via writing (journals, letters, and guide sheets) and

*Reading Aloud

*Shared Book Reading

*Reading Workshop
 Teacher-selected books for guided reading
 Student-selected books for independent reading
 Response via writing, art, drama, or other modes

*Writing Workshop

*Mini-lessons on skills

*Portfolio Assessment

FIGURE 4.37
Common features of a literature-based approach

small- and large-group sharing. They teach their district curriculum through mini-lessons built around literature, and they use both formal and informal assessment measures to evaluate progress.

Common Features of a Literature-Only Approach

From the previous descriptions of literature-based classrooms, you can see that no one model is universally followed. But common features can be found in all, and these are highlighted in Figure 4.37 and discussed in the following sections.

READING ALOUD

Reading aloud is a time when the teacher orally reads to the entire class from a book or other interesting resource. Each day the teacher reads aloud selected pieces of literature. Primary teachers usually read picture books or chapter books that interest their children or that develop a theme but are too difficult for students to read on their own. In the mid- and upper-elementary grades, teachers may read aloud excerpts to introduce new books as did Kathy Kelly or read whole books chapter by chapter in a to-be-continued fashion. As Marianne Marino did, these teachers may also read aloud picture books to offer models of good writing in condensed form and to demonstrate literary elements such as leads, plot, and resolution. Sometimes reading aloud is just a special time when teacher and students are wrapped between the pages of a good book. (See Chapter 3 for a detailed rationale for reading aloud.)

SHARED BOOK READING

Shared book reading differs from reading aloud in that all involved can see the text as the teacher reads. For novices and experimenters in the early primary grades, shared reading means big books and charts of poems, songs, and LEA stories as children read along following the print (McGee & Richgels, 1990). Students learn the conventions of print such as going left-to-right along a line; what letters, words, and sentences are; what punctuation does; and that reading is related to oral language and must make sense. (See Chapter 3 for a more detailed description of shared reading with beginners.)

For more accomplished readers, shared reading means reading aloud as students follow in individual copies of the book. When teachers read, they can model good oral reading and occasionally point out something special such as literary language, writing style, unusual vocabulary, or interesting illustrations. When students read parts in book-in-hand theater such as we saw in Bev Pilchman's class, they get the opportunity to dramatize and read for an audience.

READING WORKSHOP

Reading workshop is a place to learn a craft by experimenting with it. In reading workshop, students learn how to read by working with texts of all kinds (Atwell, 1987; Hansen, 1987). Time is spent reading, responding, and sharing. Materials can be teacher-selected or self-selected.

TEACHER-SELECTED READING

Teacher-Selected Reading can take two forms, with either the whole class or small groups reading the same book with teacher guidance. (See Chapter 3 for a discussion of how teachers guide reading with activities before, during, and after reading). Often, when the whole class reads the same book, a schedule of pages to be read each day is established; pre-reading predictions/questions are raised and confirmed/answered as the story unfolds. Through mini-lessons, the teacher can focus on specific skills appropriate for the group and demonstrated well by the text. For example, Bev Pilchman uses *The Mixed-Up Files* especially to teach students how to read and write dialogue.

Early in the year both Sue Boyd and Jean DeSantis assign children to small groups that read the same book. They match children to books they can read with teacher and peer support. Children may read individually or in pairs and then join others who are reading the same book for sharing responses. Later in the year, children may be given a choice among a group of books selected by the teacher by genre or author; in this mode, they form their own small groups but read the type of literature the teacher wants to introduce. Guided reading can be done via teacher-prepared discussion questions or activity sheets such as those used by Jean DeSantis and Sue Boyd.

SELF-SELECTED READING

Self-Selected Reading is the approach taken by Kathy Kelly and Marianne Marino for their reading workshops. Students choose from a well-stocked classroom library, the school media center, or the town library. They read during reading workshop, SSR time, and at home, responding to their books in various kinds of journals. Daily sharing in small and large groups completes their literature cycle.

Often teachers use a combination of teacher-selected and self-selected reading, going from one mode to the other. Or, like Bev, Sheila, Jean, and Sue Boyd, they select class or group books and have students reading self-selected titles simultaneously. All literature-based teachers have students reading self-selected books when they read independently during SSR time in school and for at-home reading. (See the benefits of independent reading of self-selected books in Chapter 3.)

RESPONSE TO LITERATURE

Response to Literature is an important part of every reading workshop, and the response journal appears to be the most frequently used form. After a period of silent reading, children write what they like/dislike, what they have learned, or what they question about the text. Sometimes these journal entries are just shared with other students, or they are read by the teacher on a regularly scheduled basis. Also, they may be dialogue journals in which teacher and students talk back and forth about the literary experience. Another response form is the literary letter (Atwell, 1987) in which students write to the teacher or to their classmates about the book or about their feelings as they read. Kathy Kelly uses this approach with her fourth graders.

As we saw with Sheila Hackett and Janice Markovic, children can often respond through art and dramatics. They can draw pictures, fashion puppets, and act out favorite parts. Janice's kindergarteners love to go through *Noisy Nora* behind stick puppets as others read the text. Sheila's first graders have props to act out *Mrs. Wishy-washy* (Cowley, 1980/1990).

Both beginning and accomplished readers are encouraged to engage in discussion groups about literature. Using their logs, share sheets, or pictures as prompts, they talk about a text all have read or about different books in progress. Sometimes teachers lead the groups, but ultimately the students themselves take over responsibility for their own literature response groups or "literature circles" (Harste, Short, & Burke, 1988).

For students to reconstruct their own meanings, they need to respond through talk, writing, drama, and the arts. Routman (1991) says, "The way students are asked to respond to literature in school influences their development as readers, writers, and thinkers as well as their enjoyment of literature" (p. 133).

WRITING WORKSHOP

In the same way that children learn to read by reading in reading workshop, they learn to write by experimenting with composing in a writing workshop. In **writing workshop** students write personal narrative, memoir, fiction, nonfiction, and other genres in a hands-on atmosphere in which teacher and peers receive drafts and give feedback to young authors who revise accordingly (Calkins, 1986 & 1990; Graves, 1983). In editing conferences with the teacher, they learn mechanical skills such as spelling, grammar, and punctuation as they edit selected pieces for publication in individual books or class collections. Also, in the course of publishing they gain valuable insights about text layout as they decide on pictures to illustrate a text and the placement of text on a page to achieve desired effects. They experience the thrill of authorship and begin to understand the reader-writer relationship when they share their work with peers, parents, siblings, and others rather than writing only for the teacher. Their bulging writing folders attest to their efforts, thinking, accomplishments, and what Graves (1991) calls "evidence of existence." He writes:

> In a time of uprootedness within families and communities, where there is little concrete evidence of our own creations, a folder of writing—a collection of your own expression and ideas—becomes a baseline for personal reference.
>
> "History" begins the moment I put a word on paper. . . . (Graves, 1991, p. 61)

The students in these literature-based, process-oriented classrooms are learning what writing can do for them and are gaining a sense of history about themselves.

MINI-LESSONS

According to Calkins (1986), a **mini-lesson** is a short, focused piece of direct instruction usually presented to the whole group. Often it occurs at the beginning of a workshop (reading and writing) and grows out of some need identified by the teacher or a curriculum item that must be taught. For instance, Sue Corrado gave a mini-lesson on using the context in reading because she knew students would be encountering many unusual words in their author study on William Steig; Bev Pilchman planned a mini-lesson to teach verbs in her writing workshop so that students would be familiar with a grammatical construct listed for the fifth grade curriculum and, in a more practical vein, be able to use interesting verbs in their written compositions. In a primary class a typical mini-lesson might focus on a particular sound-symbol relationship. For example, to focus on the letter *b,* Sheila Hackett uses the nursery rhyme, "Little Boy Blue Come Blow Your Horn."

While these common features (reading and writing workshop, shared reading, response to reading, and mini-lessons) are found in most literature-based programs, the actual day-to-day implementation differs widely. While some primary teachers may use some commercial materials such as *Language Arts Phonics* (Botel & Seaver, 1985) for work on skills, most use only literature and writing to implement their literacy program. In the middle grades teachers find that a literature approach makes sense because of the wide range of children's reading interests and abilities (May, 1990). Using genre, author, and theme studies permits teachers to unify the focus of their workshops and to use the mini-lesson format to teach specifics such as comprehension strategies and literary elements. With hundreds of new children's books being published each year to augment the thousands already in print, teachers are never hampered by a lack of materials. In fact, one teacher remarked that she could understand why basal readers were developed in the 19th century when books were scarce and teachers didn't know very much about literature and teaching, but she couldn't understand why today's teachers, who are well educated in general and in teaching specifically, would want to use a restricted, programmatic approach instead of the world of children's literature.

PORTFOLIO ASSESSMENT

Teachers who use literature and writing as the basis for their literacy programs generally prefer to keep portfolios of dated samples of children's work (responses to reading and original compositions) rather than to test discrete skills. However, their students usually have to participate in district-wide annual tests. How do they perform? Two administrators who encourage "whole literacy" programs told us that their students do about the same on standardized reading tests as did their counterparts of the past who had been taught by basal reading systems (Feeley, 1991a, b). Traditionally, these districts had always scored in the upper percentiles. But, these administrators were quick to add that their present students read and write much more than did students of the past, and they point to the children's portfolios to support this change. Routman (1988) reports that students in her urban district made noticeable gains on standardized tests and that they, too, read much more when her teachers made their "transition."

Literature-based, process-oriented teachers can usually document growth in many more ways than a score on a particular test. They can go to portfolios to show real evidence such as writing samples, number and kinds of books read with sample response sheets, taped samples of oral reading, observational notes, and checklists of skills mastered or being worked on. Sue Meldonian finds that dated audiotapes of her first graders' reading aloud were a valuable benchmark. Sue Boyd and Kathy Kelly involve their students in their own evaluations. Kathy has her students set goals and assess how well they have met them. All of these teachers believe that assessment is an ongoing process and keep portfolios to help paint a picture of their developing readers and writers. (See Chapter 3 for other ideas on what can go into portfolios.)

Just as interested educators and parents ask administrators and teachers in process-oriented, literature-based literacy programs how their students perform on standardized tests, we are often asked what the research literature says about these approaches. In the section that follows we will share some of our findings.

What the Research Says

In an ambitious review of many aspects of the research on learning to read through children's books, Tunnell and Jacobs (1989) conclude that a literature approach is certainly as effective as basal readers in assessing achievement via standardized test scores. From Holdaway's (1982) work on shared reading in New Zealand that led to a totally literature-based reading curriculum in that country with the highest literacy rate in the English-speaking world, to the findings of the Ohio Reading Recovery program (Boehnlein, 1987) which is based on the New Zealand model, Tunnell and Jacobs cite study after study that attest to demonstrated success for literature-based reading. The Reading Recovery studies show that 90% of the first graders whose pretest scores were in the lowest percentiles of their classes finished the 20-week program in the average or above average percentiles and never needed remediation again. Besides research that shows that literature-based approaches work for special populations such as Limited English Proficient, "at-risk" first-graders and older, "stalled" readers, Tunnell and Jacobs include studies of students in the mainstream showing that literature-based programs resulted in increased interest in reading and improved attitudes toward reading.

A growing number of small studies also supports facets of literature-based, process-oriented programs. Gunderson and Shapiro (1988) compared the vocabulary produced by first graders in a whole language classroom with the vocabulary they would have encountered in a popular basal reading series. They found that their young readers and writers produced 18 times the number of words found in the basals!

Ribowsky (1986) examined the effects of a whole language approach on the emergent literacy of 53 kindergarteners. The experimental group (whole language) followed a typical shared reading program (Holdaway, 1982) with much reading together of enlarged texts of stories, poems, chants, and songs. Along with many expressive art and drama activities, the children also regularly engaged in independent reading and writing. A comparison group was introduced to reading through a basal reading program that emphasized decoding. According to statistical procedures done on several emergent literacy factors, the whole language group made significantly greater gains than did the basal group. It was concluded that a whole language approach was more effective than a code emphasis published program for fostering emergent literacy in kindergarten.

Trachtenburg and Ferruggia (1989) used literature in shared reading activities with a "transitional" first grade. These still emerging readers and writers learned a sight vocabulary and decoding strategies through enlarged versions of favorite books such as *Corduroy* (Freeman, 1968). Significant gains were made from pre- to post-testing with the Comprehensive Tests of Basic Skills. These teacher-researchers say, "The more than double Normal Curve Equivalent gain in word attack strongly supports the whole to part instructional rationale. We trust it will prompt interested *wholists* to pursue our design" (p. 285).

Hiebert, Mervar, and Person (1990) compared the book selection strategies used in libraries by second graders in literature-based and textbook-based classrooms. While the literature children gave elaborate reasons for their selections (looked for specific authors, illustrators, genres, or topics), textbook children tended to respond simply, saying they looked for "interesting" books or books with "good pictures." Clearly, their classroom environments affected the way that these students selected books to read on their own.

This study also examined the behaviors of the less able readers, assessing word recognition strategies via interviews. The less able children from textbook classes, who demonstrated limited word recognition strategies such as "sound it out" or "ask someone," generally selected books that were one grade level higher than those chosen by their counterparts in literature classes. On the other hand, those in the literature classes, who also demonstrated more varied word recognition strategies, more often selected books that were appropriate for their reading ability and thus would be more apt to read the books chosen. The researchers conclude, "This combination of difficult books and few reading strategies probably contributes to the vicious cycle of infrequent reading and little success that characterizes less able readers" (p. 760).

Strickland, Dillon, Funkhouser, Glick, and Rogers (1989) examined the nature and quality of classroom dialogue during literature response groups in grades one, two, four, and six. These teacher-researchers looked at the functions of language, the content of the talk, and evidence of reading comprehension as children met to discuss books. The children demonstrated a growing competence in linguistic tasks such as organizing information, adjusting speech to audience and purpose, being aware of differing points of view, and sensitivity to differences between speakers' information and the backgrounds of the audience.

As for the content of the discussions, students in literature-based classrooms talked about the story line or topics of their books, the authors and their craft, literary elements (characters, setting, plot), and the relationship of the books to their own lives. It is easy to see why children in classrooms like these were more knowledgeable about selecting books as seen in the Hiebert et al. (1990) study.

Students in the Strickland et al. (1989) study also showed that they were applying a variety of comprehension strategies as they discussed their books. They were observed recalling facts and details, distinguishing between fact and fantasy, noting cause and effect relationships, comparing and contrasting, predicting and confirming, and monitoring their own comprehension. The findings supported the teachers' intuition and informal observations that literature response groups not only support literacy development but also provide an excellent vehicle for learning in general.

One of the best sources for research support that we have found is a comprehensive overview report on whole language written by Diane Stephens for the **Center for the Study of Reading**. Stephens (1991) first gives a brief history of whole language, then describes its philosophy about learning and teaching, and finally annotates 38 pieces of research that she characterizes as either case studies of individual children or descriptive and comparative classroom studies. Of the 38 studies, only seven are concerned with children above grade two; 15 address the literacy development of "at-risk" children. Stephens points out that only one study in her report was done before 1980 and 32 were conducted since 1985. As you can see, whole language is a new—but promising—area for research. We recommend this report as a starting place for educators who are searching for empirical studies on whole language.

While not an exhaustive report, Stephens's literature review of studies with a variety of designs and objectives shows that a growing body of research supports the efficacy of literature-based, whole language literacy programs.

Moving Toward a Literature-Based Program

Just as no one model exists for teaching reading and writing through literature or for designing research projects to evaluate literature-based programs, there is no one way that teachers adopt this approach. As Marianne Marino points out, "It's more of a philosophy of teaching than it is a method. If you believe that one learns to read and write by reading and writing with others in a community of language learners, then you want to plan your program for your students around literature that will appeal to them. You don't want to implement a program put together by some publisher who doesn't know you or your students and who has ordained a particular sequence of skills to be taught whether or not your children need them, or, in fact, whether or not the skills are even important!"

More than a decade ago Marianne studied with Don Graves, Nancie Atwell, and Mary Ellen Giacobbe at Martha's Vineyard when the process approach was just beginning. Later she worked with Lucy Calkins at Teachers College, Columbia, and is now pursuing a doctorate at New York University. Janice Markovic and Sheila Hackett also attended workshops and conferences offered by the Teachers College Writing Project and had their ideas validated through their graduate work at William Paterson College.

Sue Meldonian and Sue Corrado were also influenced by their graduate studies and were able to apply their philosophy when they began to teach in a district that was trying to promote "whole literacy." With Sue Boyd, a move to a new district was the impetus for her change. Fortunately, she had a colleague like Jean DeSantis and other area teachers who were in a network tied to a local university to help her set up her literature-based second grade.

Kathy Kelly acknowledges Nancie Atwell as the source of her approach. Kathy never worked with Atwell; all she did was read her book, *In the Middle,* and adapt her "reading and writing around the dining room table" model. Graves (1991) says that reading can move you to take action; this certainly was the case with Kathy.

Betsy and Cindy, the two primary teachers from Ohio, come out of a rich heritage of informal education from Froebel, Dewey, and Piaget of the past to Graves, Goodman, Clay, and other current process-oriented educators. Having done their graduate work at The Ohio State University, they espouse learning by doing, plus giving children sustained time, choice, and feedback in a literate community. In essence, these teachers and their counterparts all over the country are taking their literacy programs back from the textbook publishers and making them their own.

GETTING STARTED

While we can identify the diverse ways that teachers approach literature-based programs, some common threads do run through their stories. They are dissatisfied with the status quo reliance on published basals and workbooks that they feel are stultifying and boring and producing students who are bored and turned off to reading and writing. They want not only to teach children to read but also to teach them to enjoy reading, and they feel that literature is the only way to encourage this growth. We must admit that we experienced a feeling of joy when we visited literature-based classrooms; everyone seemed to be enjoying stories and sharing easily. This spirit was in stark contrast to one we encountered in a strict basal reader school: a boy who had several books in his desk left them to go to another room to be instructed in a higher level basal group. We asked him if he liked reading. He answered, "I hate reading [meaning reading class], but I love to read books."

Another common thread that is evident in these teachers' stories is their involvement in continuing education, either formally through colleges and universities or informally through their own professional reading and networking. This is the way we suggest you begin your own change process: become informed and knowledgeable about approaches that have worked for others. In addition to attending conferences and workshops, the easiest and most accessible route to change is to do some professional reading, and we will suggest some easy-to-read books that can get you started.

PRIMARILY FOR THE PRIMARY

Many sources are available for primary teachers. *Towards a Reading-Writing Classroom* (Butler & Turbill, 1987) is an easy-to-read source for beginners. After presenting a brief theoretical background, the authors describe how to set up a classroom in which children are immersed in print and involved in producing print from the start. *Transitions: From Literature to Literacy* (Routman, 1988) tells how the author, a reading teacher in an urban school, encouraged teachers in grades one to three to move from basals to a literature-based program. Routman gives such practical ideas and a complete list of children's books and instructional resources that teachers report they can easily use this book as a guide to setting up their own programs.

Two new, very helpful books are *Real Books for Real Reading* by two Canadian primary teachers, Linda Hart-Hewins and Jan Wells (1990), and *Children Learning Through Literature: A Teacher-Researcher Study* by a first grade teacher, June McConaghy (1990). Hart-Hewins and Wells show you how to select books for ages and stages, how to organize your classroom, and how the components (shared reading, individual reading, buddy reading, and writing) of their reading-writing program work. McConaghy shows you exactly how she created a first grade literature-based program for reading, writing, and oral language. In the Foreword to McConaghy's book, David Dillon says, "June challenges us to consider the link between children's early literacy experiences with story and becoming an independent, avid, and critical reader and writer. Can one become such a reader and writer without them?" p. ix.

A new edition of an old favorite, *Using Literature with Young Children* (Coody, 1992), is a wonderful resource for literature-based teachers. Besides suggesting titles and ideas for read-alouds and storytelling, Betty Coody offers chapters on using literature for dramatization, poetry, art, celebrating holidays, and bibliotherapy. A really unique chapter, "Better Homes and Kindergartens Cookbook," presents books that lead to cooking activities.

Sources for All Levels

The books discussed in this section are for teachers of all grades interested in making a change. Don Graves' new book, *Build a Literate Classroom* (1991), is written to get you thinking about your own teaching and how you can move into a process-oriented, literature-based approach by initiating a series of actions such as abolishing reading groups and restructuring your classroom as a literate community. His ideas were generated from years of working with teachers in transition and have all been validated by their experiences. Also, he acknowledges the role played by Jane Hansen, his colleague at the University of New Hampshire, and co-researcher in the Mast Way Elementary School project that documented a school in transition. Hansen's book, *When Writers Read* (1987), is another great source for elementary school classroom teachers, reading teachers, and administrators.

Although written about her experiences teaching seventh and eighth graders, Nancie Atwell's book, *In the Middle: Writing, Reading, and Learning with Adolescents* (1987), is one of the most frequently cited sources by elementary teachers like Kathy Kelly. They find her clearly described workshop model and many sample forms easy to adapt. One principal in an urban school used this book as a blueprint for change with his third, fourth, and fifth grade teachers (Feeley, 1991a). *Process Reading and Writing: A Literature-Based Approach* (Feeley, Strickland, & Wepner, 1991) is an edited collection of teachers' and administrators' stories about their literary programs, covering grades one through eight and special populations found in the elementary school. Written for and by teachers, it can provide models for bringing about and sustaining change. In her new book *Invitations: Changing as Teachers and Learners K–12,* Regie Routman (1991) picks up where her first book (*Transitions*, 1988) left off. While *Transitions* was targeted for primary teachers, this book is a very complete and well-organized resource for teachers at all levels who want to move away from overly structured, programmatic approaches to using literature and writing. Donna Norton's new book, *The Impact of Literature-Based Reading* (1992), is especially helpful for teachers who have had little background in literature. After describing how to develop a literature-based program, she presents in-depth chapters on literary elements such as characterization, plot, and theme, and chapters on understanding major genres such as folklore, fantasy, and realistic fiction.

For those teachers who have not yet been exposed to the writing process literature, we recommend Don Graves' *Writing: Teachers and Children at Work* (1983), Lucy Calkins' *The Art of Teaching Writing* (1986), and *Classroom Strategies that Work: An Elementary Teacher's Guide to Process Writing* (Nathan, Temple, Juntunen, & Temple, 1988). Reading any one of these books will give you an idea of how to teach writing through a workshop approach.

MOVING FORWARD

While you are building your own knowledge of how to teach reading and writing through literature, you can start your transition by doing what was suggested in Chapter 3. Begin to build your resources by accumulating a classroom library of sets of books (some for a whole class and some for small groups) and numerous individual titles appropriate for your students. Start to schedule some of the suggested literature activities such as reading aloud, shared reading, guided reading, response to reading, independent reading, and at-home reading and try them out as you are reading the professional literature. You will be learning and experimenting as you go along.

Don Graves (1991) suggests you get a friend or colleague to experiment with you so you can talk out problems and share successes. If you are fortunate enough to have teachers in your school or district who have literature-based programs, ask to spend some time in their classrooms so you can observe how they deal with organization, resources, the curriculum, and evaluation, all "hot topics" in the current literature. If you would rather go outside your district, you can probably find exemplary class-rooms by calling the education department of your local college or university; most keep a list of demonstration sites in the area. To do this, you will probably have to consult with your principal. Be prepared to discuss the advantages of literature-based reading so that your principal will know that you are serious and knowledgeable. Most of the time, administrators welcome teachers who are interested in trying new approaches and will support their efforts. Share your observations with your admin-istrators and with other teachers; everyone likes a team player.

Once you get started set up a network with other interested teachers or join one already operating in your area. Teachers making change need support, and the best kind of support comes from other teachers also engaged in pioneering efforts. Net-work sharing provides the most fertile ground for growth. Most of the teachers de-scribed in this chapter are members of networks, for example, while Sue Meldonian and Sue Corrado network within their district (as do Sue Boyd and Jean DeSantis), others, such as Sheila Hackett and Marianne Marino, have joined college or university networks.

Concluding Remarks

To summarize, if you are not happy with a basal reader approach and want to use children's books to teach reading and writing:

- Become knowledgeable by reading a few sources from the professional literature and attending conferences sponsored by colleges or universities and professional organizations such as the International Reading Association and the National Council of Teachers of English.
- Start building a classroom library of individual titles and sets of trade books.
- Begin to introduce literature activities into your present program, for example, reading aloud, shared reading, guided reading, response to reading, independent reading, and at-home reading (see Chapter 3).
- Consult with your administrators to enlist their support.
- Visit classrooms with literature-based programs to observe firsthand.
- Try to enlist at least one other teacher to experiment with you.

- Eventually start or join a network of teachers who share your philosophy and exchange ideas on a regular basis.

Although these suggestions will get you started and keep you going, they only scratch the surface. Your imagination will become more and more fertile as you internalize the principles of process teaching, let go of the basal as the mainstay of your program, and develop your own approach to using literature as "the content of your literacy program." Then you can move easily into reading workshop, writing workshop, mini-lessons for teaching skills, and portfolios to augment assessment. The pay-off comes when you see your students grow into readers and writers who are becoming literate through literature and learning to love and appreciate reading at the same time.

Questions for Discussion

1. What is your teaching philosophy? Do you agree more with Skinner and the behaviorists who break learning down into discrete skills to be taught by drill and practice, or do you align yourself with Dewey and Piaget who espouse "learning by doing"? What are the implications of your philosophy for literacy learning?
2. What do you remember about being taught to write? Where did your topics originate? What happened to your compositions? How do you feel about writing now? Compare what happened to you with what goes on in a writing workshop. Which approach do you prefer?
3. Which of the teachers described in this chapter have developed programs that appeal to you? Why? Which programs do you find difficult to accept? Why?
4. What do you remember about being taught to read? How did you feel about learning to read? What books can you remember reading in elementary school? Which was your favorite? Why?
5. What book(s) have you read recently? How many books do you read a month? a year? What else do you read?

Application Activities

1. Suppose you and some colleagues would like to use literature in your literacy programs, and your principal tells you that you must first present a statement justifying the approach. Write a rationale for using literature that you might submit to back up your request.
2. Read one professional book suggested in this chapter and list the new ideas you learn from it. Which of these new ideas could you see yourself implementing in your classroom?
3. Survey your class (or any class available to you) to find out how the students feel

about reading. Use the "Reading Survey" form at the end of these activities or devise one of your own.

4. Conduct a similar survey about writing. Use the "Writing Survey" form at the end of these activities or one of your own.

5. Review the suggestions for moving into literature-based literacy programs and plan a course of action for yourself. Write out the steps you will follow, being specific about such items as the books you will read and the places you will visit. If there is time, begin your quest, keeping a diary of your responses to the activities you plan for yourself.

READING SURVEY

NAME: _____ DATE: _____

1. How much do you like to read? (circle one) Really love it

   It's O.K.

   Maybe

   Don't like it

2. What are your favorite books? _____

   _____

3. Who are your favorite authors? _____

   _____

After tallying student responses, decide what their attitudes are. How do their attitudes reflect the way they are taught to read? What are the implications?

WRITING SURVEY

NAME: _____   DATE: _____

1. How much do you like to write? (circle one) Really love it

It's O.K.

Maybe

Don't like it

2. How often do you write the following? (check one for each selection)

	Very Often	Often	Sometimes	Not at all
books				
letters				
stories				
poems				
responses to reading				
reports				
journals				
other (write in)				

After tallying students' responses, what can you say about these young writers? How are they learning to write? Is there a relationship between how they are taught and their attitudes towards writing? What are the implications?

References

Atwell, N. (1987). *In the middle: Writing, reading, and learning with adolescents*. Portsmouth, NH: Heinemann.

Boehnlein, M. (March, 1987). Reading intervention for high risk first graders. *Educational Leadership, 44,* 32–37.

Botel, M., & Seaver, J. (1985). *Language arts phonics*. New York: Scholastic.

Butler, A., & Turbill, J. (1987). *Toward a reading-writing classroom*. Portsmouth, NH: Heinemann.

Calkins, L. M. (1986). *The art of teaching writing*. Portsmouth, NH: Heinemann.

Calkins, L. M. (1990). *Living between the lines*. Portsmouth, NH: Heinemann.

Chomsky, C. (February, 1972). Stages in language development and reading exposure. *Harvard Educational Review, 42,* 1–33.

Combs, M. (1987). Modeling the reading process with enlarged texts. *The Reading Teacher, 41,* 422–426.

Coody, B. (1992). *Using literature with young children*. Dubuque, IA: William C. Brown.

Cullinan, B. (Ed.). (1987). *Children's literature in the reading program.* Newark, DE: International Reading Association.

Cullinan, B. E. (1989). *Literature and the child.* New York: Harcourt Brace Jovanovich.

De Ford, D. (1981). Literacy: Reading, writing, and other essentials. *Language Arts, 58,* 652–658.

Eckhoff, B. (1983). How reading affects children's writing. *Language Arts, 60,* 607–616.

Eeds, M., & Wells, O. (1989). Grand conversations: An exploration of meaning construction in literature study groups. *Research in the Teaching of English, 23,* 2–24.

Feeley, J. T. (1991a). An urban school becomes a community of readers and writers. In Feeley, J. T., Strickland, D. S., & Wepner, S. B. (Eds.), *Process reading and writing: A literature-based approach* (pp. 99–107). New York: Teachers College Press.

Feeley, J. T. (1991b). Transition in a suburban district: An interview with its superintendent. In Feeley, J. T., Strickland, D. S., & Wepner, S. B. (Eds.), *Process reading and writing: A literature-based approach* (pp. 244–250). New York: Teachers College Press.

Feeley, J. T., Strickland, D. S., & Wepner, S. B. (Eds.). (1991). *Process reading and writing: A literature-based approach.* New York: Teachers College Press.

Gentry, R. (1982). An analysis of developmental spelling in "GYNS AT WRK." *The Reading Teacher, 36,* 192–200.

Graves, D. H. (1983). *Writing: Teachers and children at work.* Portsmouth, NH: Heinemann.

Graves, D. H. (1991). *Build a literate classroom.* Portsmouth, NH: Heinemann.

Gunderson, L., & Shapiro, J. (1988). Whole language instruction: Writing in first grade. *The Reading Teacher, 41,* 430–437.

Hackett, S. (1990). *Stages of spelling development in first graders' writing.* Unpublished master's project. William Paterson College, Wayne, NJ.

Hansen, J. (1987). *When writers read.* Portsmouth, NH: Heinemann.

Harste, J., Short, K., & Burke, C. (1988). *Creating classrooms for authors: The reading-writing connection.* Portsmouth, NH: Heinemann.

Hart-Hewins, L., & Wells, J. (1990). *Real books for real reading.* Portsmouth, NH: Heinemann.

Heine, P. (1991). The power of related books. *The Reading Teacher, 45,* 75–77.

Hiebert, E. H., Mervar, K. B., & Person, D. (1990). Research directions: Children's selection of trade books in libraries and classrooms. *Language Arts, 67,* 758–763.

Holdaway, D. (1982). Shared book experience: Teaching reading using favorite books. *Theory into Practice, 21,* 293–300.

Huck, C. (1977). Literature as the content of reading. *Theory into Practice, 16,* 363–371.

Huck, C. S., Hepler, S., & Hickman, J. (1987). *Children's literature in the elementary school.* New York: Holt, Rinehart & Winston.

Klein, M. L., Peterson, S., & Simington, L. (1991). *Teaching reading in the elementary grades.* Boston: Allyn & Bacon.

Leu, D. J., & Kinzer, C. K. (1991). *Effective reading instruction, K–8.* New York: Macmillan.

Marino, M. (1986). *Reading process workshop: A literature-based, whole language approach to reading.* New Jersey Governor's Grant Program: New Jersey State Dept. of Education.

Marino, M. (1991). Weaving the threads: Creating a tapestry for learning through literature. In Feeley, J. T., Strickland, D. S., & Wepner, S. B. (Eds.), *Process reading and writing: A literature-based approach* (pp. 117–129). New York: Teachers College Press.

May, F. B. (1990). *Reading as communication.* Columbus, OH: Merrill.

McConaghy, J. (1990). *Children learning through literature: A teacher-researcher study.* Portsmouth, NH: Heinemann.

McGee, L. M., & Richgels, D. J. (1990). *Literacy's beginnings: Supporting young readers and writers.* Boston, MA: Allyn & Bacon.

Meldonian, S. (1991). *Attitudes toward portfolio assessment in a first grade whole language classroom.* Unpublished master's project. William Paterson College, Wayne, NJ.

Nathan, R., Temple, F., Juntunen, K., & Temple, C. (1988). *Classroom strategies that work: An elementary teacher's guide to process writing.* Portsmouth, NH: Heinemann.

Norton, D. (1992). *The impact of literature-based reading.* Columbus, OH: Merrill/Macmillan.

O'Brochta, E. P., & Weaver, C. P. (1991). Linking reading and writing through thematic teaching in a first grade. In Feeley, J. T., Strickland, D. S., & Wepner, S. B. (Eds.), *A literature-based, process approach to teaching reading and writing.* New York: Teachers College Press.

Ogle, D. (1986). K-W-L: A teaching model that develops active reading and expository text. *The Reading Teacher, 39,* 564–570.

Ribowsky, H. (1986). *The comparative effects of a code-emphasis approach and a whole language approach upon emergent literacy of kindergarten children.* Unpublished doctoral dissertation, New York University.

Routman, R. (1988). *Transitions: From literature to literacy.* Portsmouth, NH: Heinemann.

Routman, R. (1991). *Invitations: Changing as teachers and learners K–12.* Portsmouth, NH: Heinemann.

Smith, F. (1985). *Reading without nonsense* (2nd ed.). New York: Teachers College Press.

Stephens, D. (1991). *Toward an understanding of whole language* (Technical Report No. 524). Champaign, IL: Center for the Study of Reading.

Strickland, D., with Dillon, R., Funkhouser, L., Glick, M., & Rogers, C. (1989). Research currents: Classroom dialogue during literature response groups. *Language Arts, 66,* 192–200.

Strickland, D. S., & Feeley, J. T. (1985). Using children's concept of story to improve reading and writing. In T. Harris & E. Cooper (Eds.), *Reading, thinking, and concept development* (pp. 163–175). New York: College Board.

Strickland, D., & Hiebert, E. (Producers). (1990). *The reading-writing connection* (videotape). Champaign, IL: Center for the Study of Reading.

Trachtenburg, P., & Ferruggia, A. (1989). Big books from little voices: Reaching high risk beginning readers. *The Reading Teacher, 42,* 284–289.

Tunnell, M. O., & Jacobs, J. S. (1989). Using real books: Research findings on literature-based reading instruction. *The Reading Teacher, 42,* 228–237.

Trade Books Mentioned

Aardema, V. (1975). *Why mosquitoes buzz in people's ears.* New York: Dial.

Ackerman, K. (1988). *Song and dance man.* New York: Knopf.

Adler, D. (1981). *Cam Jensen and the mystery of the dinosaur bones.* New York: Dell Yearling.

Aiken, J. (1962). *The wolves of Willoughby Chase.* New York: Dell Yearling.

Alexander, M. (1971). *Nobody asked me if I wanted a baby sister.* New York: Dial.

Andrews, J. L. (1990). *Wolves.* New York: Trumpet Books.

Asch, F. (1984). *Skyfire.* Englewood Cliffs: Prentice-Hall.

Avi. (1991). *Windcatcher.* New York: Bradbury.

Babbitt, N. (1975). *Tuck everlasting.* New York: Farrar, Straus & Giroux.

Barrett, J., & Barrett, R. (1978). *Cloudy with a chance of meatballs.* New York: Macmillan Alladin Books.

Bauer, M. B. (1987). *On my honor.* New York: Dell.

Baum, F. (1900/1972). *The wizard of Oz.* Cleveland: World.

Belanger, C. (1988). *I like the rain.* Crystal Lake, IL: Rigby.

Blume, J. (1974). *Blubber.* New York: Bradbury.

Blume, J. (1980). *Superfudge.* New York: Dutton.

Blume, J. (1981). *Tiger eyes.* New York: Dell.

Brenner, B. (1970). *Faces.* New York: Dutton.

Bulla, C. (1971). *Squanto, friend of the Pilgrims.* New York: Scholastic.

Byars, B. (1968). *Midnight fox.* New York: Viking.

Cairns, S. (1988). *Oh No!* Crystal Lake, IL: Rigby.

Christopher, M. (1973). *Mystery coach.* Boston: Little, Brown.

Cleary, B. (1973). *Socks.* New York: Dell.

Cleary, B. (1981). *Ramona, the brave.* New York: Dell.

Cohen, M. (1967). *Will I have a friend?* New York: Macmillan.

Cohlori, T. (1990). *Dancing drum.* Vero Beach, FL: Watermill Press.

Collier, J. F., & Collier, C. (1974). *My brother Sam is dead.* New York: Four Winds Press.

Cowley, J. (1980/1990). *Mrs. Wishy-washy.* San Diego, CA: The Wright Group.

Crowe, R. L. (1976). *Clyde Monster.* New York: Dutton.

Danziger, P. (1989). *Everyone else's parents said yes.* New York: Delacorte.

Dixson, F. W. (1940s–1980s). *The Hardy boys mystery series.* New York: Grossett & Dunlap.

Eckert, A. W. (1971). *Incident at Hawk's Hill.* New York: Bantam.

Ets, M. H. (1963). *Gilberto and the wind.* New York: Viking.

Flournoy, V. (1985). *The patchwork quilt.* New York: Dial.

Forbes, E. (1946). *Johnny Tremain.* Boston: Houghton Mifflin.

Frank, A. (1952). *Diary of Anne Frank.* New York: Doubleday.

Freeman, D. (1968). *Corduroy.* New York: Viking.

Gardiner, J. (1980). *Stone fox.* New York: Crowell.

George, J. C. (1984). *One day on the Alpine tundra.* New York: Crowell.

Gipson, F. (1956). *Old Yeller.* New York: Scholastic.

Grifalconi, Ann. (1987). *Darkness and the butterfly.* Boston: Little, Brown.

Grumet, R. S. (1989). *The Lenapes.* New York: Chelsea House.

Hahn, M. D. (1989). *The doll in the garden.* New York: Clarion.

Hinton, S. E. (1967). *The outsiders.* New York: Dell.

Hoberman, M. A. (1978). *A house is a house for me.* New York: Scholastic.

Howe, D., & Howe, J. (1979). *Bunnicula.* New York: Avon-Camelot.

Hoyt-Goldsmith, D. (1991). *Pueblo storyteller.* New York: Holiday House.

Hugo, V. (1831/1965). *The hunchback of Notre Dame.* New York: Signet. New American Library.

Hunt, I. (1966). *Up a road slowly.* Chicago, IL: Follett.

Hurwitz, J. (1990). *The class president.* New York: Morrow Junior Books.

Hutchins, P. (1971). *Titch.* New York: Macmillan.

Hutchins, P. (1978). *Happy birthday, Sam.* New York: Greenwillow.

Hutchins, P. (1983). *You'll soon grow into them, Titch.* New York: Greenwillow.

Irvine. (1987). *Corky the seal.* New York: Scholastic.

Keats, E. J. (1962). *The snowy day.* New York: Viking.

Keegen, M. (1991). *Pueblo boy: Growing up in two worlds*. New York: Cobble Hill Books.

Kellogg, S. (1973). *The island of the Skog*. New York: Dial.

Konigsburg, E. L. (1967). *From the mixed-up files of Mrs. Basil E. Frankweiler*. New York: Dell.

Lionni, L. (1959). *Little blue and little yellow*. New York: Astor-Honor.

Lipsyte, R. (1967). *The contender*. New York: Harper & Row.

Lipsyte, R. (1982). *The summerboy*. New York: Harper & Row.

Lipsyte, R. (1991). *One fat summer*. New York: Harper-Collins.

Lofting, H. (1967). *Doctor Doolittle: A treasury*. New York: Lippincott.

Lowry, L. (1989). *Number the stars*. Boston, MA: Houghton Mifflin.

Margolies, B. A. (1990). *Rehema's journey: A visit in Tanzania*. New York: Scholastic.

Marshall, J. (1977). *Miss Nelson is missing*. Boston: Houghton Mifflin.

Marshall, J. (1980). *Troll country*. New York: Dial.

Martin, Ann M. (1980). *The babysitters' club*. New York: Scholastic.

Martin, B., & Archambault, J. (1989). *Chicka Chicka Boom Boom*. Allen, TX: DLM.

Mayer, M. (1968). *There's a nightmare in my closet*. New York: Dial.

McCloskey, R. (1941). *Make way for ducklings*. New York: Viking.

McCloskey, R. (1952). *One morning in Maine*. New York: Viking.

McKissack, P., & McKissack, F. (1990). *James Weldon Johnson*. Chicago: Children's Press.

Mendez, P. (1989). *The black snowman*. New York: Scholastic.

Milton, J. (1987). *Marching to freedom: The story of Martin Luther King*. New York: Dell.

Naidoo, B. (1986). *Journey to Jo'burg: A South African story*. New York: Lippincott.

Osinski, A. C. (1987). *The Chippewa*. Chicago: Children's Press.

Paterson, K. (1977). *Bridge to Terabithia*. New York: Dell.

Paterson, K. (1991). *Lyddie*. New York: Dutton.

Paulsen, G. (1987). *Hatchet*. New York: Bradbury Press.

Richter, C. (1953). *The light in the forest*. New York: Knopf.

Russo, M. (1988). *Only six more days*. New York: Greenwillow.

Schoenherr, J. (1991). *Bear*. New York: Philomel.

Scieszka, J. (1991). *Knights of the kitchen table*. New York: Viking.

Showers, P. (1978). *Me and my family tree*. New York: Crowell.

Sobol, D. (1977). *Encyclopedia Brown and the case of the midnight visitor*. New York: Bantam.

Speare, E. G. (1983). *The sign of the beaver*. Boston: Houghton Mifflin.

Steig, W. (1971). *Amos & Boris*. New York: Farrar, Straus & Giroux.

Steig, W. (1986). *Brave Irene*. New York: Farrar, Straus & Giroux.

Steinbeck, J. (1937/1965). *Of mice and men*. New York: Viking.

Steinbeck, J. (1939/1951). *The grapes of wrath*. New York: Harper.

Steinbeck, J. (1947). *The pearl*. New York: Viking-Penguin.

Taylor, M. (1976). *Roll of thunder, hear my cry*. New York: Dial.

Taylor, M. (1981). *Let the circle be unbroken*. New York: Dial.

Turner, A. (1987). *Nettie's trip south.* New York: Scholastic.

Twain, M. (1881/1983). *The prince and the pauper.* New York: Puffin Books.

Van Allsburg, C. (1985). *The polar express.* Boston: Houghton Mifflin.

Viorst, J. (1972). *Alexander and the terrible, horrible, no good, very bad day.* New York: Atheneum.

Waber, B. (1972). *Ira sleeps over.* Boston: Houghton Mifflin.

Weller, F. W. (1991). *I wonder if I'll see a whale.* New York: Philomel.

Wells, R. (1973). *Noisy Nora.* New York: Scholastic.

White, E. B. (1952). *Charlotte's web.* New York: Harper & Row.

Wilder, L. I. (1932). *Little house in the big woods.* New York: Harper & Row.

Yashima, T. (1955). *Crow boy.* New York: Viking.

Yep, L. (1991). *The star fisher.* New York: Morrow.

Selected Resources for Literature-Based Teachers

CHILDREN'S BOOK CLUBS

Scholastic Book Club
PO Box 7502
Jefferson City, MO 65102

Troll Book Club
2 Lethbridge Plaza
Mahwah, NJ 07430

The Trumpet Book Club
PO Box 604
Holmes, PA 19043

JOURNALS

Book Links: Connecting Books, Libraries, and Classrooms
American Library Association
50 E. Huron Street
Chicago, IL 60611
A new bimonthly journal created to support teachers, public librarians, and library media specialists who are trying to use children's books to teach reading, writing, and the curriculum.

The Horn Book Magazine
14 Beacon Street
Boston, MA 02108
Reviews current trade books for children and young adults; contains articles by and about authors and illustrators; excellent source for keeping up on children's books.

Language Arts
National Council of Teachers of English (NCTE)
1111 Kenyon Road
Urbana, IL 61801
Offers themed issues on teaching the language arts in the elementary grades; departments include Research Directions, Bookalogues, and Leadership in the Language Arts; excellent resource for teachers who want to integrate the language arts curriculum.

The New Advocate
PO Box 809
Needham Heights, MA 02194-0006
Main focus is children's literature; reviews current children's books; offers articles by and about authors and illustrators; also contains articles about how to teach reading and writing through literature.

The Reading Teacher
International Reading Association (IRA)
800 Barksdale Road
PO Box 8139
Newark, DE 19714-8139
Focuses on practical classroom applications of the latest in literacy research for the elementary grades; departments include children's book reviews, technology, and professional book reviews; annually publishes Teachers' Choices, outstanding trade books that teachers find to be exceptional; IRA also publishes Children's Choices, an annual list of children's favorites.

NEWSLETTERS

Booklure
PO Box 70374
Pasadena, CA 91117
A quarterly that reviews "what's new and wonderful in children's literature," preschool to grade six and beyond; includes nonfiction, award winners, and gift suggestions.

The Five Owls
2004 Sheridan Avenue South
Minneapolis, MN 55405
Offers themed annotated bibliographies and reviews of current books.

The Kobrin Letter: Concerning Children's Books About Real People, Places, and Things
732 Greer Road
Palo Alto, CA 94303
Reviews nonfiction books exclusively; includes titles for preschoolers through 12-year-olds.

The WEB: Wonderfully Exciting Books
The Ohio State University
200 Ramseyer Hall
29 West Woodruff
Columbus, OH 43210
Reviews books and suggests ways they can be used in elementary school; offers a centerfold web of related books each issue; written by teachers and teacher educators.

PUBLISHERS OF BIG BOOKS AND OTHER ENLARGED TEXTS

DLM
PO Box 4000
Allen, TX 75002
1-800-527-4747

Rigby Education
PO Box 797
Crystal Lake, IL 60014
1-800-822-8661

Scholastic
PO Box 7502
Jefferson City, MO 65102
1-800-325-6149

The Wright Group
19201 120th Avenue NE
Bothell, WA 98011-9512
1-800-523-2371

PUBLISHERS OF PROFESSIONAL BOOKS

Heinemann Educational Books
361 Hanover Street
Portsmouth, NH 03801-3959
1-800-541-2086

International Reading Association
800 Barksdale Road
PO Box 8139
Newark, DE 19714-8139
1-302-731-1600

Macmillan Publishing Company
College Division
100 Front Street
Riverside, NJ 08075-1197
1-800-257-5755

National Council of Teachers of English
1111 Kenyon Road
Urbana, IL 61801
1-217-328-3870

Richard C. Owen Publishing
Box 585
Katonah, NY 10536
1-800-336-5588

Teachers College Press
Teachers College, Columbia University
New York, NY 10027
1-800-356-0409

CHAPTER
5

INCORPORATING TECHNOLOGY INTO ELEMENTARY READING

Chapter Overview

A COMPUTER LAB TEACHER in an inner-city school greets her first period class with her usual "good morning" remarks. Students sit at their computer stations and write down their assignments from the board. Some of them put their headsets on so they can use the software's speech capability. They work nonstop, reacting to what they read and often laughing at what they write. The teacher walks around, occasionally troubleshooting a problem with the software, but mostly smiling at the sight of her involved "at risk" students. Before the teacher knows it, first period ends.

Her second period class enters. Buoyed by her first period's reaction, she greets her second class with even more animation. Her students rush in excitedly to their computer stations and follow the same procedure as the first period class. Within minutes there is chaos in the lab. Eyes are everywhere but on the computer screen. Students are reacting to and laughing at everything but the software. Our once confident teacher is desperate for decorum. Her polite appeals for silence have turned into screaming threats of disciplinary action, but to no avail. She counts the minutes until the period ends.

Why would this happen? With all the research (Balajthy, 1989; Butzin, 1990; Collis, 1990; Goldman, 1988; Hague & Childers, 1986; Jenkins & Dankert, 1981; Roberts, Carter, Friel, & Miller, 1988) that indicates the motivational appeal of technology, how could two classes containing students of the same age with similar academic and environmental backgrounds react so differently? *Answer:* the software. With the first class, the teacher used a reading-writing software package that contains high-interest, low-readability, real-life stories about topics such as peer pressure, cheating, and stealing. Before students even read each story, they have the opportunity to predict what it is about. Many on-line screen options and activities are available, giving students a feeling of control over what they are doing. With the second class, the teacher used a different reading comprehension package that is written at a reportedly low level. Only this time the material is unrelated to students' background experiences. They are supposed to read about different configurations of make-believe machines so that they can arrange the machines' functions in order. Students can use the package's graphic illustrations to help them identify the correct sequence. However, too much information is presented too quickly for students to feel comfortable with the package. Hence, students' attention spans end before they actually discover the program's appeal.

Software content clearly affects students' level of motivation (Wepner, 1990/ 1991). In fact, software is no different from other printed material. As you read in the previous chapters, sterile, drill-oriented material that is written more for skill acquisition than for psychological appeal usually does not captivate students. Material that grabs students has to be written with the child's interests and abilities in mind. This same tenet applies to software.

This chapter is about, first and foremost, using software to support students' **literacy** development. At issue is not whether technology per se is valuable for learning, but rather how technology and its accompanying software can naturally complement students' development as readers and writers. (*Technology* is used interchangeably with the word *computers* in this chapter; however, **technology** is a broader term that refers to a broad range of computerized tools to make work easier and more productive.) While many factors still interfere with the widespread use of technology in the schools, we need to move beyond polemics and focus on the merits of the material that support our teaching efforts. Of course, we must get beyond some of the realities of resistance before we can carve out our own technological niches.

Factors Affecting the Use of Technology

Did you know that a recent nationwide survey reported in *The New York Times* indicates that "sophisticated use of computers in the classroom can help teachers cover more complex subjects, devote more individual attention to students, and allow students more initiative. . . ."? (Chira, 1990, p. B7). If this is so, why is it that only two to three teachers in every building use computers creatively? (Bitterhouse, 1990). Why do most teachers, if they use computers at all, use them primarily in the same way they use workbooks? The answer may be partly perception and partly experience. Many still think of the computer as today's slick answer to yesterday's basals or as yet another irrelevant time-filler (Doyle, 1988; Hancock, 1989). Others don't really know any other way, since their initial exposure to the computer was with drill-and-practice software.

Just as the basal is not inherently bad, neither is the computer. However, as with basals we often use technology without considering creative alternatives to publishers' offerings. We don't do our own cutting and pasting of activities and strategies to glean the "best" parts of the material. As a result, we sometimes see our students "ho-humming" through an on-screen lesson, and we ultimately conclude that technology is no better (yet often more expensive) than any other printed lesson. However, it may be that the technology is not the problem; rather the problem may be in the software we choose.

SOFTWARE WARS

Because of the whole language vs. subskills debate, educational publishers have been somewhat befuddled with their publishing plans. In their advertising, some companies emphasize their "whole language" products, whereas others have fortified themselves enough to proudly maintain their skill-based stance. Another dichotomy relates to some companies offering us open-ended, tool-based products, whereas others are giving us animated skill and drill on the screen. While tool-based software truly is as good as the teachers who use them, the skill-and-drill products are supposedly teacher-proof and support mandated curricula and standardized tests. If you were an elementary district administrator who was worried primarily about test scores, which type of product would you purchase for your teachers?

The unprecedented explosion of **Integrated Instructional Systems (IISs)** in the schools shows us how software money is being spent. IISs are computer-managed, comprehensive basic skills training programs that focus on skill deficiencies. Although varying in curriculum focus, pedagogy, and age range served, these systems are usually designed for elementary schools in districts that emphasize centralized decision-making, accountability, and uniform coverage of mandated curricula (Kelman, 1990; Sherry, 1990). In essence, these systems are basals on a screen. No stone has been left unturned with respect with what to teach, how to teach it, and how to assess what was taught. According to Peter Kelman, Publisher of Scholastic Software, the number of IIS-related purchases in 1990 exceeded half a billion dollars. Unfortunately, these so-called teacher-proof software systems leave little incentive for educators to experiment with software packages that promote higher level thinking and creativity. What is worse is that these packages demonstrate an insidious lack of faith in teachers' ability to decide what is effective for their students.

Fortunately, many other software publishers refuse to adopt this philosophy. Their aim is to promote students' critical and creative thinking through reading and writing. Software produced by these publishers is designed with the teacher as decision-maker in mind. There are no formulaic methods for working with these packages. Rather, these packages' chameleon-like attributes enable the software to be used in different ways and in many contexts. Although they do not guarantee increased scores on a standardized achievement test (because that is not their goal), they do appeal to students' learning curiosities and offer situations that are likely to result in more academic engaged time; this, in turn, can lead to improved reading and writing abilities.

TRAINING, TIME, AND ACCESS

Obviously, the more you know about computers, the easier it is to branch out from the workbook-on-screen mentality. Chira (1990) found that most teachers take at least five years to learn how to use computers creatively and effectively. Three factors that contribute to teachers' versatility with computers are training, time, and access. The amount of technological training one has is positively related to the kinds of computer activities the teacher implements in the classroom (Collis, 1990). This assumption is supported by a survey of 43 elementary teachers from a small northern New Jersey school district. According to Corbran (1990), the more technological training teachers have, the more frequently they use the computer as a learning tool. However, she also found that those with more training also used the computer for drill-and-practice more than those with less training, thus indicating to her that well-trained teachers are more apt to be flexible and proficient with their choice of computer activities.

Time is a second concern. Most of us don't have time to learn how to use the computer when we teach all day. We have to borrow time before and after school, often burning the midnight oil with that exasperating program that just won't work.

Access is a third concern (DeGroff, 1990). As one of our teacher friends said, "You need daily, *convenient* access to a computer and good software so you can get over the frustration humps." The survey reported in *The New York Times* also found that if teachers are to move beyond seeing computers as substitutes for skillbooks, they must have access to a variety of hardware and software to experiment with different uses.

ATTITUDE AND SUPPORT

As you would expect, Corbran (1990) also found that teachers who have a positive attitude toward the computer tend to use the computer more. Of course, those who have a positive attitude probably sought out opportunities to discover the professional and personal rewards of using technology. Yet, even with these positive attitudes, Corbran's teachers complained that imposed time constraints and scheduling problems hindered their ability to use the computer. They felt that administrators and others who don't fully understand technology see it as just another appendage to an already overloaded curriculum, rather than as a tool for enhancing existing guidelines.

Another contributing attitudinal factor is teachers' perceptions of the computer. Because the computer is often perceived as a toy, it is often undervalued. Butzin (1990) reports how she often hears teachers tell their students that they can go to the computer station *after* their work is finished. Unfortunately, even with our understanding that children are active learners, some still believe that books and pencils are the only valid form of work. In 1990 we are still being told, "Learning is documented by the quantity of papers coming home, and validated through multiple choice answers" (Butzin, 1990, p. 21). Furthermore, the organizational structure and culture of public schools are so resistant to change that the computer, as a tool for learning, is often neglected or trivialized (Turner, 1990). As a result, very little time is available for technological exploration.

This resistance has been perpetuated in the reading field by a historical lack of consensus on the role the computer should play. In addition to resisting the replacement of traditional workbooks by electronic workbooks, an increasing number of teachers have downplayed the subskill orientation of computers for more holistic approaches without the computer (Balajthy, 1988a).

Just as we need support to help us branch out from the slavish use of basals and other drill-and-practice-oriented materials, we need such support—and even more so—with the computer. We need time to understand how technology can help us attain our instructional goals. We need supportive administrators who will allow us to take risks with our instructional methodologies. We also need empathic colleagues who are dissatisfied with the status quo and are willing to work with us to find ways to use computers as an integral part of a student's learning. Because technological integration is a slow, simmering process that can be confounded by many unforeseen obstacles along the way, we need to know that our efforts are understood and encouraged.

Rationale for Using Technology

What can technology do to enhance instruction? An obvious response is the motivational appeal of technology. Our teacher at the beginning of the chapter told us that when she surveyed how her students felt about the computer in general, 97% of her students said that they liked to work with the computer all or most of the time. Even after her disappointing experience with her second period class, she told us that this same class, when threatened to be barred from the computer lab, pleaded with her to let them attend. Although they made comments like "We want to work with the software that the other class had" and "We want a different disk," they nevertheless saw the computer lab as a better option than their regular classroom work.

A friend of ours who is a principal in a suburban school related a story to us about a third grade boy who had repeated problems with self-control in the classroom. When she met with him, she told him that if he would behave well enough for a week so that he would not be sent down to her office, he would be rewarded with any activity of his choice. What do you think he chose? Yes, he told our friend that he wanted to have time on the computer.

Roberts, Carter, Friel, and Miller (1988) share their observations of inner-city fourth graders in a computer lab and in the classroom. They report how students spent the entire 40-minute period engaged in writing when they worked with word processing in the computer lab. However, in the regular class with the same type of assignment, these same students spent 30 of the 40 minutes being managed and policed by their teacher.

Why are the students in these three situations motivated to work with the computer? It's not the hardware itself, but rather what students experience while working with it. In fact, one of us has had the opportunity to observe her own elementary children work with a computer at home since they were in preschool. While initially engrossed with the glitzy, animated graphics for some of the more mundane subskill packages, they soon lost interest until they discovered that the computer was not for workbook pages only. Now, part of their "social" agenda with their guests is to go to "the computer room" to play their favorite simulation or create signs with one of the graphically adorned word processors. They also have been word processing their own school reports since third grade without ever having official keyboarding lessons. They, like the students in the three situations previously discussed, have discovered facets of technology that appeal to their interests and satisfy their needs.

What motivates students to use technology? This section explores eight factors that contribute to students' desire to use computers.

1. *Technology provides students with truly individualized instruction.* Students are in a one-to-one situation, with the computer responding to their own construction of meaning (Balajthy, 1989; Standiford, Jaycox, & Auten, 1983). The computer can help them monitor their own growth as readers and writers as they use language for their own purposes. It also is private, allowing students to progress at their own rate without feeling pressure to keep up with the rest of the class or fearing ridicule if they answer incorrectly.

2. *Technology uses immediate reinforcement to guide students.* It informs students of their progress and often allows them the freedom to redo their work without fear of reprimand or evidence of erasure. Balajthy (1989) states that because the computer interacts and responds to student inputs, it is far superior to traditional print for instruction. It also provides for increased efficiency and cost-effectiveness since it enables us to spend more time on tasks and activities that require critical and creative thinking.

   Butzin (1990) shares the story of two fourth grade boys who were working with a software package that had deleted all vowels from a passage contained in a well-known novel. Students came across "–xh– –st–d" for the word *exhausted*. After discovering that their initial attempt at identifying the second and third vowels was not correct, they looked at her for advice. She quickly looked away. They then tried to copy from two students at the next computer station, but they were already on a different screen. They then resorted to their own method of going through the vowels in alphabetical order, soon discovering that the *a* worked and one of the boy's hunches for the *u* worked next. She couldn't help but marvel at the look of discovery on these two boys' faces.

3. *Technology gives students a feeling of control.* In addition to thinking that the computer is fun, students feel they have control over what they are learning, often flipping back and forth between screens to try different program options. The computer provides students with an opportunity to explore without fear of failure and to develop a sense of self-control, power, and autonomy with their learning (Wepner, 1987, 1990/ 1991). That is, it delivers a perception of ownership.

4. *Technology supports rich social interactions.* The upright, public screen is an irresistible opportunity for students to talk spontaneously about what is displayed on the screen. As long as interaction is encouraged, students use language in richly rewarding ways as they discuss the task at hand (Cochran-Smith, Kahn, & Paris, 1988; DeGroff, 1990). Students also collaborate much more readily, often leading to improved reading and writing (Strickland, Feeley, & Wepner, 1987).

5. *Technology can assume different software-driven roles.* In addition to providing drill-and-practice and game-like activities, the computer can teach abstract concepts with the use of graphics. It also can bring realistic situations into the classroom. "It can telescope time, allowing learners to experience events through simulations" (Standiford, Jaycox, & Auten, 1983, p. x). It also serves as a versatile tool for writing, so that the drudgery of rewriting is supplanted with the ease of revising with word processing. The computer also stores and manipulates large amounts of data, enabling students to both create and access large databases. This role frees students to spend more time analyzing, synthesizing, and evaluating ideas.

6. *Technology provides access to both people and information.* Because of telecommunications, or **on-line** communication, students can transmit information from computer to computer. In addition to being able to search and access information anywhere about any topic, students can leave and receive messages from other students throughout the world (Grunwald, 1990; Milone, 1986; Rickelman & Henk, 1990; Watson, 1990). For example, one teacher in Indiana established a pen-pal system with students in Japan. Each set of students spent the year reading and writing about the other's culture.

7. *Technology provides dynamic text, offering on-screen help to readers.* Because the computer can store large amounts of information, any text can be provided in a variety of formats with a multitude of options for reading (Geoffrion & Geoffrion, 1983). Typically, when students read from a book, they read in a linear fashion. Although important concepts may be highlighted, they have to read the material as presented. They don't have choices for lowering the readability or getting animated, graphic explanations of concepts that elude them. In contrast, the computer can provide options to help students monitor their understanding of text. They can ask for definitions, pictures, overviews, and other types of supplementary infor-

mation. This is what makes for dynamic reading. When students use such **computer-mediated** options, their reading comprehension increases significantly (Reinking, 1988; Reinking & Schreiner, 1985).

8. *Technology enables students to discover and create their own meaningful learning environments.* Although still in its infancy, **hypertext**, a term for information that is linked in a nonsequential or nontraditional manner, provides opportunities for students to "navigate their own learning" (Blanchard & Rottenberg, 1990). For example, imagine that students want to rethink their reading of the book, *Blubber* (Blume, 1974a). The student begins with a Table of Contents screen that lists different facets of the book (see Figure 5.1). By clicking one of the book's MicroStories, "Blubber Gets Her Name," the student reads about this episode. On the same screen, the student sees the word *whale* because the book talks about whales in the story (see Figure 5.2). If the student clicks "whales," s/he can go to a screen that presents a set of choices for an encyclopedic discussion of whales that will follow from yet another series of screens (see Figure 5.3). At any time the student can click the "Contents" button to return to the Table of Contents. The student then can press "Major Characters" on the Table of Contents screen and read all about Wendy (see Figure 5.4) (Wepner, in press). Essentially, students can rapidly access a plethora of information in a variety of contexts by merely selecting a word or picture on a screen (Blanchard & Rottenberg, 1990).

FIGURE 5.1
Hypertext screen:
Table of contents
for *Blubber*
(Blume, 1974a)
Note. Created from
the HyperCard Pro-
gram, 1991.
HyperCard is a
trademark of Claris
Corporation regis-
tered in the U.S.
and in other coun-
tries.

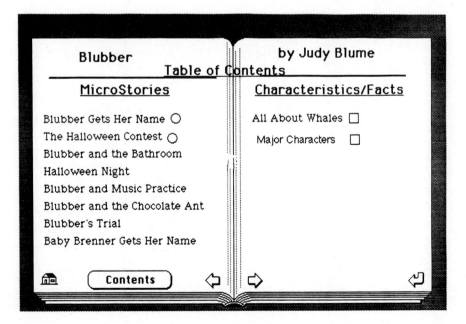

FIGURE 5.2
Hypertext screen:
One of
MicroStories from
Blubber (Blume,
1974a)
Note. Created from
the HyperCard Program, 1991.
HyperCard is a
trademark of Claris
Corporation registered in the U.S.
and in other countries.

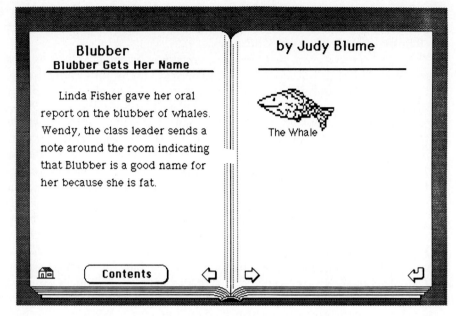

FIGURE 5.3
Hypertext screen:
Contents of
information about
whales from
Blubber (Blume,
1974a)
Note. Created from
the HyperCard Program, 1991.
HyperCard is a
trademark of Claris
Corporation registered in the U.S.
and in other countries.

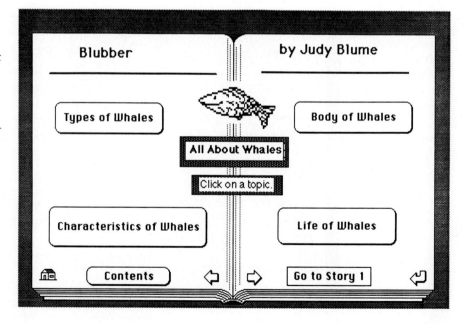

FIGURE 5.4
Hypertext screen:
Synopsis of one
character from
Blubber (Blume,
1974a)

Note. Created from
the HyperCard Pro-
gram, 1991.
HyperCard is a
trademark of Claris
Corporation regis-
tered in the U.S.
and in other coun-
tries.

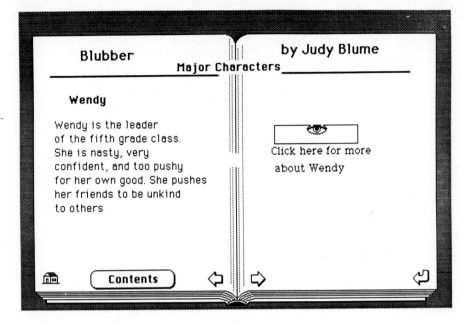

Software Considerations

However motivational new technology may be, a sound understanding of how children develop literacy should be the prime basis for making decisions about using
technology in the classroom (DeGroff, 1990; Miller, 1989). Software selection and
use should support our goals for helping students to develop as readers and writers.
Although many interesting, challenging, and innovative elementary programs are
available (Blanchard, Mason, & Daniel, 1987; Roberts, Carter, Friel, & Miller, 1988;
Scott & Barker, 1987), we should strive to identify software with the theoretical
premise that reading and writing are integral parts of natural language functioning.
We want our students to have opportunities to read and/or write whole texts as they
develop skills, for example, sequencing and identifying details (Wepner, 1990b). Software also should be compatible with the: (a) learner's needs and characteristics; (b)
teacher's needs and intentions; and (c) curriculum (Hannaford & Taber, 1982) (see
Figure 5.5).

LEARNER COMPATIBILITY

As with any other instructional material, software must be appropriate for students'
needs. Four learner needs should be considered when searching for software compatibility (Wepner, 1990/1991).

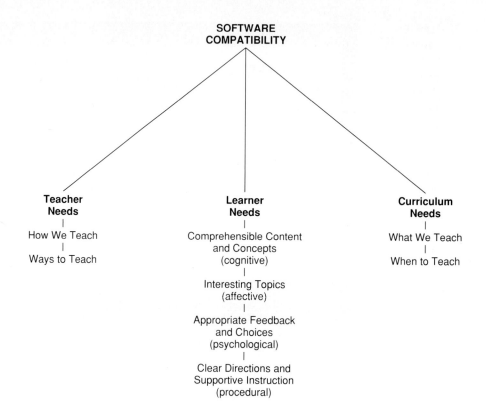

FIGURE 5.5
Software
compatibility
considerations

1. Software should be compatible with students' *cognitive* needs. Students should deal with content and concepts that are compatible with their learning experiences. Part of the problem with our students in the vignette at the beginning of this chapter was their inability to process the information about the topic presented.

2. Software should be compatible with students' *affective* needs. Since reading and writing are personal acts that develop and improve with practice, students should read and write about things that are interesting and important to them. Although writing packages do not pose this problem, many reading packages contain topics to which students cannot relate, squelching initial motivation. Again, as seen in our opening vignette, how could an abstract topic to which at-risk learners could not relate entice them when they can barely read about their own real-life events?

3. Software should be compatible with students' *psychological* needs. Appropriate feedback is one consideration. Trieschmann (1990) observed that when feedback is totally unrelated to the on-screen task at hand, students often get bored and annoyed with the feedback after a few trials. On the other hand, when the feedback is related to the task (for example, in a discrimination task, when the child chooses correctly, the part of the object that is different from the rest of the objects is animated to reinforce a response), students often talk about the object, stimulating

language skills. Activity options is another consideration. Students need to be able to make choices about the kinds of activities they can do within the same package. In our observation of students' use of software, we are invariably surprised by students' selections. When we think they will choose to write personally about what they have just read, they often choose to work with objective comprehension questions, and vice versa. But, at least they had a choice! It's important that children feel ownership for whatever they do.

4. Software should be compatible with students' *procedural* needs. Instructional directions should be brief, clear, and specific, with step-by-step guidelines and uncluttered presentations. If possible, a speech option should be included, especially for nonreaders, new readers, and disabled readers. Research indicates the positive effects of speech for reading and writing (Anderson-Inman et al., 1990; Balajthy, 1988b). Students who have access to speech while reading can read more interesting passages that otherwise might be too difficult to read (McConkie & Zola, 1987). Furthermore word recognition and passage comprehension improve with speech feedback for unknown words (Olson & Wise, 1987; Reitsma, 1988).

Part and parcel to these four considerations is the field-testing of software. A program that is effective with one student may not work with another, even if both students have similar learning needs (Smith & Vokurka, 1990).

TEACHER COMPATIBILITY

Our selection and use of software should be consonant with our understanding of teaching and learning. For example, Cochran-Smith, Kahn, and Paris (1988) found that their K–4 teachers in nine classrooms taught writing with word processors in ways similar to how they generally taught writing. However, we should not limit our use of software to only those packages that fit in with how we do things. How many times has a student read a **trade book** written at a higher grade level because the content was appealing? We need to allow technology to change or expand our visions of teaching and learning when the opportunity arises. Miller (1989) shares a vignette of a first grade teacher who was reluctant to use a database with her students because she believed that they were unable to work with this type of program. Only after "testing the waters" with a student-created database on "All About Me" did she discover that her students were quite capable of entering data, classifying, and sorting. What's most important is that the software supports the "hows" and "ways" we teach our children to read and write.

CURRICULUM COMPATIBILITY

However you use software, you need to see the "big picture" of your reading program while accounting for your own philosophy and considering your students' learning needs (Standiford, Jaycox, & Auten, 1983). Software should be considered in light of its potential to support your curriculum goals.

Project CHILD (Butzin, 1990) is an example of a three-year, K–6 project in which technology has become an integral part of students' learning. Students have been clustered as either primary (K–2) or intermediate teams (3–5). For part of each day each classroom serves as a subject area learning center with activity stations in which students work on paper-pencil, textbook, and computer activities. Each reading center has three computers, and each language arts center has six computers. Specific computer software lessons have been integrated into units that have been written and adapted from the traditional curriculum. The software for these lessons comes from at least 10 different publishers, supporting the idea of drawing the best activities from several pieces of software to satisfy student, teacher, and curricular needs.

Although this project's price tag is beyond the reach of most teachers, it demonstrates the importance of using your curricular goals as a basis for software use. Often software is ordered without considering how it will be used in the classroom. Although some software inevitably ends up being shelved, other software is used without any connection to the curriculum. Blair, Rupley, and Jones (1986) caution that this indiscriminate use usually results in the software determining what happens to the curriculum—truly the tail wagging the dog.

Plenty of software can provide sound pedagogical on-screen instruction. With a spirit for technological exploration, we can find many software packages that meet our curricular and instructional goals for developing our students as readers and writers. The next section provides examples of effective software that involves students in an active, constructive process of making meaning for themselves.

Software Examples and Applications

The division of this section into separate discussions of software for reading and software for writing is based on the software's primary use. However, we recognize this as an artificial separation, since students write in many of the reading packages and certainly read in many, if not all, of the writing packages. While not necessarily representative of the latest and greatest technology (copyright dates span 1985 to 1991), the 13 packages we cite here exemplify a range of strategies in reading and writing. (While many packages were originally developed for computers with minimal memory capacity, many publishers are now upgrading these packages to support more sophisticated computer platforms. In other words, many software packages, recognized for their sound theoretical frameworks and wide appeal, are being redesigned rather than fading into obsolescence.) For each software package we offer a brief description and a suggested activity for extending its use to other reading and writing activities.

SOFTWARE FOR READING

The seven reading packages included here focus on comprehension. However, they use different strategies to accomplish their goals: two use a combination of text, self-help options, and graphics to monitor comprehension; two use **semantic mapping**; one uses the Directed Reading-Thinking Activity (DR-TA); one uses computer-monitored cloze exercises to enhance sentence-level construction (Balajthy, 1989); and one uses computer-mediated literal comprehension activities. These packages contain reading material that ranges from stories created by the software publishers' authors to literature from basals and trade books.

COMPREHENSION-MONITORING PACKAGES

Comprehension monitoring involves a reader's awareness of what is and is not understood. Packages that support this strategy provide techniques for interacting with text. Students use these techniques to make predictions about and connections within the text (Wepner, 1989).

Tiger's Tales (Sunburst, 1986) is an example of a primary-level software package that helps students to monitor their comprehension of short, fairly simple passages about a tiger's experiences. After reading a few lines of text on the screen, students select one of three pictures to reflect what they read or predict what will happen in the next screen. Sometimes students' graphic responses determine the direction that the passage will take. (Some passages require a correct response while others accept multiple responses.) With this type of package, beginning readers have the opportunity to puzzle their way through a passage, focusing more on comprehension than on the acquisition of many subskills. Scott and Barker (1987) cite *Tiger's Tales* as an exemplary piece of software, in which children learn sight vocabulary in a meaningful context and as an outgrowth of reading.

➤ **EXTENSION ACTIVITY: Create "My Tale Booklets" with your students where they create their own tales—replete with graphics—about their own personal experiences (see Figure 5.6).**

- Share a tale of something that happened to you (for example, the loss of something special, a funny incident, a silly experience).
- Write down your tale on the chalkboard or large chart paper, illustrating highlights of three phases of your tale.
- As a few students share their tales orally, explain how they can be presented in three phases.
- Have students create their tales without putting their names on their paper.
- Collect and distribute tales to different students so that they can take turns guessing whose tale it is.
- Create a booklet to share with other primary students so that they can delight in guessing the owner of each tale.

FIGURE 5.6
"My Tale Booklet"
form for *Tiger's
Tales* (Sunburst,
1986)

_____'s Tale

The End

The Comprehension Connection (Milliken, 1987) provides strategies for comprehension monitoring from a different vantage point. Every grade level consists of 20 passages about a variety of topics such as chewing gum, bats, and electricity. Most of the passages are nonfiction. After students read the passage, they have five options for better understanding the story; reread the passage as is, reread the passage with lower readability, see animated graphic illustrations, look at main ideas for each paragraph, or get assistance with difficult vocabulary. Each option helps students comprehend the information presented. Students can choose as many options as they think they need before taking the comprehension check. With this package students use on-screen "Help" options to actively monitor their understanding of text.

➤ **EXTENSION ACTIVITY: Provoke written debates.**

• Have students write a personal reaction letter about one of the topics presented, for example the pros and cons of chewing gum.

- Use students' varied reactions to initiate an oral discussion and mini-debate.
- Once you assign students to one of the two sides of the issue, have them use resources to support their argument.
- Now the written debate begins. Have each side write a joint letter to its opposing side, explaining reasons for its argument. Have each team respond through letter writing.
- Have each side respond orally to the other side's letter.

SPECIFIC STRATEGY PACKAGES: MAPPING AND DR-TA

Mapping and the **Directed Reading-Thinking Activity (DR-TA)** have been well researched in the reading field. Mapping is a graphic representation of the connection between ideas and categories (Johnson & Pearson, 1984; Miccinati, 1988; Nagy, 1988). Useful for reading comprehension and writing preparation, mapping's visual representation serves as a mnemonic device for thought association. DR-TA is a comprehension strategy that takes students through a process of predicting, verifying, judging, and extending thought (Vacca & Vacca, 1989). Originally developed by Stauffer (1975), this strategy uses questions to guide students to think about what they are going to read so that they read with a purpose. Once they read, students refine their predictions and engage in reflective discussion and extension activities. Each of the next three packages uses one of these two strategies.

The Semantic Mapper and *The Literary Mapper* (Teacher Support Software, 1987, 1989) use mapping to help students process what they read in basals and trade books, respectively. With *The Semantic Mapper* students have opportunities to create maps of what they read in their basal texts. Main concepts and ideas from all the selections of five commonly used basals are already programmed into this package. With *The Literary Mapper* students have opportunities to do the same with trade books. Both packages contain a map disk for students to create their own on-screen maps by first brainstorming about their topics and then organizing their ideas into categories from the methodical questions posed in the package. Whereas *The Semantic Mapper* is open-ended, *The Literary Mapper* contains map shells for characters, actions, and setting.

➤ **EXTENSION ACTIVITY: Have students create a novel newspaper for one of the stories or books they have read.**

- Once students have mapped their story ideas, have them decide which parts of the story or book they want to include in a newspaper.
- Present possible newspaper components that can be included in a group-developed newspaper. Have students decide which to include (e.g., news story about the book, editorial, book review, crossword puzzle, horoscope for one of the characters, advertisement for the book, TV listing of book-related shows).
- Have students divide up and work in small groups, based on their self-selected tasks.

- Assign a few students to oversee how the newspaper is put together.
- Celebrate with a Newspaper Publishing Party.*

Reading Realities Elementary Series (Teacher Support Software, 1990) uses DR-TA as a framework for reading and writing about real-life issues and concerns. For each of the 45 stories students predict what the story is about and select options for reading each story. The options include speech, rate assessment, and strategy (e.g., whole screen, phrases, or word-by-word). They then follow up their reading with four reading and writing comprehension options (multiple choice, cloze, discussion questions, or creative writing questions). The story topics for the package's three strands—School Issues, Personal Issues, and Family Issues—are based on nearly 1,000 children's surveys about things that concern them. Face-to-face interviews with children in grades 2 through 6 provide the content for each story so that children talk to other children about similar feelings, events, and issues through the selections.

➤ **EXTENSION ACTIVITY: Create "Dear Friend" postcards with your class. These are similar to "Dear Abby"-type correspondences where students give advice to story characters about what they would do in their situations.**

- Select a story from this package for the students to role-play.
- Have one student assume the role of the major character who has some type of problem; have the other assume the role of Dear Abby who will give advice to the character. Have students role-play their respective parts.
- Have students write a "Dear Friend" postcard to that character, giving advice on how to resolve his or her dilemma.
- Have students share their responses.

LITERATURE-BASED SOFTWARE

Unlike those in the first two categories, the software in this category uses literature in traditional print form as a foundation for on-screen activities. Books accompany the next two packages so that students have opportunities to read the book before or after working with the software. Although not necessarily representing the best use of on-screen comprehension strategies, these packages are "state of the art" in that their initiatives do create literature-technology connections.

Micro Tales (Troll Associates, 1987) uses the fairy tale genre as the basis for its 15 modules. Each module contains a paperback book and a disk containing three skill-

---

*Maureen Armour (1990, July 7), Personal Communication.

based activities that relate to the book; for example, understanding sequence, following directions, and recalling details. Some of the titles in the series include: *Beauty and the Beast, The Frog Prince, Rapunzel,* and *Thumbelina.* (See page 264 for a description of how one teacher uses this package.)

➤ **EXTENSION ACTIVITY: Have students rewrite a fairy tale in a modern setting using a round-robin storytelling format (Wepner, 1990a).**

- Have students stage the tale in a modern setting. For example, students might stage the tale *Beauty and the Beast* so that Beauty and her two jealous sisters live with their once-affluent father in an overcrowded apartment. Beast might live in a luxury home with a three-car garage.
- Form small groups. Have each student in a group write a paragraph to start the story and then pass it along for the next person to continue writing (Tway, 1985).
- After all students have had a turn and the story is finished, have each group share its modern tale with the other groups.

Success with Reading (Scholastic, 1985) uses nonfiction and fiction paperback books, for example *If You Grew Up with George Washington* (Gross, 1982) and *The Pinballs* (Byars, 1977), as a foundation for its on-screen cloze activities. Once students read a selected book, they work with passages from it on the screen with whole-word deletions keyed to important language cues in the text. According to a class of fourth graders in Demarest, New Jersey, students also may enjoy doing the on-screen activity before reading the book (Feeley, 1986). You also can type in your own selected literature, including passages in French, Spanish, and German with the foreign language editor. Students then can use this package to reinforce their comprehension of any story read in or out of the classroom.

➤ **EXTENSION ACTIVITY: Create "Bag-A-Book" with your students.***

- Have students bring in a brown bag and decorate it to reflect the title of a book.
- Have them collect all kinds of objects that are related to their book and put them in their bag. (For example, with *The Pinballs* they can bring in a miniature, toy pinball machine to introduce Carlie and her feelings about foster homes; a tiny, toy microphone to introduce the second foster child, Thomas J, who previously lived with elderly, nearly deaf twin women; and an ace bandage or some other leg support to introduce Harvey, whose alcoholic father ran over his leg with his car.)

---

*Bonnie Jernigan (1990, September 20), Personal Communication.

- As students retell their book, they should pull out objects that relate to that segment of the book.

SOFTWARE FOR WRITING

Software for writing usually includes some type of word processing capability. Other than drill-and-practice software, word processing is the most frequently used type of software in the classroom. An impressive body of research has begun to show the salutary effects of word processing (Balajthy, 1989; Collis, 1990). Students write and revise more, possibly following different strategies for revising with a word processor than with paper or pencil. Students also edit more carefully, resulting in pieces with fewer errors (Daiute, 1985). However, as with any other software, the teacher determines the success or failure of using word processing for writing. In addition to demonstrating the mechanics of word processing, teachers need to spend time on the process and content of writing itself (Collis, 1990; Wagner, O'Toole, & Kazelskis, 1985).

The six writing programs described in the following sections contain more than word processing capabilities. Generic and theme-based graphics, fonts, speech, sound, and music enhance the variety of presentation formats. In addition to creating, for example, mini-books, bordered stories, booklets, newspapers, letters, and big books, students get a taste of "multimedia" with on-screen slide shows and **interactive stories. (Multimedia** is a combination of media—for example, audio, video, and print—in which a microcomputer is at the hub of the system [D'Ignazio, 1989].) As with the reading programs already cited, we include extension activities with each writing package. Each activity uses a trade book so you can see how easily tool-based software can be blended with literature-based reading programs.

Muppet Slate: The Word and Picture Processor (Sunburst, 1988) provides primary students with desktop publishing capabilities and an alphabetized graphics library of 126 pictures. As young students type with this package's primary print, they can access the graphics library at any time to intersperse their ideas with pictures; they can also replace words with pictures to create rebus-like stories. When students are ready to print what they created, they can choose from 10 different borders to surround their writing and illustrations. A Muppet Slate Poster accompanies this disk so that students can easily see their picture options. In addition to working with the regular keyboard, this package also works with *Muppet Learning Keys,* a keyboard designed for young children that has upper and lower case letters arranged in alphabetical order.

➤ **EXTENSION ACTIVITY: Create "My Environment" rebus stories.**

- Select a book that focuses on a particular setting. For example, the Caldecott award book *Make Way for Ducklings* (McCloskey, 1969) is about a family of ducks trying to find a safe place to live in the Boston area.

- Read and discuss the book, focusing on the good and bad parts of the duck's environment.
- Have students discuss the good and bad parts of their own environment.
- Have students create and print their own bordered, rebus stories about their environment (see Figure 5.7). Create your own story too.
- Display on "Our Environment" bulletin board.

Make-A-Book (Teacher Support Software, 1991) is a newly released talking word processing program that enables students to print out their writing in booklet form. Along with the 5 book sizes (for example, mini-book, fanfold book, and big book) and 14 font choices, there is also a speech component. Anything that the child writes can be read back in a variety of ways: letters, words, sentences, and paragraphs. Students can hear how their books sound before production.

➤ **EXTENSION ACTIVITY: Create family portfolios.**

- Select a book that focuses on some facet of the family. For example, *The Pain and the Great One* (Blume, 1974b) realistically portrays sibling rivalry from two different perspectives with the older sister (the Great One) and the younger brother (the Pain) sharing their feelings about each other in two separate tales.
- Have students discuss how the Pain and the Great One feel about each other; then have them describe ways in which each could help the other feel better.
- On the chalkboard or large chart paper, write down the word *Family*. Have students brainstorm ideas about what a family is and what it means to them.

FIGURE 5.7
Rebus story from *Muppet Slate: The Word and Picture Processor* (Sunburst, 1988)
Note. From screen from *Muppet Slate: The Word and Picture Processor,* 1988. Copyright 1988 by Sunburst Communications. Reprinted by permission.

I get to play with the 🚤 🐟 and the 🐢. I love the 〰️ and my 🏠, just like the ducks.

- Have students create and print a family portfolio with this package.
- Have students draw or paste pictures above their description of each family member in their booklets.

The Children's Writing & Publishing Center (The Learning Company, 1989) is an easy-to-use **desktop publishing program** for elementary students. A variety of communication forms (for example, newsletters, signs, awards, stories, reports, and letters) accompany the graphic and font options so that students can choose among many ways to publish their writing. In addition to a quasi-theme-based library of 137 pictures that can be included within the body of the text, there are 22 predesigned graphic headings that correspond to the pictures and can be used in the heading workspace of each communication form. Pictures from other graphic programs can also be used.

➢ **EXTENSION ACTIVITY: Create book-specific journals for your students to keep as they read a bibliotherapeutic book that helps them understand problems.**

- Select a book that lends itself to recording how a character learns to cope with a painful situation. For example, *The Divorce Express* (Danziger, 1982) describes how an initially traumatized ninth grader named Phoebe learns how to create her own niche in life as a child of divorced parents.
- Have students help you create a title and format for their journals with this package. For example, they could create "The Divorce Express-ion" with space created for writing in the chapter(s), setting, characters, events, Phoebe's reaction, and their reaction.
- Depending on the number of computers available, have students either work with the journal on- or off-line.
- Dialogue back either on- or off-line to students.

Story Starters: Science (Pelican, 1989) is a content-specific, graphics-adorned word processor that talks. Unlike the title suggests, this package does not have "story starters" per se; rather, it provides a wide variety of graphics related to science to stimulate students' writing. Clip art and story backgrounds are available for life science (plants, animals, and ecology), physical science (matter and energy), earth science (earth, space, and weather), and the human body. Students can listen to and print their own science scenarios. In addition to a colorful array of graphics that students can flip around on the screen, students can print out dialogue and screens of text in seven different formats, including a miniature and big book version.

➤ **EXTENSION ACTIVITY: Create science fiction fantasies.**

- Select a book or series of science fiction books. For example, *The Visitor from Outer Space* (Rauch, 1989), the first of five books, shares what happens when a 10-year-old boy named Barnaby Brown meets his look-alike friend B.B. from the planet Erehwon.
- As students read the book, highlight vocabulary and information related to the solar system.
- After students read, have them take turns retelling the adventures of Barnaby Brown.
- Have students re-create the story with this package. In addition to designing their own solar system with the software's space backgrounds and space clip art, students can create their own rendition of the tale with the people clip art, speech bubbles, and text (see Figure 5.8).
- Print out big book versions for students to share with a class of younger students.

FIGURE 5.8
Screen for *The Visitor from Outer Space* from *Story Starters: Science* (Pelican, 1989)
Note. From screen for *The Visitor from Outer Space,* 1989. Copyright 1989 by Pelican Software, a division of Queue. Reprinted by permission.

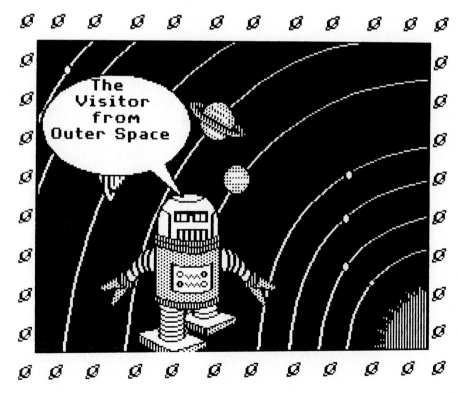

Slide Shop (Scholastic, 1988) enables students to create dynamic, on-screen slide presentations about any topic by first designing individual screens and then connecting them. Students appreciate this package's multimedia flavor as they orchestrate how the thematic-based backgrounds and clip art, fonts, music, sound, and special effects are used. Storyboard forms are provided with the program so that students can map out the components of each slide.

When Rosemary Alesandro had her gifted and talented students in West New York, New Jersey, create four-slide scripts about their in-school activities to share with their parents during "Back to School Night," she said that the creative juices were really flowing. (See page 264 for a description of Alesandro's two other projects.)

Dan Lake (1990) shares how his fifth grade son learned to use *Slide Shop* at home for a book report presentation. Within a few hours Patrick learned how to create a variety of colorful backgrounds and objects for his 10-slide presentation of his book, *Kon Tiki* (Heyerdahl, 1960). Although Patrick met with some initial resistance from his teacher who didn't like computers, Patrick impressed his class and other teachers so much that 10 copies of the program were purchased for the building. Ironically, Lake is a region-wide trainer responsible for teaching teachers how to integrate computers into the classroom, and it took his son to convince his local school about the value of this new multimedia program.

➤ **EXTENSION ACTIVITY: Create "Scenes from. . . ."**

- Select a book that is rich in description about a place that a character lives or visits. For example, *Jelly Belly* (Smith, 1981) is a story about the heaviest kid in the fifth grade, Ned, who is sent to Camp Lean-Too for the summer to try to lose weight. Ned vividly describes his experiences and feelings about the camp.
- As students read the book have them note details about the camp.
- Introduce students to this package's *summer, welcome, calendar, graph,* and *sports* templates; *people* and *speech/thought bubble* clip art; reveille music; and other speech and sound effects so that students are aware of the various media they can use (Wepner, 1990b).
- Have groups of students create their own "Scenes from Camp Lean-Too" slide shows.
- Have student groups share their shows with each other.
- As a follow-up, have the same student groups create their own imaginary "Scenes from . . ." slide shows to share with the other groups.

Super Story Tree (Scholastic, 1989) provides the same multimedia options as *Slide Shop;* however, students create interactive, branching stories. Rather than planning for a linear presentation of screens, students plot their stories so that they branch out from one beginning to many possible endings. Three branching options are available; a *continue* link takes users directly to the next page; a *choice* link gives the user up to eight alternative paths to follow; and a *chance* link sends the user to one of two different pages. Because a comprehensive on-screen tutorial accompanies this package, it is much easier for students to understand and appreciate how to create their own stories. According to Balajthy (1989), this type of software "is particularly effective in teaching students story structure" (p. 7).

> ➤ **EXTENSION ACTIVITY: Create historical fiction adventures.**

- Select some type of adventure book. For example, *The Whipping Boy* (Fleischman, 1986), a Newbery award-winner, tells about the adventures of a runaway prince and his whipping boy.
- As students read the book have them take notes about the two main characters' experiences as runaways.
- Have students discuss these experiences and then brainstorm alternative experiences.
- After students finish reading have them brainstorm alternative endings.
- On the chalkboard or large chart paper create a multi-stage story structure that includes students' brainstormed ideas. Explain how this format serves as the framework for this package.
- Introduce students to this package's *herald* title screens, castle backgrounds, *prince* and *boy* clip art, castle borders, background music, and sound effects so that students are aware of the various media they can use (see Figure 5.9).
- Have groups of students use the story structure to create their own interpretation of the prince and whipping boy's tales.
- Have each group share with each other before sharing with other classes.

   Any of the activities just described can be done with only one computer in the classroom. The following options can help you to decide how to best use your computer: (a) create a daily schedule to ensure equitable access; (b) pair two to four students at a time for programs and ongoing projects that lend themselves to group decision-making; (c) use an aide or parent volunteer to type in students' paper-and-pencil writing; (d) use a large color monitor projection device to work with the whole class (Balajthy, 1987a); (e) use a learning center approach so that while some students are working on a computer project, other students are working on a different project; and (f) bargain with other teachers to borrow additional computers for a specified period of time.

   Even if you have to share a computer all the time, DeGroff (1990) suggests that you cluster time as a temporary solution. If, for example, you are scheduled for the

FIGURE 5.9
Screen for *The Whipping Boy* from *Super Story Tree* (Scholastic, 1989)

Note. From screen from *The Whipping Boy* from *Super Story Tree.* Copyright 1989 by Scholastic. Reprinted by permission.

computer one day a week, try to exchange your weekly time slot for an extended period of time at some point during the year when you want to connect technology to your reading or writing program.

Technology, Basals, and Trade Books: Where We Are and What We Can Do

Although the previous section's extension activities for writing focused more on using trade books than basals, we believe that any good piece of literature, whether found in basals or other resources, can be blended with technology. We also believe that technology is not here to replace basals or any other type of printed material. Technology and other rich resources should be carefully combined to provide appropriately challenging learning experiences for students. However, technology's role as an afterthought or academic frill is no longer satisfactory, especially in light of the expanding use of technology in almost every aspect of 21st-century America (Mecklenburger, 1990). We need to examine how reading publishers are using technology so that we know what to ask for in the future.

BASAL CONNECTIONS

Computer programs are now being developed with basal programs (Rickelman & Henk, 1989). A few years ago Balajthy (1987b) found that only two companies were incorporating instructional computing into their basal programs. One company adapted existing software to its basal program from a software company that was its subsidiary, while the other basal company developed software that could be used with any basal series.

In our recent analysis of seven basals' Teachers' Manuals, we found that four of the basals had software for reading, four had software for writing, and only two basals had software for both (see Table 5.1). (We are not including management systems here because these programs assess instruction rather than provide it.)

One company provided specific recommendations in the manual about which reading software to use; another company did the same for writing. However, nowhere was there a picture that displayed what was on the computer screen. It was, therefore, difficult to discern the software's format and theoretical premise. Moreover, more often than not, directions for using the software were vague at best, leading us to conclude that reading and writing software was not considered the learning resource of choice. One company did include an annotated description of 55 software packages in the back of the manual; however, there seemed to be no information in the rest of the manual about when or how to use these packages.

The basal publishers' half-hearted effort to include technology into their manuals is communicating a strong message. Basal publishers will continue to treat technology as a stepchild to paper-and-pencil workbooks and skillpads until software becomes more profitable for them. Apparently, we are not demanding that technology be in the forefront of our instructional strategies. We also are not demanding that the software includes **dynamic text** features so that students are reading strategically on the screen. Now that basal publishers have begun to expand their repertoire of reading selections to include literature from trade books that is not chopped up to fit a readability formula, they must begin to view technology with the same holistic eye. In addition to including authors who know something about technology, as one company did, they need to look at how existing, exemplary software packages can be integrated into their reading framework or create other packages that are not merely technological dressing. They then need to work with educators and students so that they know how the software supports the mainstay of their program and creates

TABLE 5.1 Comparison of reading and writing software in seven basal series	BASALS						
	SF	H	MM	HBJ	SBG	HM	MH
Software for Reading	●		●		●	●	
Software for Writing	●	●	●	●			

bridges to other literary resources. Comprehensive guidelines, including sample software screens, should be included in the manual so teachers can evaluate the effectiveness of the format. Although some may laugh at the idea of adding yet more bulk to the heavyweight manuals, we believe that some of the instructional fat can be trimmed to make room for this important learning component.

If publishers would follow these guidelines, it would be much easier for teachers to integrate technology with basals. Currently, we suggest using software companies that may extend basal material.

TRADE BOOK CONNECTIONS

Although connecting technology to trade books is a more difficult task than making those connections to basals, it is very gratifying. To create this connection, start by assessing your knowledge and objectives. If you know children's literature, search for software that extends students' thinking about the book. If you already are using tool-based software, analyze your objectives for each trade book to determine which software packages meet these needs. Once you have identified software packages (or parts of them), generate ideas for adapting them to your plans (Wepner, 1990c). Consider the following four areas as you develop your ideas:

1. *Software to Support the Book's Genre.* Whether working with realistic fiction, fairy tales, science fiction, nonfiction, adventure, historical fiction, or poetry, you can find software to support your students' genre-based reading. In addition to the software and applications mentioned in the previous section, many other packages are also available. For example, *Big Book Maker: Favorite Fairy Tales and Nursery Rhymes* (Pelican, 1990) complements students' work with fairy tales; *Story Starters: Social Studies* (Pelican, 1989) enhances students' experiences with adventure, historical fiction, and content-related nonfiction. However, software need not be genre-specific. Many packages, especially those with theme-oriented graphic libraries, support creative genre-based projects.
2. *Software to Support the Book's Theme.* Use software to help students look at themes across books within the same genre. For example, students could use *The Literary Mapper* (Teacher Support Software, 1989) to analyze the similarities and differences in the characters in both *The Pain and the Great One* (Blume, 1974b) and *Oh, Brother* (Wilson, 1988) as part of their analysis of the books' sibling rivalry theme.
3. *Software to Support Content Area Learning.* Use software to support students' acquisition of information from books. For example, the book *Silver* (Whelan, 1988) has to do with a child's relationship with a dog, but it also includes a great deal of information about Alaska. In studying this book, students might use *The Semantic Mapper* (Teacher Support Software, 1987) to make connections with what they know and what they learn and then work with the simulation *Where in the USA*

is Carmen SanDiego? (Broderbund, 1986) to apply and expand their knowledge of geography.

4. *Software to Support Students' Skills.* Open-ended software packages that allow you to enter your own data support this endeavor. For example, *The Sequencer* (Teacher Support Software, 1989) is useful for reinforcing students' ability to sequence episodes from any book.

By now, you must be exhausted from the litany of "coulds" and "shoulds" surrounding technology. It is time to take a look at what teachers actually are doing for their students and themselves to connect technology to their instructional situations.

The Proof is in the Pudding: Teachers' Applications

This section provides a glimpse of reality. While some teachers use software to support existing classroom structures, others have restructured their classrooms to support technology. As some are just getting their feet wet with the drill-and-practice mode, others are entrenched in multimedia. Although not always on the cutting edge, these teachers' initiatives are working for them right now. As we interviewed and observed these teachers in their classrooms, we asked them to characterize how they teach: primarily basal, a combination of basals and trade books, trade books only. We, therefore, present to you what a dozen teachers and one reading/language arts supervisor are doing for their K–3 and 4–6 students within each configuration. Inner-city, suburban, and suburban-rural districts are represented. While some have ideal hardware set-ups, others don't. While some have software choices, others have to use what is available. However, we hope you see yourself somewhere in (or, better yet, beyond) the examples that follow.

TECHNOLOGY WITH STUDENTS IN GRADES K–3

Uses Technology with Basals

Even though first grade teacher Edith Green, whom you read about in Chapter 2, only has one computer in her classroom one week of every four, she makes sure that her students use it during their reading and enrichment periods. With the advice of colleagues, she found software that complements some of the concepts from her basal reading program with two of the three Curious George software packages, *Curious George Goes to the Library* and *Curious George in Outer Space* (DLM, 1989). Because primary students love to read and are successful with the Curious George series (Richek & McTague, 1988), they get to read a familiar story line about Curious George getting lost until the man with the yellow hat finds him. They also reinforce their concepts of position (for example, up-down) and comparison (for example, tall-taller-tallest) respectively.

Second grade teacher Ann Carline, whom you also read about in Chapter 2, is fortunate enough to have two computers in her classroom. Despite pressure to cover the basal and work with the district's "Literature in the Classroom" program, she manages to have each of her students work with the computer two to three times a week. Ann typically has students work in pairs for computer time so that more able students work with less able students. One of her students' favorite packages is Troll's *The Magic String* (1985), a reading lab module with a 32-page hardcover book, a matching read-along audiocassette, and a software program with learning activities keyed to the book.

Similarly, second grade teacher Dana Licameli finds that her students love packages from Troll because they get to read the book and listen to the tape before they use the computer. She feels that her students love to work on the computer to reinforce vocabulary skills from the basal. To schedule all 23 of her students to use the computer every two or three days, she devises a checklist. Students check off their names when they complete their computer assignment and then tell the next student to go.

Although all three teachers wish they had more time, software, hardware, and staff development, they are working successfully with what they have. They have taken a first step in discovering ways in which the computer can support their basal reading program.

USES TECHNOLOGY WITH BASALS AND TRADE BOOKS

Kindergarten teacher Maria Conway takes her students to the computer room once a week to work with software from the Minnesota Educational Computing Consortium (MECC) that is related to word recognition skills from her basal workbook. Because her goal "is for children to be excited about books and the stories that we hear and create," she has spent the last five years collecting trade books to supplement her school's reading program. While she takes great pride in her vast and varied collection, she never really developed an organizational system for connecting all her books to her instructional goals. After taking a semester-long in-service course on computers, she realized that if she put all of her books into a **database program**, she would have an open-ended system for sorting her books. After searching for appropriate and available database programs and talking to colleagues who could help her trouble-shoot, she decided to use the *Bank Street School Filer* (Sunburst, 1986). Weeks later, she had every one of her 214 classroom books in her file, along with subjects to consider for teaching and creative activities to accompany each book (see Figure 5.10). She also can sort her books in the following ways:

Alphabetically by title	Social problem-solving books
Alphabetically by author	Winter books
Alphabet books	Specific authors with multiple books (for example,
Animal books	Asch, Berenstain, Carle, Hoban, Keats, Lionni,
Apple books	Moore, Prelutsky)
Bear books	

FIGURE 5.10
A page from a kindergarten teacher's database of trade books using *Bank Street School Filer* (Sunburst, 1986) *Note.* From "Database of Trade Books," 1991. Copyright 1991 by Maria Conway. Software program used is *Bank Street School Filer.* Copyright 1986 by Sunburst Communications. Reprinted by permission.

```
TITLE: ARABELLA THE SMALLEST GIRL IN THE WORLD
AUTHOR: FOX
SUBJECT: SIZES
SUBJECT2: MATH
SUBJECT3: MEASUREMENT
SUBJECT 4:

COMMENT:
CHART WEIGHT AND HEIGHT COMPARE
SIZES OF STUDENTS.


================================================================


TITLE: BABAR AND THE GHOST
AUTHOR: DE BRUNHOFF
SUBJECT: ELEPHANT
SUBJECT2: GHOST
SUBJECT3: HALLOWEEN
SUBJECT4:

COMMENT:
MAKE TISSUE GHOST. VIEW TAPE "BABAR,
THE LITTLE ELEPHANT." MAKE PAPER
PLATE ELEPHANT MASK.


================================================================


TITLE: BASIL BRUSH BUILDS A HOUSE
AUTHOR: FIRMIN
SUBJECT: FOXES
SUBJECT2: MOLES
SUBJECT3: HOME
SUBJECT 4: CO-OPERATION

COMMENT:
BUILD A BLOCK VILLAGE.


================================================================


TITLE: BASIL BRUSH GOES BOATING
AUTHOR: FIRMIN
SUBJECT: FOXES
SUBJECT2: MOLES
SUBJECT3: TRANSPORTATION
SUBJECT4: CAMPING

COMMENT:
LIST THINGS YOU WOULD NEED FOR A
CAMPING TRIP.


================================================================
```

First grade teacher Julie Smith did her own research on ways to complement her basal program with trade books and technology. She reads to her students every day so that they, in turn, want to read their own books. After students read a book, they receive a train car that is put around the room. Each year, her classroom goal is to have the train go completely around the room. Because she has volunteer parents working alongside her, her students have the opportunity to work with the computer at least three times a week. They often dictate stories to the parents with the *Muppet Slate: The Word and Picture Processor* (Sunburst, 1988). Students work with the parents to read, revise, and edit their stories. Interestingly, while she has used skill-based software with her students, she told us that they are much more enthusiastic about writing on the computer. As a result, Julie decided to teach keyboarding. Students have laminated keyboards at their desks that they take home for additional practice.

Connects Technology to Trade Books

Primary teacher Shana Leib uses her daily read-alouds and follow-up computer activities to help her inner-city children note details. For instance, after reading Robert N. Munsch's *The Paper Bag Princess* (1980), a book about a liberated princess, students create their own images of the princess from the story and write descriptive stories about the princess with Spinnaker's *Facemaker: Gold Edition* (1986) (see Figure 5.11).

If you have access to a **CD-ROM (compact disk read-only memory)** player and a Macintosh computer, you can have students reread *The Paper Bag Princess* (Discis, 1990) on the computer as often as they like. A new company called Discis has created an identical book in text and pictures. The only difference is that this company has added phrase-by-phrase narration, in-context word explanations, and identification of picture elements—all presented orally—to aid students' understanding (see Figure 5.12 for a sample screen). Although this book does not include a second language translation, some of the nine other books from the company have translations in Spanish, French, and Cantonese. (See *The Paper Bag Princess* entry under the "Software Mentioned" section at the end of this chapter for a listing of other books available by Discis.)

Virginia Modla, a supervisor of language arts, has created a unit on rainbows that integrates technology. Seventeen different software packages are used with over 45 rainbow books. Whether students listen to a book read aloud, read to themselves, or write about a book, they work with some facet of technology to share their ideas. For example, after the teacher reads *The Wizard and the Rainbow* (Vickers, 1987), a story about a wizard who takes a little boy on a carpet ride to rainbow town where everything is made of rainbows, students have a copy of a small wizard from *SuperPrint II* (Scholastic, 1989) to draw a picture of a rainbow and themselves with a wizard. They then complete the sentence, "The wizard and I will travel on our rainbow to _____ ." Students' papers are then put on a laminated, poster-size wizard that is created with the same program.

FIGURE 5.11
Students' ideas for *The Paper Bag Princess* using *Facemaker: Gold Edition* (Spinnaker, 1986) *Note.* From students' work on computer, 1991. Copyright 1991 by Marquita Ferguson, Ari Lester, and Jeffrey Zacharie. Software program used is *Facemaker: Gold Edition.* Copyright 1986 by Spinnaker. Reprinted by permission.

This is Princess Zelda. She is from a castle in Florida. Zelda always likes to smile. She is nice and friendly. She has long, curly hair and she likes a king. The king's name is Ronald. And they will get married on Monday. And she will have a little boy named Raphael.
By: Marquita F. Ari L. and Jeffrey Z.

Every nook and cranny of the classroom also contains some reminder of students' work with rainbows and technology. In the rainbow reading corner there is a poster created with *Clifford's Big Book Publisher* (Scholastic, 1990) showing Clifford reading a book with "Read with Clifford" printed below. A chart entitled "Rainbow Books Read to Us" is created with *The Print Shop* (Broderbund, 1984) so that children can record the books they have read next to their names. After children return their rainbow book that has been read aloud to them by their parents and then complete the "My Rainbow Book Report" form (see Figure 5.13) created with *The Children's Writing & Publishing Center* (The Learning Company, 1988), the teacher places a rainbow sticker next to that child under the appropriate title.

As a supervisor Modla feels that her role is to support her teachers' use of technology. Because she herself has worked with every piece of suggested software, creating rainbow bulletin boards and posters for her teachers, she has helped her teachers to appreciate how readily software supports their unit plans.

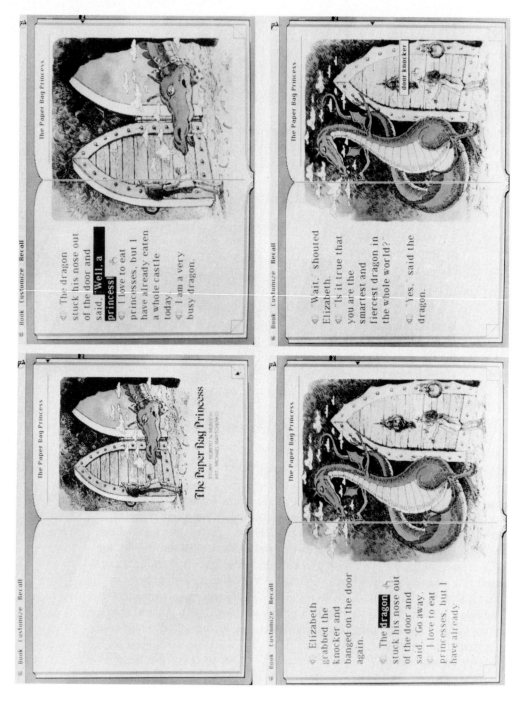

FIGURE 5.12

Four screens from *The Paper Bag Princess* (Discis, 1990)

Note. From screens from *The Paper Bag Princess*, 1990. Copyright 1990 by Discis. Reprinted by permission.

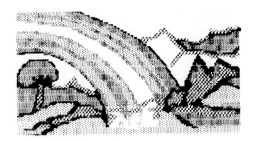

My Rainbow Book Report

Name of book_____

Author_____

This book is:

_ **Funny**   _ **Scary**   _**Interesting**

_**Boring**

FIGURE 5.13
Book report activity form for a kindergarten unit on rainbows using *The Children's Writing and Publishing Center* (The Learning Company, 1989)
Note. From "Book Report Activity for Rainbow Unit," 1991. Copyright 1991 by Virginia Modla. Software program by The Learning Company, 1989. Reprinted by permission.

TECHNOLOGY WITH STUDENTS IN GRADES 4–6

USES TECHNOLOGY WITH BASALS

After toying with the idea of technology for seven years, fourth grade teacher Frank Massaro found his computer niche with word processing. He uses *Milliken Word Processor* (1984) because of the **icon menu** (images, as opposed to words, to represent options) and simple one-letter commands that students use to access different program components. Although he believes that one of the child's most difficult problems is to become familiar with the keyboard, he finds that poetry is an excellent way to start students with a word processor, since "poems do not have to be lengthy to be good, and apprehensive writers may be more daring" (Massaro, 1990, p. 3). He starts by having a class discussion about secret hiding places where students like to be alone. They then write poetry on the computer about where they like to go to think. He encourages his students to illustrate and entitle their poems (see Figure 5.14).

Although Frank teaches primarily with the basal, he requires students to read at least two self-selected trade books each month. Currently he is setting up a Book Report file with a database program so that students can enter their opinions of the books read. He feels that this helps students to see how others feel about what they are reading, and it helps him to identify students for small-group book talks.

USES TECHNOLOGY WITH BASALS AND TRADE BOOKS

Rosemary Taylor, whom you read about in Chapter 3, continues to branch out from her basal reading series with trade books and technology. She feels comfortable combining both to help her students acquire skills and give them opportunities to "really read." Taylor's experimentation with technology grows out of her college course work. As she continues to learn about new products, she tries them with her class. Two of her noteworthy technology projects are described in the following paragraphs.

During one of her sessions with process writing in which students wrote about an area of interest, she noticed that most of her students wrote about pets. She decided to use *The Children's Writing & Publishing Center* (The Learning Company, 1989) to create a class newsletter because of this program's "animal" graphics library. She had each student create an illustrated pet story. Afterward two students edited the stories and created a pet newsletter to share with other classes (Wepner, 1990b).

Recently Taylor linked a poetry unit to a multimedia plan. Students first read the poems in Paul Fleischman's (1988) *Joyful Noise, Poems for Two Voices*, a Newbery Award book, to understand each poem's main idea and to interpret its figurative language. They practiced reading a selected poem with a partner and presented their poems on videotape. They then used *VCR Companion* (Broderbund, 1988) to create introductory screens, identifying the poem's title and the poem's readers for their own class presentation of poetry reading (Wepner, 1990c).

CONNECTS TECHNOLOGY TO TRADE BOOKS

About three years ago, Barbara Chertoff decided that her days of teaching her third graders with the basal were over. She worked closely with the district's reading coordinator to select class sets of five different trade books: *Charlotte's Web* (White, 1952), *James and the Giant Peach* (Dahl, 1961), *Charlie and the Chocolate Factory* (Dahl, 1964), *Ramona the Pest* (Cleary, 1968), and *The Cricket in Times Square* (Selden, 1960). She follows the same pattern by preparing her students to read with questions and new vocabulary words and discussing predictions and vocabulary after reading. She usually uses technology to do book-related projects. One project that her students enjoy is creating crossword puzzles with *Crossword Magic* (Mindscape,

FIGURE 5.14

Student's first experience with word processing using *Milliken Word Processor* (Milliken, 1984)

Note. From "My Favorite Place," 1990. Copyright 1990 by Asha S. White. Software program by Milliken Publishing, 1984. Reprinted by permission.

1985). Students create clues for their accumulated vocabulary lists. They then create puzzles, run them off, and disseminate them to other students to complete. As she said, "It's fun!"

Fifth grade teacher Bernard Ready has been using trade books since the early 1970s. He says, "My ultimate goal is to get my students to read books." Although he used basals along with his literature-based reading program for many years, he abandoned basals (but not skill development) in 1986 when he discovered *The Electronic Bookshelf* through his principal.

The Electronic Bookshelf (1984) is a management system for over 2,500 trade books. Fifteen to 30 books are included in each title disk. Title disks include such themes as Newbery Awards, Popular Pre-Teen Authors, Fun-To-Read Intermediates, and Caldecott Honors to accommodate the K–12 population. After students read books from a title disk, students take a 10-item multiple choice quiz to assess their comprehension. Points are awarded for mastery. Although the point system (1 point for easy books, 2 points for middle level books, and 3 points for hard books) has already been rated by the publishing company, the mastery level is established by the teacher. Students can attempt to pass the book quiz three times before this management system indicates that they have failed a book. Students get printouts, indicating their total points and the number of books passed and failed (see Figure 5.15). Although *Bookshelf*'s pass/fail system for assessing students' book understanding is somewhat controversial, it nevertheless involves students in the world of computers via trade book reading.

When we meet with Ready he reported that the average student in his room reads 53 books each year, with every student reading at least 40 books by the end of the year. His 50- to 60-minute long class of heterogeneously grouped students does not spend the entire time doing *Bookshelf*. He uses the following teaching pattern every day:

- He begins his class by reading to his students for about 10 minutes.
- He then has all students engage in Sustained Silent Reading. He takes 15 seconds to 2 minutes to talk to each student about what he or she is reading. He firmly believes that this effort shows his students that he cares about what they are reading.
- He then calls up a small group of students who are reading the same trade book from the program to hone vocabulary and comprehension skills. Since each of the books from the disk comes with 8 to 10 copies, he usually has enough students working on the same book to form a group. Because he determined which skills from his former basal series needed to be addressed at this grade level, he weaves these skills into his small-group sessions.
- He then sits and reads with them. At this time, students who are ready to work with *Bookshelf* go to the classroom computer to take their tests.

Ready makes an effort to help all his students read at least 10 three-point books during the year. At the end of each year, he also has his students vote for the top 10

FIGURE 5.15

Student's progress report using *The Electronic Bookshelf* (The Electronic Bookshelf, 1984)

Note. From "Progress Report," 1991. Copyright 1991 by Leigh A. Daigneault. Software program by Electronic Bookshelf. Copyright 1984. Reprinted by permission.

```
LEIGH A DAIGNEAULT                    READY B

TOTAL POINTS . . . . . 77
BOOKS PASSED . . . . . 38
BOOKS FAILED . . . . .  0
TOTAL BOOKS ATTEMPTED  38
LEVEL. . . . . . . . .  0

    SCORE       TRIES       POINTS
    -----       -----       ------

    8/10          1           2      TALES OF FOURTH GRADE NOTHING
    9/10          1           2      BUNNICULA
    8/10          1           2      CELERY STALKS AT MIDNIGHT
    9/10          1           2      TRAMP STEAMER AND THE SILVER B
    9/10          1           3      PUSHCART WAR
   10/10          1           2      CHARLOTTE'S WEB
    8/10          1           2      HOW TO EAT FRIED WORMS
    9/10          1           2      RAMONA THE BRAVE
    8/10          1           2      CRICKET IN TIMES SQUARE
   10/10          1           2      RAMONA AND HER FATHER
    8/10          1           2      CHRISTMAS CAROL
    8/10          1           2      BASEMENT BASEBALL CLUB
    8/10          1           2      THE MOUSE AND THE MOTORCYCLE
   10/10          1           2      RUNAWAY RALPH
    8/10          1           2      NIGHTY NIGHTMARE
    9/10          1           2      MY SIDE OF THE MOUNTAIN
    7/10          1           2      RAMONA AND HER MOTHER
    7/10          1           2      THE TRUMPET OF THE SWANS
   10/10          1           2      WAR WITH GRANDPA
    9/10          1           3      HARRIET THE SPY
    7/10          1           2      RABBIT HILL
   10/10          1           2      RALPH S. MOUSE
   10/10          1           2      CHARLIE AND THE GREAT GLASS EL
   10/10          1           2      ALDO APPLESAUCE
   10/10          1           2      KEY TO THE TREASURE
    9/10          1           1      SARAH, PLAIN AND TALL
    8/10          2           2      HELEN KELLER
    8/10          1           2      INDIAN IN THE CUPBOARD
   10/10          1           2      MR. POPPER'S PENGUINS
    9/10          1           2      BETSY'S LITTLE STAR
   10/10          1           2      SECRET LIFE OF THE UNDERWEAR C
    9/10          1           2      GREAT BRAIN DOES IT AGAIN
    8/10          1           3      JUST AS LONG AS WE'RE TOGETHER
   10/10          1           2      THE VAMPIRE MOVES IN
    8/10          1           2      IT'S NOT THE END OF THE WORLD
   10/10          1           2      B IS FOR BETSY
   10/10          1           2      PIPPI LONGSTOCKING
    9/10          1           1      WHIPPING BOY

-------------------------------------------
```

books so that he doesn't have to keep using the same books year after year. He also sends parents any printout that the student gets so that they know what their children are reading and how they are progressing. As Ready says, "I was not always a computer fan. [But], it has taken technology to get kids to read books."

Susan McGrath and Celia Einhorn (1990) have spent the last few years mixing and matching their tool-based software to spice up their reading lessons with trade books for K–6 students. One exciting example is what they have done with Judith Viorst's *Alexander and the Terrible, Horrible, No Good, Very Bad Day* (1972). After they read the book to their students, they have them identify what happens to Alexander during different parts of the day—early morning, mid-morning, noon, afternoon, and evening—so that students can create visual time lines with the *Timeliner* (Tom Snyder Productions, 1986). Since this program allows students to create time lines for different periods of time, students select the one-day option to delineate Alexander's day. Because the time lines print out sideways in a large, clear banner format, students get to display these murals around the room. Afterwards students create their own rendition of their terrible, horrible day with the *Timeliner* (see Figure 5.16) and *The Children's Writing & Publishing Center* (The Learning Company, 1989). They then design a slide show of their day with *Slide Shop* (Scholastic, 1988). The entire project takes about seven hours or one solid week of the language/reading time slot.

A recently published software package that could also be used with this book is *Alexander and the Terrible, Horrible, No Good, Very Bad Day* (Sunburst Communications, 1991), a collection of 15 lesson plan ideas about the book that is used with *Magic Slate II* (Sunburst, 1988), 40-column version. As students learn to work with different word processing features, they strengthen their comprehension of the book by writing in, for instance, poetic, letter, and story form.

TECHNOLOGY WITH SPECIAL NEEDS STUDENTS

Although not all types of special needs students are represented in this section, we share with you samples of what three teachers are doing with their special education, English as a Second Language, and gifted and talented populations. Since these teachers did not identify themselves within a special configuration, we share their initiatives more globally.

SPECIAL EDUCATION

Jane Beaty, a fourth grade special education teacher in Hermitage, Tennessee, uses technology for every one of her literature-based plans. Unlike most of us, Beaty is part of the Apple Classroom Teacher Of TomorrowSM (ACOTSM) nationwide research project funded by Apple Computer, enabling her and her students to have access to their own Apple IIgs computers. However, Jane started out like the rest of us with what is now a low-level machine in her home that she could pound away at during her spare time. Because many of her students have had frustrating academic experiences and difficult home lives, she has always combed professional books for captivating ideas and searched through catalogues for "must reading" trade books. When she discovered how intrigued her students were with the one computer in her

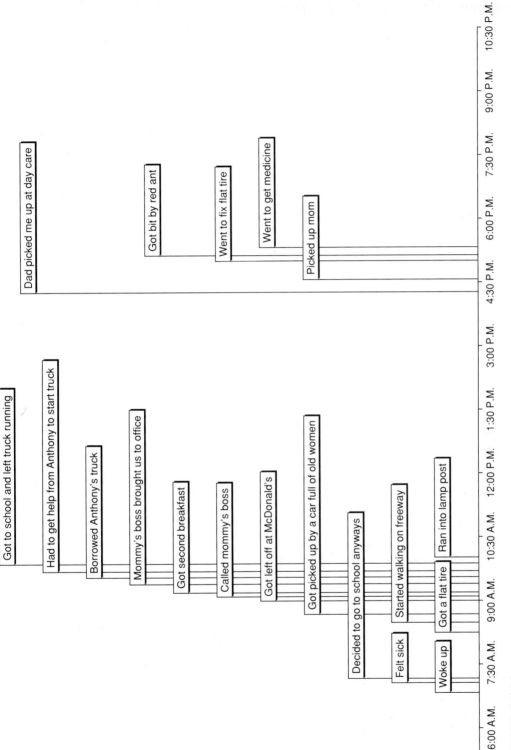

FIGURE 5.16

Student's personal time line about her terrible, horrible, no good, very bad day using *Timeliner* (Tom Synder Productions, 1986)

Note. From "Personal Time Line," 1991. Copyright 1991 by Elizabeth Einhorn. Software program by Tom Snyder Productions, 1986. Reprinted by permission.

classroom, she realized that she had stumbled on the perfect marriage for instruction: literature and technology.

Beaty embeds technology into every one of her literature-based plans. Here is an example of one of her lessons from her book *A Link to Literature* (Beaty, 1988). One of the trade books from her plans, *The Courage of Sarah Noble* (Dalgliesh, 1954), is about a young girl who leaves the rest of her family to accompany her father from New England to a Connecticut wilderness. As she waits for her father to build a new family home, she makes friends with the Indians to help her overcome her fears and loneliness. Before actually reading the story, Beaty uses *The Semantic Mapper* (Teacher Support Software, 1987) to help her students brainstorm and organize their ideas about pioneer life. Then she has her students write about life in pioneer days. She displays students' writing and their maps. After discussing the book's theme, she reviews the meaning of difficult vocabulary in the book from a chart that she created with the *Language Experience Recorder Plus* (Teacher Support Software, 1987), 20-column editor. She uses the 20-column editor so that the printout is chart size. She then has her students complete vocabulary sheets of words from the book that she created with the *Word Works Utility* (Teacher Support Software, 1987), an open-ended software program for vocabulary development. She reads the book to them, pausing at certain points to clarify concepts and vocabulary. After reading, she has her students write a summary of the book with the *Language Experience Recorder Plus*, 40- or 80-column editor.

English as a Second Language (ESL)

ESL teacher Marcia Diamantis created a fairy tale unit for her primary students because they had little or no exposure to this genre. She wanted to help enrich her students' understanding and use of language by exposing them to a genre that has become a part of American culture. After she created her unit, she decided that she wanted to use technology because of its ability to promote interaction and build self-confidence. She searched for fairy tale software that would help her students to better comprehend the stories. When she discoverd that *Micro Tales* (Troll, 1987) had four of the fairy tales that she was using, *Cinderella, The Elves and the Shoemaker, Jack and the Beanstalk,* and *Rumplestiltskin,* she decided to use these software packages as part of her unit. She first reads a fairy tale to her students—often using a big book version—and then uses fairy tale software to reinforce what she read. Because her students are at different reading levels, she uses their responses to each package to help her decide which facets of each package to emphasize. She has found that her students enjoy the computer activities so much that they want to work with the computer again and again (Diamantis, 1989).

Gifted and Talented

Rosemary Alesandro, a teacher of gifted and talented students in grades one through eight, connects technology to the majority of her reading/language arts lessons. Primarily inspired by her college courses, she looks for software packages that extend the lessons that can be found in books. The following two examples demonstrate how she incorporates software with her unit themes for primary and elementary students. She uses the 20-column version of *Magic Slate II* (Sunburst, 1988) word processor with her first grade students to create cloze-like stories with this package's fill-in features. After students listen to animal stories and discuss each animal's features, habitats, and habits, they dictate a story into a tape recorder. Each student dictates two sentences. She transcribes what they dictated onto *Magic Slate II,* deleting key words with this package's fill-in feature. Once students complete the story, they print it out and design animal title pages.

She helps her fourth grade students understand the concept of "testimonials" in advertising with *Create with Garfield!* (DLM, 1987), a cartoon-maker program. Students actually use Garfield as the starring personality to create testimonial ads. Rosemary said that before she used this program, she was extremely frustrated by her students' inability to understand this concept (Alesandro, 1989).

Guidelines

In addition to the suggestions that are interspersed throughout this chapter, we offer the following eight guidelines to help you get started or continue with your technology plans.

1. Find someone with whom you can brainstorm, ask questions, and seek advice. Don't be afraid to ask what you consider to be a silly question. All of us involved with technology know about those moments of trepidation and frustration.
2. Make sure you have good software to use. In other words, the software should be grounded in theory and strategies that support your teaching philosophy. If you are a beginner, don't try to work with software that is too complicated. Make sure that one hour is all that is required to learn the thrust of the program. Once you know the program's basics, go back to learn its intricacies.
3. Keep in mind that you need not feel locked into using entire packages. Sometimes an activity or a reading selection within a package may be the only useful component for your plan.
4. Once you have identified one to three pieces of software, generate ideas for adapting them to your instructional plans. Think of using reading software in lieu of an occasional story from the basal. Alternatively, consider ways that the topics from the reading software can support and extend stories from the basal or other reading selections. Use writing software to support students' reading of any type of literature and to enhance their writing efforts.
5. Introduce new programs to the entire class so that you can go through its operation. Have students work through packages with you. Although they may not

receive the full benefits of technology immediately, this procedure will help them to see how to work a program. If you are working with software for reading, make sure that students are aware of all the useful options in a package. If you are working with software for writing, demonstrate how to use the package's set of commands. Bonnie Prohaska, a special needs/computers and reading teacher, dumps selected software screens onto a videotape so that she can highlight facets of the software package that are most important to her students. She believes that this method helps students to know what to look for when they get to the keyboard.

6. Find student assistants or teacher aides to help students as they begin working on the program. They can handle the frequent low-level questions about program operation.

7. Encourage teamwork with software, especially for the writing software.

8. Keep a class library of disks as part of the regular classroom so that students consider software an integral part of their learning experience.

Concluding Remarks

In a summary of a research article entitled "Computers are Great But I . . . ," Collis (1990) bemoans the fact that technology has become an "in" thing like exercise and dieting: we know we should be using it, feel guilty if we're not, plan to start using it next week, but we cannot use it now. And, of course, we never get around to that "must-do" technology plan. On the other hand, many of us are proud of our technology efforts until we read a magazine or journal article that crushes our confidence about our state-of-the-art instruction. Part and parcel of these ne'er-do-well-feelings is the rapid rate at which technology changes. Why bother to start or keep trying if we think that what we are doing today will become obsolete tomorrow? Although these fears are not completely unfounded, we must never forget that our mission is to prepare our students to deal with life's realities, one of which is that we live in a nation that is increasingly dependent on computer technology.

Although we may not be ready to tackle Mecklenburger's (1990) admonishment to look at education in the context of the technologies of the 20th and 21st century, we need to ensure that our students benefit from technology. For us, this means using software that helps our students to become more literate. It means using technology for the same fundamental purpose that we use books—to help our students understand and appreciate the joys of communicating with print. Yet, it also means helping our students to see how communication can be more easily facilitated with technology.

As with any other regimen, once we begin to see the positive effects of our software applications, we become more and more motivated to continue. Think back to the teacher in our chapter opening vignette. Even though her second period class was a disaster, her first period class was so rewarding that she discovered how best to use technology to communicate to her students. Although she may not have had the latest and greatest hardware and software, she found her technological niche. Amid the shrill sound of educational, political, and technological debates, we need to consider software within the context of our own literacy goals. And we must be prepared for psychological bumps and bruises along the way. However, if we find ways to govern what we do with technology, rather than allowing it to govern us, we won't feel the need to procrastinate any longer.

Questions for Discussion

1. Why is it important to integrate technology into reading and writing programs?
2. How can hypertext be useful for literacy development?
3. What should reading teachers look for in reading and writing software?
4. What role should basal companies play in supporting technology?
5. How can we encourage teachers to use technology as an integral part of their reading and writing program?

Application Activities

1. Find a piece of software for reading. Record the publisher's stated purpose for developing the software. Then experiment with the software to see if it supports the publisher's statements. Record whether you agree or disagree with the purpose. Give reasons for your conclusion.
2. Use the following rating scale for this activity:

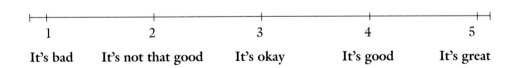

1	2	3	4	5
It's bad	It's not that good	It's okay	It's good	It's great

Experiment with a piece of software. Rate it with this rating scale. Find a student for whom the software package is intended. Have your student experiment with the software and rate it with the same scale. What happened?
3. Find a software package that you would like to use. Create an extension activity for it. Give it a title and write a description of your activity for others to follow.
4. Identify a creative writing project that your students could do with writing soft-

ware. Devise a plan so that all your students get to use the computer. Specify the details of the project, the amount of time each student or set of students need to spend at the computer, and the length of time the project will take.

5. Select a piece of literature that you would like to use. Identify a software package that you could use with your story or book. Create an activity that connects the software to the trade book. Give your activity a title and write a description of your activity for others to follow.

References

Alesandro, R. (1989). *Language arts, computers, and the gifted student.* Unpublished manuscript, William Paterson College, Wayne, NJ.

Anderson-Inman, L., Adler, W., Cron, M., Hillinger, M., Olson, R., & Prohaska, B. (1990). Speech: The third dimension. *The Computing Teacher, 17* (7), 35–40, 53.

Balajthy, E. (1987a). Only one computer in the classroom? *The Reading Teacher, 41,* 210–211.

Balajthy, E. (1987b). What are basal publishers doing with computer-based instruction? *The Reading Teacher, 41,* 344–345.

Balajthy, E. (1988a). Computers and instruction: Implications of the rising tide of criticism for reading education. *Reading Research and Instruction, 28,* 49–59.

Balajthy, E. (1988b). Voice synthesis for emergent literacy. *The Reading Teacher, 42,* 72.

Balajthy, E. (1989). *Computers and reading: Lessons from the past and the technologies of the future.* Englewood Cliffs, NJ: Prentice Hall.

Beaty, J. (1988). *A link to literature.* Gainesville, FL: Teacher Support Software.

Bitterhouse, J. (1990, May). *Overview of state of computers and language arts.* Paper presented at the meeting of the International Reading Association, Atlanta, GA.

Blair, T. R., Rupley, W. H., & Jones, M. P. (1986). Microcomputers: Another false prophet? *Reading Research and Instruction, 26* (1), 58–61.

Blanchard, J. S., Mason, G. E., & Daniel, D. (Eds.). (1987). *Computer applications in reading* (3rd ed.). Newark, DE: International Reading Association.

Blanchard, J. S., & Rottenberg, C. J. (1990). Hypertext and hypermedia: Discovering and creating meaningful learning environments. *The Reading Teacher, 43,* 656–661.

Butzin, S. M. (1990). Project CHILD: "Not boring school, but work that's fun and neat." *The Computing Teacher, 17* (6), 20–23.

Chira, S. (1990, September 5). Making computers better teachers. *The New York Times,* p. B7.

Cochran-Smith, M., Kahn, J., & Paris, C. L. (1988). When word processors come into the classroom. In J. L. Hoot & S. B. Silvern (Eds.), *Writing with computers in the early grades* (pp. 43–74). New York: Teachers College Press.

Collis, B. (1990). *The best of research windows: Trends and issues in educational computing.* Eugene, OR: International Society for Technology in Education.

Corbran, E. (1990). *The effect of attitude and training in computer technology on teachers' use of computers for instruction.* Unpublished master's thesis, William Paterson College, Wayne, NJ.

Daiute, C. (1985, March). *Word processing and writing: The state of the art.* Paper presented at the Writing, Reading, and Computers Conference, William Paterson College, Wayne, NJ.

DeGroff, L. (1990). Is there a place for computers in whole language classrooms? *The Reading Teacher, 43,* 568–572.

Diamantis, M. (1989). *Computer time in a fairy tale unit.* Unpublished manuscript, William Paterson College, Wayne, NJ.

D'Ignazio, F. (1989). *Classroom multimedia.* New York: Scholastic.

Doyle, C. (1988). Creative applications of computer-assisted reading and writing instruction. *Journal of Reading, 32,* 236–239.

Feeley, J. T. (1986). Software review of *Success with Reading. The Reading Instruction Journal, 30* (1), 30–32.

Geoffrion, L., & Geoffrion, O. (1983). *Computers and reading.* Menlo Park, CA: Addison-Wesley.

Goldman, J. M. (1988). *The use of computers versus basal readers for reading comprehension in the primary grades.* ERIC Document Reproduction Service No. ED 299 548.

Grunwald, P. (1990). The new generation of information systems. *Phi Delta Kappan, 72,* 113–114.

Hague, S., & Childers, N. (1986, October). *Micros and reading: What do secondary reading teachers say?* Paper presented at the College Reading Association, Knoxville, TN.

Hancock, J. (1989). Learning with databases. *Journal of Reading, 32,* 582–589.

Hannaford, A. E., & Taber, F. M. (1982). Microcomputer software for the handicapped: Development and evaluation. *Exceptional Children, 49* (2), 137–142.

Jenkins, T. M., & Dankert, E. J. (1981). Results of a three-month PLATO trial in terms of utilization and student attitudes. *Educational Technology, 21,* 44–47.

Johnson, D. S., & Pearson, P. D. (1984). *Teaching reading vocabulary* (2nd ed.). New York: Holt, Rinehart & Winston.

Kelman, P. (1990). *Alternatives to integrated instructional systems.* Unpublished manuscript.

Lake, D. (1990). Patrick's visual: A book report using presentation software. *The Computing Teacher, 17* (8), 54–55.

Massaro, F. (1990). *Tool applications in the classroom.* Unpublished manuscript. William Paterson College, Wayne, NJ.

Mecklenburger, J. A. (1990). Educational technology is not enough. *Phi Delta Kappan, 72,* 104–108.

McConkie, G. W., & Zola, D. (1987). Two examples of computer-based research on reading: Eye movement monitoring and computer-aided reading. In D. Reinking (Ed.), *Computers and reading: Issues for theory and practice* (pp. 97–107). New York: Teachers College Press.

McGrath, S., & Einhorn, C. (1990, March). *Software to spice up your reading lessons.* Paper presented at the meeting of the Tenth Annual Microcomputers in Education Conference, Arizona State University, Tempe, AZ.

Miccinati, J. L. (1988). Mapping the terrain: Connecting reading with academic writing. *Journal of Reading, 31,* 542–552.

Miller, L. (1989). Sometimes the tail should wag the dog. *The Reading Teacher, 42,* 428.

Milone, M. (1986). On-line communication: A revolution in reading? *The Reading Instruction Journal, 29* (3), 17–19.

Nagy, W. E. (1988). *Teaching vocabulary to improve reading comprehension.* Newark, DE: International Reading Association.

Olson, R., & Wise, B. (1987). Computer speech in reading instruction. In D. Reinking (Ed.), *Computers and reading: Issues for theory and practice* (pp. 156–177). New York: Teachers College Press.

Reinking, D. (1988). Computer-mediated text and comprehension differences: The role of reading time, reader preference, and estimation of learning. *Reading Research Quarterly, 23*, 484–498.

Reinking, D., & Schreiner, R. (1985). The effects of computer-mediated text on measures of reading comprehension and reading behavior. *Reading Research Quarterly, 20*, 536–552.

Reitsma, P. (1988). Reading practice for beginners: Effects of guided reading, reading-while-listening, and independent reading with computer-based speech feedback. *Reading Research Quarterly, 23* (2), 219–235.

Richek, M. A., & McTague, B. K. (1988). The "Curious George" strategy for students with reading problems. *The Reading Teacher, 42*, 220–226.

Rickelman, R. J., & Henk, W. A. (1989). Meeting tomorrow's challenge. *The Reading Teacher, 43*, 78–79.

Rickelman, R. J., & Henk, W. A. (1990). Telecommunications in the reading classroom. *The Reading Teacher, 43*, 418–419.

Roberts, N., Carter, R. C., Friel, S. N., & Miller, M. S. (1988). *Integrating computers into the elementary and middle school.* Englewood Cliffs, NJ: Prentice-Hall.

Scott, D., & Barker, J. (1987). Guidelines for selecting and evaluating reading software: Improving the decision-making process. *The Reading Teacher, 40*, 884–887.

Sherry, M. (1990). Implementing an integrated instructional system: Critical issues. *Phi Delta Kappan, 72*, 118–120.

Smith, R., & Vokurka, J. F. (1990). A software selection model for the special student. *The Computing Teacher, 17* (5), 36–38.

Standiford, S. N., Jaycox, K., & Auten, A. (1983). *Computers in the English classroom: A primer for teachers.* Urbana, IL: ERIC Clearinghouse on Reading and Communication Skills and the National Council of Teachers of English.

Stauffer, R. G. (1975). *Directing the reading-thinking process.* New York: Harper & Row.

Strickland, D. S., Feeley, J. T., & Wepner, S. B. (1987). *Using computers in the teaching of reading.* New York: Teachers College Press.

Trieschmann, M. (1990). Drill-and-practice software: What is appropriate feedback? *The Computing Teacher, 17* (5), 53–55.

Turner, J. (1990). Image processing: A complement to text. *The Computing Teacher, 17* (6), 24–26.

Tway, E. (1985). *Writing is reading: 26 ways to connect.* Urbana, IL: National Council of Teachers of English.

Vacca, R. T., & Vacca, J. A. L. (1989). *Content area reading* (3rd ed.). Glenview, IL: Scott, Foresman.

Wagner, W. G., O'Toole, W. M., & Kazelskis, R. (1985). Learning word processing skills with limited instruction: An exploratory study with college students. *Educational Technology, 25* (2), 26–28.

Watson, B. (1990). The wired classroom: American education goes on-line. *Phi Delta Kappan, 72*, 109–112.

Wepner, S. B. (1987). Connecting computers and reading disabilities. *Journal of Reading, Writing, and Learning Disabilities International, 3* (4), 297–307.

Wepner, S. B. (1989). Stepping forward with reading software. *Journal of Reading, Writing, and Learning Disabilities International, 5* (1), 61–83.

Wepner, S. B. (1990a). Computers and whole language: A "novel" frontier. *The Computing Teacher, 17* (5), 24–28.

Wepner, S. B. (1990b). Holistic computer applications in literature-based classrooms. *The Reading Teacher, 44*, 12–19.

Wepner, S. B. (1990c, October). Technology between the lines. *Teaching preK–8*, pp. 61–63.

Wepner, S. B. (in press). Computers and the gifted: How can they be challenged? *Proceedings from the Thirty-fifth Annual Convention of the International Reading Association.* Microcomputers and Reading

Special Interest Group, Newark, DE: International Reading Association.

Wepner, S. B. (1990/1991). Computers, reading software, and at-risk eighth graders. *Journal of Reading, 34,* 264–268.

Trade Books Mentioned

Blume, J. (1974a). *Blubber.* New York: Dell.

Blume, J. (1974b). *The pain and the great one.* New York: Dell.

Byars, B. (1977). *The pinballs.* New York: Harper & Row.

Cleary, B. (1968). *Ramona the pest.* New York: Morrow.

Dahl, R. (1961). *James and the giant peach.* New York: Knopf.

Dahl, R. (1964). *Charlie and the chocolate factory.* New York: Knopf.

Dalgliesh, A. (1954). *The courage of Sarah Noble.* New York: Charles Scribner's Sons.

Danziger, P. (1982). *The divorce express.* New York: Dell.

Fleischman, P. (1988). *Joyful noise, poems for two voices.* New York: Harper & Row.

Fleischman, S. (1986). *The whipping boy.* Mahwah, NJ: Troll Associates.

Gross, R. B. (1982). *If you grew up with George Washington.* New York: Scholastic.

Heyerdahl, T. (1960). *Kon Tiki.* Chicago: Rand McNally.

McCloskey, R. (1969). *Make way for ducklings.* New York: The Viking Press.

Munsch, R. (1980). *The paper bag princess.* Toronto, Canada: Annick Press.

Rauch, S. J. (1989). *The visitor from outer space.* Roslyn, NY: Berrent Publications.

Selden, G. (1960). *The cricket in Times Square.* New York: Farrar, Straus & Giroux.

Smith, R. K. (1981). *Jelly Belly.* New York: Dell.

Vickers, K. (1987). *The wizard and the rainbow.* San Diego: The Wright Group.

Viorst, J. (1972). *Alexander and the terrible, horrible, no good, very bad day.* New York: Atheneum.

Whelan, G. (1988). *Silver.* New York: Random House.

White, E. B. (1952). *Charlotte's web.* New York: Harper & Row.

Wilson, J. M. (1988). *Oh, brother.* New York: Scholastic.

Software Mentioned

TITLE: *Alexander and the Terrible, Horrible, No Good, Very Bad Day* (1991)
PUBLISHER: Sunburst Communications, 101 Castleton Street, Pleasantville, NY 10570-3498; 1-800-628-8897
PRICE: $59
HARDWARE: Apple

TITLE: *Bank Street School Filer* (1986)
PUBLISHER: Sunburst Communications, 101 Castleton Street, Pleasantville, NY 10570-3498; 1-800-628-8897
PRICE: $99
HARDWARE: Apple

TITLE: *Big Book Maker: Favorite Fairy Tales and Nursery Rhymes* (1990)
PUBLISHER: Pelican; distributed by Queue, Inc., 338 Commerce Drive, Fairfield, CT 06430; 1-800-232-2224
PRICE: $49.95
HARDWARE: Apple, MS-DOS

*All prices and hardware platforms subject to change.

TITLE: *The Children's Writing & Publishing Center* (1989)
PUBLISHER: The Learning Company, 6493 Kaiser Drive, Fremont, CA 94555; 1-800-852-2255
PRICE: $69.95
HARDWARE: Apple, MS-DOS, Macintosh (called *The Writing Center*)

TITLE: *Clifford's Big Book Publisher* (1990)
PUBLISHER: Scholastic Inc., 2931 East McCarty Street, P. O. Box 7502, Jefferson City, MO 65102; 1-800-541-5513, 1-800-392-2179 (MO)
PRICE: $39.95
HARDWARE: Apple, MS-DOS

TITLE: *The Comprehension Connection* (1987)
PUBLISHER: Milliken Publishing, 1100 Research Blvd., P.O. Box 21579, St. Louis, MO 63132-0579; 1-314-991-4220
PRICE: $150 for each grade level (grades 4–9)
HARDWARE: Apple

TITLE: *Create with Garfield!* (1987)
PUBLISHER: DLM Teaching Resources, One DLM Park, Allen, TX 75002; 1-800-527-4747
PRICE: $29.95, $39.95 (deluxe edition)
HARDWARE: Apple, Commodore, MS-DOS (deluxe edition only)

TITLE: *Crossword Magic* (1985)
PUBLISHER: Mindscape, P.O. Box 1167, Northbrook, IL 60062; 1-800-999-2242
PRICE: $59.95
HARDWARE: Apple, MS-DOS, Macintosh, Commodore/Atari

TITLE: *Curious George in Outer Space* and *Curious George Goes to the Library* (1989). (Third package in the series not mentioned is *Curious George Goes Shopping*.)
PUBLISHER: DLM Teaching Resources, One DLM Park, Allen, TX 75002; 1-800-527-4747
PRICE: $24.95
HARDWARE: Apple (MS-DOS and Tandy for *Curious George Goes to the Library* only)

TITLE: *The Electronic Bookshelf* (1984)
PUBLISHER: The Electronic Bookshelf, Inc., Rt. 9, Box 64, Frankfort, IN 46041; 1-317-324-2182
PRICE: $179.95 (program disk), $49.95 (each title disk)
HARDWARE: Apple

TITLE: *Facemaker: Gold Edition* (1986)
PUBLISHER: Spinnaker; distributed by Queue, Inc., 338 Commerce Drive, Fairfield, CT 06430; 1-800-232-2224
PRICE: $39.95 or $44.95 (for MS-DOS)
HARDWARE: Apple, MS-DOS, Commodore

TITLE: *Language Experience Recorder Plus* (1987)
PUBLISHER: Teacher Support Software, 1035 N.W. 57th Street, Gainesville, FL 32605-4483; 1-800-228-2871
PRICE: $99.95
HARDWARE: Apple, MS-DOS, Macintosh

TITLE: *The Literary Mapper* (1989)
PUBLISHER: Teacher Support Software, 1035 N.W. 57th Street, Gainesville, FL 32605-4483; 1-800-228-2871
PRICE: $129.95 for each level (K–3 or 4–6) or $159.95 for both levels
HARDWARE: Apple

TITLE: *The Magic String* (1985)
PUBLISHER: Troll Associates, 100 Corporate Dr., Mahwah, NJ 07430; 1-201-529-4000 x 119
PRICE: $39.95
HARDWARE: Apple

TITLE: *Make-A-Book* (1991)
PUBLISHER: Teacher Support Software, 1035 N.W. 57th Street, Gainesville, FL 32605-4483; 1-800-228-2871
PRICE: $59.95
HARDWARE: MS-DOS, Macintosh

TITLE: *Magic Slate II* (1988)
PUBLISHER: Sunburst Communications, 101 Castleton Street, Pleasantville, NY 10570-3498; 1-800-628-8897
PRICE: $65 for each version (20-column, 40-column, and 80-column)
HARDWARE: Apple

TITLE: *Micro Tales* (1987)
PUBLISHER: Troll Associates, 100 Corporate Dr., Mahwah, NJ 07430; 1-201-529-4000 (x 119)
PRICE: $39.95 for each of the 15 modules
HARDWARE: Apple

TITLE: *Milliken Word Processor* (1984)
PUBLISHER: Milliken Publishing, 1100 Research Blvd., P.O. Box 21579, St. Louis, MO 63132-0579; 1-314-991-4220
PRICE: $70
HARDWARE: Apple

TITLE: *Muppet Slate: The Word and Picture Processor* (1988)
PUBLISHER: Sunburst Communications, 101 Castleton Street, Pleasantville, NY 10570-3498; 1-800-628-8897
PRICE: $75
HARDWARE: Apple

TITLE: *The Paper Bag Princess* (1990)
OTHER TITLES: *A Long Hard Day on the Ranch, Cinderella, Heather Hits Her First Home Run, Moving Gives Me a Stomach Ache, Mud Puddle, Scary Poems for Rotten Kids, The Tale of Benjamin Bunny, The Tale of Peter Rabbit,* and *Thomas' Snowsuit*
PUBLISHER: Discis, 25 Sheppard Ave. East, Suite 802, Toronto, Ontario, Canada M2N 5W9; 1-416-250-6537
PRICE: $69.95
HARDWARE: CD-ROM drive and Macintosh

TITLE: *The Print Shop/The New Print Shop* (updated version) (1984)
PUBLISHER: Broderbund Software, 17 Paul Drive, San Rafael, CA 94903-2101; 1-800-521-6263
PRICE: $49.95–$69.95 (depending on hardware and version)
HARDWARE: Apple, MS-DOS, Macintosh (*The Print Shop*)

TITLE: *Reading Realities Elementary Series* (1990)
PUBLISHER: Teacher Support Software, 1035 N.W. 57th Street, Gainesville, FL 32605-4483; 1-800-228-2871
PRICE: $169.95 (Apple)/$179.95 (MS-DOS) for each package (School, Family, or Personal)
HARDWARE: Apple, MS-DOS

TITLE: *The Semantic Mapper* (1987)
PUBLISHER: Teacher Support Software, 1035 N.W. 57th Street, Gainesville, FL 32605-4483; 1-800-228-2871
PRICE: $254.95 (for basal package), $99.95 (for utility disk)
HARDWARE: Apple

TITLE: *The Sequencer* (1989)
PUBLISHER: Teacher Support Software, 1035 N.W. 57th Street, Gainesville, FL 32605-4483; 1-800-228-2871
PRICE: $284.95 (for basal package), $99.95 (for utility disk)
HARDWARE: Apple

TITLE: *Slide Shop* (1988)
PUBLISHER: Scholastic Inc., 2931 East McCarty Street, P.O. Box 7502, Jefferson City, MO 65102; 1-800-541-5513, 1-800-392-2179 (MO)
PRICE: $69.95
HARDWARE: Apple, MS-DOS

TITLE: *Story Starters: Science* (1989)
PUBLISHER: Pelican; distributed by Queue, Inc., 338 Commerce Drive, Fairfield, CT 06430; 1-800-232-2224
PRICE: $49.95
HARDWARE: Apple

TITLE: *Story Starters: Social Studies* (1989)
PUBLISHER: Pelican; distributed by Queue, Inc., 338 Commerce Drive, Fairfield, CT 06430; 1-800-232-2224
PRICE: $49.95
HARDWARE: Apple

TITLE: *Success with Reading* (1985)
PUBLISHER: Scholastic Inc., 2931 East McCarty Street, P.O. Box 7502, Jefferson City, MO 65102; 1-800-541-5513, 1-800-392-2179 (MO)
PRICE: $99.95 for each grade (3–8)
HARDWARE: Apple, Commodore

TITLE: *SuperPrint II* (1989)
PUBLISHER: Scholastic Inc., 2931 East McCarty Street, P.O. Box 7502, Jefferson City, MO 65102; 1-800-541-5513, 1-800-392-2179 (MO)
PRICE: $69.95
HARDWARE: Apple, MS-DOS

TITLE: *Super Story Tree* (1989)
PUBLISHER: Scholastic Inc., 2931 East McCarty Street, P.O. Box 7502, Jefferson City, MO 65102; 1-800-541-5513, 1-800-392-2179 (MO)
PRICE: $79.95
HARDWARE: Apple, MS-DOS

TITLE: *Tiger's Tales* (1986)
PUBLISHER: Sunburst Communications, 101 Castleton Street, Pleasantville, NY 10570-3498; 1-800-628-8897
PRICE: $65
HARDWARE: Apple, Commodore

TITLE: *Timeliner* (1986)
PUBLISHER: Tom Snyder Productions, 90 Sherman Street, Cambridge, MA 02140; 1-800-342-0236
PRICE: $59.95/$69.95 (Macintosh version)
HARDWARE: Apple, MS-DOS, Macintosh (called *MacTimeliner*)

TITLE: *VCR Companion* (1988)
PUBLISHER: Broderbund Software, 17 Paul Drive, San Rafael, CA 94903-2101; 1-800-521-6263
PRICE: $49.95 (Apple)/$54.95 (MS-DOS)
HARDWARE: Apple, MS-DOS

TITLE: *Where in the USA is Carmen SanDiego?* (1986)
PUBLISHER: Broderbund Software, 17 Paul Drive, San Rafael, CA 94903-2101; 1-800-521-6263
PRICE: $39.95/$49.95 (depending on hardware)
HARDWARE: Apple, MS-DOS, Macintosh

TITLE: *Word Works Utility* (1987)
PUBLISHER: Teacher Support Software, 1035 N.W. 57th Street, Gainesville, FL 32605-4483; 1-800-228-2871
PRICE: $59.95
HARDWARE: Apple, MS-DOS

*Additional Software**

TITLE: *BIG and Little* (1990)
PUBLISHER: Sunburst Communications, 101 Castleton Street, Pleasantville, NY 10570-3498; 1-800-628-8897
PRICE: $59
HARDWARE: Apple
DESCRIPTION: Creates big books, little books, cards, and posters with *Muppet Slate: The Word and Picture Processor*.

TITLE: *BannerMania* (1990)
PUBLISHER: Broderbund Software, 17 Paul Drive, San Rafael, CA 94903-2101; 1-800-521-6263
PRICE: $69.95
HARDWARE: Apple, MS-DOS, Macintosh
DESCRIPTION: Creates banners, posters, and bumper stickers with its 19 different fonts, 27 different shapes, and array of special effects.

TITLE: *Charlie and the Chocolate Factory* (1989)
PUBLISHER: Sunburst Communications, 101 Castleton Street, Pleasantville, NY 10570-3498; 1-800-628-8897
PRICE: $59
HARDWARE: Apple
DESCRIPTION: Contains 18 language arts lessons, including writing advertisements, poetry, letters, acrostics, newspaper articles, dialogue, descriptive paragraphs, and announcements that go along with Roald Dahl's *Charlie and the Chocolate Factory* (1964). Used with *Magic Slate II*-40 column.

TITLE: *Choices, Choices: On the Playground* (1988)
PUBLISHER: Tom Snyder Productions, 90 Sherman Street, Cambridge, MA 02140; 1-800-342-0236
PRICE: $89.95
HARDWARE: Apple, MS-DOS

---

*While many other excellent software packages are available, these are some of the packages that we have had the opportunity to use successfully. We encourage you to try these packages with your students and share your experiences with us.

DESCRIPTION: Provides dilemma about a new kid at school who doesn't fit in and students have to decide whether to invite him to play ball with them. As students make different choices, they learn about cause and effect relationships through the different consequences that appear.

TITLE: *Dinosaur Days Plus* (1989)
PUBLISHER: Pelican; distributed by Queue, Inc., 338 Commerce Drive, Fairfield, CT 06430; 1-800-232-2224
PRICE: $49.95 (Apple)/$39.95 (MS-DOS, Macintosh)
HARDWARE: Apple, MS-DOS, Macintosh
DESCRIPTION: Contains prehistoric background scenes and clip art of dinosaur parts and other creatures for students to create their own dinosaur scenes and diaries in seven print sizes, including big book. Includes speech for Apple only.

TITLE: *Great Beginnings* (1987, 1991)
PUBLISHER: Teacher Support Software, 1035 N.W. 57th Street, Gainesville, FL 32605-4483; 1-800-228-2871
PRICE: $99.95
HARDWARE: Apple, MS-DOS
DESCRIPTION: Contains library of graphics and descriptive words for approximately 40 topics organized around four themes (Animals and Nature, Seasons and Holidays, Things I Like and Do, People and Places) to stimulate students' writing. Includes speech.

TITLE: *Explore-a-Classic: The Three Little Pigs* (1989); *Explore-a-Classic: Stone Soup* (1989)
PUBLISHER: William K. Bradford, 310 School Street, Acton, MA 01720; 1-800-421-2009
PRICE: $75 for each package
HARDWARE: Apple, MS-DOS
DESCRIPTION: Presents these classic fairy tales much like an animated, pop-up book, enabling students to move characters and objects around on the screen as they read each part of the tale. Includes "Story Maker" for retelling the story with own characters and text and set of "Activities" related to the tale.

TITLE: *Explore-A-Folktale: Pecos Bill and Slue-foot Sue* (1990); *Explore-A-Folktale: The Tales of Ananse the Spider* (1990)
PUBLISHER: William K. Bradford, 310 School Street, Acton, MA 01720; 1-800-421-2009
PRICE: $75 for each package
HARDWARE: Apple, MS-DOS
DESCRIPTION: Presents these folktales with pop-up windows and story text. Students can move characters, objects, and scenery on the screen. Includes "Story Maker" for retelling the folktale with own characters and text and "Writer's Workshop" for developing folktale writing.

TITLE: *Explore-a-Science: Animal Watch: Whales* (1988); *Explore-a-Science: A Closer Look: The Desert* (1987)
PUBLISHER: William K. Bradford, 310 School Street, Acton, MA 01720; 1-800-421-2009
PRICE: $75 for each package
HARDWARE: Apple, MS-DOS
DESCRIPTION: Key science concepts are explored as students use printed storybooks as a guide for moving through the computer screens. Objects can be manipulated and used in students' science story creations.

TITLE: *HyperScreen* (1990)
PUBLISHER: Scholastic Inc., 2931 East McCarty Street, P.O. Box 7502, Jefferson City, MO 65102; 1-800-541-5513, 1-800-392-2179 (MO)
PRICE: $99.95
HARDWARE: Apple, MS-DOS
DESCRIPTION: Creates interactive presentations or screen-by-screen "stacks" with graphic backgrounds, fonts, sound, clip art, and drawing tools.

TITLE: *Katie's Farm* (1991)
PUBLISHER: Broderbund Software, 17 Paul Drive, San Rafael, CA 94903-2101; 1-800-521-6263
PRICE: $39.95
HARDWARE: Apple IIgs, MS-DOS, Macintosh, Amiga
DESCRIPTION: A little girl named Katie and her cousin McGee explore Katie's farm—the pond, the chicken coop, the barn, and the garden—and engage in a variety of activities that students select.

TITLE: *Kid Pix* (1991)
PUBLISHER: Broderbund Software, 17 Paul Drive, San Rafael, CA 94903-2101; 1-800-521-6263
PRICE: $59.95
HARDWARE: Macintosh
DESCRIPTION: Easy-to-use, full-faceted paint program that is full of surprises. Includes talking alphabet, dozens of "rubber stamps," magical screen transformations, and over 20 Wacky brushes for painting.

TITLE: *McGee* (1990)
PUBLISHER: Broderbund Software, 17 Paul Drive, San Rafael, CA 94903-2101; 1-800-521-6263
PRICE: $39.95
HARDWARE: Apple IIgs, MS-DOS, Macintosh, Amiga
DESCRIPTION: A little boy named McGee engages in 36 different activities in five areas in and around his house. Students decide how McGee explores his house.

TITLE: *Monsters & Make-Believe* (1987, 1989)
PUBLISHER: Pelican; distributed by Queue, Inc., 338 Commerce Drive, Fairfield, CT 06430; 1-800-232-2224
PRICE: $49.95 (Apple)/$39.95 (MS-DOS, Macintosh)
HARDWARE: Apple, MS-DOS, Macintosh
DESCRIPTION: Creates monster screens and stories with monster body parts, monster backgrounds, and fonts that can be printed in seven sizes, including big book. Speech included for Apple. Also has Spanish version for Apple without speech.

TITLE: *Pow! Zap! Ker-Plunk!* (1989)
PUBLISHER: Pelican; distributed by Queue, Inc., 338 Commerce Drive, Fairfield, CT 06430; 1-800-232-2224
PRICE: $49.95
HARDWARE: Apple, MS-DOS
DESCRIPTION: Creates comic books with speech bubbles, sound and special effects, super props, heros and heroines. Can purchase additional disk of comic book art album.

TITLE: *The Playroom* (1989)
PUBLISHER: Broderbund Software, 17 Paul Drive, San Rafael, CA 94903-2101; 1-800-521-6263
PRICE: $49.95–$59.95 (depending on hardware)

HARDWARE: Apple, MS-DOS, Macintosh
DESCRIPTION: As children explore a playroom of different objects, they engage in a variety of activities related to early learning.

TITLE: *Reading Magic Library: Jack and the Beanstalk* (1988)
PUBLISHER: Tom Snyder Productions, 90 Sherman Street, Cambridge, MA 02140; 1-800-342-0236
PRICE: $44.95
HARDWARE: Apple, MS-DOS
DESCRIPTION: An interactive, whimsical retelling of this classic fairy tale in which students make choices about how the tale progresses.

TITLE: *Robot Writer* (1990)
PUBLISHER: Pelican; distributed by Queue, Inc., 338 Commerce Drive, Fairfield, CT 06430; 1-800-232-2224
PRICE: $49.95 (Apple)/$39.95 (MS-DOS, Macintosh)
HARDWARE: Apple, MS-DOS, Macintosh
DESCRIPTION: Contains futuristic background scenes and clip art of a family of robots and futuristic friends to create robot scenes and reports that can be printed in seven different print sizes, including big book. Speech included for Apple only.

TITLE: *Solve It!* (1988)
PUBLISHER: Sunburst Communications, 101 Castleton Street, Pleasantville, NY 10570-3498; 1-800-628-8897
PRICE: $75
HARDWARE: Apple
DESCRIPTION: Provides six mysteries in which students, acting as detectives for the Solve It Detective Agency, have to access, analyze, and synthesize data to solve the mystery.

TITLE: *The Velveteen Rabbit* (1989)
PUBLISHER: Sunburst Communications, 101 Castleton Street, Pleasantville, NY 10570-3498; 1-800-628-8897
PRICE: $59
HARDWARE: Apple
DESCRIPTION: Provides 12 language arts lessons, including writing poetry, letters, dialogue, and descriptive sentences for Margery Williams' book, *The Velveteen Rabbit* (1986). Used with *Magic Slate II-*20 column.

TITLE: *Watership Down* (1990)
PUBLISHER: Sunburst Communications, 101 Castleton Street, Pleasantville, NY 10570-3498; 1-800-628-8897
PRICE: $59
HARDWARE: Apple
DESCRIPTION: Contains 20 language arts lessons for writing poetry, memoirs, dialogues, character descriptions, journals, eulogies, short stories, and proverb stories for Richard Adams' book, *Watership Down* (1972). Used with *Magic Slate II*-40 column.

TITLE: *Where in America's Past is Carmen San-Diego?* (1991)
PUBLISHER: Broderbund Software, 17 Paul Drive, San Rafael, CA 94903-2101; 1-800-521-6263
PRICE: $59.95
HARDWARE: MS-DOS
DESCRIPTION: Students, acting as detectives for the Acme Detective Agency, use the package's "Chronoskimmer 450SL" and Gorton Carruth's *What Happened When: A Chronology of Life and Events in America* (1989) to stop Carmen and her cohorts from heisting priceless treasures and historical landmarks.

TITLE: (1) *Write On! Peter Rabbit* (1989); (2) *Write On! Sleeping Away* (1987); (3) *Write On! Great Wild Imaginings* (1987)
PUBLISHER: Humanities Software, 408 Columbia Street, Suite 222, P.O. Box 950, Hood River, OR 97031; 1-800-245-6737
PRICE: $75
HARDWARE: Apple, MS-DOS, Macintosh
DESCRIPTION: *Write On!* series, with these three titles as examples, include writing activities for specific books that are accessed with word processing software. (1) Contains 11 writing activities including group writing of a tale, for Beatrix Potter's book, *The Tale of Peter Rabbit* (1902). (2) Contains 7 writing activities, including writing ghost stories, for Bernard Waber's book, *Ira Sleeps Over* (1972). (3) Contains 11 writing activity files, including chant and journal writing, created for Maurice Sendak's book, *Where the Wild Things Are* (1963).

CHAPTER
6

EXTENDING MATERIALS TO CONTENT AREA LEARNING

Chapter Overview

M R. D. HAS BEEN TEACHING his Early American social studies curriculum according to the book for nearly a decade. He assigns his fifth grade students a segment of a chapter to read for homework with subsequent check-up questions to answer. He uses students' purported at-home preparation as a springboard for his lecture-style introduction to new concepts and content. Mr. D. follows this procedure for two-week intervals, give or take a few days, at which time he tests students for their knowledge acquisition.

Mr. D. realizes that his students are emotionally asleep during his social studies lessons. The lively, coherent picture of history that Mr. D. has in his head is a collage of disjointed pieces of information in his students' minds. Students do not read their text with the historian's panoramic view of our country's foundation; rather, they go straight to the checkups to complete their homework. Important historical figures are nothing more than names to be memorized, because students do not know enough about them as people to relate to them personally. Early American artifacts mean little to these students, because they have not had the opportunity to touch and feel anything remotely similar to these tools of the past.

Mr. D. realizes that his social studies curriculum is a complete contradiction to a major part of his instructional day. In his reading and writing classes, students are using trade books. Contrary to the boredom they feel during social studies lessons, his students are animated as they discuss issues related to reading and writing that touch their daily lives. They see characters as people who share similar concerns about family, ideas, and events. Yet here they are in social studies class, personally removed from critical historical events that impact on their everyday lives.

How many other Mr. D.'s are there who have converted from traditional reading programs to process-oriented reading and writing classrooms, but have not yet allowed their new materials and strategies to spill over into the content areas? They exercise judgment and make decisions about content and procedures for reading and writing instruction, yet they continue to allow published content-area books to dictate how students will learn in the content areas. Students' exposure to content material in social studies texts or other content area texts often fails to evoke feelings of excitement toward a subject. Although students inevitably learn facets of content from their trade book reading and writing, they are not learning how to learn about content through books; instead, they see reading and content area learning as two separate entities.

This chapter shares ways to begin to transfer what you have discovered about reading and writing instruction to content area instruction.

Materials for Content Area Instruction

No matter what material is used, the key to effective teaching is to make it easy for students to understand content area material in relation to the real world. For example, in studying about communism, memorizing its definition is not nearly as important as understanding its implications for the people who have lived with it. Alternatively, in studying about the human body, memorizing the function of each part serves little purpose unless students understand how the parts and body function as a whole.

One of us had the opportunity to watch a few children study for a science test on the human body. The students' ability to regurgitate the information from their notebooks was commendable. Yet, these students didn't really relate what they were reciting to their own bodies. Not until someone stopped them and said, "Wait, I want you to imagine that I am the blood in your body. Tell me where I go in your body and why," did the light bulb turn on for these youngsters! They undoubtedly would do fine in their test, but they would leave the exam without any appreciation for what they had studied.

As you read the next section, keep in mind that instructional materials should serve as resources for the "whole" picture rather than as conduits for bits and pieces of data. In other words, students need to learn *how* to learn with content material (Konopak, Martin, & Martin, 1990).

CONTENT AREA TEXTBOOKS

Content area textbooks contain chapter-by-chapter presentations of factual information. Organized by topics, these textbooks systematically introduce students to many facts and generalizations about a specific subject (Moss, 1991; Moore, Moore, Cunningham, & Cunningham, 1986). Although textbooks provide helpful organizational features for reading (for example, introductory statements, graphic aids, and engaging anecdotes), their distilled and serious discussion of content area information does not often whet students' appetites for reading (Brozo & Simpson, 1991). Textbooks are designed to cover a body of knowledge whose parameters are defined by the curricula (Sebesta, 1989). Most students labor over the expository material presented, often bypassing material that they think will be explained by the teacher. For this reason, it is simply not enough to assign students to read and learn from this material.

Guided reading strategies that support basal and trade book reading also need to be in place for textbook reading so that students are stimulated and prepared to read textbook topics. Teachers need to set aside time to activate, assess, and build relevant prior knowledge, set meaningful purposes for reading, and pre-teach critical concepts and vocabulary. Language experience activities, **learning logs**, role-playing, **simulations**, and pre-reading guides are some of the many activities that contribute to students' readiness to learn (Atwell, 1990; Brozo & Simpson, 1991; Kinney, 1985).

Content area textbook reading poses problems for many children because they are unfamiliar with how the text is structured (Englert & Hiebert, 1984; Spiro & Taylor, 1980). The same students who are very familiar with the structure of stories often cannot decipher their textbook codes. One reason may be that these students' preschool and primary-level reading experiences have helped them to develop, refine, and expand their schemata for the structure of stories where characters perform actions in a setting that leads to a desired goal (Hennings, 1982; Piccolo, 1987). Similar exposure to expository reading found in textbooks may have been sparse or missing altogether.

Another reason for students' difficulty in reading content area textbooks is the mismatch between the way information is presented and the cognitive processing tools that students bring to the information. In other words, textbook authors often presume that students have the necessary background knowledge for making connections between what is actually stated and what is really needed to fully comprehend the significance of a concept or event. In an interesting study, Beck, McKeown, Sinatra, and Loxterman (1991) showed how four passages about the American Revolution in a fifth grade social studies textbook could be revised to better correspond to 10-year-old readers' text processing abilities. For each textbook statement, Beck et al. analyzed what they thought the text authors intended and what a reader should know in order to construct meaning. They then revised the text, often adding statements in narrative form to make connections more explicit. For example, the first sentence in the original textbook was "In 1763 Britain and the colonies ended a 7-year war with the French and Indians." The revision by Beck et al. was

> About 250 years ago, Britain and France both claimed to own some of the same land, here, in North America. This land was just west of where the 13 colonies were. In 1756, Britain and France went to war to see who would get control of this land. Because the 13 American colonies belonged to Britain, the colonists fought on the same side as Britain. Many Indians fought on the same side as France. Because we were fighting against the French and Indians, the war has come to be known as the French and Indian War. The war ended in 1763. (p. 257)

Beck et al. found that the fourth and fifth graders who read the revised text were able to recall more information and answer more questions correctly than students who read the original text. However, even with their successful attempts to improve students' understanding with more "comprehensible" text, the researchers still found that students need several opportunities to work with the same content to fully understand it.

As publishers grapple with ways to make textbooks more comprehensible, there are techniques that we can use to facilitate students' reading. Piccolo (1987) found from her work with fifth grade students that their textbook comprehension improved when she included three instructional strategies: (a) direct explanation of the structure of a text (for example, *description,* in which a specific topic and its attributes are presented; *cause-effect,* in which supporting details are used to tell why statements in topic sentences are made; and *problem-solution,* in which supporting details are used to describe a problem—stated in the topic sentence—its causes and solutions); (b) a graphic organizer to help in visualizing and writing about the text; and (c) use of writing as an instructional technique. Other researchers also have found that direct instructional approaches for working with **text structure** have proven effective in minimizing students' frustration with content area reading, especially if the instruction is begun in the middle grades (Armbruster & Anderson, 1980; Flood, Lapp, & Farnan, 1986; McGee & Richgels, 1985; Piccolo, 1987; Taylor & Beach, 1984).

Armbruster, Anderson, & Ostertag (1989) describe how their instructional method with problem-solution text structures improved fifth grade students' reading

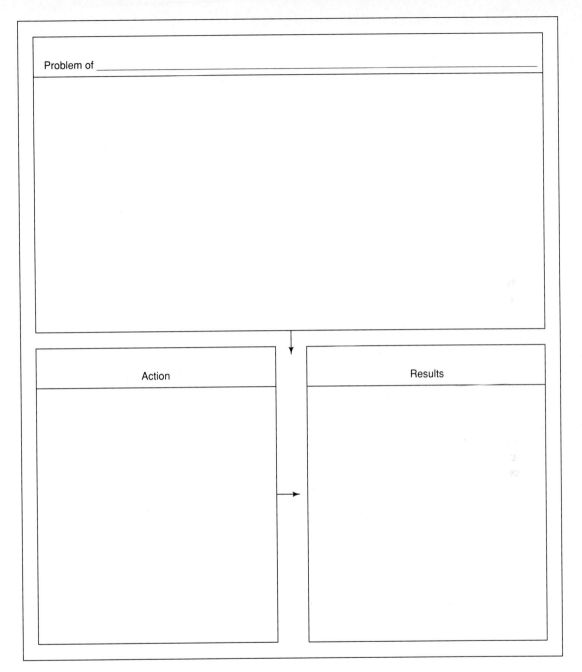

Problem = something bad; a situation that people would like to change
Action = what people *do* to try to solve the problem
Results = what happens as a result of the action; the effect or outcome of trying to solve the problem

FIGURE 6.1

Problem-solution text structure: frame and definition

Note. From Figure 1 from "Teaching text structure to improve reading and writing" by B.B. Armbruster, T.H. Anderson, and J. Ostertag, 1989, *The Reading Teacher,* Nov. 1989, pp. 130–137. Reprinted with permission of the International Reading Association.

comprehension and summary writing skills. In addition to using teacher modeling, guided practice, teacher monitoring, and independent practice, they provided problem-solution frames (see Figure 6.1, p. 283) for passages from social studies texts written with this structure. They then provided students with guidelines for summarizing problem-solution passages (see Figure 6.2). They believe that the instructional benefits of **frames**—the graphic representations of ideas and relationships in text— are superior to the various suggestions in teachers' manuals.

Although the study just described dealt with social studies, Armbruster (1991) describes how framing can be used just as effectively for science texts. She explains how two questions help to develop frames: "What are the important categories of information associated with the topic?" and "How might these categories be subdivided?" While similar to the process of producing an outline, framing focuses more on a visual representation of the structure of the text material. A frame can be used to set a purpose before reading, act as a structured format for taking notes during reading, and serve as a point of reference after reading.

How to Summarize Problem-Solution Passages

Sentence 1—Tells who had a problem and what the problem is
Sentence 2—Tells what action was taken to try to solve the problem
Sentence 3—Tells what happened as a result of the action taken

Pattern for Writing a Summary of a Problem-Solution Passage

_____ had a problem because _____

Therefore, _____

As a result, _____

Guidelines for Checking Summaries of Problem-Solution Passages

Check to see that:
1. Your summary has all of the information that should be in a summary of a problem-solution passage. (See "How to Write a Summary of a Problem-Solution Passage.") Compare your summary with the original problem-solution passage to make sure that the summary is accurate and complete.
2. You have used complete sentences.
3. The sentences are tied together with good connecting words.
4. The grammar and spelling are correct.

FIGURE 6.2

Guidelines for summarizing problem-solving passages

Note. From Figure 2 from "Teaching text structure to improve reading and writing" by B.B. Armbruster, T.H. Anderson, and J. Ostertag, 1989, *The Reading Teacher,* Nov. 1989, pp. 130–137. Reprinted with permission of the International Reading Association.

TRADE BOOKS AND OTHER RESOURCES

Despite well-organized instructional plans for reading content area texts, students still need the content to come to life through their own reading of **narrative text**. Trade books, when they pertain to a curricular topic, may bridge the gap between **efferent** (for learning) and **aesthetic** (for fun) **reading** related to the content areas (Rosenblatt, 1978; Sebesta, 1989). As you will see from many of the teachers whose stories appear in this chapter, trade books have become part of content area instruction because they narrow the chasm between trade book-based reading instruction and textbook-based content area instruction.

Blending textbooks and trade books serves important functions for schema-building and organized instruction. Stories written in familiar narrative style provide background information and call to mind related ideas that build the foundation for easier assimilation of textual information (Brozo & Simpson, 1991). In using trade books to augment students' experience with textbooks, two lines of information conjoin to make a "unit" (Sebesta, 1989). When carefully selected, books also serve as long-lasting reminders of important attitudes, feelings, and concepts emanating from content area learning (Troy, 1977).

Fifth grade teacher Beverly Pilchman, whom you will read about later in this chapter and whom you read about in Chapter 4, says, "It would be torture for me to have to use commercial materials all the time. I don't think that people who write these materials understand them through children's eyes." As she searches for trade books to make her content area textbook come alive, she always asks herself, "What is it that makes a child want to learn?"

In addition to using fictional trade books, nonfiction sources can also be used. Any nonfiction text—whether an autobiography, biography, true experience, informational book, essay, journal, letter, historical document, newspaper, or news magazine—can add to students' knowledge about a particular topic. Hittleman (1991) recommends asking the following questions to help students appreciate nonfiction:

1. What might this passage be about?
2. How does the passage make you feel?
3. What makes you feel this way?
4. What seems especially real to you?
5. What words are used unusually?
6. What is said about human behavior?
7. What can you use in your writing?

Unlike the easy-to-follow instructional regimen of textbooks, trade books and other sources present additional organizational pressure for the teacher. Questions arise, such as, "How do I find books and other sources to support what I'm supposed to teach?" "When should I use these materials?" or "How do I use them?" These questions, among other issues related to organizing content area instruction, are addressed in the next section.

Organizing Content Area Materials

Take a moment to look at Figure 6.3. It shows one possible set of steps to follow while organizing for content area instruction.

STEP 1

Identify appropriate themes, concepts, main topics, subtopics, or questions for your unit of study. Use a **web** or other graphic device to help organize your ideas (Bromley, 1991; Brozo & Simpson, 1991). The hub of a web includes a content area concept or content and the spokes of the web include its subtopics. As you may recall from Chapter 3, and you will see later in this chapter, kindergarten teacher Elsie Nigohosian uses webs to create her weekly plans for all content areas.

STEP 2

Find materials and resources that you want to use. Ask yourself, "Do I want to use my district's content-based textbook?" Notwithstanding a textbook's somewhat lifeless portrayal of dynamic events and concepts, it nevertheless may cover important curricular objectives that cannot be found in trade books.

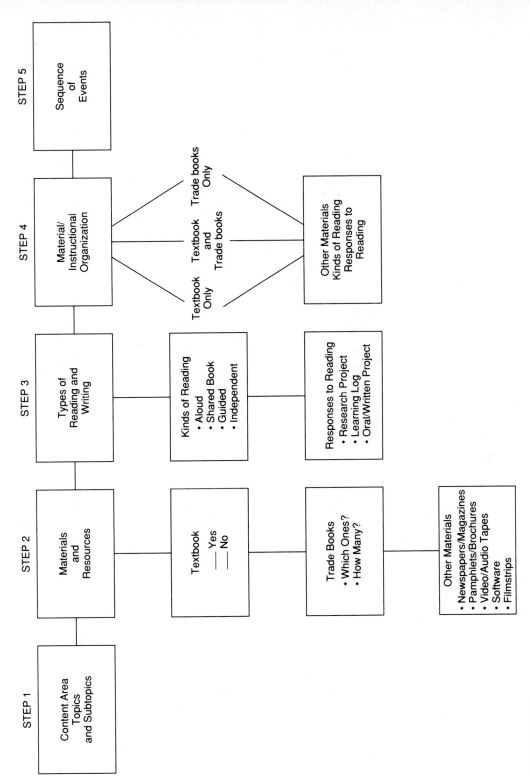

FIGURE 6.3
Steps for organizing content-based materials

287

Search for trade books relevant to a curricular topic. This search should cut across genres and levels of readability (Sebesta, 1989). Some professional books that include the names of trade books across curricular areas are *Children's Literature in the Elementary School* (Huck, Hepler, & Hickman, 1987), *Through the Eyes of a Child: An Introduction to Children's Literature* (Norton, 1991), *Coming to Know: Writing to Learn in the Intermediate Grades* (Atwell, 1990), *Using Literature in the Elementary Classroom* (Stewig & Sebesta, 1989), and *Webbing with Literature: Creating Story Maps with Children's Books* (Bromley, 1991). The Children's Book Council (CBC) also collaborates with national organizations to create lists of trade books. Just as CBC and the International Reading Association publish "Children's Choices" every October in *The Reading Teacher,* CBC and the National Science Teachers Association published "Outstanding Science Trade Books for Children in 1990," an annotated bibliography of books identified by topic (for example, Animals, Space Science, and Astronomy). These books are judged for their accuracy, readability, format, and illustrations. Similarly, CBC, in conjunction with the National Council for the Social Studies, published "Notable 1990 Children's Trade Books in the Field of Social Studies," which is also divided into topics such as North American History, Culture, and Life; The American Frontier and The Revolutionary War; and The Civil War and the African-American Experience. Single copies of these lists are available free with a self-addressed, stamped envelope from CBC, 568 Broadway, New York, NY 10012.

Reference books in the library that help in selecting trade books by topic are

- *Children's Books in Print 1990–1991 Subject Guide: A Subject Index to Children's Books* (See Figure 6.4 for some sample entries.)
- *Elementary School Library Collection: A Guide to Books and Other Media, Seventeenth Edition* (Winkel, 1990)
- *Children's Catalog: Fifteenth Edition* (Isaacson, Hillegas, & Yaakov, 1986)
- *A to Zoo: Subject Access to Children's Picture Books* (Lima, 1986)
- *Books Kids Will Sit Still For: The Complete Read-Aloud Guide* (Freeman, 1990)

The last four reference books listed here offer helpful annotations as a guide for selection. In addition to teaming up with other teachers to identify books, you might also work with your school, district, or community librarian.

Place selected books into your web so you have an idea of how your selection matches your unit topics. Figure 6.5 is an example of a topic-trade book web created for slavery in the United States. The main topics in the web come from a fifth grade social studies curriculum.

Locate other materials that introduce, reinforce, and present other points of view about your topic. *Coming to Know: Writing to Learn in the Intermediate Grades* (Atwell, 1990) includes an appendix of resources across curricular areas. *Magazines for Children* (Stoll, 1990) provides an annotated list of magazines for just about every conceivable topic that is also indexed by subject and age/grade. Moreover, *Using Children's Magazines in the K–8 Classroom* (Seminoff, 1990) not only provides an annotated listing of children's magazines but also offers K–2, 3–5, and 6–8 across-the-curriculum activities, including reproducibles, for incorporating magazines into literature, mathematics, science, social studies, and study skills.

SLAVE TRADE

Fox, Paula. The Slave Dancer. Eros, Keith, illus. LC 73-80642. 192p. (gr. 5–8). 1973. 10.95 (ISBN 0-02-735560-8). Bradbury Pt.

Killingray, David. The Transatlantic Slave Trade. 64p. (gr. 6–8). 1987. 17.95 (ISBN 0-7134-5469-5, Pub. by Batsford England). David & Charles.

Meltzer, Milton. All Times, All Peoples: A World History of Slavery. Fisher, Leonard E., illus. LC 79-2810. 80p. (gr. 5–9). 1980. 12.701 (ISBN 0-06-024186-1); PLB 12.89 (ISBN 0-06-024187-X). HarpJ.

Sterne, Emma G. The Slave Ship. Lockhart, David, illus. 192p. (Orig.). (gr. 4–6). 1988. pap. 2.50 (ISBN 0-590-40621-3). Scholastic Inc.

SLAVERY-FICTION

Anderson, Paul L. Slave of Catiline. LC 57-9446. 255p. (gr. 7–11). 1930. 15.00 (ISBN 0-8196-0101-2). Biblo.

Collier, James L., & Collier, Christopher. Jump Ship to Freedom. LC 81-65492. 192p. (gr. 4–6). 1981. pap. 13.95 (ISBN 0-385-28484-5). Delacorte.

—Who Is Carrie? LC 83-23947. 192p. (gr. 4–6). 1984. 14.95 (ISBN 0-385-29295-3). Delacorte.

Endore, Guy. Babouk. rev. ed. Kincaid, Jamaica & Trouillot, Michel-Rolphintro. by. 352p. (gr. 9–12). 1988. 20.00 (ISBN 0-85345-759-X); pap. 7.50 (ISBN 0-85345-745-X). Monthly Rev.

Hurmence, Belinda. A Girl Called Boy. 180p. (gr. 3–6). 1982. 12.95 (ISBN 0-395-31022-9, Clarion). HM.

Levy, Elizabeth. Running Out of Time. Mars, W. T., illus. LC 79-28064. 128p. (gr. 3–6). 1980. lib. bdg. 4.99 (ISBN 0-394-94422-4); pap. 1.95 (ISBN 0-394-84422-X). Knopf.

Miner, Jane C. Corey, No. 22. 192p. (Orig.). (gr. 5–10). 1987. pap. 2.50 (ISBN 0-590-40395-8, Sunfire). Scholastic Inc.

FIGURE 6.4
Sample entries from a *Subject Index to Children's Books*

STEP 3

Decide what kinds of reading and writing experiences you want your students to have with your selected materials and resources. In a nutshell, and as you may recall from Chapter 3, reading aloud is a teacher's opportunity to read orally from any type of material; shared book reading is a teacher-directed read-along, similar to bedtime story reading. Guided reading is a teacher-facilitated reading experience with opportunities for pre-reading, during-reading, and after-reading activities. Independent reading is student-engaged free reading. Whether using textbooks, trade books, or other resources, these three types of reading experiences should be included in some capacity.

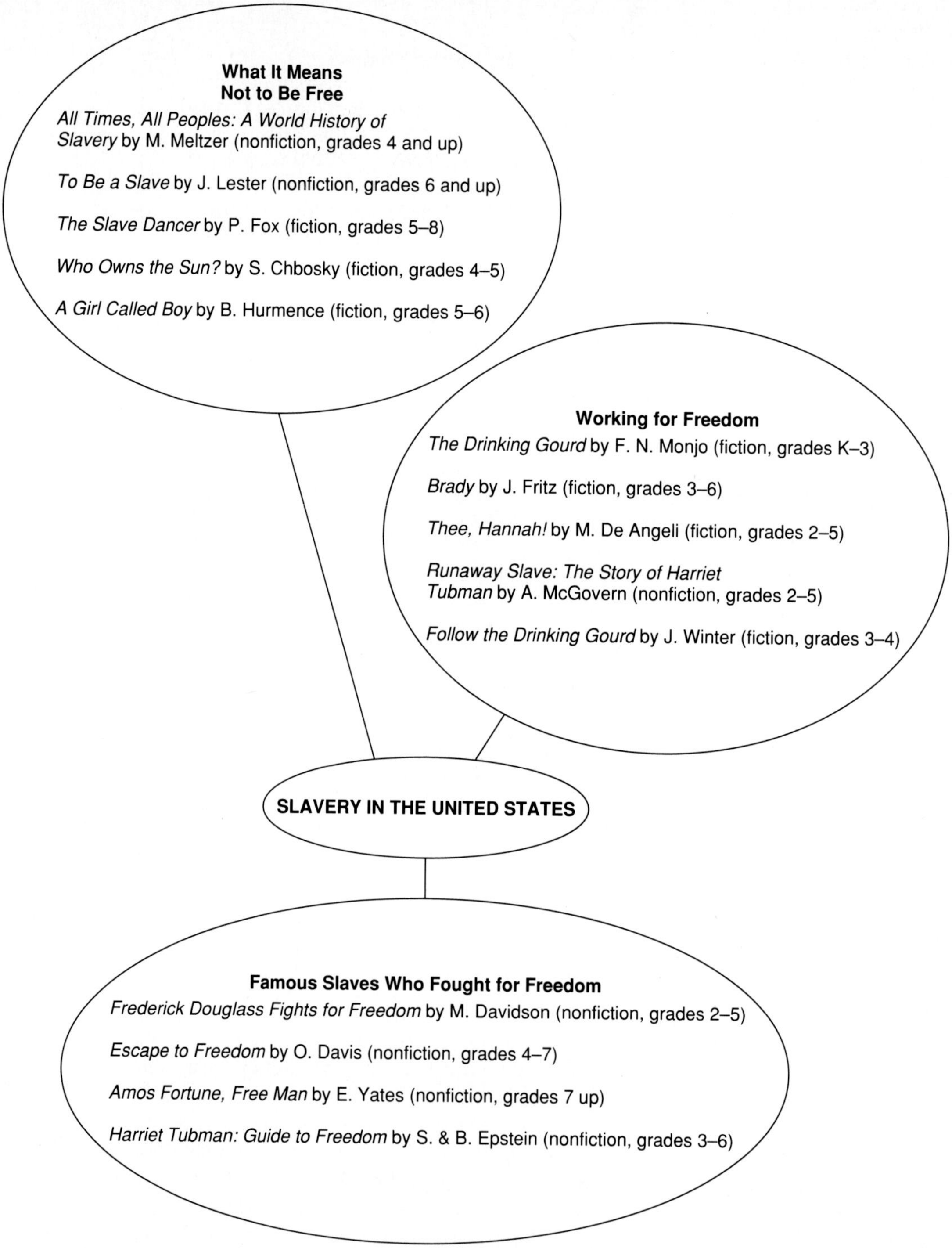

**What It Means
Not to Be Free**

*All Times, All Peoples: A World History of
Slavery* by M. Meltzer (nonfiction, grades 4 and up)

To Be a Slave by J. Lester (nonfiction, grades 6 and up)

The Slave Dancer by P. Fox (fiction, grades 5–8)

Who Owns the Sun? by S. Chbosky (fiction, grades 4–5)

A Girl Called Boy by B. Hurmence (fiction, grades 5–6)

Working for Freedom

The Drinking Gourd by F. N. Monjo (fiction, grades K–3)

Brady by J. Fritz (fiction, grades 3–6)

Thee, Hannah! by M. De Angeli (fiction, grades 2–5)

*Runaway Slave: The Story of Harriet
Tubman* by A. McGovern (nonfiction, grades 2–5)

Follow the Drinking Gourd by J. Winter (fiction, grades 3–4)

SLAVERY IN THE UNITED STATES

Famous Slaves Who Fought for Freedom

Frederick Douglass Fights for Freedom by M. Davidson (nonfiction, grades 2–5)

Escape to Freedom by O. Davis (nonfiction, grades 4–7)

Amos Fortune, Free Man by E. Yates (nonfiction, grades 7 up)

Harriet Tubman: Guide to Freedom by S. & B. Epstein (nonfiction, grades 3–6)

FIGURE 6.5
Web of trade books on slavery in the United States

Responses to reading include oral and written presentations. This can occur before, during, or after reading any materials or resources. Short-term or long-term research projects for the whole class, small groups, or individual students—with or without teacher-directed frameworks—can be used along with or in lieu of learning logs and projects. (See the next section "Some Strategies That Work" for a description of some research-oriented frameworks.) Figure 6.6 provides ideas to use for each of the content areas presented in this chapter. Many of these ideas emanate from the teachers in this chapter as well as from the work of Atwell (1990) and Thompson (1990).

STEP 4

Determine which material/instructional configuration is best for you: textbook only, a combination of textbook and trade books, or trade books only. Incorporate your ideas about materials and resources and types of reading and writing from Steps 2 and 3 into your selected configuration. Figure 6.7 provides an example of instructional patterns for each configuration. Each pattern shows how two types of materials or resources can be cycled with concept introduction/discussion and response to reading. The order of events can be interchanged; however, some type of concept introduction/discussion or schema activation should precede textbook reading so that students can bring background knowledge to their textbook reading. Concept introduction/discussion can include a teacher-directed presentation of salient concepts and content, a pre-reading strategy such as framing, a writing activity, a cooperative learning activity, or a discussion with the whole class or in small groups. This phase helps you to assess what students know and need in order to be prepared for subsequent reading. Vocabulary and concepts taken for granted by trade books and textbooks may need to be developed.; on the other hand, you may learn that students already know much of what is covered in the textbook. Your decisions about the kinds of reading and writing experiences that students have within each instructional pattern probably will be determined by the type of material you use. For example, you may plan a shared book experience with an informational book without any follow-up writing as well as a guided reading experience with a magazine article to which students respond in their learning logs.

STEP 5

Flesh out your instructional pattern from Figure 6.7 to include specific information about your flow of events. For example, given that you are using the trade book-textbook pattern with your web of books for slavery (see Figure 6.5), you could do the following:

1. Read aloud *All Times, All Peoples: A World History of Slavery* (Meltzer, 1980), a powerful, yet comprehensible document about the history and implications of slavery. Use ideas from this book to introduce the concept and development of slavery.
2. Move into "concept introduction/discussion" with such questions as: "What is

Survey of people's attitudes toward current events
Oral interview between two historical figures
Class newspaper with articles, editorials, or other activities related to time and place in history
Identity cards for historical figures
Annotated catalog of artifacts
List of *do's* and *don'ts* for living in a certain time and place

Summary of issue or situation presented from a book or from the news
Trade book written by students to depict an important historical person, era, or event
Update of ideas learned
Dress-up biography of an important historical figure
Illustrations of people, places, and events studied
Evaluation of inventions and contributions of a historical era
Skit of a historical era

Science fiction stories set in the future or on another planet
Calendar of events during the life cycle of animal
Individual bound book about an important scientific discovery
Environmental postage stamp for a selected country
News broadcast of a scientific discovery
Campaign to preserve a plant or animal
Environmental debate about issues facing community

Mathematics concept books told as a short story or picture book
Activity book of mathematics games
Television program about mathematics in the real world
How-to book for doing certain computations or problem-solving
Essay about "What I learned in mathematics"
Mystery stories using problem-solving clues
Appendix of mathematics tricks
Tree diagram of mathematics problems for other students to solve
Inventory of items at home or in school
Collage of places where mathematics may be used
Shopping spree

Article about a favorite song
Retelling of a favorite book about music
Time line of famous artists or musicians
Scene for a play

FIGURE 6.6
Content-based oral and written presentation ideas

FIGURE 6.7
Instructional patterns for textbook only, textbook and trade books, and trade books only

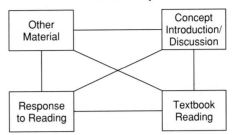

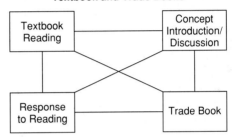

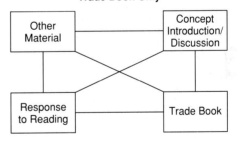

slavery?" "What do you think happens to people who are slaves?" "How does slavery affect people's lives?"

3. Read aloud segments of *To Be a Slave* (Lester, 1968) to help students visualize how slaves felt about themselves and their situations.

4. Have students write in their journals about what slavery means to them.

5. Have students read the textbook portion on slavery and discuss what it means.

6. Have students read as a class the Newbery Medal book, *The Slave Dancer* (Fox, 1973), a historical fictional portrayal of the experiences of Jesse, a kidnapped 13-year-old boy who is forced to play his fife for slaves being brought from Africa on a slave ship in the 1700s. Alternate between guided reading strategies and independent reading in school and at home. Encourage students to read aloud sections of the book to each other. Have students write a summary of the main character's problem.

7. Have students read a section in the textbook that discusses what people did to fight for freedom.
8. Have students read at home one of the biographies listed in Figure 6.5 (or any other appropriate biography) under "Famous Slaves Who Fought for Freedom." Have students dress up as their characters and share what they learned in an oral presentation.
9. Have students select one of the books listed in Figure 6.5 (or any other appropriate book) under "Working for Freedom" or "What it Means not to be Free." Divide class into groups accordingly. Use guided reading strategies to work with each book.

Once students complete this unit, they will have read three trade books on the topic of slavery: the same historical fiction book, *The Slave Dancer;* and two self-selected books, one during class and one at home. Obviously, this plan can be streamlined or altered in any way, based on the amount of time you think should be devoted to this topic and the number of resources available. Field trips and assemblies can be used in lieu of or in addition to any component of this plan. For example, Nancy Letteney, a principal of a K–6 school, provided an assembly in which a woman portrayed Harriet Tubman. While she discussed her life—replete with authentic dialect and dress—she involved the students in her escape to freedom with the underground railroad. Ms. Letteney felt that the students came away from the assembly with a new understanding of what *underground railroad* means. What is most important is that, because of students' experiences with trade books or other resources, students' images of this concept (or any other concept) is much more vivid than one developed with straight textbook reading. Important facts are not forfeited; they are just woven into a rich experience of reading and writing about a significant event in history.

Some Strategies That Work

Strategies are neither effective nor ineffective. They vary in their degree of effectiveness with respect to the material, grade level, and reading ability of students (Alvermann & Swafford, 1989). The reading-writing strategies described in the following section help to assess students' prior knowledge about the topic. They also help students to consider new ideas and understand the structure that binds these ideas together (Konopak, Martin, & Martin, 1990; Readance, Bean, & Baldwin, 1989). The quality of content-based lessons improves when students think strategically about what they are reading, visually organize their ideas, and respond in writing to what they are learning. There is nothing especially magical about the three strategies described herein, but we have seen teachers work with them successfully. Other validated reading and writing strategies that engage students work equally well.

GRAPHIC ORGANIZERS

Did you realize that every chapter in this book begins with the components for a **structured overview**, one type of graphic organizer, to help you "see" more clearly—

and before you read—how the chapters' contents are organized? **Graphic organizers**—whether they are semantic maps, webs, **networks,** clusters, frames, or structured overviews—help students to visualize relationships among key concepts and terms. Graphic organizers are visual representations or diagrams of categories of information and their relationships. They help students to appreciate how words and ideas relate to overarching concepts (Bromley, 1991; Heimlich & Pittelman, 1986). (See Johnnie Cole's use of different graphic organizers for social studies in the "Examples of Teacher Applications" section. Also see the end-of-book glossary for definitions of different types of graphic organizers.)

To appreciate the effectiveness of graphic organizers, imagine that you were about to study the animal kingdom and the words from Figure 6.8 were presented in a similar fashion in a textbook. How would you feel? How do you think your students with little or no prior knowledge about the animal kingdom would feel? Now take a look at Figure 6.9. Would this organizational display of words ease some of your frustration?

If we merely asked students to brainstorm words related to the animal kingdom without helping them to organize what they already know, they are not as readily able to see how their existing knowledge fits together. They also have more difficulty fitting new information into an organizational pattern for learning.

Graphic organizers help to promote comprehension because they graphically relate the new to the known. They help to organize students' knowledge base into loosely constructed hierarchies of information so that more vivid images of the connection between ideas and concepts are created. Graphic organizers also help to prepare students for textbook or trade book reading.

If you have students create graphic organizers before they start a unit or area of study, you can assess the information they bring to the session while promoting personal involvement. The following three sixth grade content area teachers shared with us how they use **clustering** to introduce their units. The math teacher uses clustering to note students' strengths and weaknesses with the concept of "division" before deciding how to proceed with her lesson plans. The health teacher uses clustering to get

FIGURE 6.8
List of words about the animal kingdom

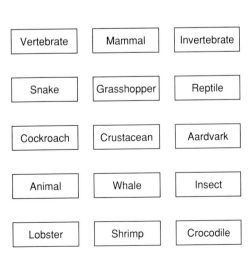

FIGURE 6.9
Structured
overview of
animal kingdom
words

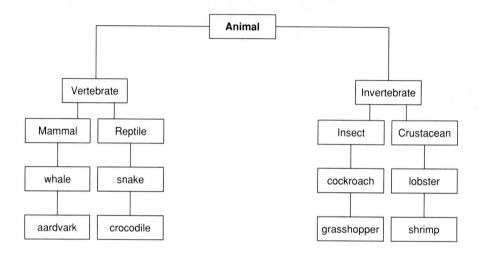

her students to present an autobiographical sketch of themselves before beginning a unit on self-awareness. The art teacher uses clustering to facilitate students' art work. She has her students cluster "What I Am Most Scared of" before illustrating their fears. She then teaches her students a specific art technique, watercolor wash (crayon resist), to use with their illustrations. She finds that clustering helps students to verbalize and organize their ideas before portraying them in art form.

Using graphic organizers during any reading phase encourages students to connect their existing knowledge to new information. As schema theory tells us, what we comprehend and learn from what we read or hear is directly related to what we already know and bring to a given situation (Bromley, 1991). Graphic organizers help to visually mesh what students already know with what they learn.

BEFORE-DURING-AFTER READING GUIDE

As expressed throughout this book, guided reading needs to be in place to help students move beyond superficial reading practices. Awareness of what is to be read facilitates introspective reading which, in turn, encourages a more critical retrospective analysis of what was read. Many strategies can facilitate **before-during-after reading** thinking, for example, Directed Reading Activity (see Chapter 2), Directed Reading-Thinking Activity (see Chapter 5), and **Guided Reading Procedure**, a strategy that helps students to reconstruct what they read in order to elaborate thoughtfully on the text and its implications (Manzo, 1975). Another technique for guiding students' reading, K-W-L, is described in the following section.

K-W-L

K-W-L, a procedure that helps students become active readers of expository text, consists of three basic cognitive steps: (a) accessing what I <u>K</u>now; (b) determining what I <u>W</u>ant to learn; and (c) recalling what I <u>L</u>earned as a result of my reading (Carr

& Ogle, 1987; Ogle, 1986). Although created for expository text, it can also be used successfully when students read narrative text or pursue research interests.

Before students read, whether it is a passage from a textbook or a chapter or set of chapters from a trade book, students brainstorm what they know about a particular topic. To help students brainstorm, the teacher poses a specific question about the topic. For example, before reading a passage about mammals, the teacher might say, "What do you know about mammals?" rather than "What do you know about animals?" to help students focus on the topic (Marzola & Freund, 1989). Students' generated ideas are discussed and placed in the "What I (or we) Know" column (see Figure 6.10).

Students then generate questions that they would like to see answered as they read. These questions are based on the unresolved information discovered during a discussion of students' brainstormed ideas. For example, in trying to find out more about mammals, students might generate a question such as "Do any mammals live in water?" Students record their questions in the "What I (or we) want to find out" column of the same K-W-L worksheet. Students read in search of answers to their questions. Answers to their questions are recorded in the "What I (or we) learned

K—WHAT WE KNOW	W—WHAT WE WANT TO FIND OUT	L—WHAT WE LEARNED AND STILL NEED TO LEARN
• Dogs are mammals. • Mammals have live babies. • Some mammals are tame. • Some mammals live in the zoo. • Cats are mammals. • Cats eat meat and fish.	• Do any mammals live in water? • Do any mammals fly? • Do all mammals have hair or fur? • Do mammals eat vegetables? • What mammals live in my neighborhood? • What is the largest mammal?	• Whales live in water. • Tigers, camels, koalas, seals, gerbils, and rats are mammals. • All mammals have fur or hair. • Marsupials grow in their mother's pouch. • The blue whale is the largest mammal. • Dogs, cats, and horses are mammals in our neighborhood. • Baby mammals are nourished by their mothers.

FIGURE 6.10

Use of K-W-L for mammals

Note. From "Becoming an Active Reader: K-W-L and K-W-L Plus" by Eileen S. Marzola and Lisa A. Freund, 1989, *The Reading Instruction Journal, 33,* p. 32. Copyright 1989 by the New Jersey Reading Association. Adapted by permission.

and still need to learn" column (refer to Figure 6.10). After reading, students discuss which questions were answered and what they learned. They can use other sources to find answers to any unanswered or newly generated questions.

A videotape entitled *Literacy in Content Area Instruction* (Raphael & Au, 1991) demonstrates how third grade teacher Laura Pardo uses K-W-L for a whole-class lesson on newspapers that is discussed in students' social studies textbook.

Eventually, through teacher modeling, students can use this strategy on their own. Cooperative groups are ideal for helping students to learn and extend their expertise about a content topic (Brozo & Simpson, 1991). The next section shares how cooperative group writing can be used to help students experience the writing process as they share what they know about a subject.

COOPERATIVE GROUP LEARNING WITH PROGRESSIVE WRITING

One semester when one of us was team teaching with a language arts teacher from a neighboring school, we created a **cooperative group learning** strategy we called "Progressive Writing" to help teachers experience each stage of writing in a nonthreatening atmosphere. An adaptation of the Progressive Dinner, at which a group of people eat each part of a five-course meal in a different home, **"Progressive Writing"** provides the same progressive movement in writing as groups of participants go from table to table to experience each writing stage. Here is how you can implement this strategy:

1. Bring in five objects or artifacts related to a topic or theme. For instance, for our concept of slavery discussed in the "Organizing Content Area Materials," you could bring in a toy log house, cotton, map of escape routes along the underground railroad, a Harriet Tubman doll, and a fife. Better yet, Sam Sebesta (personal communication, July 16, 1991) recommends that students can make their own objects to use for this activity. Put one object on each table with five pieces of large chart paper. Divide students into five groups. Have one student from each group volunteer to be the recorder.
2. Introduce this strategy as a collaborative writing assignment and require all group members to participate at each writing stage. Explain that each group can contribute to one facet of every piece of writing for each of the five objects in the room. They will rotate clockwise to experience a different writing stage for a different piece of writing every 5 to 7 minutes.
3. (Prewriting) Have each group of students jot down words, such as *long* or *secretive,* related to an object on the table (5 minutes). Entire group moves to the next table, which has a different object.
4. (Writing) Have each group write a story related to the new object, using the words or ideas written by the previous group during prewriting (7 minutes). Entire group then moves to the next table.
5. (Revising) Have each group revise (add/delete/reorganize) the story written by the previous group (7 minutes). Entire group moves to the next table.

6. (Editing) Have each group edit for mechanics (grammar and spelling) the revised story of the previous group (5 minutes). Entire group moves to the next table.
7. (Creating Final Copy) Have each group create a final copy of the edited piece written by the previous group (5 minutes). Entire group moves to the original table.
8. (Reseeing) Have each group look at the story created for its object and share reactions (Wepner, 1991).

Teachers who have used this technique commented that students' group work provided the physical and mental involvement needed to experience each stage of the writing process. A science teacher uses this technique to tie together several exercises on photosynthesis. First, students experiment with geraniums to see the effect of the lack of light on starch production, using iodine and chlorophyll. Subsequently, students use progressive writing to write about five objects: a flowering geranium plant, a bottle of iodine, a flask of chlorophyll solution, a single geranium leaf, and a box of cornstarch. This teacher finds that this strategy helps students to further their understanding of complex science concepts (Andreano & Wepner, 1991).

Examples of Teacher Applications

This next section shares how teachers are using many of the ideas discussed from the previous sections. The reasons that these teachers moved away from traditional textbook-oriented teaching emanated from their desire for students to gravitate more toward thinking about a topic rather than toward memorizing disjointed pieces of information. Although a picturesque array of resources and strategies are represented in the examples that follow, there is no perfect blend across curricular areas. Teachers, in trying to make content area instruction exciting for their students and themselves, searched for their own strategic ways to combine reading and writing materials and activities.

Two important ideas come out of our work with teachers in this chapter: (a) while process-oriented instruction with a writing-to-learn focus applies across curricular areas, literature-based reading does not fit in as readily; and (b) teachers need to be just as discreet with their integration of literature-based reading as they are with other concepts and frameworks. For example, one teacher who uses trade books at every possible juncture said, "You know, I could use trade books for science, but my students cannot be reading trade books all day long. They need other options for discovering the meaningfulness of learning about a content area." When we heard that, we understood that, as with everything in life, there needs to be a balance. We hope that as you read what teachers shared with us you find your own balance of materials and strategies.

SOCIAL STUDIES

MULTICULTURAL TRADE BOOKS IN THE PRIMARY CLASSROOM

Vicki Contente wants her culturally diverse first grade students to have a picture of the world that is broader than their immediate surroundings. As she follows her state-wide social studies curriculum and uses her school's social studies textbook about the community, she exposes her students to multicultural literature. In her mind, literature is the medium that enables students to see the world through a number of different windows. Vicki has scoured her countryside looking for her current library of books that support her multicultural strand.

When Vicki introduces students to Native American culture, she uses books such as *The Legend of the Blue Bonnet* (de Paola, 1983), *Knots on a Counting Rope* (Martin & Archambault, 1987), *On Mother's Lap* (Scott, 1972), and *The Story of the Jumping Mouse* (Steptoe, 1972). When Vicki launches her study of Asian American culture, she uses books such as *Crow Boy* (Japanese) (Yashima, 1955), *How My Parents Learned to Eat* (Japanese) (Friedman, 1984), *Angel Child, Dragon Child* (Vietnamese) (Surat, 1983), *Toad is the Uncle of Heaven* (Vietnamese) (Lee, 1985) and *Nine-In-one grr! grr!* (Hmong) (Xiong, 1989). And when Vicki opens students' eyes to African American customs, she reads books such as *Mufaro's Beautiful Daughter* (Steptoe, 1987), *Darkness and the Butterfly* (Grifalconi, 1987), *Lord of the Dance* (Tadjo, 1988) and *Tell Me a Story, Mama* (Johnson, 1989).

Of course, these are just a few of the hundreds of books that Vicki uses for her social studies units. As she follows her curriculum, she identifies books from different cultures to support a theme. For example, when she discusses mothers, she reads books about mothers in different cultures so that students become aware of the universality of mothering. Alternatively, she creates an entire unit around a cultural celebration such as the lunar new year so that students learn more about Chinese and Vietnamese practices.

Vicki finds that the books that touch her the most are the books that affect her children in the most positive ways. She truly believes that students' exposure to the customs of diverse cultures sensitizes them to the effects of stereotyping in and around their communities. She and Johnnie Cole, whom you will read about in a later section, actually put together a listing of multicultural books for thematic and seasonal units of study. For more information, write to Head of Curriculum Development (currently Ms. Pat Masonheimer), Elk Grove Unified School District, 8820 Elk Grove Boulevard, Elk Grove, California, 95624. Another excellent resource, *Multicultural Children's and Young Adult Literature: A Selected Listing of Books Published Between 1980–88* (Kruse & Horning, 1989), provides an annotated listing of multicultural books by category.

USING TRADE BOOKS AND SIMULATIONS FOR HANDICAP AWARENESS

Second grade teachers Janis Young and Virginia Baird created a social studies unit on handicap awareness so that their students would become more sensitized to the needs and feelings of children with physical disabilities. They use four books for shared book reading: *The Balancing Girl* (Rabe, 1981), a story about a physically disabled girl who proves that she is a capable person; *Howie Helps Himself* (Fassler, 1978), a narrative about a boy with cerebral palsy who tries to move his wheelchair by himself; *Knots on a Counting Rope* (Martin Jr. & Archambault, 1987), a poetic story about a blind boy's preparation for a horse race; and *Anna's Silent World* (Wolf, 1977), a book about a deaf girl's experiences in school and with friends.

Students discuss each book as a class and in small groups before responding in their reaction journals. They work in small groups to generate questions for interviewing their mayor and school principal to find out how the town and school are meeting the needs of people with handicapping conditions. They also engage in a variety of activities to appreciate what it is like to live with a handicap: watching part of a TV program with the sound turned off; going through a simple obstacle course in class blindfolded; finger painting blindfolded; communicating a simple message with sign language; and miming a scene from *The Balancing Girl*.

Students then select a book about someone with a special need to read independently. Janis and Virginia help them to select one of the following four culminating writing projects to do in response to their independent reading:

1. List three ways the character dealt with his/her special needs.
2. Compare/contrast that person with yourself.
3. Write an entry in that person's diary pretending you are that person.
4. Design an invention to benefit the life of this person.

Cross-Curricular Unit for Japan

Fourth grade teacher Susan M. Dammeyer created a 5-week unit on Japan to help her students understand its culture, geography, and history. Although designed to broaden the fourth grade social studies curriculum, this unit taps into science, language arts and art. Figure 6.11 indicates the cross-curricular objectives identified and materials/resources used for this unit.

Susan's students read two novels as a whole class: *The Big Wave* (Buck, 1947), a tale about two boys in Japan, one of whom has to deal with losing his family to a tidal wave; and *Sadako and the Thousand Paper Cranes* (Coerr, 1977), a tale of a young Japanese girl who, while suffering from leukemia, spends her time folding paper cranes in the hopes that this superstitious behavior will help to cure her.

Before students read these books, Susan uses films, maps, and posters to help students learn about Japan. She also reads aloud from the books listed in Figure 6.11 to encourage students to learn more information about Japan. She incorporates both written assignments and art projects into students' reading and listening experiences.

When students read the third book, *Volcanos and Earthquakes* (Lauber, 1985), a visually descriptive and informative book about the causes of volcanos and earthquakes, Susan has the fourth grade science teacher work with her students so that they understand the similarities and differences between volcanos and earthquakes. Susan uses this science lesson as an introduction to students' research in the library where they read books and take notes to create an outline of volcanos. An excellent

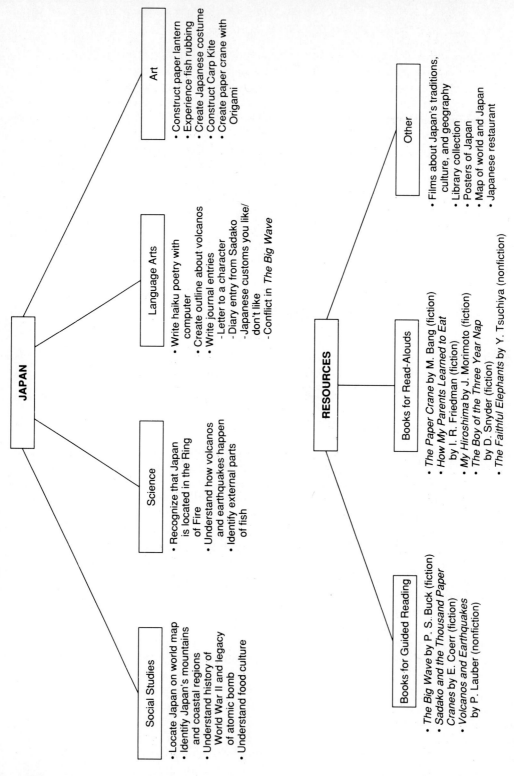

JAPAN

Social Studies
- Locate Japan on world map
- Identify Japan's mountains and coastal regions
- Understand history of World War II and legacy of atomic bomb
- Understand food culture

Science
- Recognize that Japan is located in the Ring of Fire
- Understand how volcanos and earthquakes happen
- Identify external parts of fish

Language Arts
- Write haiku poetry with computer
- Create outline about volcanos
- Write journal entries
  - Letter to a character
  - Diary entry from Sadako
  - Japanese customs you like/don't like
  - Conflict in *The Big Wave*

Art
- Construct paper lantern
- Experience fish rubbing
- Create Japanese costume
- Construct Carp Kite
- Create paper crane with Origami

RESOURCES

Books for Guided Reading
- *The Big Wave* by P. S. Buck (fiction)
- *Sadako and the Thousand Paper Cranes* by E. Coerr (fiction)
- *Volcanos and Earthquakes* by P. Lauber (nonfiction)

Books for Read-Alouds
- *The Paper Crane* by M. Bang (fiction)
- *How My Parents Learned to Eat* by I. R. Friedman (fiction)
- *My Hiroshima* by J. Morimoto (fiction)
- *The Boy of the Three Year Nap* by D. Snyder (fiction)
- *The Faithful Elephants* by Y. Tsuchiya (nonfiction)

Other
- Films about Japan's traditions, culture, and geography
- Library collection
- Posters of Japan
- Map of world and Japan
- Japanese restaurant

FIGURE 6.11

Cross-curricular objectives and resources for a fourth grade unit on Japan

Note. From "Cross-Curricular Objectives and Resources," 1991. Copyright 1991 by Susan M. Dammeyer. Adapted by permission.

book for this research is *Volcano—The Eruption and Healing of Mount St. Helens* (Lauber, 1986), a vivid description of the 1980 event, with dramatic photographs of the volcano before and after its eruption.

Susan concludes the unit with a field trip to a local Japanese restaurant in which students, dressed in costumes that they created as an art project, have a Japanese feast.

EARLY AMERICA WITH TRADE BOOKS AND TECHNOLOGY

Fifth grade teacher Johnnie Cole is responsible for the same social studies curriculum as Mr. D. in our opening vignette. Although she expressed the same concerns as Mr. D. a few years ago, she recently discovered that her trade book-based reading plan could extend to her social studies curriculum. In fact, she decided that she would not only use trade books to teach social studies but would also use technology to enhance students' social studies experiences.

COLONIAL ARTIFACTS

Writing Situation: You are an archaeologist in Williamsburg, Virginia. You have been working in a dig and have discovered an object that you believe existed during Colonial times.

Writing Directions: Draw an accurate illustration of your artifact in the rectangle below. Include as much detail as possible. Under the illustration, write a paragraph including the following information:
- the name you would give to the artifact
- how it was used during Colonial times
- what materials it was made of
- what kinds of tools we use today to perform the same function

When you have finished, you will be asked to read your paragraph and show your illustration to the class.

FIGURE 6.12
Prereading activity for fifth grade unit on early American artifacts
Note. From "Prereading Activity for Early American Artifacts," 1991. Copyright 1991 by Johnnie Cole. Reprinted by permission.

She begins the unit by bringing in a bag of Early American artifacts (for example, beeswax, wooden needle, and curlers). Students select an artifact, study it, and pretend that they are archaeologists in Williamsburg, Virginia, who have just dug up their objects from colonial times. They have to illustrate and write a paragraph about their artifacts (see Figure 6.12, p. 303). Ms. Cole uses *If You Lived in Colonial Times* (McGovern, 1980) to give students more information about their artifacts. Students then do a presentation to the rest of the class about their ideas.

Students read three books for this unit: (a) *The Secret Soldier: The Story of Deborah Sampson* (McGovern, 1975); (b) *And Then What Happened, Paul Revere?* (Fritz, 1973) and (c) *The Sign of the Beaver* (Speare, 1983). With the first book, they write about colonial homes and colonial women and imagine themselves as the main character. When they complete the book, students generate a list of questions they would like to ask Deborah. They then pretend to be Deborah in order to respond to their own questions.

With the second book, students create an individual census and class census, contrast modern American and Colonial American message delivery systems, engage in cooperative learning, and create silversmith art. With the third book, students engage in a variety of activities related to the animals mentioned in the book. They also work with five different graphic organizers: **weave**, **topical net**, **story graph**, **Venn diagram**, and **branching hierarchy** to organize and react to what they read (see Figures 6.13 through 6.17 for examples).

In between reading these three books, students create their own hornbooks, colonial houses, mob caps, and weather vanes. They work with the *Colonial Times Database* from the *Bank Street Beginner's Filer* (Sunburst, 1985) to learn how to browse, sort and find information about colonial times. They publish a class book about beavers with *Magic Slate II* (Sunburst, 1988). (See Chapter 5, "Software Mentioned" for software publishers' addresses.)

FIGURE 6.13
Example of weave graphic organizer for fifth grade social studies unit
Note. From "Weave Graphic Organizer," 1991. Copyright 1991 by Johnnie Cole. Reprinted by permission.

	How They Feel	What They Do	How They Look
Matt	impatient superior angry at self lonely foolish	taught Attean how to read learned to hunt for food waited for family to come taught Attean to spell	tall thin brown hair
Attean	scornful superior suspicious brave satisfied	taught Matt to hunt without a gun found his manitou went North with his tribe	tall straight, black hair black eyes darker than Matt

FIGURE 6.14
Example of topical net graphic organizer for fifth grade social studies unit
Note. From "Topical Net Graphic Organizer," 1991. Copyright 1991 by Johnnie Cole. Reprinted by permission.

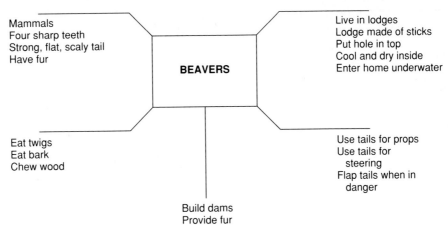

Mammals
Four sharp teeth
Strong, flat, scaly tail
Have fur

BEAVERS

Live in lodges
Lodge made of sticks
Put hole in top
Cool and dry inside
Enter home underwater

Eat twigs
Eat bark
Chew wood

Use tails for props
Use tails for steering
Flap tails when in danger

Build dams
Provide fur

FIGURE 6.15
Example of story graph graphic organizer for fifth grade social studies unit
Note. From "Story Graph Graphic Organizer," 1991. Copyright 1991 by Johnnie Cole. Reprinted by permission.

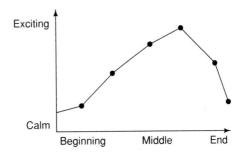

FIGURE 6.16
Example of Venn diagram graphic organizer for fifth grade social studies unit
Note. From "Venn Diagram Graphic Organizer," 1991. Copyright 1991 by Johnnie Cole. Reprinted by permission.

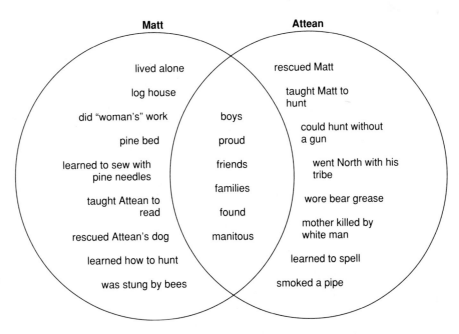

Matt

Attean

lived alone

log house

did "woman's" work

pine bed

learned to sew with pine needles

taught Attean to read

rescued Attean's dog

learned how to hunt

was stung by bees

boys

proud

friends

families

found

manitous

rescued Matt

taught Matt to hunt

could hunt without a gun

went North with his tribe

wore bear grease

mother killed by white man

learned to spell

smoked a pipe

FIGURE 6.17
Example of branching hierarchy graphic organizer for fifth grade social studies unit
Note. From "Branching Hierarchy Graphic Organizer," 1991. Copyright 1991 by Johnnie Cole. Reprinted by permission.

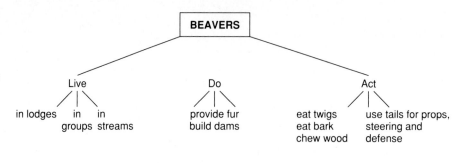

Students culminate their study of this unit with a Colonial Christmas celebration that includes colonial food, costumes, project presentations, songs, dances, and games. Although these are the only books that Ms. Cole uses with her class, she has generated a list of other books for a study of Early American literature: *The Many Lives of Benjamin Franklin* (Aliki, 1988), *James Monroe, Young Patriot* (Bains, 1986), *Everyday Dress of the American Colonial Period* (Copeland, 1975), *The Story of Benjamin Franklin, Amazing American* (Davidson, 1988), *An Early American Christmas* (de Paola, 1987), and *Young Thomas Jefferson* (Sabin, 1986).

Another book that a teacher friend says is a "must" when talking about our nation's history is *A Visit to Washington, D.C.* (Krementz, 1987), an informative narrative and photographic journey of major and out-of-the ordinary sights in Washington.

RESEARCHING THE AMERICAN REVOLUTION WITH TRADE BOOKS AND OTHER RESOURCES

Fifth grade teacher Beverly Pilchman, who appears in Chapter 4 as a "trade books only" teacher, finds it quite natural to include her social studies curriculum with her literature-based plan so that she does not have to clock-watch or move students from one subject to another. She established three goals for her students' study of the American Revolution: (a) use multiple resources—not just a textbook—to learn about this period; (b) involve students in age-appropriate research in which they are able to learn from one another; and (c) help students establish their own learning goals by encouraging them to identify a topic to learn in depth and publish their expert knowledge in a format of their choice. She also decided to use her Literary Study Group format as a framework for instruction in which she would

- begin each period with a short teacher-directed lesson
- enable students to read independently and respond in their reading logs for 20 minutes
- confer with students during independent reading time
- form small heterogeneous discussion groups for 10 to 15 minutes in which stu-

dents would rotate as notetakers to record the content and process of each group's discussion
• meet with the whole class to discuss, share, and ask questions

Her first step was to decide which lessons, activities, or textbook readings were necessary. As Beverly says, "It was the first time I gave myself permission to weed." She works closely with her school's media specialist to develop a booklist of rich historical fiction appropriate for a wide range of students. She tries to include at least two copies of each book so that students have the opportunity for paired interaction. Two books that she selected to read aloud to students are *King George's Head Was Made of Lead* (Monjo, 1974) and *Can't You Make Them Behave, King George?* (Fritz, 1977). She uses these books to bring the class together to model discussion, encourage inquiry, and foster comparisons. Although these are the books that Beverly uses, many other nonfiction and poetry books about this period in American history could be used for read-alouds. Some of the books include *Paul Revere* (Gleiter, 1987), an illustrated biographical description of Paul Revere's famous ride; *Paul Revere and the Minutemen* (Charles, 1975), a narrative poem in picture book format that details reasons for Paul Revere's famous ride; *The American Revolutionaries: A History in Their Own Words, 1750–1800* (Meltzer, 1987), a collection of letters, diaries, interviews, and speeches of people who fought in the Revolutionary War; and *With Flying Colors: Highlights of the American Revolution* (Buranelli, 1969), an illustrated biography of famous figures and an account of major events from the American Revolution.

Students then begin their independent reading and responses to self-selected books. Students read, for example, *Mr. Revere and I* (Lawson, 1953), *Johnny Tremain* (Forbes, 1943), *Early Thunder* (Fritz, 1967), and *The Mystery Candlestick* (Bothwell, 1970). By using reading logs as a vehicle for self-expression, she finds that students' record their own thoughts before being influenced by the thoughts of others. Students' insights and responses to influential historical figures and documents such as the Bill of Rights and the Declaration of Independence communicate a personal attachment to their meaning.

Once students finish reading their book, Beverly has them write book reviews. She reads aloud a sample of children's book reviews from *The New York Times* so that, together as a class, they can analyze the reviews for salient components to include. Students know that they are writing these reviews for future fifth graders to help them in their selection of books.

To move students forward in their ability to complete a more complex task than a review of a single book, Beverly initiates a research project so that students can develop and answer research questions by organizing information into a meaningful format. She, along with her media specialist, created a format for students to follow. She begins by brainstorming with the class possible topics to research for this historical period. Once students select a topic, she invites them to write down everything they know or think they know about their topics. All students have a different topic so that they can learn from one another. Students then generate a list of questions about what else they would like to know. Beverly then creates a graphic organizer to help students see how different topics relate to each other. She uses this graphic organizer to form writing groups so that students can meet daily to offer suggestions, ask for clarification, confirm ideas and help writers become aware of their audiences. For example, one writing group that is working with "Battles and Military Leaders" includes such topics as the Battle of Lexington and Concord, the Battle of Bunker Hill, the Boston Massacre, General Thomas Gage, and General George Washington. These writing groups remain together throughout the project so that students can help each other with questions about their topics and concerns about their writing.

Students write all their notes on 5 × 7 cards to prepare for an oral report. This occurs before any writing is done. Beverly has a student who is ready to share his/her information give an oral report in front of the whole class so that Beverly can model for the students how to outline their information for their written report. All other oral reports are given in the writing groups. Beverly confers with students about their progress so that they become ready to write about what they have internalized rather than what they can copy. Because students have choices for presenting their research, some write historical fiction, some write question-and-answer books, and some write newspapers reflective of the time period (see Figure 6.18) (Pilchman, 1991). As evi-

The Boston Gazette

Interview with Jonathan Lyte Tremain

by
Sara
Stanley

Sara: Hello! I am here with a member of The Boston Tea Party, Jonathan Lyte Tremain. Now, Johnny, how do you feel about being the boy who signaled the "indians" to go aboard the ships, Dartmouth, Beaver, and The Eleanor?

Johnny: Well, I'm quite proud of being chosen by Rab, my good friend, to blow the whistle and get the "indians" aboard the ships.

Sara: Why don't you tell our readers how Rab and you met.

Johnny: Very well. Rab and I met after I was sent away by my master, Mr. Lapham, to find a new job. Mr. Lapham is now dead.

Sara: Why did you get sent away?

Johnny: John Hancock asked my master and I to make a suger basin to match his tea set. Dove, Mr. Lapham's other assistant handed me a broken crucible to get back at me for being "mean". I was heating the silver on the furnace when the crucible broke and I burned my hand. The next thing I new I was lying in the birth and death room with my hand in a bandage.

Sara: Oh, how tragic.

Johnny: Please do not dwell on the past, think of the present.

Sara: Now for the last question. How do you feel about Cilla being your future bride?

Johnny: Well, I'd love to marry her but I don't know if it will happen with Mr. Laphem and all. I'll only marry her in my drea-

Sara: We better stop before I start crying again. Goodbye.

The Battle of Lexington and Concord

The Battle of Lexington and Concord was one of the many battles between the English and the Colonists. This acount is of one boy, Johnny Tremain.

Johnny had dressed up as an Englishman to sneak into the battle. He had no weapons, but his main objective was to find his friend Rab. After many hours of searching, he found Rab, along with his friend, Dr. Warren. Rab was deathly wounded, for he had been shot on the front line. Rab ordered Johnny to go to Silsbee's cove and find his family. They were not there, and when Johnny got back, Rab was dead. Dr. Warren did fix Johnny's hand, but not his feelings, as those would last forever

The Boston Tea Party

The Boston Tea Party was a massive raid of the tea from England's ships. The Sons of Liberty and whigs from all over organized it.

One fifteen year old boy named Johnny Tremain was the signaler. After Josiah Quincy said, "...and to that God who rides the whirlwind and directs the storm, I commit my country..." that was his signal to blow the whistle so the tea party could begin. The participators dressed up as indians and chopped open the chests of tea and dumped them into the harbor. They dumped three ship fulls of tea.

After that, King George closed the harbor and sent over some of his troops. He also said that no ship could come in or go out from Boston until the tea was paid for.

That was one of the events that lead up to the battle of Lexington and Concord.

Advertisments

NEW! Paul Revere crubicles!
LOW, LOW, LOW, PRICE!!

Special Offer!!!!
Get 4 bars of Franklin Soap for only 1 pence!!

Get the BIG SIG quill pen!
It's the same kind John Hancock used to sign the Declaration of Independence!

FIGURE 6.18

Newspaper written by fifth grade students

Note. From original student writing, 1991. Copyright 1991 by Becki Baron, Ana Christa Boksay, Matthew Glaser, Jessie Shacklette, and Sara Stanley. Reprinted by permission.

denced by this unit, Beverly knows that her goal of creating learners who know what they want to learn and know how to search for it is being accomplished.

SCIENCE

As Jeffry V. Mallow (1991), professor of physics at Loyola University of Chicago, has stated, science anxiety, science avoidance, and science illiteracy pervade our society. Much of this fear and ignorance has been caused by misconceptions about learning science. It just is not the same as reading literature or other content area material. For this reason, science instruction at the elementary level must be presented in a way that intrigues students to want to continue learning in this area. In addition to getting ideas from the teacher examples that follow, you may want to look at a recently published text, *Science Learning: Processes and Applications* (Santa & Alvermann, 1991), a collection of articles written by science and reading teachers about helping students to acquire **scientific literacy.**

THEMATIC UNIT FOR ENDANGERED SPECIES

Kindergarten teacher Elsie Nigohosian, whom we talked about earlier and discussed in Chapter 3, decided to modify one of her required science units—endangered species—to include other content areas and a variety of genres: poetry, fables, informational books, and fiction. With this month-long unit, students learn about many kinds of endangered species, reasons why these animals are becoming extinct, and ways to help preserve some of them.

As with her basal-trade book plan, Elsie used a web to create this **thematic unit.** But, instead of using a letter for her hub, she used her endangered species theme to set concept goals, identify related books, and create activities.

As you can see in Figure 6.19, Elsie weaves six content area activities into her day. (See Figure 3.1 in Chapter 3 to get an idea of her weekly organizational plans.) Let's look at science for a moment to see what she does. As she reads *Animals Do the Strangest Things* (Hornblow, 1964), a humorous reference book about the characteristics of different kinds of animals, she discusses the unique features of each animal. Students then become "animal experts" for their favorite animals and write big books containing the following information: what the animal looks like; how the animal moves; what makes the animal special; and where the animal lives.

As she reads *All Kinds of Babies* (Selsam, 1967), an informational book describing baby animals and their physical similarities to their parents, she has her students compare and contrast likenesses and differences between each baby and adult animal. She then creates a graph with the class to show students' comparisons visually.

She reads and discusses the following books over several days, *Animals in Danger* (Whitcomb, 1988), *Cheetah* (Arnold, 1989), *Gordy Gorilla* (Irvine, 1990), *Gorilla* (Brown, 1983) so that students begin to understand what is causing animals to be endangered. She makes a semantic web with her class, identifying and describing

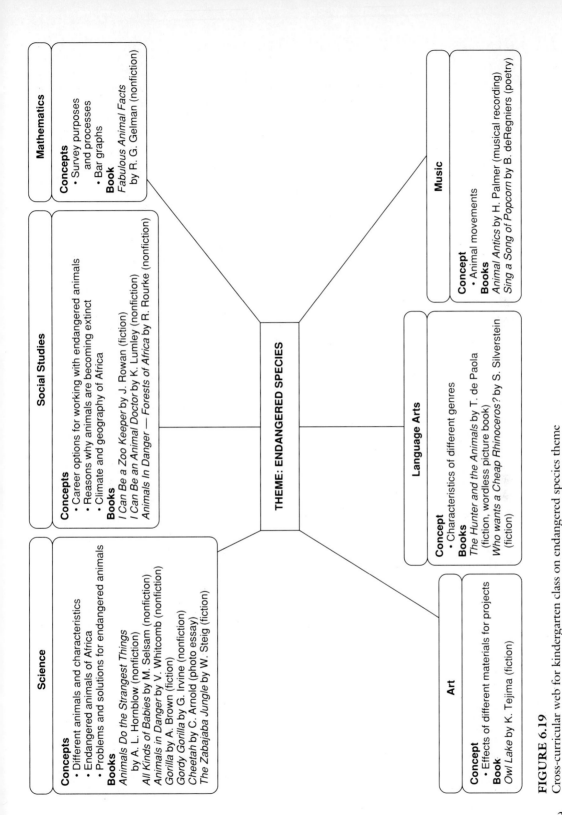

Science

Concepts
- Different animals and characteristics
- Endangered animals of Africa
- Problems and solutions for endangered animals

Books
Animals Do the Strangest Things by A. L. Hornblow (nonfiction)
All Kinds of Babies by M. Selsam (nonfiction)
Animals in Danger by V. Whitcomb (nonfiction)
Gorilla by A. Brown (fiction)
Gordy Gorilla by G. Irvine (nonfiction)
Cheetah by C. Arnold (photo essay)
The Zabajaba Jungle by W. Steig (fiction)

Social Studies

Concepts
- Career options for working with endangered animals
- Reasons why animals are becoming extinct
- Climate and geography of Africa

Books
I Can Be a Zoo Keeper by J. Rowan (fiction)
I Can Be an Animal Doctor by K. Lumley (nonfiction)
Animals In Danger — Forests of Africa by R. Rourke (nonfiction)

Mathematics

Concepts
- Survey purposes and processes
- Bar graphs

Book
Fabulous Animal Facts by R. G. Gelman (nonfiction)

THEME: ENDANGERED SPECIES

Art

Concept
- Effects of different materials for projects

Book
Owl Lake by K. Tejima (fiction)

Language Arts

Concept
- Characteristics of different genres

Books
The Hunter and the Animals by T. de Paola (fiction, wordless picture book)
Who wants a Cheap Rhinoceros? by S. Silverstein (fiction)

Music

Concept
- Animal movements

Books
Animal Antics by H. Palmer (musical recording)
Sing a Song of Popcorn by B. deRegniers (poetry)

FIGURE 6.19

Cross-curricular web for kindergarten class on endangered species theme

Note. From "Cross-Curricular Web of Endangered Species Theme," 1991. Copyright 1991 by Elsie Nigohosian. Adapted by permission.

311

factors that contribute to extinction. Students then brainstorm various ways to call attention to the notion of endangered species (for example, write a letter, make a poster) before selecting one activity to do.

The last book that she reads for the science portion of her unit is *The Zabajaba Jungle* (Steig, 1987) to help her students acquire a more vivid picture of Africa, its terrain, and its plant and animal life. Students make a mural of Africa and then complete a language experience chart on Africa using the cloze procedure and a word bank.

Let's look at how Elsie handles the other content areas. For social studies Elsie reads *I Can Be a Zoo Keeper* (Rowan, 1985), *I Can Be An Animal Doctor* (Lumley, 1985), and *Animals in Danger—Forests of Africa* (Rourke, 1982). She also uses newspaper and magazine articles dealing with animal rights, pollution, and recycling. Students visit a zoo, meet with a veterinarian, create a map of Africa, and write letters to restaurants and chemical companies to request information about how these companies address recycling and pollution.

For mathematics Elsie reads aloud *Fabulous Animal Facts* (Gelman, 1981). Students create their own word problems, survey each other on animal rights, and work with Elsie to graph their results. For music students learn animal songs from Palmer's (1986) musical recording of *Animal Antics* and move like animals to the music. They also dramatize poems that are put on charts from *To Sing a Song of Popcorn: Every Child's Book of Poems* (deRegniers, et al., 1988).

For language arts Elsie uses examples of different genres from the books already mentioned as well as other books—*The Hunter and the Animals* (de Paola, 1981), *Who Wants a Cheap Rhinoceros?* (Silverstein, 1983), *Please Send a Panda* (Orbach, 1977), and *A Zoo for Mr. Muster* (Lobel, 1962)—to help students identify why books represent different genres. She also has students retell stories on tape, dramatize, make advertisements for animals, and rewrite stories to fit a specific genre.

For art Elsie notes Tejima's (1987) woodcut drawing techniques for the pictures in *Owl Lake* as a springboard for students' creation of their own animal drawings. Students also use their art time to create stick puppets for their dramatizations during language arts and music and murals of endangered species in Africa for science. Elsie concludes the unit with a "What I Learned About Endangered Species" question from K-W-L to help students summarize all that they learned from the unit.

FROGS, TRADE BOOKS, AND OTHER ACTIVITIES

With a more narrow curricular focus, first grade teacher Pat Piech created a science **learning center** for the life cycle of a frog. Students actually participate in nine frog-related activities. They (a) create frog folders; (b) work with frog words; (c) record their observations of a frog hatching in the center's hatchery tank; (d) illustrate the life cycle of a frog (using picture books and reference books for assistance) (see Trade Books Mentioned for Science); (e) sequence the frog's life cycle with sentence strips; (f) listen to Arnold Lobel's frog and toad stories (see Trade Books Mentioned); (g) measure the sizes of laminated tadpoles; (h) create paintings and recite poetry to distinguish between frogs and toads; and (i) write factual books about frogs in frog-shaped books (Piech, 1991). Students are acting like scientists and learning the scientific process as they go through this interesting and engaging unit.

K-W-L FOR PENGUINS AND SHARKS

Second grade teacher Maryanne Crowley, one of our teachers from Chapter 3, discovered that her method for combining basals and trade books could be used to blend textbooks and trade books in science. In addition to using her science textbook as a resource for district-wide curricular objectives, she is using trade books to extend her science curriculum. She recently developed two units, one for penguins and one for sharks. She went to her community and school library to find books that are appropriate for second graders.

Maryanne's framework for introducing her penguin unit is K-W-L. She begins by asking students, "What do we know about penguins?" After she lists students' brainstormed ideas, she asks, "What do we want to learn about penguins?" She then uses students' ideas as a springboard for reading from various sections of trade books such as *Emperor Penguin* (Deguine, 1974), *Penguins* (Darling, 1956), *Penguins Live Here* (Eberle, 1974), *Adelbert the Penguin* (Hutchins, 1969), *Penguins: A New True Book* (Lepthien, 1983), and *A Pocketful of Penguins* (Falla, 1970). She also reads sections of penguin articles from *National Geographic World* (Washington, DC) and *Ranger Rick* (National Wildlife Federation, Vienna, VA).

As Maryanne reads and discusses the information from the books and magazines, she helps to build students' "penguin" vocabulary (for example, *rookery*). Once she's spent many days with shared book reading, she generates an outline of students' new ideas and organizes the information into different categories on the chalkboard, for example, "types of penguins," "what they look like," "how they mate," and "sounds of penguins." Her students then write for several weeks, conferencing periodically. For a culminating art project, students make 3-foot penguins out of construction paper, dress them, and put them in a rookery where their penguin-shaped writing is attached.

Maryanne's shark unit proceeds similarly for her seven shark books (see Trade Books Mentioned for books about sharks). Student pairs complete this unit with a cooperative learning art experience in which they create 2- to 3-foot sharks that they put together in a huge mural underwater scene. Students also create shark poetry to illustrate what they learned.

Although both units initially focused on expanding students' content-based reading and writing experiences, Maryanne finds that the art projects bring out unexpected excitement in students' responses to what they are learning.

CURRENT EVENTS, PERSONAL OBSERVATION, AND WRITING

Susan McGrath, a teacher of special education students in grades two through five, created a science project on the January, 1991, oil spill in the Persian Gulf. She brought in copies of the *Los Angeles Times'* headline story about the oil spill. After reading the article to her class, she gave each student a plastic foam cup filled with water. Students added salad oil and food coloring to their cups. They stirred, mixed, and observed. Susan then recorded their observations on the chalkboard as they discussed what they saw.

Each student then put a feather from a feather duster into their oil and water mixture. Again, Susan recorded students' observations as they discussed what they saw. She and her students then brainstormed ways in which they could clean the feathers, relating it to the task of cleaning the animals in the Gulf. Students wrote their own stories from the viewpoint of the animal caught in the mess; in other words, how it would feel and what the animal would want done (see Figure 6.20). They wrote their stories with pen and paper and then typed them into the computer. Using hard copy printouts, she did group editing with her students. "Does every sentence begin with a capital letter?" "Does every sentence end with a period?" Once students revised and printed their stories, they printed out two copies, one for the classroom library and one for themselves to take home.

Susan says, "It has been a real battle with special education students to get them to express their thoughts, to let them know there is more than one right answer to many things, that they have something valuable to contribute and that it's a safe environment to contribute in." She believes that the more these students are afforded reinforcing opportunities to express their views about science through discussion and writing, the more open they will be to assimilate new ideas.

So far, our four teachers of science—Elsie Nigohosian, Pat Piech, Maryanne Crowley, and Susan McGrath—have used different types of animals as a basis for their science instruction. In a moment we'll read about how another science teacher, Leslie Young, uses different science principles to get her students to write. Before we do, though, we want to share with you some other informational books about animals in Figure 6.21 that other teachers we know recommend using for science.

I was a bird and oil got stuck to my wings and I had no food for a whole entire week. Nobody notices me. Then somebody picked me up and brought me in their garage and got a bucket of water. They dried the oil off of me. Then gave me a nice place to sleep. Then they gave me a lot of food so I could build my strength up. They let me go.

BY JOSH LANE

FIGURE 6.20
Student's story about the oil spill
Note. From original student writing, 1991. Copyright 1991 by Josh Lane. Reprinted by permission.

•*CREATURES OF THE SEA*

Starfish (Hurd, 1962) is a poetic informative book about characteristics of the starfish.

Seahorse (Morris, 1972) is an easy-to-read, illustrated description of what the seahorse eats, the sounds it makes, the way it hides from its enemies, and the way it gives birth to its young.

Dive to the Coral Reefs (Tayntor, 1986) is an explanation, along with photographs, about how the coral reef is created from the tiny animals that actually make up the mounds, boulders, and branches.

•*ANIMALS ALL AROUND US*

Busy Beavers (Brownell, 1988) is an informative text with photographs about how beavers search for food, build their dams, and care for their young.

Can You Find Me? A Book About Animal Camouflage (Dewey, 1989) is an illustrated book about how a wide variety of animals in their natural environment— fish, insects, birds, reptiles, and mammals—use camouflage to survive.

Monarch Butterfly (Gibbons, 1989) is an illustrated story of the monarch butterfly and how it is transformed from a worm to a stained-glass window wonder.

Spiders (Petty, 1985) is a fascinating description of spiders and their architectural skills.

•*EXTINCT ANIMALS*

Wild and Woolly Mammoths (Aliki, 1977) is an excellent source of information about the mammoth and how it has been found frozen in glaciers, allowing scientists to learn more about these animals.

Creatures that Really Lived (Selsam, 1987) is an overview of the major creatures who are no longer with us.

FIGURE 6.21
Informational books about animals

USE OF RESOURCES FOR PERSUASIVE WRITING

Although sixth grade teacher Leslie Young does not really use trade books, she nevertheless believes in providing multiple sources for her students' processing of information. Each of her science units follows a similar format:

- Introduce information about a topic so that students have a common reference point.
- Use material related to a topic (for example, newspaper and/or magazine article, filmstrip, listening tape, or visual).
- Launch writing activity with provocative sentence starter, idea, or debatable issue that is discussed in small groups or as a whole class.

- Have students write about a topic. Once students write, they share their ideas with each other and then create a finished product that is based on sharing.

Leslie's unit on English scientist Sir Isaac Newton's Law of Motion and Inertia highlights how this format works for her. From the outset of Leslie's teacher-directed instruction, she connects the idea of using seat belts to Newton's ideas of preventing inertia-related injuries. Students then read a few newspaper articles about the pros and cons of using seat belts. Students interview each other about their feelings toward seat belts, and then they discuss what they discovered. They also listen to a tape of teenagers who collide while driving an automobile. Her students have to decide whether the teenagers were wearing seat belts or not.

Leslie then asks her students to think about what they read and heard before writing on a piece of paper "Yes" or "No" to the statement that "seat belts are important for preventing automobile-related injuries." Once students respond, they have to write three supporting statements to back up their argument. After students turn to a neighbor to share ideas and elicit feedback, they write a persuasive essay that is shared with a voluntary editorial board of three students who judge the impact of students' arguments. (She finds that this type of peer-editing encourages students to think for themselves about important science topics and issues.) Persuasive essays that are judged highly are published in the school's student newspaper.

Another application of Leslie's process-oriented approach is obvious with her introduction to Swiss mathematician Daniel Bernouilli's principle of lift. Again, after students listen to her presentation of how airplane wings create the upward force called *lift* and read a few articles from other sources about this topic, they build their own paper airplanes. (An excellent informational book for the study of flight is *The Glorious Flight* [Provensen & Provensen, 1983], the story of Bleriot's flight across the English Channel in a plane he had built.) Students from each table group of four then share their products with each other. Each table group must decide which planes will fly successfully through a hoop the greatest distance. Once students test their hypotheses, they write in their learning logs what they discovered. Ms. Young then reads students' ideas and generates a list of about 30 to 40 statements from the learning logs. She gives this list to each table group so that they can write a "summary by consensus" of what was learned about Bernouilli's principle.

Even though 142 students pass through her classroom each day, Leslie strongly believes in using reading and writing activities to which her students can relate so that they think about science content critically and creatively. Exposure to multiple sources of information combined with realistic writing assignments contributes to students' ownership of the material.

MATHEMATICS

A PIECE OF THE WHOLE: WRITING ABOUT DECIMALS

Beverly Pilchman, our fifth grade teacher from the social studies section, finds that just as her students need megadoses of real-world reading experiences in social studies and language arts, they also need similar amounts of discovery-oriented opportunities in mathematics. As she sees it, her mathematics textbook is just one small part of her total math program. She relies heavily on other resources such as *Family Math* (Stenmark, Thompson, & Cossey, 1986), *A Collection of Math Lessons, From Grades 3–6* (Burns, 1987), *Fraction Factory* (Holden, 1986), and *Mental Math in the Middle Grades* (Hope, Reys, & Reys, 1987), and *The Problem-Solver 5* (Moretti, Stephens, Goodnow, & Hoogeboom, 1987).

With each math unit students write before, during, and after their learning discoveries. For example, before students even work on a decimal unit, she says to them, "Write everything you know or think you might know about decimals: the way they are used, what they might mean, or where you have seen them. You can use writing, diagrams, or illustrations to indicate what you know." Students then do a variety of decimal-related activities. One such activity is students' search for all the different places where decimals are used. Students soon discover that decimals crop up in the library, in their cars, and on the radio. They create a decimal booklet of pictures and corresponding explanations, indicating their discoveries of decimals' ubiquity. Students soon learn more about decimals in the real world when they go on a hypothetical shopping spree in which they have $200 to spend for family gifts, with no more than $25 allotted for each gift, including tax. As they leaf through a variety of catalogues from local stores, they cut out pictures of selected gifts and write reasons for their purchase of each gift. The need for understanding and using decimals becomes that much more obvious as they simulate shopping in the real world.

Students' ability to think about decimals through writing is also part of Beverly's assessment procedures. For instance, when students have to place numbers correctly on a number line, including decimals, they first do the activity and then write down how they decided to put in their numbers on the number line.

Beverly finds that her mathematics teaching parallels her process-oriented instructional approach in every other content area. She uses such publications as *New Directions for Elementary School Mathematics: 1989 Yearbook* (Trafton & Shulte, 1989) to help her think about ways in which students can use language to understand the meaning of numbers and how they are used. A few trade books that complement Beverly's approach to challenging students' mathematical thinking are *Brain-Teasers and Mind-Benders* (Brandreth, 1979), *Devilish Bets to Trick Your Friends* (Churchill, 1985), and *263 Brain Busters: Just How Smart Are You, Anyway?* (Phillips, 1985). Each of these books offers refreshing collections of "puzzlers" that encourage students to think logically and creatively about mathematical ideas.

THEMATIC READING AND WRITING

Leah Richards, a teacher of seventh grade students (11-year-olds) in Adelaide, Australia, has set up her mathematics program around broad themes such as time and number. Each theme is organized into three phases: *pretheme work* in which she and her students prepare by establishing goals and organizing resources; *investigation* in which children work individually, in pairs, or groups to investigate theme-related ideas and share their discoveries through group conferences and class sharing; and *tie-*

up in which students share their findings through writing (for example, creating a big book), evaluation forms, and tests.

Because of her **inquiry-oriented approach,** students read and write daily about mathematics. Although students do not really read mathematics-related trade books, they do read the following: books produced by children themselves, including such things as instructions, explanations, definitions, applications, and reports; mathematics dictionaries and other published books with mathematical topics; discoveries, goals, and problems posted on a bulletin board; information and mathematical terms on charts and labels in the classroom; and newspapers. On the other hand, because she expects students to keep a record of their learning in their mathematics books, they experience all kinds of writing, for example, *summaries* of findings and processes, *translations* of definitions and concepts, *reports* of work they have done, *personal writing* of feelings, *instructions* for solving problems, and *predictions* of outcomes (Richards, 1990).

Richards believes that the more frequently students use language to communicate their mathematical understandings, the more likely they will be to apply mathematical ideas to their everyday lives—which should be the cornerstone of mathematics instruction.

MORE BOOKS AND IDEAS FOR MATHEMATICS

Although fewer trade books exist for mathematics than social studies or science, and fewer teachers use trade books for mathematics instruction, there still are many books that can be used for lesson starters. *Gator Pie* (Matthews, 1979), a book about two alligators who must divide a pie into more and more parts to share with their friends, is ideal for introducing a unit on fractions. Three books—*The Line Up Book* (Russo, 1986), *How Big Is a Foot?* (Myller, 1969), and *Inch by Inch* (Lionni, 1962)—are good lead-ins to measurement activities. And *The King's Chessboard* (Birch, 1988), a story about a wise man who, as a reward from the king, chooses a grain of rice to be doubled each day for 64 days (the number of squares on a chessboard) is a wonderful introduction to the concept of exponents.

Numerous rhyming and narrative counting books that can be used with primary students to support their concept of number correspondence are also available. Figure 6.22 provides a briefly annotated list of some of the books that can be used.

Webre (1989, 1991) also found that Children's Choices, the annotated list of books chosen by children and published in the October issue of *The Reading Teacher* each year since 1975, contains books that can be included in mathematics instruction: *Roman Numerals* (Adler, 1977), *The I Hate Mathematics! Book* (Burns, 1975), *How Much Is a Million?* (Schwartz, 1985), and *Sums: A Looking Game* (Vreuls, 1977). She describes how, for example, students can use the amazing facts from *How Much Is a Million?* to trigger the creation of their own amazing-but-true facts and then bind them into a class book for the math table. Similarly, students could use Schwartz's (1989) sequel about how money, banks, and interest work in *If You Made a Million* to generate their own ideas about investing their future fortunes!

Anno's Counting Book (Anno, 1977)
A landscape of buildings, trees, trains, boats, and people in a village keep increasing from 0 (no real village) to 12.

Anno's Counting House (Anno, 1975)
Ten little people move to an empty house next door to their furnished house and take their things with them.

One Crow: A Counting Rhyme (Aylesworth, 1988)
Counting rhyme of 1 to 10 farm animals, first in summer and then in winter scenes.

The Very Hungry Caterpillar (Carle, 1969)
A very hungry caterpillar eats his way through the pages with one apple, two pears, etc., until he becomes a butterfly.

Five Little Monkeys Jumping on the Bed (Christelow, 1989)
Rhyme about monkeys with one falling off and bumping his head.

The April Rabbits (Cleveland, 1988)
Number of rabbits corresponds to each day in the month of April.

Ten Black Dots (Crews, 1986)
Counting rhyme from 1 to 10 black dots.

Dancing in the Moon: Counting Rhymes (Eichenberg, 1975)
Counting rhyme about 1 to 20 animals doing different things.

1 Hunter (Hutchins, 1982)
A hunter's humorous walk through the jungle of hidden animals.

A Number of Dragons (Leedy, 1985)
Rhyme about dragons, 10 to 1 and back again.

One Was Johnny: A Counting Rhyme (Sendak, 1962)
Counting rhyme about Johnny and his plight with his intruders of his peace and quiet.

Who Wants One? (Serfozo, 1989)
Rhyming animals and objects from 1 to 10.

FIGURE 6.22
Counting books for primary students

Fictional stories about students' experiences with mathematics also can be used to prompt students to talk about their own feelings. And the books don't have to have mathematics in the title! For example, although *What a Wimp!* (Carrick, 1983) is about Barney, a new boy in school who is having trouble coping with his "wimpish" behavior in front of an older boy, the book weaves Barney's frustration with mathematics into the overriding theme of learning to cope with stressful situations. Students could use Barney's experiences with mathematics to talk about their own and then brainstorm ways to help Barney (and themselves) like mathematics more.

THE ARTS

Teachers in this section share how they use reading and writing opportunities to work with art and music.

READING ABOUT THE NINJA TURTLES AND OTHER ART MASTERS

Kathryn Bernardis teaches art to elementary students (grades one through six) with a four-phase, literature-based program:

Phase 1, "Leonardo Wasn't just a Ninja Turtle," is a unit in which students study Renaissance art and artists, especially Donatello, Michelangelo, Raphael, and Leonardo da Vinci, the names of the four Ninja Turtles. Ms. Bernardis introduces this phase by reading to them excerpts from *Art for Children* (Raboff, 1988), a series of 16 picture books, with each book devoted to a specific artist. She also reads from other sources. For example, during the 1990–91 school year, she used an article about the renovation of the Sistine Chapel, painted by Michelangelo, from *National Geographic* magazine. Another book that she provides as a resource is *Getting to Know the World's Greatest Artists* (Venezia, 1988). Along with studying the artists of this era, students study the "science of art" and get involved with color mixing, prisms, and color theory. Students also have the opportunity to create portraits of each other to simulate the work of Renaissance artists.

Kathryn introduces art museums to her students with a film and two books, *Visiting the Art Museum* (Brown & Brown, 1986) and *Let's Go to the Art Museum* (Levy, 1983), so that students understand the etiquette of attending art museums.

Inasmuch as Kathryn sends a newsletter to the classroom teachers to inform them of her annual plans, classroom teachers actually plan some of their literature around her art phases. For example, during this phase a fifth grade classroom teacher had her students read *The Mixed-Up Files of Mrs. Basil E. Frankweiler* (Konigsburg, 1967) because of the book's focus on Michelangelo's work.

Phase 2, "A Different Way of Seeing European Artists, 1900–1930," invites students to study different art forms. She begins this unit with the Picasso book from *Art for Children* (Raboff, 1988) as well as *Who Said Red?* (Serfozo, 1988) to prepare students for color blending. She also reads *Meet Matisse* (Munthe, 1983) to explain Matisse's work with cut-out paper during the last 20 years of his career before students actually create their own decoupage, a technique of using paper cut-outs.

Phase 3, "Multicultural Unit on Asian Art," is designed to have students examine 10 prints from the Asian Art Museum in San Francisco. Kathryn introduces this phase with multicultural folktales. Students then study and do Chinese Brush Painting, Indian Mehndi Hand (an Indian tradition of painting one's hand for special celebrations), and Persian lettering. Ms. Bernardis believes that this phase of her art program is critical for helping students to develop an appreciation and cultural understanding of all art forms.

Phase 4, "Modern Masters" is a unit in which students study such modern artists as Andy Warhol and Roy Lichtenstein. Although Ms. Bernardis doesn't use specific books for this phase, she expands students' use of language from different content areas to describe the 10 reproductions of modern masters displayed around the room. Here's what she does. She writes six words on cards pertaining to each content area (for example, she will write math words such as *add, subtract,* or *pattern;* or science words such as *earth*). Each group of students, with one set of content cards, has to decide which words to use for the reproductions. For instance, the science group might use the word "earth" to describe a reproduction that uses earth colors and is very somber. Since all six words have to be used, students actively search for ways to connect their knowledge of content vocabulary with their newfound understanding of art. Students then create their own work of art from a variety of common objects.

After every single project Kathryn has students write poetry, prose, or stories to describe their creations. She finds that students are remarkably fluent in verbalizing ideas because of their extended personal involvement with their projects. Because she also believes that the process is more important than any product, all her students succeed at some level.

PICTURE BOOKS WITH MUSICAL THEMES

Lamme (1990) shares how one school in Florida uses picture books with musical themes as an integral part of its curriculum. For example, one fourth grade teacher introduces students to the study of musical instruments with the book, *Song and Dance Man* (Ackerman, 1988), a story about a grandfather who provides his grandchildren with an impromptu musical performance. This teacher has volunteer parents and a grandparent visit her class to play their musical instruments. Students then create a musical instrument museum in their classroom with instruments on loan from a used instrument store. Students research different types of instruments and create an informational class book about musical instruments. Along the way, this teacher reads aloud from an array of nonfiction and fiction books on musical instruments. (See Trade Books Mentioned for examples of books about musical instruments.)

MUSICAL RESEARCH AND TEAM TEACHING

Music teacher Carl Howard is fortunate to be in a middle school where his principal encourages teachers to take advantage of the school's media specialist. Carl has developed a research project with his media specialist that is incorporated into his regular sixth grade music program. This project occurs four times a year since each student has music for only one nine-week cycle.

During students' first class session, Carl lists a series of topics on the board, for example, composers, instruments, instrumentalists, and types of music. He has students brainstorm what they know about these topics to generate excitement about their impending research project and to get to know more about his students' musical backgrounds. By the end of this first class, students self-select a topic to research.

During the next two class periods, Carl and his students go to the library so that the media specialist can discuss basic research techniques and introduce books about students' self-selected topics. The media specialist manages to acquire books for just about every topic by working with other libraries in the state. For the next 10 days, students visit the library before and after school to use the library's resources, including an electronic encyclopedia. The media specialist works closely with students as they acquire information for their reports.

Once students write their reports, they make oral presentations to their music class. Some type of music accompanies each presentation. If students research a composer, Carl helps students to find a record or tape of the composer's music to play during the presentation. If students research an instrument that they know how to play, they actually play their instrument during the presentation.

In addition to the library project, Carl uses reading and writing as an integral part of his regular class instruction. He supplements his music textbook with a series of articles from the magazine, *Music Alive: For the General Music Classroom* (Cherry Lane Music Company, Portchester, New York). Each time that Carl introduces a different musical era from the textbook, he has students read about a famous musician of that era from the "Composer of the Month" section of the magazine.

As with his library project, Carl uses brainstorming to find out what students know about each composer. Once students read and discuss the magazine article, they listen to a tape of the composer's music and then use percussion instruments to play a few of the composer's simple tunes. Although Carl often feels that there's just too much to do in nine weeks, he manages to help his students appreciate music through the language arts.

SUMMARY

The teachers whose teaching ideas we have described here recognize the positive relationship between the quality of learning experiences and the degree of students' content area literacy. Consequently, they have sought out materials and strategies that help them branch out from the "standard" regimen of textbooks. While some still suffer from inadequate resources, external pressures, and organizational problems, they have discovered paths to follow that help to create better instructional climates for their students and themselves.

Final Considerations for Content Area Instruction

Although there is no surefire way to design the ideal plan for content area instruction, consideration of the following areas helps to enrich students' learning expriences: (a) topics and subtopics within a content area that need to be covered; (b) materials and resources that address the topics and subtopics; (c) types of reading and writing experiences that support students' work with materials and resources; (d) organization of the lesson or unit to encompass the first three areas; (e) organizational patterns of students (whole class, small groups, or individual) for the lesson or unit; and (f) assessment of students' assimilation and organization of knowledge.

Ideas for thinking about the first four areas are addressed in the section found earlier in this chapter entitled "Organizing Content Area Materials," which, by the way, represents merely one of many procedures to help you organize instructional materials. If, in fact, you choose to use trade books, you need to decide what is available (for example, trade books for mathematics are more limited than trade books for social studies) and the number of books to acquire for each title. This decision reflects how you want to use these books in your classroom:

1. You can have different students reading different books, sometimes with a few students reading the same book.
2. You can select one book for all to read and create activities related to this book. The other books can be suggested for independent reading.
3. You can read one of the books to the entire class, similar to shared book reading, especially if students have copies of the book.
4. You can create student-directed, cooperative learning groups where the formation of groups is based on students' book selection.
5. You can use all of the aforementioned options.

While making decisions about how you want to use trade books, you also are making decisions about organizational patterns, the fifth area of consideration. Somewhere along the line—whether with trade books, textbooks, or other resources—students need to experience a combination of teacher-led, whole-class groups, cooperative small groups, and independent learning. (Current beliefs about the need to move away from ability grouping during reading instruction parallel recent discoveries about the benefits of moving away from whole-class instruction for content area learning [Pardo & Raphael, 1991].) Each organizational pattern provides different instructional benefits. Teacher-led, whole-group learning develops the learning community and provides an opportunity for students to use a shared vocabulary to express ideas and experiences. It also enables the teacher to introduce new strategies and concepts. Cooperative, small-group learning empowers students with common interests to work toward a common goal as they practice newly learned strategies and apply newly learned concepts. Independent learning gives students private time for reflection and sustained reading and writing without feeling pressure to communicate with a larger community (Berghoff & Egawa, 1991; Pardo & Raphael, 1991). Laura Pardo, the third grade teacher mentioned earlier in this chapter in the "K-W-L" section, describes how she weaves in and out of all three organizational patterns for social studies while incorporating such strategies as K-W-L, mapping, and journal writing (Pardo & Raphael, 1991).

Shedding the traditional textbook with the whole-class model of content area instruction creates questions about assessment. Given that the purpose of assessment is to aid instruction, naturalistic assessment techniques illuminate students' progress more than traditional paper-and-pencil tests, particularly those devised commercially. *Observation, verbal reporting,* and *oral and written retellings* are a few of the assessment techniques that can be used to reveal essential information about students' characteristics as readers and writers (Brozo & Simpson, 1991). For instance, if students ask good questions about what they read and provide many plausible responses to questions about what they read, they typically have a good grasp of what they are reading. Similarly, if students' written responses demonstrate an understanding of salient points made in the text, they are demonstrating equally commendable comprehension.

How you organize content area instruction depends on the purposes of your lesson or unit, the content to be learned, the materials to be used, and the strategies needed to enhance reading and writing (Pardo & Raphael, 1991).

Concluding Remarks

Our goal for this chapter is to help you understand that students' *desire* to learn content area information is just as important—if not more so—than students' acquisition of knowledge to satisfy curricular objectives. Textbooks alone are more informational than inspirational. Their serious, didactic tone is meant to transmit facts rather than stir feelings and emotions about historical nuances, idiosyncratic behaviors, or accidental discoveries. As with basal texts, content area texts are written with the whole hemisphere as their audience. Content is written to satisfy the norm. Students' geographical, sociological, academic, and personal background experiences are not accounted for in textbooks. For instance, a textbook's presentation of the characteristics of the seashore in general may be quite appropriate for students living in Kansas, yet superfluous for students living in Puget Sound. It would be better for students living near the shore to spend their time reading books about different shore areas (Sebesta, 1989).

As with the other chapters in this book, we believe that our mission as teachers is to find whatever it takes to help students appreciate the joys of learning. This challenge is particularly acute for content area instruction since we often hear teachers complain about students' inability to make the transition to this type of reading.

We often think of a friend of ours, Eddie, who has been a gifted carpenter since childhood. When he talks about his school days, he bemoans the "cut and dried" instructional approaches of his academic teachers. He cannot recall one teacher who tried to relate his interest in carpentry to what they were trying to teach. Although exceedingly bright (just talk to him and you know), he often failed his courses—not because he couldn't do it but because he chose not to. Today, as a masterful builder, he knows he applies the basic mathematical and scientific concepts that he was supposed to learn in school. And he spends his spare time taking all types of courses and reading history to better understand architectural trends. Unfortunately, his appreciation of learning came after his formal schooling because his teachers did not understand the urgency of opening his eyes to the relevancy of what they were trying to teach.

Although impossible to reach out to all the Eddies of the world, we must look beyond curricular objectives to "see" how what we think we have to teach relates to where our children are in their thinking. We also need to apply to content area instruction what we know works for reading instruction so that teachers like Mr. D. from our opening vignette are not afraid to extend their instructional discoveries to social studies and other content areas. We also need to keep in mind that, while content area textbooks serve a noble purpose for informing and explaining, rarely do they contain enough "juicy" reading material to entice children to curl up and read them for leisure. If we want our students to become a part of the life of a notable scientist or mathematician or revel in the behind-the-scene events of an eventful historical era, we need to provide our students with books that massage our rich language into candidly vivid portrayals of real-world people and events. Although it is unquestionably more time consuming to search and screen for books and resources that nurture our students' content area interests, the preparatory time and effort expended will provide endless opportunities for developing students' content area literacy.

Questions for Discussion

1. How do you think content area instruction can be improved to help students become more skillful at learning and organizing content area information?
2. Do you think that trade books should become part of content area instruction? If yes, why? If no, why not?
3. Think of each of the four content areas listed here. Which material/instructional configuration is or would be most suitable for you and your students? Select one per content area and write a rationale for each choice.

Content Area	Material/Instructional Configuration		
Social Studies	Textbook Only	Textbook and Trade Books	Trade Books Only
Science	Textbook Only	Textbook and Trade Books	Trade Books Only
Mathematics	Textbook Only	Textbook and Trade Books	Trade Books Only
The Arts	Textbook Only	Textbook and Trade Books	Trade Books Only

4. Which reading and writing strategies do you think are important to use during content area instruction? Why?
5. Look back at the "Examples of Teacher Applications" section. Which teachers exemplify innovative yet sound instructional practices to you? What are they doing in their classroom situations that you would like to use?

Application Activities

1. Select a content area and a concept, unit, or topic of interest within that content area. Review the section entitled "Organizing Content Area Materials." Follow the steps listed in this section so that you
   - Create a web of ideas for your topic.
   - Identify and place materials and resources into your web.
   - Decide which reading and writing experiences you want your students to have.
   - Prepare a plan within one of the material/instructional configurations (textbook only, textbook and trade books, or trade books only).
   - Create a sequence of events to follow.
2. Use the plan that you created in question #1 to do one of two things: (a) implement the plan with a small or large group of children; or (b) share your plan (including how all materials would be used) with your college class. What happened?
3. Visit a teacher who is using trade books for content area instruction. Observe this teacher at work with students. Record your observations of this teacher's instructional techniques as well as students' reactions.
4. Interview the same teacher observed in question #3. Find out how the teacher's method for organizing content area instruction is similar to or different from the plan described in this chapter. What did you discover?
5. Examine a yearlong curriculum guide in a selected content area. Compare this guide with a content area textbook that is supposedly aligned with a curriculum guide to see how the concepts and content are developed. Identify which areas in the textbook are developed adequately and which are not. Identify trade books and other resources that can be used to supplement the textbook's less-than-adequate coverage of content.

References

Alvermann, D. E., & Swafford, J. (1989). Do content area strategies have a research base? *Journal of Reading, 32,* 388–394.

Andreano, V., & Wepner, S. B. (1991, April). From process to practice: Writing techniques that work for all. *NJEA Review, 64* (8), 17–21.

Armbruster, B. B. (1991). Framing: A technique for improving learning from science texts. In C. M. Santa & D. E. Alvermann (Eds.), *Science learning: Processes and applications* (pp. 104–113). Newark, DE: International Reading Association.

Armbruster, B. B., & Anderson, T. H. (1980). *The effect of mapping on the free recall of expository text* (Tech. Rep. No. 160). Urbana-Champaign, IL: University of Illinois, Center for the Study of Reading.

Armbruster, B. B., Anderson, T. H., & Ostertag, J. (1989). Teaching text structure to improve reading and writing. *The Reading Teacher, 43,* 130–137.

Atwell, N. (Ed.). (1990). *Coming to know: Writing to learn in the intermediate grades.* Portsmouth, NH: Heinemann.

Beck, I. L., McKeown, M. G., Sinatra, G. M., & Loxterman, J. A. (1991). Revising social studies text from a text-processing perspective: Evidence of improved comprehensibility. *Reading Research Quarterly, 26,* 251–276.

Berghoff, B., & Egawa, K. (1991). No more "rocks": Grouping to give students control of their learning. *The Reading Teacher, 44,* 536–541.

Bromley, K. D. (1991). *Webbing with literature: Creating story maps with children's books.* Boston: Allyn & Bacon.

Brozo, W. G., & Simpson, M. L. (1991). *Readers, teachers, learners: Expanding literacy in secondary schools.* Columbus, OH: Merrill/Macmillan.

Burns, M. (1987). *A collection of math lessons, from grades 3–6.* New Rochelle, NY: Cuisinaire CO. of America.

Carr, E., & Ogle, D. (1987). K-W-L plus: A strategy for comprehension and summarization. *Journal of Reading, 30,* 626–631.

Englert, C. S., & Hiebert, E. (1984). Children's developing awareness of text structures in expository materials. *Journal of Educational Psychology, 76,* 65–74.

Flood, J., Lapp, D., & Farnan, N. (1986). A reading-writing procedure that teaches expository paragraph structure. *The Reading Teacher, 39,* 556–562.

Freeman, J. (1990). *Books kids will sit still for: The complete read-aloud guide* (2nd ed.). New York: R. R. Bowker.

Heimlich, J. E., & Pittelman, S. D. (1986). *Semantic mapping: Classroom applications.* Newark, DE: International Reading Association.

Hennings, D. G. (1982). A writing approach to reading comprehension-schema theory in action. *Language Arts, 59,* 8–17.

Hittleman, D. (1991, March). *Personal and aesthetic response to informational literature.* Paper presented at Linking Reading and Writing in the Classroom Conference at Rutgers University, New Brunswick, NJ.

Holden, L. (1986). *Fraction factory.* Oaklawn, IL: Creative Publications.

Hope, J. A., Reys, B. J., & Reys, R. E. (1987). *Mental math in the middle grades.* New Rochelle, NY: Cuisinaire CO. of America.

Huck, C. S., Hepler, S., & Hickman, J. (1987). *Children's literature in the elementary school* (4th ed.). Fort Worth, TX: Holt, Rinehart & Winston.

Isaacson, R., Hillegas, F., & Yaakov, J. (Eds.). (1986). *Children's catalog: Fifteenth edition.* New York: The H. W. Wilson Company.

Kinney, M. A. (1985). A language experience approach to teaching expository text structure. *The Reading Teacher, 38,* 854–856.

Konopak, B. C., Martin, S. H., & Martin, M. A. (1990). Using a writing strategy to enhance sixth grade students' comprehension of content material. *Journal of Reading Behavior, 22,* 19–37.

Kruse, G. M., & Horning, K. T. (1989). *Multicultural children's and young adult literature: A selected listing of books published between 1980–88.* Madison, WI: Cooperative Children's Book Center, University of Wisconsin-Madison.

Lamme, L. L. (1990). Exploring the world of music through picture books. *The Reading Teacher, 44,* 294–300.

Lima, C. W. (1986). *A to zoo: Subject access to children's picture books.* New York: R. R. Bowker, a division of Reed Publishing USA.

Mallow, J. V. (1991). Reading science. *Journal of Reading, 34,* 324–338.

Manzo, A. V. (1975). Guided reading procedure. *Journal of Reading, 18,* 287–291.

Marzola, E. S., & Freund, L. A. (1989). Becoming an active reader: K-W-L and K-W-L Plus. *The Reading Instruction Journal, 33* (1), 29–35.

McGee, L. M., & Richgels, D. J. (1985). Teaching expository text structure to elementary students. *The Reading Teacher, 38,* 739–748.

Moore, D., Moore, S. A., Cunningham, P., & Cunningham, J. (1986). *Developing readers and writers in the content areas.* New York: Longman.

Moretti, G., Stephens, M., Goodnow, J., & Hoogeboom, S. (1987). *The problem-solver 5*. Oaklawn, IL: Creative Publications.

Moss, B. (1991). Children's nonfiction trade books: A complement to content area texts. *The Reading Teacher, 45,* 26–32.

Norton, D. E. (1991). *Through the eyes of a child: An introduction to children's literature* (3rd ed.). New York: Macmillan.

Ogle, D. (1986). K-W-L: A teaching model that develops active reading of expository text. *The Reading Teacher, 39,* 564–570.

Pardo, L. S., & Raphael, T. E. (1991). Classroom organization for instruction in content areas. *The Reading Teacher, 44,* 556–565.

Piccolo, J. A. (1987). Expository text structure: Teaching and learning strategies. *The Reading Teacher, 40,* 838–847.

Piech, P. (1991). Science learning centers: Seatwork alternatives. *The Reading Teacher, 44,* 446–447.

Pilchman, B. (1991). Extending reading and writing process to the teaching of social studies. In J. T. Feeley, D. S. Strickland, & S. B. Wepner (Eds.), *Process reading and writing: A literature-based approach* (pp. 88–98). New York: Teachers College Press.

Raphael, T., & Au, K. (Producers) (1991). *Literacy in content area instruction.* [Videotape]. Urbana-Champaign, IL: Center for the Study of Reading, University of Illinois.

Readance, J., Bean, B., & Baldwin, R. S. (1989). *Content area reading: An integrated approach* (3rd ed.). Dubuque, IA: Kendall/Hunt.

Richards, L. (1990). Measuring things in words: Language for learning mathematics. *Language Arts, 67* (1), 14–25.

Rosenblatt, L. (1978). *The reader, the text, and the poem.* Carbondale, IL: Southern Illinois University Press.

Santa, C. M., & Alvermann, D. E. (Eds.). (1991). *Science learning: Processes and applications.* Newark, DE: International Reading Association.

Sebesta, S. L. (1989). Literature across the curriculum. In J. W. Stewig & S. L. Sebesta (Eds.), *Using literature in the elementary classroom* (revised and enlarged ed.) (pp. 110–128). Urbana, IL: National Council of Teachers of English.

Seminoff, N. E. (1990). *Using children's magazines in the K–8 classroom.* Logan, IA: The Perfection Form Company.

Spiro, R. J., & Taylor, B. M. (1980). *On investigating children's transition from narrative to expository discourse: The multidimensional nature of psychological text classification.* (Tech. Rep. No. 195). Urbana-Champaign, IL: University of Illinois, Center for the Study of Reading.

Stenmark, J. K., Thompson, V., & Cossey, R. (1986). *Family math.* New Rochelle, NY: Cuisinaire CO. of America.

Stewig, J. W., & Sebesta, S. L. (Eds.). (1989). *Using literature in the elementary classroom* (revised and enlarged ed.). Urbana, IL: National Council of Teachers of English.

Stoll, D. R. (Ed.). (1990). *Magazines for children.* Glassboro, NJ: Educational Press Association of America and International Reading Association.

Taylor, B. M., & Beach, R. W. (1984). The effects of text structure instruction on middle grade students' comprehension and production of expository text. *Reading Research Quarterly, 19,* 134–146.

Thompson, A. (1990). Letters to a math teacher. In N. Atwell (Ed.), *Coming to know: Writing to learn in the intermediate grades* (pp. 87–93). Portsmouth, NH: Heinemann.

Trafton, P. R., & Shulte, A. P. (Eds.). (1989). *New directions for elementary school mathematics: 1989 yearbook.* Reston, VA: National Council of Teachers of Mathematics.

Troy, A. (1977). Literature for content area learning. *The Reading Teacher, 30,* 470–474.

Webre, E. C. (1989). *Content-area-related books recommended by children: An annotated bibliography selection from Children's Choices 1975–1988.* Lafayette, LA: University of Southwestern Louisiana. (ERIC Document Reproduction Service No. ED 303 775)

Webre, E. C. (1991). Using Children's Choices books to enhance math and health instruction. *The Reading Teacher, 44,* 445–446.

Wepner, S. B. (1991). Ten best ideas for reading teachers. In E. Fry (Ed.), *Ten best ideas for reading teachers* (pp. 125–127). Menlo Park, CA: Addison-Wesley.

Winkel, L. (1990). *The elementary school library collection: A guide to books and other media, seventeenth edition.* Williamsport, PA: Brodart.

Trade Books Mentioned

SOCIAL STUDIES

Aliki (1988). *The many lives of Benjamin Franklin.* New York: Simon & Schuster.

Bains, R. (1986). *James Monroe, young patriot.* Mahwah, NJ: Troll.

Bang, M. (1985). *The paper crane.* New York: Greenwillow.

Bothwell, J. (1970). *The mystery candlestick.* New York: Dial.

Buck, P. S. (1947). *The big wave.* New York: Harper & Row.

Buranelli, M. (1969). *With flying colors: Highlights of the American Revolution.* London: Collier-Macmillan Limited.

Charles, C. (1975). *Paul Revere and the minutemen.* Chicago: Children's Press.

Chbosky, S. (1988). *Who owns the sun?* Kansas City, MO: Landmark Editions.

Coerr, E. (1977). *Sadako and the thousand paper cranes.* New York: Dell.

Copeland, P. F. (1975). *Everyday dress of the American Colonial Period.* New York: Dover.

Davidson, M. (1988). *The story of Benjamin Franklin, amazing American.* New York: Dell.

Davidson, M. (1989). *Frederick Douglas fights for freedom.* New York: Scholastic.

Davis, O. (1990). *Escape to freedom.* New York: Penguin.

De Angeli, M. (1949). *Thee, Hannah!* New York: Doubleday.

de Paola, T. (1983). *The legend of the blue bonnet.* New York: Scholastic.

de Paola, T. (1987). *An early American Christmas.* New York: Holiday House.

Epstein, S., & Epstein, B. (1968). *Harriet Tubman: Guide to freedom.* New York: Garrard.

Fassler, J. (1978). *Howie helps himself.* Chicago: Albert Whitman.

Forbes, E. (1943). *Johnny Tremain.* Boston: Houghton Mifflin.

Fox, P. (1973). *The slave dancer.* New York: Bradbury Press.

Friedman, I. R. (1984). *How my parents learned to eat.* Boston: Houghton Mifflin.

Fritz, J. (1960). *Brady.* New York: Coward McCann.

Fritz, J. (1967). *Early thunder.* New York: Coward McCann.

Fritz, J. (1973). *And then what happened, Paul Revere?* New York: Coward-McCann.

Fritz, J. (1977). *Can't you make them behave, King George?* New York: Coward-McCann.

Gleiter, J. (1987). *Paul Revere.* Milwaukee: Raintree.

Grifalconi, A. (1987). *Darkness and the butterfly.* Boston: Little, Brown.

Hurmence, B. (1982). *A girl called boy.* New York: Clarion.

Johnson, A. (1989). *Tell me a story, Mama.* New York: Orchard.

Krementz, J. (1987). *A visit to Washington, D.C.* New York: Scholastic.

Lawson, R. (1953). *Mr. Revere and I.* Boston: Little, Brown.

Lee, J. (1985). *Toad is the uncle of heaven*. New York: Henry Holt & Company.

Lester, J. (1968). *To be a slave*. New York: Dial.

Martin, Jr. B., & Archambault, J. (1987). *Knots on a counting rope*. New York: Henry Holt & Company.

McGovern, A. (1965). *Runaway slave: The story of Harriet Tubman*. New York: Scholastic.

McGovern, A. (1975). *The secret soldier: The story of Deborah Sampson*. New York: Four Winds Press.

McGovern, A. (1980). *If you lived in Colonial Times*. New York: Scholastic.

Meltzer, M. (1980). *All times, all peoples: A world history of slavery*. New York: Harper & Row.

Meltzer, M. (1987). *The American Revolutionaries: A history in their own words, 1750–1800*. New York: Crowell.

Monjo, F. N. (1970). *The drinking gourd*. New York: Harper & Row.

Monjo, F. N. (1974). *King George's head was made of lead*. New York: Coward McCann.

Morimoto, J. (1987). *My Hiroshima*. New York: Viking.

Rabe, B. (1981). *The balancing girl*. New York: Dutton.

Sabin, F. (1986). *Young Thomas Jefferson*. Mahwah, NJ: Troll.

Scott, A. H. (1972). *On mother's lap*. New York: McGraw-Hill.

Snyder, D. (1988). *The boy of the three-year nap*. New York: Houghton Mifflin.

Speare, E. (1983). *The sign of the beaver*. New York: Houghton Mifflin.

Steptoe, J. (1972). *The story of the jumping mouse*. New York: Mulberry.

Steptoe, J. (1987). *Mufaro's beautiful daughter*. New York: Lothrop, Lee & Shepard.

Surat, M. M. (1983). *Angel child, dragon child*. Milwaukee: Raintree.

Tadjo, V. (1988). *Lord of the dance*. New York: Lippincott.

Tsuchiya, Y. (1951). *The faithful elephants*. Boston, MA: Houghton Mifflin.

Winter, J. (1989). *Follow the drinking gourd*. New York: Knopf.

Wolf, B. (1977). *Anna's silent world*. New York: Lippincott.

Xiong, B. (1989). *Nine-In-one grr! grr!* San Francisco: Children's Book Press.

Yashima, T. (1955). *Crow boy*. New York: Viking.

Yates, E. (1950). *Amos Fortune, free man*. New York: Dutton.

SCIENCE

Aliki. (1977). *Wild and woolly mammoths*. New York: Crowell.

Arnold, C. (1989). *Cheetah*. New York: Morrow Junior Books.

Blumberg, R. (1976). *Sharks*. New York: Franklin Watts.

Brown, A. (1983). *Gorilla*. New York: Knopf.

Brownell, B. (1988). *Busy beavers*. Washington: National Geographic Society.

Cole, J. (1980). *A frog's body*. New York: Morrow.

Darling, L. (1956). *Penguins*. New York: Morrow.

de Paola, T. (1981). *The hunter and the animals*. New York: Holiday House.

Deguine, J. C. (1974). *Emperor penguin*. Brattleboro, VT: Stephen Greene Press.

Dewey, J. (1989). *Can you find me? A book about animal camouflage*. New York: Scholastic.

Eberle, I. (1974). *Penguins live here*. New York: Doubleday.

Falla, M. (1970). *A pocketful of penguins*. Sydney, Australia: A. H. & A. W. Reed.

Florian, D. (1986). *Discovering frogs.* New York: Macmillan.

Freedman, R. (1985). *Sharks.* New York: Holiday House.

Gibbons, G. (1989). *Monarch butterfly.* New York: Holiday House.

Hogan, P. Z. (1979). *The life cycle of the frog.* Milwaukee: Raintree.

Hornblow, A. (1964). *Animals do the strangest things.* New York: Random House.

Hurd, E. T. (1962). *Starfish.* New York: Crowell.

Hutchins, R. E. (1969). *Adelbert the penguin.* Chicago: Rand McNally.

Irvine, G. (1990). *Gordy gorilla.* New York: Simon & Schuster.

Lauber, P. (1985). *Volcanos and earthquakes.* New York: Scholastic.

Lauber, P. (1986). *Volcano—The eruption and healing of Mount St. Helens.* New York: Bradbury.

Lepthien, E. U. (1983). *Penguins: A new true book.* Chicago: Children's Press.

Lobel, A. (1962). *A zoo for Mr. Muster.* New York: Harper & Row.

Lobel, A. (1976). *Frog and Toad all year.* New York: Harper & Row.

Lobel, A. (1979). *Frog and Toad are friends.* New York: Harper & Row.

Lobel, A. (1984). *Days with Frog and Toad.* New York: Harper & Row.

Lumley, K. (1985). *I can be an animal doctor.* Chicago: Children's Press.

McGovern, A. (1976). *Sharks.* New York: Four Winds Press.

McGovern, T. (1977). *Album of sharks.* New York: Checkerboard Press.

Morris, D. (1977). *Read about frogs and toads.* Milwaukee: Raintree.

Morris, R. (1972). *Seahorse.* New York: Harper.

Orbach, R. (1977). *Please send a panda.* New York: Philomel.

Penzler, O. (1976). *Hunting the killer shark.* Mahwah, NJ: Troll.

Petty, K. (1985). *Spiders.* New York: Watts.

Provensen, A., & Provensen, M. (1983). *The glorious flight.* New York: Viking.

Rourke, R. (1982). *Animals in danger—Forests of Africa.* Windermere, FL: The Rourke Corp.

Rourke, R. (1982). *Animals in danger—Forests of the seas.* Windermere, FL: The Rourke Corp.

Rowan, J. (1985). *I can be a zoo keeper.* Chicago: Children's Press.

Selsam, M. (1967). *All kinds of babies.* New York: Scholastic.

Selsam, M. (1987). *Creatures that really lived.* New York: Scholastic.

Silverstein, S. (1983). *Who wants a cheap rhinoceros?* New York: Macmillan.

Simon, S. (1969). *Discovering what frogs do.* New York: McGraw-Hill.

Steig, W. (1987). *The Zabajaba jungle.* New York: Michael DiCapua Books.

Tayntor, E. (1986). *Dive to the coral reefs.* New York: Crown.

Waters, J. F. (1973). *Hungry sharks.* New York: Crowell.

Whitcomb, V. (1988). *Animals in danger.* New Market, England: Brimax Books.

Zim, H. S. (1950). *Frogs and toads.* New York: Morrow.

Zim, H. S. (1966). *Sharks.* New York: Morrow.

MATHEMATICS

Adler, D. (1977). *Roman numerals.* New York: Crowell.

Anno, M. (1975). *Anno's counting house.* New York: Crowell.

Anno, M. (1977). *Anno's counting book.* New York: Crowell.

Aylesworth, J. (1988). *One crow: A counting rhyme.* Philadelphia: Lippincott.

Birch, D. (1988). *The king's chessboard.* New York: Dial.

Brandreth, G. (1979). *Brain-teasers and mind-benders.* New York: Sterling.

Burns, M. (1975). *The I hate mathematics! book.* Boston, MA: Little, Brown.

Carle, E. (1969). *The very hungry caterpillar.* New York: Philomel.

Carrick, C. (1983). *What a wimp!* New York: Clarion.

Christelow, E. (1989). *Five little monkeys jumping on the bed.* New York: Clarion.

Churchill, R. E. (1985). *Devilish bets to trick your friends.* New York: Sterling.

Cleveland, D. (1988). *The April rabbits.* New York: Scholastic.

Crews, D. (1986). *Ten black dots.* New York: Greenwillow.

Eichenberg, F. (1975). *Dancing in the moon: Counting rhymes.* New York: Harcourt Brace Jovanovich.

Freeman, J. (1990). *Books kids will sit still for: The complete read-aloud guide* (2nd ed.). New York: R. R. Bowker.

Gelman, R. G. (1981). *Fabulous animal facts.* New York: Scholastic.

Hutchins, P. (1982). *1 hunter.* New York: Greenwillow.

Leedy, L. (1985). *A number of dragons.* New York: Holiday House.

Lionni, L. (1962). *Inch by inch.* New York: Astor-Honor.

Matthews, L. (1979). *Gator pie.* New York: Dodd, Mead.

Myller, R. (1969). *How big is a foot?* New York: Atheneum.

Phillips, L. (1985). *263 Brain busters: Just how smart are you, anyway?* New York: Viking.

Russo, M. (1986). *The line up book.* New York: Greenwillow.

Schwartz, D. (1985). *How much is a million?* New York: Lothrop.

Schwartz, D. (1989). *If you made a million.* New York: Lothrop.

Sendak, M. (1962). *One was Johnny: A counting book.* New York: Harper & Row.

Serfozo, M. (1989). *Who wants one?* New York: Macmillan.

Vreuls, D. (1977). *Sums: A looking game.* New York: Viking.

THE ARTS

ART

Brown, L. K., & Brown, M. (1986). *Visiting the art museum.* New York: E. P. Dutton.

Konigsburg, E. L. (1967). *The mixed-up files of Mrs. Basil E. Frankweiler.* New York: Atheneum. (used along with study of Renaissance artists)

Levy V. (1983). *Let's go to the art museum.* New York: Harry N. Abrams.

Munthe, N. (1983). *Meet Matisse.* Boston: Little, Brown.

Raboff, E. (1988). *Art for children* (3rd ed.). New York: Harper & Row.

Serfozo, M. (1988). *Who said red?* New York: Scholastic.

Tejima, K. (1987). *Owl lake.* New York: Philomel.

Venezia, M. (1988). *Getting to know the world's greatest artists.* Chicago: Children's Press.

MUSIC

Ackerman, K. (1988). *Song and dance man.* New York: Knopf.

deRegniers, B., et al. (1988). *To sing a song of popcorn: Every child's book of poems*. New York: Scholastic.

Dupasquier, P. (1985). *Dear Daddy.* . . . New York: Bradbury. (instrument: piano)

Fleischman, P. (1988). *Rondo in C*. New York: Harper & Row. (instrument: piano)

Isadora, R. (1979). *Ben's trumpet*. New York: Greenwillow.

Palmer, H. (1986). *Animal antics* [Musical recording]. Freeport, NY: Educational Activities.

Schick, E. (1954). *A piano for Julie*. New York: Greenwillow.

Williams, V. B. (1983). *Something special for me*. New York: Greenwillow (instrument: accordion)

Williams, V. B. (1984). *Music, music for everyone*. New York: Greenwillow. (instruments: accordion, drum, flute, fiddle)

CHAPTER
7

CLIMATE FOR CHANGE

Chapter Overview

RATIONALE FOR CHANGE

EXAMPLES OF CHANGE

BOTTOM-UP EFFORTS / TOP-DOWN EFFORTS / EFFORTS FROM THE
BOTTOM AND THE TOP

CONSIDERATIONS FOR IMPLEMENTING CHANGE

CURRICULUM / INSTRUCTION / ASSESSMENT / SUPPORT SYSTEMS

GUIDELINES FOR INITIATING CHANGE

FOR TEACHERS / FOR ADMINISTRATORS

Feeling "burned out" and dissatisfied with the strictly basal program she had been using for 12 years, Ms. S., a third grade teacher in a suburban district, attended a conference on using trade books and writing in the reading program. Her students learned to read and did well on the standardized tests for which she drilled them, but they didn't seem to have time to read for pleasure in her classroom. She hoped she would find some new ideas at this conference. She came away so impressed with the simple, sensible approach the presenters, mostly teachers like herself, shared that she enlisted two primary grade teachers in her school to join her in a summer workshop course on teaching reading and writing through literature at a local university.

That fall the three teachers started to change their way of working: they began reading to their students daily, offering them time to read books independently, and making time for writing workshop in which children wrote about their own topics for various audiences. Time was the most pressing factor, and they found time by abandoning the step-by-step use of their language arts texts and skipping many basal workbook pages.

In the teachers' lounge they excitedly shared pieces their children had written and books they were reading to their classes. Soon, other teachers began asking how they might breathe new life into their language arts programs. Ms. S. loaned them professional books, visited their rooms to demonstrate what she was doing, and regularly shared journal articles with the whole staff. The principal had observed all three teachers several times and liked what she saw, giving tacit approval "as long as those test scores remain high."

When the superintendent asked for volunteers to update the reading-language arts curriculum the following summer, Ms. S. and a cadre of teachers, who were all experimenting with literature-based instruction, signed up. They were able to persuade the superintendent and others on the committee that their existing curriculum, structured on their basal's scope and sequence chart, was too rigid and overly prescriptive, allowing no room for teacher innovation.

The new curriculum that emerged suggested general goals for each grade and encouraged greater use of literature and increased time for reading and writing. Although the curriculum committee was also charged with searching for a new basal, they decided to put off the search so they could use their allotted funds to purchase multiple copies and class sets of trade books to support the new thrust. During subsequent summers, committees developed book lists, guides, literature units, and thematic units that teachers could use to get started. They eventually did adopt a new basal but made its use voluntary: the basal was just another resource that teachers could use in their literacy program.

They now have a network of over 20 teachers (a neighboring district has joined in) who meet monthly to share children's literature, professional books, and teaching/organizational ideas. The administration supports them by sending representatives to conferences and workshops and supplying staff development courses to help with the implementation of the new curriculum. They have come a long way, and one teacher, Ms. S., started it all!

Ruth (1991) predicts that the United States in the 1990s may finally be entering "the age of the teacher" (p. 106). In fact, White (1988) probably had teachers like Ms. S. in mind when she said, "The primary teacher, when in sole charge of a class, has the power to reshape the curriculum" (p. 9). Although laws, regulations, and curricula can be made at national, state, and district levels, Ruth calls teachers, "the ultimate policymakers," who must make informed decisions day-by-day and hour-by-hour in their classrooms. Since students are not cut from the same mold, teachers must constantly adjust their teaching to fit the students, the goals of the schools, and what is known about good teaching/learning practices.

Rationale for Change

We think good teachers everywhere have always balanced students' needs with prescribed curricula, but it is the third element, keeping abreast of current research, that sometimes passes them by. If they are not reading the professional literature, attending conferences, taking courses, or being exposed to well-chosen staff development experiences, teachers can easily get in a rut and accept ready-made "compleat" programs such as those supplied by the basal publishers. Add to this the fact that some districts promote children based on performance on basal level tests and annual standardized tests (which are often from the same publishers who market the basals), and you can understand why teachers feel "bound to the basals" and reluctant to change.

To break out of the status quo, Monson and Pahl (1991) say that teachers need to undergo a fundamental change in their belief systems about the culture of the classroom. They call this change a "paradigm shift" away from a **transmission model**, in which teachers transmit discrete knowledge and skills to students, toward a **transaction model**, in which students learn by interacting between the known and unknown. Figure 7.1 (Monson & Pahl, 1991, p. 52) shows the contrasting models they describe. Note that the transmission model fits an older, traditional orientation with heavy reliance on a basal program: it is defined, teacher-centered, and skills-based, promoting passive learning that is assessed by mastery tests. On the other hand, the transaction model is process-oriented, student-centered, and concept-based, promoting active learning that is assessed by demonstrated competencies.

Monson and Pahl maintain that making a paradigm shift of this magnitude is not easy since it requires a reconceptualization of the context for learning and teaching. They say, "For practitioners, it means breaking down the prevailing norms of isolation and control and replacing them with the new norms of collaboration and responsibility" (p. 53).

We agree that change of this sort is difficult and doesn't come about without a constant search for new knowledge anchored in the best of what we already know. Teachers have to keep up with current research about validated practices by reading the professional literature and attending conferences, as did the teachers in our vignette. They also need to have a philosophy or internalized theory of good teaching/learning conditions from which to judge their present teaching situations and what is

TRANSMISSION MODEL ⟵――――――⟶ TRANSACTION MODEL		
	What Is Learned	
Defining what we know	*Objective*	Interacting with the unknown
Acquisition of knowledge	*Purpose*	Construction of meaning
Fact-orientation	*Outcome*	Thinking process
	How It Is Learned	
Teacher-centered instruction		Student-centered learning
Part to whole	*Strategy*	Whole to part
Skills-based	*Content*	Concept-based
One dimensional	*Context*	Multi-dimensional
Dissemination of information	*Teacher role*	Catalyst for problem solving
Passive learning	*Learner role*	Active learning
Mastery	*Assessment*	Demonstrated competence

FIGURE 7.1

Paradigm shift required of the whole language philosophy

Note. From Figure 1 from "Charting a New Course with Whole Language" by R.J. Monson and M.M. Pahl, 1991, *Educational Leadership, 48* (6): 52. Copyright 1991 by ASCD. Reprinted with permission of the Association for Supervision and Curriculum Development. All rights reserved.

being proposed by current trends. And, they must be willing to experiment to see what works for them and their students, given their particular needs and interests. Graves (1991) suggests that teachers take certain "actions," such as noting the amount of time wasted when all children have to wait for the teacher before starting to read and write and recording the amount of actual reading and writing students do in a day if they are in three-group basal programs. By analyzing routines objectively, teachers can begin to rethink how the transmission model often wastes precious learning time.

In an opinion piece on the whole language movement's effect on the schools, MacGinitie (1991) begins by saying, "This is a time of great change in the teaching of reading . . . again" (p. 55). Reminiscing about trends of the past 40 years that have come and gone, such as the emphasis on the whole child in the 1950s and the mastery learning movement of the 1970s, he says that one reason that "new" ideas don't last may be because we constantly try to "reform" rather than "improve" education. We force ourselves into extreme camps: those who want a complete revolution and those who want no change whatsoever. Instead, we should be constantly looking for ways to improve, to do what we do better.

MacGinitie says that often new movements don't last because we don't profit from the past. Frequently, advocates of new trends choose to ignore the past and don't know that their "new" ideas have been suggested previously, for example, Jan Veatch (1959, 1968, 1978), who has been a long-time advocate of literature-based reading, is rarely cited by whole language enthusiasts. It is important for those involved in change to know their roots and to learn from the past. Over 30 years ago Veatch advocated teaching beginners to read through the Language Experience Approach (LEA) and children's books. She espoused Individualized Reading (IR) in which students grew as readers by self-selecting books from a wide array of the best of literature. Whereas literature-based programs of today, such as the California Language Arts Framework (Honig, 1988), recommend the use of trade books and integrated language arts strategies such as LEA, they differ from earlier approaches in several ways. Beginners are taught through many shared reading experiences and are encouraged to write early in an invented spelling/writing workshop approach. While students self-select books for independent and at-home reading, all choice is not always left up to them; often, teachers select titles and guide students in group reading/responding situations. Research in literature-response groups (Eeds & Wells, 1989; Harste, Short, & Burke, 1988; Samway et al., 1991; Strickland, Dillon, Funkhouser, Glick, & Rogers, 1989) documents the value of shared response to promote a deeper understanding of text than that which might be attained when reading alone.

MacGinitie also addresses two other issues: the teaching of phonics and the inclusion of nonfiction in the literature mix offered to children. He cautions, "Because whole language is entering the scene in the guise of a replacement, many will interpret whole language as a total rejection of phonics, and the progression of fads will continue. To avoid the excesses of the skills-based movement, we should continue to help students know and use the meaningful system that relates our written language to our spoken language" (p. 58). While some whole language proponents reject phonics, most teachers we have observed are not anti-phonics but want to see phonics and other skills taught in context rather than through the endless completion of mindless worksheets.

Lauding the "reborn emphasis" on writing and seeing this as counteracting those teachers who ignore phonics, MacGinitie says, "At a very basic level constructing words with letters emphasizes the phonemic structure of language—that is, it clarifies that there is a sound system of the language that is represented in alphabetic writing" (p. 58). We heartily agree with MacGinitie on the place of phonics and writing in the total language program.

Expressing fear that literature-based approaches may give short shrift to nonfiction in their emphasis on narratives and story structure, MacGinitie points out the need for children to learn to read and write expository text. He says that good writing in science, math, history, and other informational areas may be overlooked. We find this a needless concern. Most literature-based teachers we know include nonfiction as a genre study (see Sue Boyd in Chapter 4) and use examples of well-written nonfiction in their writing workshops (Ziegler, Stampa, & Klicka, 1991). In fact, Chapter 6 deals exclusively with ways teachers use both fiction and nonfiction in the content areas. Also, one teacher cited in Chapter 4 (Jean DeSantis) was doing exactly what MacGinitie suggests: helping students to appreciate good nonfiction writing by reading to her class from Jean Craighead George's *One Day on the Alpine Tundra* (1984).

With the caveats to beware of ignoring the past and of not seeking to replace but rather to improve your reading/writing program through a solid knowledge base and experimentation, we turn now to some real stories of change that may make a lasting impact on literacy instruction in the schools and districts described.

Examples of Change

In the "schools in transition" literature, when superintendents, principals, and curriculum coordinators initiate instructional change, the thrust is said to be coming "from the top" and thus is termed **"top-down."** When teachers, who are at the bottom of the educational hierarchy, seek modifications in the teaching/learning environment, the thrust is said to be **"bottom-up."** Suggestions for change can be top-down (coming from the administrators), bottom-up (coming from the teachers), or a combination of the two, which is more likely the case. The stories we will share can be loosely fitted into one of these three categories, but eventually all become "combinations" to remain and flourish. Most administrators and teachers in the 1990s, the decade of **"empowerment,"** agree that you cannot mandate change of this nature but have to "invite" educators to become informed and "buy into" a new conceptualization of the classroom culture (Ruth, 1991). At the same time, to make a lasting contribution, you don't want change for change's sake but rather to improve what you are doing in real ways (MacGinitie, 1991).

BOTTOM-UP EFFORTS

Much of the movement to teach writing through a process approach and to use literature for reading has come through the grassroots, the teachers themselves. Two suburban New Jersey communities, Closter and Glen Rock, are examples of districts that were encouraged to change by teachers, much like the district in our opening vignette.

CLOSTER, NEW JERSEY

Edie Ziegler and her teaching partner, Lyn Stampa, in Closter's Tenakill School have been using an individualized reading program à la Jan Veatch (1959, 1968, 1978) since the 1970s. Philosophically, they have always felt that they can develop readers better by offering children a variety of books and helping them to read them rather than by using a basal program developed by publishers who do not know them or their students.

In the summer of 1981 both teachers were introduced to the concept of the writing process through the New Jersey Writing Project under Janet Emig at Rutgers University. That fall they began adding writing workshop to their individualized reading program, quickly seeing the natural connection between reading and writing. Wanting to learn more about teaching with a process approach, they enrolled in the summer workshop led by Lucy Calkins at Columbia University's Teachers College (TC). The next fall they invited three other teachers from their district to informal weekly dinner meetings at which they would share what they learned at TC and what they were doing in their classrooms; this became their first network.

The two principals in the district were supportive because these were seasoned teachers who were well grounded in theory and practice; they had built a solid knowledge base through reading, studying with leaders in the field, and experimenting.

Parents and children were pleased, and—the bottom line—test scores held at their usual high level.

In the mid-1980s Edie was awarded a TC Writing Project teacher-researcher grant to study the effect of networking on teachers' classroom practices. To do this she expanded her original network to include 16 teachers from the Northern Valley, the surrounding area schools that fed into one regional high school. After one year of regular share sessions, she found that networks like this positively affected the attitudes and behaviors of the teachers involved. As for behaviors, they began holding writing workshops in their classrooms and writing along with their children. They wanted to share with other teachers, dispelling the sense of isolation they had felt for years. As for attitudes, they began to develop a new philosophy about teaching and learning; they saw these new ideas as not "just another fad" but as real improvements in their literacy programs.

A fortuitous event occurred about this time when the New Jersey Department of Education instituted the High School Proficiency Test (HSPT), a statewide requirement for receiving a high school diploma. The language test, influenced by the New Jersey Writing Project, included a writing sample worth 60% of the writing subtest. Since the test was taken by ninth graders in the regional high school, the cry went out that the elementary schools from sending districts should emphasize writing. In Closter, Edie's group was enlisted to train teachers in holistic scoring so that writing samples could be systematically evaluated. This led to staff development sessions on running writing workshops and eventually to a new language arts curriculum.

In 1987 Edie Ziegler and two fellow teachers, who presently teach a cross-graded group of second, third, and fourth graders in Tenakill School, received a New Jersey Governor's Grant to write a detailed description of their program. The result was the publication of the booklet, *Building Communities of Readers and Writers* (Klicka, Stampa, & Ziegler, 1987), which was designed to guide others who were interested in moving toward a literature-based, reading-writing program.

The movement begun by these pioneers in Closter has been quietly spreading to adjoining districts through teachers who participated in their networks. Recently, a survey of the first grade teachers in the Northern Valley found a significant increase in the frequent use of trade books, big books, and the language experience approach, especially among the newer teachers. Those hanging on to a basal program with little attention to children's literature were more likely to be teachers with 20 or more years of experience (Pesce, 1990).

GLEN ROCK, NEW JERSEY

Almost simultaneously, a parallel story was emerging in another northern New Jersey community. In Glen Rock, Marianne Marino, whose literature-based reading program is described in Chapter 4, had been using trade books for several years when, in 1984 and 1985, she and four colleagues attended the summer writing workshops led by Donald Graves at Martha's Vineyard. They brought the concept of writing workshop back to Glen Rock and suggested that the district hire consultants to help

them teach writing as a process. A series of staff development workshops taught by writing researchers such as Mary Ellen Giocobbe, Joanne Curtis, and Shelley Harwayne, followed.

Meanwhile, Marianne began attending sessions at TC's Writing Project, receiving teacher-researcher grants to conduct classroom research (1986) and to study the teacher as change agent (1987). She also won a New Jersey Governor's Award that enabled her to purchase hundreds of trade books for her expanding literature collection. By this time her school and one other in the district were mainly using a literature-writing approach; a third school had some teachers who were moving in that direction.

In 1987 an outside evaluator lauded this grassroots movement and recommended that the district rewrite its language arts curriculum to reflect what was actually going on in many of the elementary school classrooms. The evaluator also suggested regularly scheduled district-wide grade level meetings as well as the appointment of an instructional leader to implement the new curriculum and coordinate the grade level networks. These recommendations have been carried out, and it appears that the grass is still growing in Glen Rock.

TOP-DOWN EFFORTS

In some districts change has come from the administration. For example, in Leonia, another New Jersey suburb not too far from Closter and Glen Rock, a deputy superintendent in charge of curriculum, initiated change, starting with the middle school. A new principal in a Brooklyn, New York, K–5 school was the spark that moved the middle grade teachers to seek to expand their reading-writing program. A reading supervisor in a large New Jersey district has begun to ask teachers directly to read good literature with and to their students on a regular basis.

LEONIA, NEW JERSEY

Inspired by the work that his wife Edie Ziegler was doing in Closter, Deputy Superintendent Irv Ziegler wanted his Leonia teachers to try teaching writing as a process, but he met with strong resistance. He decided to work with the most respected and, initially, most resistant middle grade teacher. He actually taught the "how to" of writing workshop himself by demonstrating for this teacher in her sixth grade class for six weeks. While previous output had been one piece of writing per month, at the end of that period the students had bulging writing folders and had published several pieces of writing that amazed students, teacher, and Irv Ziegler!

This previously reluctant teacher not only continued writing workshop and started a network among interested middle school teachers but also became the cheerleader for change. As in Closter, Ziegler also took advantage of the state mandated HSPT to offer district staff development on holistic scoring. This staff development program focused attention on writing as communication and the need to have children write frequently, learning to revise and edit as they move favorite pieces through the writing process. Language textbooks gave way to teacher-led workshops; now literature, long a staple in the middle school, provided models from which students learned to write throughout the grades.

To help the elementary school teachers move away from their basal, skill-driven program, Irv Ziegler established the position of language arts coordinator, hiring a reading-writing workshop teacher and staff developer who had been a part of Edie Ziegler's network from the start. Having also spent summers at Martha's Vineyard with Donald Graves, Nancie Atwell, and others, he was well prepared for his new assignment.

Taking the lead from Irv Ziegler, the new coordinator began by teaching reading and language arts in a third grade class for part of his day and working with teachers in their classrooms the rest of the time. Now he works full time as a staff developer for English (K–12) and leads a network in his district. Leonia, Closter, and Tenafly belong to a staff development network at the Writing Project (TC) through which they are exposed to internationally known speakers such as Lee Jacobs for literature, Don Murray and Nancie Atwell on writing, and Ken and Yetta Goodman and Don Holdaway on holistic teaching.

P.S. 321, BROOKLYN

When Peter Heaney arrived at P.S. 321, a mid-sized, urban school that serves a diverse population of children from all socioeconomic levels and many ethnic backgrounds, he found a mix of literacy programs and practices. While primary teachers (K–2) were using big books, LEA, and literature to teach reading, the middle grade teachers (3–5) were still using basals and workbooks. To him, this was an anomaly since it is usually the primary teachers who feel the need for the structure provided by basals and the middle grade teachers who opt for trade books. He soon learned that the vice-principal, who had arrived on the scene three years earlier, was responsible for the shift in the primary. Having been a teacher and staff developer for bilingual programs and a specialist in process reading-writing, the vice-principal (for K–2), had demonstrated and modeled for her teachers the holistic techniques that had proved so successful for bilingual learners; her teachers abandoned the highly structured, phonics-based materials they had been using for immersion reading and writing practices with children's literature (Feeley, 1991a).

Heaney decided to move these practices into the middle grades, but he didn't want his efforts to be perceived as a top-down directive. He began by seeking advice from the upper level Program Improvement Committee, a **site-based management** team of teachers, parents, and administrators. Staff development for organizing writing workshops was the first need identified. Some teachers had been introduced a few years back when the TC Writing Project had done workshops in the district, but others who were new to the school knew nothing about process writing. This need was addressed by bringing in a consultant to work with teachers who wanted help in their classrooms.

Next, Heaney decided to use Laura Kotch, a fourth grade teacher who had been successfully using literature, as a role model for encouraging further change in the middle grades. He invited all teachers of grades three to five to bi-monthly, noontime meetings (at which he supplied lunch) to dialogue with him about how they were teaching reading and writing. They shared information about their goals for their classes and how their writing workshops were going. They began to raise questions about their reading programs. Most were not happy with the basals they used "just because they were there" and wanted to hear about another approach to teaching. Their goals of developing real readers who read on their own and who could discuss books and authors were not being met. Heaney pointed to Laura Kotch's program as an alternative and offered to help interested teachers to move in that direction.

The meetings were then switched to workshops, with teachers receiving a letter from Heaney beforehand that indicated what the focus would be (e.g., literature discussion groups, response logs, or the choice of sure-fire authors and titles). At the meetings teachers would break into grade level or interest groups to discuss how they might deal with the issue. Finally, groups would share at the end of the session.

It soon became evident that the teachers didn't know children's books and authors, certainly essential knowledge for literature-based reading. Accordingly, Mr. Heaney had Laura Kotch and Leslie Zackman, the teacher resource center consultant, bring in books to share, and he asked the teachers to read Roald Dahl's *The Witches* (1983) so he could use one piece of literature to model how to teach with trade books. Through mini-lessons the teachers developed webs, story maps, character profiles, and engaged in other post-reading activities such as dramatizations and art projects. Through the book talks and their own experiences with response logs, they were learning to teach with books and were enjoying reading good literature at the same time!

Soon two questions arose: How could they be sure they were consistently teaching skills? Where would they get the stock of trade books needed for a literature program?

Laura and Leslie volunteered to write a guide that would show how all the goals for the New York City language arts curriculum (*Essential Learning Outcomes: The Communication Arts,* 1988) could be met through reading-writing workshops. The resulting handbook now serves as a teacher's guide, replete with models of strategies drawn from the luncheon meetings.

As for books, Heaney told the teachers they could use their textbook budget to buy multiple copies of trade books. He found a nearby vendor who allowed the teachers to browse through his warehouse of children's paperbacks with reinforced covers to select titles they would like to read with their students. By the end of that school year they had spent $10,000 and had dozens of sets of wonderful books in their school ready to be used the next fall. (See Figure 7.2 for a sampling of the titles they purchased.) Given the opportunity, training, and materials, all the teachers in grades three to five opted to go for a literature-based program for the next year.

Books by James L. Collier and Christopher Collier

My Brother Sam Is Dead (1974). New York: Four Winds Press.
The Bloody Country (1976). New York: Scholastic.
Decision in Pennsylvania: The Constitutional Convention of 1787 (1987). New York: Ballinger.

Books by Roald Dahl

The Twits (1981). New York: Knopf.
The BFG (1982). New York: Farrar.
The Witches (1983). New York: Farrar.
Matilda (1988). New York: Viking.

Books by Jean Craighead George

My Side of the Mountain (1959). New York: Dutton.
Who Really Killed Cock Robin? (1971). New York: Dutton.
Julie of the Wolves (1972). New York: Harper & Row.
Water Sky (1987). New York: Harper & Row.
On the Far Side of the Mountain (1990). New York: Dutton.

Books by Scott O'Dell

Island of the Blue Dolphins (1960). Boston: Houghton Mifflin.
Sing Down the Moon (1970). Boston: Houghton Mifflin.

Books by Katherine Paterson

Bridge to Terabithia (1977). New York: Scholastic.
Lyddie (1991). New York: Dutton.

FIGURE 7.2
Sampling of books purchased by teachers in P.S. 321

The next fall all classes started the day with 90 minutes of reading-writing workshop. While some began with whole-class novels so they could demonstrate the strategies learned in their lunchtime sessions, others began with small groups reading the same books, and still others followed Laura Kotch and developed a completely individualized program. The common elements were plenty of time to read, respond, write, and share (Feeley, 1991a).

For continuing staff development Heaney released Laura Kotch from some class time so that she could work with teachers in their classrooms. Laura and Leslie led grade-level meetings every three weeks to answer teachers' questions and address problems encountered in class visits. Leslie continues to give book talks and information on authors and new titles. Teachers share what works, and together they develop book guides and thematic units as they grow as a literary community of learners and teachers.

EAST BRUNSWICK, NEW JERSEY

Phil Caccavale is the reading supervisor for East Brunswick, a suburban school district that has eight elementary schools, a middle school, a junior high, and a senior high. His district has been tied to a basal program for decades, and teachers are generally reluctant to try innovations. He does want his district to produce lifetime readers, but he doesn't see many suggestions coming from the ranks. Accordingly, he has set a minimum of one book per marking period that children must read and respond to in various ways. To encourage teachers to try this limited foray into literature, he has written book guides to serve as models and hopes teachers will develop their own. Some teachers are reacting by using the assessment tests of the basals as pretests and having students do only those basal exercises they need, thus making more time for literature and doing more than the minimum.

In the middle school Caccavale established an elective reading course in which students read and write about 8 to 10 different kinds of books, studying the genres in depth. To further encourage literature he brought in local authors who write for this age group such as Jan Marino, author of *Eighty-Eight Steps to September* (1989). Students are manifesting their interest in these kinds of experiences by signing up for this course in record numbers. To increase teachers' appetite for using literature, Caccavale has arranged staff development workshops with experts such as M. Jerry Weiss, children's literature professor from Jersey City State College. These small but positive steps are moving the literacy program in this district in a new direction.

EFFORTS FROM THE BOTTOM AND THE TOP

In this last group of districts efforts for change came from both directions, often starting with teachers but supported and encouraged by strong administrators. From a small New Jersey suburb to schools in rural Montana and finally to an urban California district we shall hear stories of teacher initiative and mutual planning.

RIVER EDGE, NEW JERSEY

In the mid-1980s Erika Steinbauer, a reading teacher in River Edge, New Jersey, a 700-student district in two K–6 schools, became aware of the writing process movement through conferences and a summer institute at TC's Writing Project. She interested some teachers in joining in her investigations, and they started experimenting with writing workshop in their classrooms. When they sought help from Superintendent John LaVigne, he encouraged them to follow the lead of an earlier group of teachers, the Thinking Skills Committee, who had established a precedent for teacher "empowerment" by working with the staff, administration, and board. Thus, the Writing Process Committee was born. LaVigne said, "We gave the Writing Process Committee our support. It didn't need as much as the Thinking Skills group because we had learned so much from their work. Our teachers now knew they had power, that they had some control over what they do in their classrooms" (Feeley, 1991b).

The writing committee brought in consultants, mainly teachers from other districts like Glen Rock, who taught summer workshops in process writing. They wrote a new curriculum guide and made writing the focus of staff development sessions. In addition to the superintendent, they sold the board, the parents, and a number of other teachers on the new writing curriculum.

In 1987 LaVigne created the new position of Staff Development Coordinator, promoting Erika Steinbauer to the slot. At this time the writing committee became the Reading-Writing Committee as the teachers realized they needed to look at reading along with writing. They found that the basals no longer seemed adequate and wanted to look into using trade books. Steinbauer led the teachers in summer sessions that combined curriculum revision with the creation of guides for favorite books and thematic units encompassing reading, writing, and content areas.

Steinbauer has since become principal of one of the two schools in the district but continues to teach staff development courses on writing process and to lead a network of over 40 teachers from River Edge and an adjoining district. The network meets once a month to share ideas, hear speakers, and exchange information on both professional and children's books. Out of the network has come a common philosophy of teaching children, not programs, and focusing on process, not product.

LaVigne realized that he couldn't completely throw out the basals since some teachers simply couldn't get along without them. He continues to order basals for those who want them but suggests that teachers look carefully, ordering only those components they absolutely need, for example, the student texts. He discourages the use of workbooks and disposables; teachers may use basal monies to purchase trade books, professional books, and journals. While teachers are not required to buy the process philosophy in toto, they are strongly encouraged and supported in their efforts to try new ideas.

LaVigne reports that the children and parents appear happy with the new emphasis because interest in books is at an all time high. The board is satisfied since standardized test scores have remained constant, with students scoring consistently in the 80th and 90th percentiles. He and his teachers continue to search for new ways to evaluate what is happening such as checklists of behaviors, reading logs, and portfolios of student work (see Meldonian in Chapter 4). When teachers retire he looks for new teachers in tune with the child-centered, process. philosophy that has emerged in his district (Feeley, 1991b).

KALISPELL, MONTANA

Carol Santa, the language arts coordinator for the Kalispell public schools, began promoting a more holistic approach to developing literacy in the early 1980s. She offered reading and writing summer institutes, college courses in the district, and support to teacher-researchers who wanted to use trade books more and workbooks less. While not all teachers were eager for change, things seemed to be moving along smoothly (Santa, 1991).

Then a polarization of philosophies surfaced in the form of a dispute between a first and a second grade teacher. The second grade teacher, who had continued to use the basal according to the manual, complained openly about the students who came from the process-oriented first grade. He didn't like invented spelling and was upset because the children didn't know how to complete worksheets and operate in basal ability groups. Santa and the school principal met with the two teachers to hear both sides. It was decided that this was a real problem reflecting an undercurrent of uneasiness that needed to be addressed by the district-wide language arts committee, composed of teachers and administrators from all grade levels in all schools.

The committee generated a yearlong research plan that included the development of a consistent philosophy, the collection of data on student performance and preferences, and a curriculum-plus-assessment plan congruent with the philosophy. First, the committee used standardized test scores to see if student performance was affected by being in either a literature-based or basal classroom. At every grade level the average percentile ranks for the literature-based groups were 2 to 7 percentile points higher than the basal classes. Next, Santa surveyed every class to ask students whether they preferred to learn to read through basals (displaying a new basal in one hand) or through books (displaying a trade book in the other hand). Trade books won out, with 96% to 100% favoring them over basals.

To develop a district philosophy Santa and the committee surveyed the K–6 teachers to see what they believed about literacy learning. The form had two parts: the first asked about current practices, and the second asked the teachers to dream about the literacy program they would like to see in place in the 1990s. On the first part of the survey the primary teachers responded very differently from the middle grade staff: they used a combination of basals and trade books. Fourth grade teachers were evenly divided between basals and trade books. By the fifth and sixth grades, most simply taught reading through literature.

Responses to the second part ("dreams") were similar to those on the first: the primary teachers wanted access to a basal along with other materials, whereas most middle grade teachers wanted to expand their trade book approaches. Few teachers at any level wanted a traditional basal program tied to a publisher's scope and sequence chart. Despite their programs, all used some basal assessment tests, but most were not satisfied with them. Clearly, assessment would have to be a consideration in any future plan.

Since assessment emerged as a major issue, the committee interviewed all teachers to see what could be done. They decided that they needed their own scope and sequence chart of reading and writing behaviors. Instead of the multitude of skill clusters found in basals, Santa and her teachers came up with four categories: phonics, main ideas, literary learnings, and reference strategies. They loosely specified behaviors by grade levels and then submitted the draft to the teachers at large to make revisions and refinements. The final scope and sequence chart was then translated into products that could document the behaviors and become the basis for their district portfolio assessment.

Calling the emerging curriculum and assessment portfolio the most critical part of their change, Santa (1991) confided:

> Even if individual teachers differed philosophically, we now had a common strand for evaluating according to district expectations. Documenting expected literacy behaviors provided needed security to whole language teachers and helped others to cut loose from the basal programs. . . . Because accountability was reduced to just a few things at each grade level, teachers felt free to move ahead. . . . (p. 239)

As for materials, the district has been adding sets of trade books and has developed a graded book list of favorite titles. Like River Edge, the language arts committee has continued to have a basal available in each building for teachers who want to use them, but no money has been authorized for workbooks or skillpads.

As Santa (1991) points out, what happened in Kalispell was more evolutionary than revolutionary. Although she started the new ideas, she needed the collaboration of all the teachers to develop a common philosophy, curriculum, and assessment procedure that they could accept before the ideas could take root.

THE FAIR OAKS STORY

Fair Oaks is a successful bilingual, whole language school in Redwood City, California. Ninety-five percent of its students come from immigrant families who live below the poverty line. Although a majority come speaking no English, most can speak, read, write, and learn in English by grade four (Bird, 1989).

But it was not always this way. In fact, in the late 1970s Fair Oaks was targeted by the State Department of Education for its poor performance on state tests and urged to seek help to improve. Gloria Norton, a resource teacher in the school, had heard about the psycholinguistic model of the Goodmans in nearby Arizona. After reading the professional literature and visiting schools with this approach of learning to read by reading real books and learning to write by writing for real purposes, in 1980 she and another teacher set up the psycholinguistic reading lab for fourth through sixth graders. "This meant no basal texts, no workbooks, only real books from which children could select their own reading material" (Norton, 1989, p. 107).

To get a wide selection of books and tapes in both English and Spanish for their immersion language lab, the school asked Raychem, a local company that makes wire, cable, and tubing, to fund the project. Once opened, the "reading room" was a huge success; students came during nonassigned hours, and, to the delight of the initiators, hundreds of paperbacks were "lost" as students took them home to read, thus bringing print to an even wider audience. Test scores further documented improvement: by the end of the second year, the fourth through sixth graders were showing an annual growth of from 1.1 to 1.8 years on the California Tests of Basic Skills (CTBS).

After this success, the primary teachers began to adapt the lab techniques to their literacy programs, and it appeared that the work of the two teachers would become schoolwide. However, a problem arose when some of the bilingual teachers saw the new holistic approach as a threat to bilingual education. This issue was settled when the Goodmans' protege, Barbara Flores, was brought in from Arizona State to assure the staff that bilingual education and holistic literacy programs were indeed compatible. Some teachers who could not accept the new philosophy left the school, and the administration helped out by hiring new teachers amenable to trying a different approach. Through continued support from Raychem, staff development was continued, and Lois Bird, co-editor of *The Whole Language Catalog* (Goodman, Goodman, & Bird, 1991), was hired as a regular consultant (Norton, 1989).

Principal Norm Smith is justly proud of his school. Fair Oaks has recorded the highest attendance rate in Redwood City for the past three years. Bilingual students transfer to English instruction in grade three rather than grade four. While previously only 10% to 15% of his students passed the Redwood City writing proficiency test, 82% passed after five years of the immersion reading-writing program. Also, scores on the CTBS continue to climb, with students in the new program the longest doing the best (Smith, 1989).

Kenneth Hill (1989), Superintendent of Redwood City schools, is quick to admit that authoritarian leadership and fiscal constraints caused by Proposition 13 all but choked California schools in the late seventies. When he arrived on the scene, he hoped to develop a system that would encourage teachers and principals to take control of their school programs, seek outside funding, and improve the schools with the students as the center of focus. He said, "The Fair Oaks experiment was our first attempt to release the reins and say to a school, 'Go to it'" (p. 124).

Along with the teachers and principal of Fair Oaks, Hill also became a learner. Together they visited bilingual, whole language schools in Phoenix and brought back ideas for continued staff development. Soon the school became the model for the district. Hill states that the Fair Oaks experiment was a success because there was congruence between its goals and those of the district. Staff members were empowered by the district's school-based management plan, and there was genuine verification that the program, based on sound research, really worked (Hill, 1989). The pioneering efforts of the teachers and administrators at Fair Oaks have made the school a visitation site for others looking to improve literacy programs, especially for bilingual and minority children.

Considerations for Implementing Change

As you can see from the preceding accounts, when teachers and administrators want to bring about change to improve test scores as in Fair Oaks, or student attitudes toward reading as in River Edge and P.S. 321, or teachers' attitudes toward an expanded vision of literacy teaching/learning as in Kalispell, they end up having to deal with what Bean (1989) calls the three essential elements of a literacy program: curriculum, instruction, and assessment. They also have to seek support from outside the school. This section will deal with these concerns.

CURRICULUM

Districts usually have a reading curriculum that states their goals and what is to be taught at various levels. The curriculum is often written around the scope and sequence chart of the adopted basal reading program. In many cases a separate writing or language arts curriculum reflects the topics in the language arts series purchased for the district. Goals and curricula are tied to the published materials in use. Publishers have a powerful impact on what is taught in American schools (Goodman, Shannon, Freeman, & Murphy, 1988; Ruth, 1991).

Teachers and administrators cannot ignore the curriculum since parents, school boards, and state departments rely on it to evaluate what a school is supposed to be doing. If teachers want to use more literature and writing, they can as long as they follow the curriculum in a general way. For instance, if the curriculum specifies the teaching of verb endings, verbs and how they change can be made the focus of a mini-lesson, and children's written work can be checked to see if they understand this convention. In Chapter 4 we saw Beverly Pilchman and Kathy Kelly using checklists to show they were covering their districts' curricula.

Better still, if enough teachers find a total mismatch between the curriculum and what they are doing in the classroom, it is probably time for curriculum review. As seen in our district stories from Kalispell, River Edge, and Glen Rock, teachers and administrators need to collaborate on constructing a curriculum that is broad and flexible, reflecting a common philosophy and consistent goals. Before dealing with materials and teaching strategies, Carol Santa and the teachers in Kalispell began by hammering out a "consensus philosophy," and Peter Heaney in Brooklyn first led his teachers to define their goals for reading instruction.

Materials come next. While basals have dominated the scene for decades, they no longer have to be the centerpiece. As we have seen in River Edge and Kalispell, even though literature is emphasized, there is still a place for basals. Teachers should have the option of choosing the right mix for their needs and those of their students; in addition to basals and trade books, the whole gamut of authentic print such as computer software, magazines, newspapers, catalogs, and informational pamphlets should round out classroom resources.

INSTRUCTION

Instruction deals with how the curriculum is delivered: the organization of the classroom and strategies for teaching/learning (Bean, 1989). When a flexible, more collaboratively developed curriculum drives a school's instructional program, the door is opened for all kinds of organizational patterns. Berghoff and Egawa (1991) argue for a change from the tracking that has become endemic in school reading programs. Instead of the rigid three-group plan promoted by sole reliance on the basals, teachers can elect to do more whole-group teaching of essential skills via mini-lessons, brief but focused direct instruction, followed not by worksheets but by direct application in the accompanying reading-writing workshop. Transfer is not a problem because skill lessons are put directly into a real context. In the primary grades, the whole group can read a big book or write a language experience story together; in the middle grades, students can work with a class novel as in Bev Pilchman's fifth grade.

Keegan and Shrake (1991) maintain that literature study groups provide an excellent alternative to ability groups. Students reading the same book or story in a basal can work in small groups to permit the exchange of ideas and to allow students to help each other. They can learn to summarize and come to consensus so they will be able to share with the whole class. They can write in small support groups, helping each other with spelling, mechanics, and content/organization.

Pairs of students can read together, with younger children taking turns reading aloud and older children reading silently, then discussing as they go along. If teachers elect to use some skill sheets for practice or reinforcement, having children complete them in pairs makes great sense. This is especially helpful with phonics, which should

be see-say-hear activities in which children help each other to make sense of sound-symbol relationships. Topping (1989) has suggested combining the two powerful techniques of peer tutoring and paired reading.

Students should also have opportunities to work alone. Silent Sustained Reading (SSR) and self-selected, at-home reading with individual response logs supply needed independent reading time. Writing in journals first thing in the morning or at the start of workshop sessions and writing in learning logs during content area study offer sustained, individual writing time. Reutzel and Cooter (1991) suggest various grouping patterns, including independent reading, for structuring reading workshops.

Teachers can choose from a vast array of strategies. Instead of being tied to the suggestions in a basal's manual, teachers should try to internalize a guided reading strategy such as the Directed Reading-Thinking Activity (DRTA). For example, when reading to or with a group, they should encourage prediction *before,* interaction with text *during,* and response *after* the reading. This models what effective readers do and will soon become a part of what students do when they read independently (Robb, 1991).

In fact, modeling is one of the most effective strategies that teachers can use. For example, before having students write responses to literature in reading logs, teachers should show them how by sharing their own written reactions and modeling by actually doing some together, perhaps after shared reading. In effect, the teacher is saying, "This is how I do it."

Metacognitive strategies that lead students to monitor their own reading and learning can be taught through all-class mini-lessons or small groups. For instance, students can be shown how to get the meaning of unfamiliar words from context or to think aloud via learning logs or think sheets as they read content area texts. Also in the content areas, teachers can model how to use the metacomprehension strategies described in Chapter 6 such as K-W-L (What do I *K*now? What do I *W*ant to know? What did I *L*earn?) (Ogle, 1986).

Rather than a few prescribed practices found in publishers' manuals, teachers need to be aware of many strategies that they can use to help readers negotiate text throughout the school day.

ASSESSMENT

According to Bean (1989), a third element to be considered in program development is assessment. There must be some realistic way to verify that students are developing in literacy abilities. Bean identifies two kinds of assessment: external and internal. External assessment is supplied by standardized tests and is used to let a district know how its students compare with a state or national sample. Many districts are rethinking giving such tests annually; the use of such tests with very young children (before grade three) is especially being questioned. Stallman and Pearson (1990) analyzed the content of current readiness and first grade reading tests and reported that most of these tests measured children's performances on isolated skills such as letter and word recognition, sound-symbol correspondences, and perception of shapes. Children were not asked to produce language or actively construct meaning, two performances consistent with an emergent literacy point of view.

Constant testing at all grade levels encourages teaching to the test, eventually destroying the validity of the norms. Recently, a physician from West Virginia reported some interesting data from a study of standardized test results (Pikulski, 1989). He found that 82% of 3,503 districts surveyed and 100% of the 32 states that have mandated testing programs reported their *average* scores as being *above average*. Since *average* means that 50% are below and 50% above, the norms are now skewed and meaningless. Yet valuable instructional time is used up as teachers prepare students to score well on tests rather than to read for real, functional purposes.

Unless a state requires annual testing, one answer to the assessment problem is to test with external measures less frequently, perhaps at benchmarks such as third, sixth, and ninth grades. Fortunately there is a movement in the testing establishment to develop new tests that may yield new information and give students a better chance to show their abilities (theme issue of *The Reading Instruction Journal*, Spring, 1990; Vacca, Vacca, & Gove, 1991). States such as Michigan, Illinois, California, and Maryland are taking the lead. The new tests use longer passages, focus on information central to the structure of the passage, and attempt to assess students' prior knowledge, interests, and metacognitive knowledge as well as their ability to answer traditional multiple choice questions.

While external assessment is in a state of flux, internal assessment is receiving much attention as teachers are seeking other ways to demonstrate student growth. Note how teachers such as Gerry Wahlers (Chapter 3) and those in Kalispell continue to rely on basal reading level tests even when they don't use the basals! They feel that these test results can at least help them to report to parents and administrators, but they are quick to admit that they would like to replace these anachronisms. Kalispell answered the need by developing simple assessments tied to their new broadly written curriculum.

Kathy Kelly (Chapter 4) uses some district-made tests along with many checklists and observational notes to describe how well her students perform as readers and writers. Sue Meldonian (Chapter 4) is in tune with the portfolio movement as she develops her portfolio for first graders around dated writing samples, journal entries, lists of books read, dated audiotapes, and anecdotal records of literacy behaviors. Flood and Lapp (1989) suggest a "comparison portfolio" to demonstrate progress to parents. In addition to writing samples and achievement levels attained on texts, they include charts showing the number of books read voluntarily and samples of books read at specific times. As seen in Chapter 4, many teachers are now using reading response journals, learning logs, interest inventories, and quantitative and qualitative information on what and how children write and read as they compile portfolios to assess growth patterns.

Graves (1991) drives home the importance of helping students to keep good records of their own achievement and encouraging them to participate in the evaluation process. As we can see from Chapter 4, teachers are asking students to evaluate themselves. Sue Meldonian has first graders commenting on their audiotapes done over time; Sue Boyd and Kathy Kelly have their students evaluate their own reading and writing behaviors and products through various rating scales.

Curriculum, instruction, and assessment are so intertwined that it is difficult to talk about them separately, but it is definitely the last element, assessment, that is occupying center stage at this time. In their new text on teaching reading, Reutzel and Cooter (1992) include a very complete chapter on assessing progress in literacy. Besides addressing the positive and negative features of traditional assessment approaches, they give comprehensive coverage to newer "naturalistic-holistic assessment strategies" such as observational techniques and portfolios.

Also, new publications are emerging to help teachers in their quest for appropriate assessment tools to validate their students' growth in literacy. Among them are *Monitoring Children's Language Development: Holistic Assessments in Classrooms* (Daly, 1990); *Whole Language Evaluation: Reading, Writing, and Spelling* (Eggleton, 1990); *The Whole Language Evaluation Book* (Goodman, Goodman, & Hood, 1988); *Assessment and Evaluation in Whole Language Programs* (Harp, 1991); *Assessment for Instruction in Early Literacy* (Morrow & Smith, 1990); and *Portfolio Assessment in the Reading-Writing Classroom* (Tierney, Carter, & Desai, 1991).

SUPPORT SYSTEMS

When school districts are in the process of changing their way of delivering instruction, they must look for support from outside the schools—from parents, the Board of Education, colleges and universities, and the community at large.

Instead of being "outsiders" who run cake sales and help out on class trips, parents can be made important adjuncts to their children's learning. First and foremost, teachers need to keep parents informed by means of newsletters and informal sessions about the goals, practices, and assessment techniques being used. Feeley, Wahlers, and Jones (1990) invited parents of second and fourth graders to participate in writing workshops to show how children learn to write. They followed up each session with a newsletter for those parents who couldn't make the evening sessions. When a "Celebrate Writing" assembly was held at the end of the year, over 100 parents and siblings came to hear the children read from their pieces and to receive copies of an anthology of stories written by parents. Several volunteered to help out during their children's writing workshops. Donald Graves (1983) and Jane Hansen (1987) describe wonderful parent involvement in their New Hampshire writing projects. If they are not free to help during school hours, parents can promote reading at home by being reading models and showing interest in their children's at-home reading (see Chapters 3 and 4 for teachers who include at-home reading in their programs).

Board of Education members should be kept informed and involved in a school's attempts to improve its reading-writing instruction. In River Edge, the superintendent told the teachers to sell their ideas to the board. And they did, winning philosophical approval and budgetary support. Pat Brown (1989), a Redwood City board member assigned to monitor Fair Oaks, became a researcher with the teachers and their principal. She attended staff development courses in the school and read the professional literature, especially citing the effect that reading Weaver's *Psycholinguistics and Reading: From Process to Practice* (1980) had on her ability to better understand how spoken and written language is learned. Having visited Fair Oaks classrooms and the exemplary sites in Arizona with the staff, she helped them write a grant proposal to seek further funding. The mission statement that she helped draft says

> The Redwood City School District will work in partnership with parents and the community to help youth develop a positive vision of the future and acquire the attitudes, knowledge, and skills necessary to become successful, contributing participants in a rapidly changing world. (Brown, 1989, p. 134)

Instead of an Us-Them stance often fostered by salary negotiations, teachers can gain the respect of and enlist the support of their Board of Education members by taking their plans, dreams, and formative evaluations directly to the board and making them partners in improvement plans.

Pat Brown (1989) talks about "continual renewal" to keep the momentum of innovation going. Here's where local colleges and universities can be helpful. Schools should try to affiliate with colleges to provide continued staff development and consultation for teachers who are experimenting with new approaches. Fair Oaks had established ties to Sonoma State College through Jayne Delawter and to Arizona State through Barbara Flores. Closter and Leonia have maintained ties to Lucy Calkins and Shelley Harwayne at Teachers College, Columbia. Over 20 districts in northern New Jersey have joined the North Jersey Writing Consortium at William Paterson College. The Rutgers University Literacy Curriculum Network, under the leadership of Dorothy Strickland, has more than 30 school districts in its group. Besides supplying consultants, the colleges offer conferences and workshops, bringing to the area renowned speakers that districts couldn't afford to tap on their own. For example, while the Rutgers Network has invited reading researchers such as Harold Herber and Roger Farr and literature experts such as Bee Cullinan and M. Jerry Weiss, William Paterson has brought writing researchers such as Dixie Goswami and Peter Elbow to New Jersey. The Writing Project at Teachers College has featured speakers from all over the world. Besides Americans such as Graves, Atwell, and Hansen, they have brought Clay, Cambourne, and Holdaway from New Zealand and numerous language and literacy experts from Canada and Britain. The Ohio State University has a nationwide network of teachers who keep informed about children's literature through its fine newsletter, *The WEB: Wonderfully Exciting Books* (see resources in Chapter 4).

Colleges and universities can also provide help with teacher-researcher projects, for example, the following William Paterson studies: Regina Pesce's (1990) survey of the teaching methods in the Northern Valley schools in New Jersey; our second grade teacher's experiment showing how the addition of trade books, with time to read them, significantly improved her urban students' standardized test scores and attitudes toward reading; and Gerry Wahlers' and Barbara Jones' (Feeley, Wahlers, and Jones, 1990) writing workshops for parents project. The Writing Project at Teachers College has funded and guided several studies in the New Jersey districts of Glen Rock, Closter, Tenafly, and Leonia. The Rutgers Network has spawned a number of teacher-researcher studies in central and northern New Jersey.

Instead of operating in a "closed system," teachers and administrators can also seek support from their local communities. Fair Oaks has maintained a wonderful relationship with Raychem. In addition to money grants, workers from Raychem tutor students and read to classes during lunchtime and breaks. In some of the New Jersey communities, women's clubs, the town libraries, and service organizations have purchased multiple sets of trade books for the schools, sponsored authors-in-the-classroom projects, and offered reading and writing incentives such as displays of children's writing and reading awards.

As teachers feel empowered to work with administrators to design and implement their own literacy programs for their own students, they need to reach out to parents, boards of education, colleges and universities, and the community at large to gain support for their efforts to establish broad-based literate communities.

Guidelines for Initiating Change

Keeping in mind the experiences and stories of the educators shared in this book and the information found in the professional literature, we would like to close by offering guidelines to teachers and administrators who are interested in promoting change in their literacy programs. While they are not meant to be followed in any exact order, they can provide ideas for getting started and moving forward. Since this is the age of teacher empowerment (Ruth, 1991), we will address teachers first, then administrators.

FOR TEACHERS

Despite the new emphasis on teacher empowerment, we all know that teachers have always had a great deal of control over what they do in the classroom once "they close the door." We suggest you use that decision-making power to try out some of the new (and not so new) ideas described in this book, starting in small ways and gradually expanding; if they bring about improvement in the affective or cognitive domains and if the climate is right in your school or district, you can be a catalyst for enduring change.

1. Begin by having *reading aloud, shared reading* and *SSR* every day and *writing workshop* at least three times a week. You can find time by eliminating some skill sheets and workbook pages; teach the skills through mini-lessons in writing workshop.
2. If your district insists on basals, use them mainly for *guided reading,* developing your own instructional strategy for reading with a group, for example, Predict (from prior knowledge)-Confirm (by reading)-Interact (during reading)-Respond (after reading). Once comfortable with such a strategy, you will no longer feel the

need to depend on the manual. You can also use basal stories to model and practice working in reader *response* groups and with *response* logs. Instead of doing workbook pages and answering questions over a text, students can discuss stories in small groups and write individual responses in reading logs. Students can learn to make choices if you occasionally allow them to select stories and form groups by story choice.

3. Enlist at least one teacher to experiment with you. Share ideas and visit each other's classrooms. If you hear of an exemplary teacher in your area, request time to visit and observe. Join any existing networks in your area or start one with your fellow experimentor and any others you can interest in joining you.

4. Continue to build your knowledge base by attending conferences and workshops and reading the professional literature. Again, it's good to have a friend with whom to share these activities. If we had to recommend basic texts, we would suggest Routman (1988, 1991), Atwell (1987), Graves (1983, 1991), and Calkins (1986).

5. Build your resources so that your room will reflect the literate environment you want to create. Consult your librarian, read book columns in journals such as *The Reading Teacher, Language Arts, The New Advocate,* and *The Horn Book,* and subscribe to newsletters such as *The WEB: Wonderfully Exciting Books* (see resources at the end of Chapter 4). Ask your principal if you may spend workbook allowances to purchase sets of children's books; ask parent groups to buy books and sponsor authors-in-the-classroom programs.

   Once available, use sets of books for your *guided reading* one or two times a week; if your students have been working in response groups with the basal, this will present no problem. You can also try paired reading and whole-class reading of a book in this way.

6. Consider new ways of working in the content areas. Pick a unit in social studies or science that you know well and would like to expand. Teach reading, writing, and the content together by collecting appropriate resources (fiction, nonfiction, technology, and audiovisuals) and planning a themed unit occupying a block of time as was done by teachers described in Chapter 6.

7. Expand your use of technology. Interweave useful software packages with basals, trade books, and content area texts. Technology, including multimedia software, can be a valuable tool in any literacy program. For example, word processing and desktop publishing programs can facilitate publishing in writing workshop; content area information can be learned nonlinearly and at will from software programs that contain databases, reflecting real-life informational systems.

8. Keep your administrators and parents informed about any instructional changes you make, explaining what you hope to accomplish and enlisting their help. For example, ask your principal to help you find copies of trade books to build your classroom book sets and to provide needed staff development. Offer to lead staff development workshops for others. Inform your students' parents by occasional meetings and newsletters; invite them to help out during writing workshop publishing or reading workshop response groups. Explain their role in any *at-home reading* program you may start.

9. Volunteer to work on curriculum revision so that you can influence the goals, curriculum, and assessment procedures that are put in place for your district. As you foray further into creating your own literacy program, you will probably begin to undergo the paradigm shift described by Monson and Pahl (1991) from a teacher-centered, skills-based, part-to-whole transmission model to a more student-centered, whole-to-part, meaning-based transaction model. You need to be a model for others, making positive contributions toward the establishment of broad goals rather than being an elitist who has found a "better" way to teach reading and writing and looking down on others still "bound to the basal." Routman (1991) warns against any orthodoxies that proclaim there is only one way to teach. She says

> When I first gave up basals and workbooks, I spent years as a 'basal basher' with minimal tolerance for basal users and publishers. As a literature 'purist,' I spent a lot of time pointing out the bad features of basal texts. Over the past several years, however, I've come to realize that the basal is not the enemy. The basal text is, at best or worst—like any other material—a resource. In the hands of a knowledgeable professional, it can be used holistically and intelligently, particularly if the worksheets are set aside. . . . It is the literacy model the teacher holds that determines the type of instruction that goes on in the classroom. (p. 26)

FOR ADMINISTRATORS

As we have seen from the stories presented here, change can be initiated from administrative levels even though such efforts are frequently teacher-driven. Superintendents, principals, reading supervisors, or curriculum coordinators often become aware of new thinking and interested in making improvements in their literacy programs. To administrators we offer the following guidelines:

1. Build your knowledge base by visiting exemplary sites, networking with administrators involved with new programs, and reading the professional literature. We would recommend some of the same titles suggested for teachers, namely, Atwell (1987), Graves (1983, 1991), and Routman (1991) as well as *Becoming a Whole Language School: The Fair Oaks Story* (Bird, 1989) and *The Administrator's Guide to Whole Language* (Heald-Taylor, 1989).

2. Support teachers who are experimenting by giving approval. Encourage all staff members to experiment. Principal Fred Burton (1991) promotes what he calls the "professional quest," through which teachers identify one problem and search for ways to solve it. Toward the end of a school year, he and his staff gather to share their "quests" and how they will pursue answers through such avenues as taking summer courses, reading books and journals, and preparing special materials for the next term. Sometimes they get into "small circles" to work on a common problem; Burton facilitates and participates wherever he can. The "quests" are brought to closure the following year when the teachers share their projects via videotapes, informal research reports, a "portfolio of a journey," and other presentations.

3. Offer regular staff development workshops and courses dealing with new approaches to teaching reading and writing. Seek suggestions for presenters from teachers who are experimenting since they will probably know of local consultants and university people who can be tapped.

4. Appoint an "instructional leader" to help teachers within your school or district. Leonia and River Edge made new full-time staff development positions; P.S. 321 and Closter provided present staff members with released time to work with teachers in their classrooms; Kalispell and Fair Oaks had instructional leaders in the form of their resource teacher (Norton) and language arts coordinator (Santa).

5. Share curriculum review with your staff. First establish common goals (you may want to survey teachers as did Heaney and Santa) and then aim to develop a flexible, broad-based curriculum to carry out those goals (see the New York City curriculum guide, *Essential Learning Outcomes: The Communication Arts,* 1988). As you review your curriculum, deal with assessment so that your assessment procedures will be congruent with your curriculum. De-emphasize standardized testing, especially before grade three, and encourage teachers to develop appropriate internal assessment tools through reading the literature and informal research (see Meldonian, Chapter 4).

6. Give teachers more control over the school budget. Allow those who want to try using more literature with their classes to spend their portion of textbook funds on sets of trade books rather than on basal components they may not want to use. In the spirit of *Becoming a Nation of Readers* (Anderson et al., 1985), you can discourage the use of workbooks and worksheets but should not go to extremes; if some teachers really want a basal with some of its adjuncts, allow them to spend their share of funds for materials accordingly. The best way to undermine a program is to insist that everyone do the same thing at approximately the same time.

7. Encourage networking within your school or district by providing time during the school day or, if not possible, by having after-school meetings with refreshments.

8. Keep board members informed by having teachers report on what they are doing and share samples of students' work. Too often, board members are isolated from everyday happenings in the school. One of us remembers fondly a presentation made to a board that included books published by children from their district. The board members were amazed at the quality and sophistication of the children's writing and were delighted to be able to support further staff development in the teaching of writing.

9. Keep parents informed by suggesting speakers for PTA meetings, encouraging teachers to keep informal lines of communication open, and sending home newsletters explaining your rationale for change and what you and your teachers are trying to accomplish.

10. Seek outside support for your efforts. Certainly, local colleges and universities can provide consultants and access to world-renowned researchers through campus offerings. Many colleges and universities have established networks for school districts to keep the momentum of transition going.

The local community can support your efforts, too. Like Fair Oaks with Raychem, you may be able to find businesses in the area that would fund literacy projects and provide volunteers to tutor students. Town libraries, service organizations, and chambers of commerce can be tapped to make promoting literacy a community concern.

Concluding Remarks

A **National Assessment of Educational Progress** (NAEP) report (Langer, Applebee, Mullis, & Foertsch, 1990) reveals that in the United States today the major emphasis in beginning reading is on narrowly focused, skills-driven, basal reader instruction. Even through grade four, teachers tend to teach with a single basal reader with heavy, daily use of workbooks and skillsheets. Trade books are used as supplements, if at all, and students are rarely asked to discuss what they read in small groups. Teachers admit that they use skill materials more than any other resources and that there is little time to have students analyze, discuss, or write about what they read. Yet, this and other NAEP reports show that while reading proficiency, as measured by questions on surface level meaning and details, increases through the grades, students do poorly on tasks requiring higher level reasoning at all grade levels. It appears that the results of skills-driven instruction are as limited as the instruction: we get what we teach.

The NAEP report also indicates that our students do very little reading for school (often fewer than 10 pages a day) and even less for personal reasons. There appears to be an inverse relationship between interest in reading and grade level: while 75% of the fourth graders read for enjoyment once a week, only half of the 12th graders read for pleasure on a weekly basis. This pattern is mirrored in library use: whereas a majority of fourth graders frequent a library weekly, only 25% of the eighth graders and 12% of high school seniors use a library regularly. Citing her work on **voluntary reading** and that of other researchers in the 1980s, Morrow (1991) concludes that substantial numbers of children and adults read neither for pleasure nor for information. Although they can read, students in today's American schools are not readers.

And what does the NAEP report say about our teachers? One interesting finding is that although teachers are well trained and experienced, their expertise is frequently not trusted by administrators. More often than not, administrators expect teachers to follow closely the curriculum that is usually written around a basal reader scope and sequence chart. Teachers report that while they have control over the sequence of instruction, they feel they have very little choice over what to teach.

Changing the status quo that has produced such NAEP findings is what this book is all about. We hope that teachers and administrators will use the stories told in this book and the guidelines for action that are based on those stories to effect change in their districts, change that will improve students' ability to read at both surface and deep structure levels and their attitudes toward reading as a self-enriching, lifetime activity. We hope this book will help administrators and teachers become learners together by sharing decision-making and becoming better able to balance basals, books, and the world of print to provide the very best literate environment and instructional program for the students entrusted to them.

Questions for Discussion

1. What literacy skills do you believe citizens of the 21st century will need? Do you think current reading programs, as described by the recent NAEP report, are providing students with these skills?
2. Describe your present program or the one in effect in the elementary school you attended. Do you think this program would prepare students adequately for the 21st century?
3. If asked to "dream" about the kind of classroom, materials, and support you would like to have to develop your students as readers and writers, what would you say?
4. How does your school or district plan curriculum, instruction, and assessment? Is there truly shared decision-making or is decision-making limited by policy statements such as, "We will all be involved in revising our reading/language arts curriculum, but you must pick a current basal as the core resource"?
5. How does your school (or any school you know about) use support sources such as parent groups, businesses, and community service organizations?

Application Activities

1. Collect reading and writing curriculum guides from two or three districts in your area. How do the guides differ? Which appear to be written from basal scope and sequence charts? Which appear to be broadly written, with reading, writing, speaking, and listening behaviors presented in an integrated manner? What do the guides tell you about the philosophies of the districts?
2. Look over the guidelines for teachers (or administrators) presented in this chapter. Which might you be able to follow immediately? in one year? in three years? Plot a plan of action for yourself.
3. Write a proposal to an outside support resource such as a local business, the Chamber of Commerce, or the town's Women's Club and request help with your literacy program. Specify your goals and how they can help, for example, by purchasing trade books or supplying a small budget to attract authors to visit your school. Be sure to tell them that you will seek publicity opportunities to tell the world about their good works.
4. Read at least one of the basic books suggested in this chapter with another teacher. Discuss ideas that you might like to try in your classrooms.
5. Survey the teachers in your school or a school in your area to find out how they teach reading and writing. Note if there are differences related to grade levels

taught or to years of teaching. To collect your information, use the following form or design one yourself.

SURVEY

SCHOOL: _____

GRADE: _____

TEACHER: _____ YEARS TEACHING: _____

A. Describe your reading program:
   How much time is spent on reading each day? _____
   What materials do you use? _____
   _____

   How does a typical session go? _____
   _____

   How do you assess achievement? _____
   _____

B. Describe your writing program:
   How much time do students spend writing each day? _____
   _____

   What do students write (answers to questions or journals, narratives, reports, etc.) _____
   _____

   How does a typical writing session go? _____
   _____

   How do you assess growth? _____
   _____
   _____

C. What are the goals of your literacy program? _____
   _____
   _____

References

Anderson, R. C., Hiebert, E. H., Scott, J. A., & Wilkinson, I. A. G. (1985). *Becoming a nation of readers: The report of the Commission on Reading.* Champaign, IL: The National Academy of Education, The National Institute of Education, The Center for the Study of Reading.

Atwell, N. (1987). *In the middle: Reading, writing, and learning with adolescents.* Portsmouth, NH: Heinemann.

Bean, R. M. (1989). Effective reading program development. In S. B. Wepner, J. T. Feeley, & D. S. Strickland, *The administration and supervision of reading programs* (pp. 1–21). New York: Teachers College Press.

Berghoff, B., & Egawa, K. (1991). No more "rocks": Grouping to give students control of their learning. *The Reading Teacher, 44,* 536–541.

Bird, L. B. (Ed.). (1989). *Becoming a whole language school: The Fair Oaks story.* Katonah, NY: Richard C. Owen.

Brown, P. (1989). A school board perspective. In L. B. Bird (Ed.), *Becoming a whole language school* (pp. 129–134). Katonah, NY: Richard C. Owen.

Burton, F. R. (1991). Learning to read through literature: An administrator's perspective. In J. T. Feeley, D. S. Strickland, & S. B. Wepner (Eds.), *Process reading and writing: A literature-based approach* (pp. 42–48). New York: Teachers College Press.

Calkins, L. (1986). *The art of teaching writing.* Portsmouth, NH: Heinemann.

Dahl, R. (1983). *The witches.* New York: Farrar.

Daly, E. (1990). *Monitoring children's language development: Holistic assessments in classrooms.* Portsmouth, NH: Heinemann.

Eeds, M., & Wells, O. (1989). Grand conversations: An exploration of meaning construction in literature study groups. *Research in the Teaching of English, 23,* 2–24.

Eggleton, J. (1990). *Whole language evaluation: Reading, writing, and spelling.* San Diego, CA: The Wright Group.

Essential learning outcomes: The communication arts. (1988). New York: Office of Curriculum Development and Support, New York City Board of Education.

Feeley, J. T. (1991a). An urban school becomes a community of readers and writers. In J. T. Feeley, D. S. Strickland, & S. B. Wepner (Eds.), *Process reading and writing: A literature-based approach* (pp. 99–107). New York: Teachers College Press.

Feeley, J. T. (1991b). Transition in a surburban district: An interview with its superintendent. In J. T. Feeley, D. S. Strickland, & S. B. Wepner (Eds.), *Process reading and writing: A literature-based approach* (pp. 244–250). New York: Teachers College Press.

Feeley, J. T., Wahlers, G., & Jones, B. (1990, May). *Helping parents understand the writing process.* Paper presented at the International Reading Association Convention, Atlanta, GA.

Flood, J., & Lapp, D. (1989). Reporting reading progress: A comparison portfolio for parents. *The Reading Teacher, 42,* 508–514.

George, J. C. (1984). *One day on the Alpine tundra.* New York: Crowell.

Goodman, K. S., Goodman, Y. M., & Bird, L. B. (Eds.). (1991). *The whole language catalog.* Santa Rosa, CA: American School Publishers.

Goodman, K. S., Goodman, Y. M., & Hood, W. J. (Eds.). (1988). *The whole language evaluation book.* Portsmouth, NH: Heinemann.

Goodman, K. S., Shannon, P., Freeman, Y. S., & Murphy, S. (1988). *Report card on basal readers.* Katonah, NY: Richard C. Owen.

Graves, D. (1983). *Writing: Teachers and children at work.* Portsmouth, NH: Heinemann.

Graves, D. (1991). *Build a literate classroom.* Portsmouth, NH: Heinemann.

Hansen, J. (1987). *When writers read.* Portsmouth, NH: Heinemann.

Harp, B. (Ed.). (1991). *Assessment and evaluation in whole language programs.* Norwood, MA: Christopher-Gordon.

Harste, J., Short, K., & Burke, C. (1988). *Creating classrooms for authors: The reading-writing connection.* Portsmouth, NH: Heinemann.

Heald-Taylor, G. (1989). *The administrator's guide to whole language.* Katonah, NY: Richard C. Owen.

Hill, K. G. (1989). Nurturing a metamorphosis. In L. B. Bird (Ed.), *Becoming a whole language school* (pp. 123–128). Katonah, NY: Richard C. Owen.

Honig, W. (1988). The California reading initiative. *The New Advocate, 1,* 235–240.

Keegan, S., & Shrake, K. (1991). Literature study groups: An alternate to ability grouping. *The Reading Teacher, 44,* 542–547.

Klicka, J., Stampa, M., & Ziegler, E. (1987). *Building communities of readers and writers.* New Jersey Governor's Grant Program. Trenton, NJ: New Jersey State Department of Education.

Langer, J. A., Applebee, A. N., Mullis, I. V. S., & Foertsch, M. A. (1990). *Learning to read in our nation's schools: Instruction and achievement in 1988 at grades 4, 8, and 12.* Princeton, NJ: National Assessment of Educational Progress.

MacGinitie, W. H. (1991). Reading instruction: Plus, ca change . . . *Educational Leadership, 48,* 55–58.

Margolis, H. (Ed.) (1990). Entire issue. *The Reading Instruction Journal, 33*(3).

Marino, J. (1989). *Eighty-eight steps to September.* Boston: Little, Brown.

Monson, R. J., & Pahl, M. M. (1991). Charting a new course with whole language. *Educational Leadership, 48,* 51–53.

Morrow, L. M. (1991). Promoting voluntary reading. In J. Flood, J. M. Jensen, D. Lapp, & J. R. Squire (Eds.), *Handbook of research on teaching the English language arts,* (pp. 681–690). New York: Macmillan.

Morrow, L. M., & Smith, J. K. (1990). *Assessment for instruction in early literacy.* Englewood Cliffs, NJ: Prentice Hall.

Norton, G. (1989). What does it take to ride a bike? In L. B. Bird (Ed.), *Becoming a whole language school: The Fair Oaks story* (pp. 105–114). Katonah, NY: Richard C. Owen.

Ogle, D. (1986). K-W-L: A teaching model that develops active reading and expository text. *The Reading Teacher, 39,* 564–570.

Pesce, R. (1990). *First grade reading instruction: Current trends in the Northern Valley regional district.* (Report No. CS 010-112). ERIC Document Reproduction Service No. ED 320-118).

Pikulski, J. (1989). Questions and answers. *The Reading Teacher, 7,* 533.

Reutzel, D. R., & Cooter, R. B. (1991). Organizing for effective instruction: The reading workshop. *The Reading Teacher, 44,* 548–553.

Reutzel, D. R., & Cooter, R. B. (1992). *Teaching children to read: From basals to books.* New York: Merrill/Macmillan.

Robb, L. (1991). Building bridges: Eighth and third grades read together. *The New Advocate, 4,* 151–161.

Routman, R. (1988). *Transitions.* Portsmouth, NH: Heinemann.

Routman, R. (1991). *Invitations: Changing as teachers and learners K–12.* Portsmouth, NH: Heinemann.

Ruth, L. (1991). Who decides? Policymakers in English language arts education. In J. Flood, J. M. Jensen, D. Lapp, & J. R. Squire (Eds.), *Handbook of research on teaching the English language arts* (pp. 85–109). New York: Macmillan.

Samway, K. D., Whang, G., Cade, C., Gamil, M., Lubandina, M. A., & Phommachanh, K. (1991). Reading the skeleton, the heart, and the brain of a book: Students' perspectives on literature study circles. *The Reading Teacher, 45,* 196–205.

Santa, C. (1991). Cutting loose: A district's story of change. In J. T. Feeley, D. S. Strickland, & S. B. Wepner (Eds.), *Process reading and writing: A literature-based approach* (pp. 232–243). New York: Teachers College Press.

Smith, N. (1989). The view from the principals' desk. In L. B. Bird (Ed.), *Becoming a whole language school: The Fair Oaks story* (pp. 115–122). Katonah, NY: Richard C. Owen.

Stallman, A. C., & Pearson, P. D. (1990). Formal measures of early literacy. In L. M. Morrow & J. K. Smith (Eds.), *Assessment for instruction in early literacy* (pp. 7–44). Englewood Cliffs, NJ: Prentice Hall.

Strickland, D., with Dillon, R., Funkhouser, L., Glick, M., & Rogers, C. (1989). Research currents: Classroom dialogue during literature response groups. *Language Arts, 66,* 192–200.

Tierney, R. J., Carter, M. A., & Desai, L. E. (1991). *Portfolio assessment in the reading-writing classroom.* Norwood, MA: Christopher-Gordon.

Topping, K. (1989). Peer tutoring and paired reading: Combining two powerful techniques. *The Reading Teacher, 42,* 488–494.

Vacca, J. L., Vacca, R. T., & Gove, M. (1991). *Reading and learning to read*. New York: Harper-Collins.

Veatch, J. (1959). *Individualizing your reading program*. New York: G. P. Putnam.

Veatch, J. (1968). *How to teach reading with children's books*. Katonah, NY: Richard C. Owen.

Veatch, J. (1978). *Reading in the elementary school*. Katonah, NY: Richard C. Owen.

Weaver, C. (1980). *Psycholinguistics and reading: From process to practice*. Portsmouth, NH: Heinemann.

White, J. (1988). *Changing practice: A collaborative study* (Part I). Slough, England: National Foundation for Education and Research.

Ziegler, E., Stampa, M., & Klicka, J. (1991). Triskadekaphobia and other uncommon nonfiction interests. In J. T. Feeley, D. S. Strickland, & S. B. Wepner (Eds.), *Process reading and writing: A literature-based approach* (pp. 62–72). New York: Teachers College Press.

Appendix

Analysis of Skillwork for Seven Popular Basals

Figures A.1 and A.2 show the type of skillwork suggested for the three sample lessons for both levels. Skillwork denotes either workbooks or skillbooks (referred to in Chapter 2 as Skill Practice Books). Five of the seven basals combine workbooks and skillbooks. Workbooks play a more major role than skillbooks; yet, miniaturized replicas of each are displayed in the teachers' guides.

To help you read these figures, let's look at an example from Figure A.1. Take a look at the two columns for D. C. Heath. The first column indicates the number and type of workbook pages; the second column indicates the number and type of skillbook pages. If you look at D. C. Heath's decoding skills (signified by D), you see that D. C. Heath has 6 decoding workbook pages [6 D U] and 9 decoding skillbook pages [9 D U] that are *unrelated* (does not connect with what students are reading) to the student text. It has only 1 decoding workbook page [1 D R] that is *related* (connects with what students are reading) to the student text.

The following conclusions reflect what you see in these two figures:

First Grade

- *Type of Skillwork:* As already indicated in Chapter 2, decoding prevails as the skill activity of choice for the first grade lessons with **39%** of the activities devoted to some type of word study. Comprehension (**31%** of the activities), vocabulary (**21%**) and study skills (**9%**) follow as second, third, and fourth choices respectively.

  Scott, Foresman and Macmillan do not include study skills at all.

  Macmillan and Silver Burdett & Ginn are the only two series that include more comprehension activities than any other area.

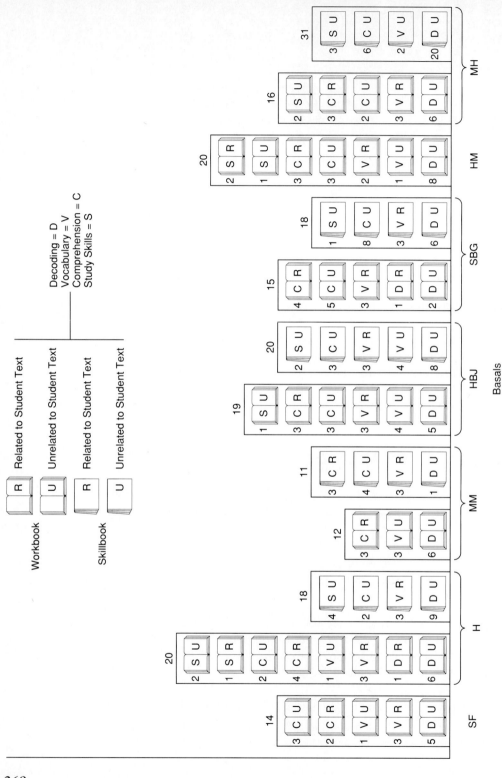

FIGURE A.1
Workbook and skillbook pages for three sample stories for first grade in seven basal series

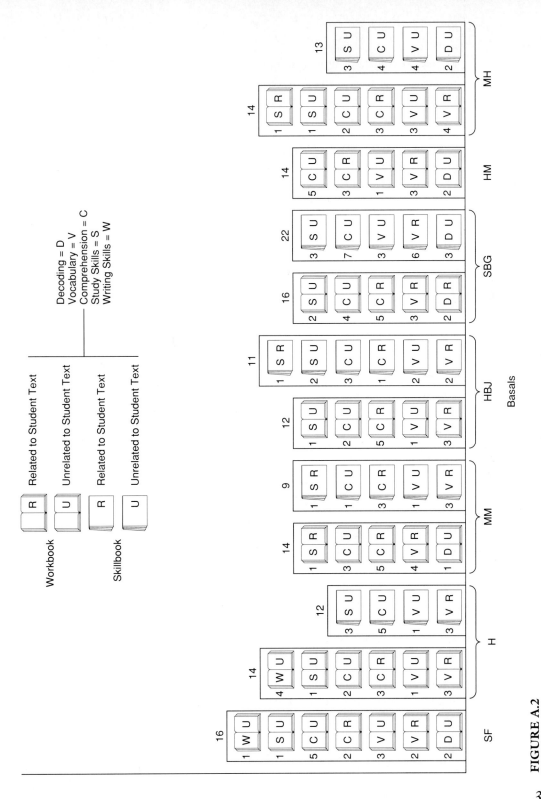

FIGURE A.2
Workbook and skillbook pages for three sample stories for fourth grade in seven basal series

- *Content of Skillwork:* As already indicated, 72% of all the skillwork is unrelated to what students are reading. In other words, the skillwork could be used for any reading material from a trade book or a basal without diminishing its usefulness.

  Twenty-eight percent of all the skillwork (60 out of 214 skill sheets) is related to what students are reading; however, because 3% of the skillwork (2 of the 60 related skill sheets) focuses on decoding or word study, these skill sheets really are only peripherally related to what students are reading. Therefore, only 27% of all the skillwork (58 out of 214 skill sheets) uses the vocabulary and/or content from the student text for skillwork.

  Nearly 38% of the 116 workbook pages is related to what students are reading whereas only 15% of the 98 skillbook pages is related to what students are reading.

Fourth Grade

- *Type of Skillwork:* As already indicated in Chapter 2, comprehension prevails as the skill activity of choice for the fourth grade lessons with 43% of the activities devoted to some type of comprehension activity. Vocabulary is the second most concentrated skill (34%). Study skills (13%), decoding (7%), and writing (3%) follow as third, fourth, and fifth choices respectively.

  Whereas all the basals spend about the same percentage of time on vocabulary activities, they vary in the amount of time spent on comprehension, with Houghton Mifflin spending as much as 57% and McGraw-Hill as little as 33%.

- *Content of Skillwork:* As already indicated, 57% of all the skillwork is unrelated to what students are reading.

  Forty-three percent of all the skillwork (72 out of 167 skill sheets) is related; however, because 3% of all the skillwork (2 of the 72 related skill sheets) focuses on decoding or word study, only 41% of all skillwork (69 out of 167 skill sheets) uses the vocabulary and/or content from the student text for skillwork.

  Nearly 52% of the 100 workbook pages is related, whereas only 30% of the 67 skillbook pages is related to what the students are reading.

What does this particular analysis tell us? A greater portion of first grade skillwork is devoted to decoding, whereas a greater portion of fourth grade skillwork is devoted to comprehension. As discussed in Chapter 2, approximately one-fourth and two-fifths of the skillwork for first grade and fourth grade, respectively, reflect what the students are reading; the rest could be done in any other context. While slightly more than one-third of the first grade workbook pages and slightly more than one-half of the fourth grade workbook pages are closely aligned to the student text, only one-sixth of the first grade skillbooks and nearly one-third of the fourth grade skillbooks are. In general, there are more workbook pages related to what students are reading than skillbook pages; however, most skill activities do not require students to read the student text to respond correctly. And, although not reflected in Figures A.1 and A.2, many of the workbook pages and skillbook pages are not well constructed.

Words are not used in context. Comprehension strategies require merely matching or multiple choice responses.

Analysis of Scope and Sequence Charts for Seven Popular Basals

NUMBER OF SKILLS

Table A.1 shows the number of skills we counted in each series for first grade. There is a difference of 68 skills between the highest number of skills (HBJ lists 98) and the lowest number of skills (Houghton Mifflin lists 30). Whereas Houghton Mifflin and McGraw-Hill seem to address very few skills, Scott, Foresman and HBJ address nearly 100 skills. This is somewhat deceptive because most of the skills addressed in Scott, Foresman and HBJ also are addressed in Houghton Mifflin and McGraw-Hill's skill-work, yet they are not really identified in their scope and sequence charts.

Table A.2 shows that there is a difference of 93 skills between the highest number of skills (Scott, Foresman lists 130) and the lowest number of skills (Houghton Mifflin has 37). Again, similar patterns emerge, with the same basals in the fourth grade having correspondingly high and low numbers in their scope and sequence.

There also is a greater number of skills identified for Decoding/Phonics and Comprehension than for Vocabulary and Study Skills in first grade. However, there were more skills identified for comprehension and study skills than for decoding/phonics and vocabulary in fourth grade. Those basals that identify thinking strategies, literature, and language in their scope and sequence chart for both levels have far more

TABLE A.1
Number of skills for first grade in seven basal series

SKILLS	BASALS						
	SF	H	MM	HBJ	SBG	HM	MH
Decoding and Phonics*	11	11	14	22	12	5	20
Vocabulary	6	6	4	8	7	4	4
Comprehension	17	15	12	14	10	13	7
Study Skills	11	4	7	8	5	2	3
Other (includes Thinking Strategies, Literature, and Language)	52	40	28	46	38	6	--
Total	97	76	65	98	72	30	34

*Skills are not necessarily listed in this order or with these exact category names.

TABLE A.2
Number of skills for fourth grade in seven basal series

SKILLS	BASALS						
	SF	H	MM	HBJ	SBG	HM	MH
Decoding and Phonics*	10	2	9	9	6	5	6
Vocabulary	11	9	7	11	9	4	7
Comprehension	24	20	15	18	13	14	8
Study Skills	22	17	11	20	21	7	15
Other (includes Thinking Strategies, Literature, and Language)	64	69	32	64	57	7	9
Total	130	117	74	122	106	37	45

*Skills are not necessarily listed in this order or with these exact category names.

skills for the "other" category than for the four categories for which workbook and skillbook activities are created.

TYPE OF SKILLS

Tables A.3 to A.6 identify the specific skills taught across basals for decoding and phonics, vocabulary, comprehension, and study skills.

DECODING AND PHONICS

Table A.3 identifies the 19 decoding and phonics skills that are covered in first and fourth grades. Eleven skills appear in four or more of the first grade basals' scope and sequence: (a) recognizing and using consonants, (b) consonant clusters at the beginning and end of words (for example *bl* and *st* at the beginning of words and *ld* and *pt* at the end of words), (c) consonant digraphs (for example, *th* and *ch*), (d) short vowels, (e) long vowels, (f) vowel digraphs (for example, *ey* and *oa*), (g) recognizing and understanding inflectional endings (for example, *-ed* and *-ing*), (h) contractions, (i) spelling changes, (j) compound words, and (k) context clues.

Only five skills appear in a majority of the fourth grade basals: (a) inflectional endings, (b) suffixes and prefixes, (c) base words, (d) compound words, and (e) syllable patterns. As expected, decoding at this level is not emphasized as much as it is in first grade.

VOCABULARY

Table A.4 identifies the 15 vocabulary skills addressed for both grades. Four areas—word meaning, synonyms/antonyms, multiple meanings/homographs, and classifi-

TABLE A.3
Scope and sequence for decoding and phonics

	FIRST GRADE		FOURTH GRADE	
	In Four or More Basals	In Three or Less Basals	In Four or More Basals	In Three or Less Basals
1. Consonants	✓			✓
2. Consonant Clusters	✓			
3. Consonant Digraphs	✓			✓
4. Short Vowels	✓			
5. Long Vowels	✓			
6. Vowel Digraphs	✓			
7. R-Controlled Vowels		✓		✓
8. Vowel Variants		✓		
9. Vowel Patterns		✓		
10. Phonograms		✓		
11. Inflectional Endings	✓		✓	
12. Contractions	✓			✓
13. Spelling Changes	✓			✓
14. Suffixes/Prefixes		✓	✓	
15. Base Words		✓	✓	
16. Compound Words	✓		✓	
17. Syllable Patterns		✓	✓	
18. Context Clues	✓			✓
19. Long Word Decoding Strategies				✓

cation—appear in four or more of the first grade basals. These same skills, plus homophones and connotation/denotation, appear in the fourth grade scope and sequence for four or more basals.

COMPREHENSION

Table A.5 identifies the 23 comprehension skills for first and fourth grades. Six skills are emphasized in practically all first grade basals: (a) main ideas/details, (b) sequence,

TABLE A.4
Scope and sequence for vocabulary

	FIRST GRADE		FOURTH GRADE	
	In Four or More Basals	In Three or Less Basals	In Four or More Basals	In Three or Less Basals
1. Word Meaning	✓		✓	
2. Synonyms/Antonyms	✓		✓	
3. Multiple Meanings/Homographs	✓		✓	
4. Homophones		✓	✓	
5. Classification	✓		✓	
6. Analogies		✓		✓
7. Semantic Mapping		✓		✓
8. Semantic Feature Analysis		✓		✓
9. Content Area Vocabulary		✓		✓
10. Context Clues		✓		✓
11. Idioms		✓		✓
12. Referents		✓		✓
13. Connotation/Denotation			✓	
14. Etymologies				✓
15. Figurative Language				✓

(c) comparison/contrast, (d) drawing conclusions, (e) predicting outcomes, and (f) cause/effect. These same six skills, plus summarizing, elements of fiction/nonfiction, and fact/opinion, are covered in the fourth grade basals.

STUDY SKILLS

Table A.6 lists the 21 study skills for the basals' first and fourth grade scope and sequence. Four of these skills—(a) following directions, (b) parts of a book, (c) alphabetical order, and (d) dictionary/glossary—are consistently addressed across basals for first grade. (We included dictionary/glossary under the Study Skills category because most basals include it here. However, HBJ includes this skill under its vocabulary category.) In addition to those skills listed for first grade, nine skills appear frequently for fourth grade: (a) locating information in books, (b) special graphic

TABLE A.5
Scope and sequence for comprehension

	FIRST GRADE		FOURTH GRADE	
	In Four or More Basals	In Three or Less Basals	In Four or More Basals	In Three or Less Basals
1. Picture Details		√		
2. Main Ideas/Details*	√		√	
3. Sequence*	√		√	
4. Word Referents		√		√
5. Comparison/Contrast*	√		√	
6. Drawing Conclusions	√		√	
7. Predicting Outcomes	√		√	
8. Cause/Effect*	√		√	
9. Inferences		√		√
10. Summarizing		√	√	
11. Paraphrasing		√		√
12. Story Mapping		√		√
13. Evaluating Text		√		√
14. Visualizing		√		√
15. Categorize		√		√
16. Prediction Strategies		√		√
17. Reality/Fantasy		√		√
18. Make Judgments		√		√
19. Elements of Fiction/Nonfiction		√	√	
20. Punctuation/Typographical Features/Sentence Logic		√		√
21. Fact/Opinion			√	
22. Problem-Solution				√
23. Make Generalizations				√

*Appears in all seven basals for both grades.

TABLE A.6
Scope and sequence for study skills

	FIRST GRADE		FOURTH GRADE	
	In Four or More Basals	In Three or Less Basals	In Four or More Basals	In Three or Less Basals
1. Following Directions	✓		✓	
2. Content Area Reading		✓		✓
3. Parts of a Book	✓		✓	
4. Alphabetical Order	✓		✓	
5. Dictionary/Glossary	✓		✓	
6. Locating Information in Books		✓	✓	
7. Special Graphic Aids		✓	✓	
8. Forms/Applications		✓		✓
9. Calendar		✓		✓
10. Test-Taking Strategies		✓	✓	
11. Mapping Ideas		✓		✓
12. Maps and Globes		✓	✓	
13. Life Skills		✓	✓	
14. Varying Reading Rate		✓		✓
15. Skimming/Scanning		✓	✓	
16. Bibliography		✓		✓
17. Organizes Information		✓	✓	
18. Library Resources			✓	
19. Study Techniques			✓	
20. Research Techniques				✓
21. Summaries/Reports				✓

aids, (c) test-taking strategies, (d) maps and globes, (e) life skills, (f) skimming/scanning, (g) organization of information, (h) library resources, and (i) study techniques. Some of the basals make an attempt to relate study skills to the student text (see Figures A.1 and A.2). Generally, though, study skill coverage varies greatly from basal to basal.

In summary, 25 (or 36%) of the skills listed in Tables A.3 to A.6 are similar across first grade basals; 44 (or 64%) of the skills are represented unevenly across basals. Decoding and phonics is the only skill area where more than half (61%) of the skills are consistently addressed. Vocabulary (31%), comprehension (30%) and study skills (22%) vary considerably from basal to basal in first grade. Thirty-three (or 46%) of the skills identified for fourth grade are similar across basals; 38 (or 54%) of the skills are represented unevenly across basals. Study skills is the only area where more than half (62%) of the skills are consistently addressed. (We noted, though, that the amount of skillwork for study skills is not commensurate with the large number of skills listed in the scope and sequence.) Decoding (41%), comprehension (40%), and vocabulary (38%) vary considerably.

Glossary

Aesthetic Reading: a type of reading in which the reader focuses on what is being lived through during reading, what feelings are stirred up, the rhythm of the words, and the past experiences that these words elicit (Rosenblatt, 1978).

All-Group Share: a class activity in which students share their writing by reading it to a group and inviting response.

Alphabetic Principle: the assumption underlying writing systems having an alphabet that phonemes or speech sounds are related to graphic symbols.

At-Home Reading: time spent alone or with parents, guardians, or others in the home reading aloud or silently.

Basal: a sequential, grade-specific set of reading texts (student readers) in a basal reading program that usually contains controlled vocabulary and is written at a specific grade level.

Before-During-After Reading Guide: a set of protocols of well-formulated techniques and strategies that are used at appropriate intervals to help with the comprehension of text.

Bibliotherapeutic: helping the reader, through the use of books and other texts, to grow in self-awareness or to solve personal problems.

Big Books or Enlarged Print: children's books that are printed in large type so that a group of students can readily see the text and read along with the teacher.

Bottom-Up: a reference to initiatives for change in the schools that start with the teachers; also can refer to an approach to teaching and writing by starting with letters and sounds.

Branching Hierarchy: a type of graphic organizer that is similar to a structured overview in which the main topic is further divided into divisions and subdivisions.

CD-ROM (Compact Disk-Read Only Memory): an output device that combines the storage capabilities of compact disks and the printing capabilities of a laser printer. A CD- (compact disk) player is connected to a computer to use the CD-ROM disk (Flake, McClintock, & Turner, 1990).

Center for the Study of Reading: a research center established at the University of Illinois (since 1976) by the National Institute of Education; its major focus is to study the complex processes of reading comprehension and the relationship between reading and writing.

Clustering: a type of graphic organizer in which ideas and concepts are held together, or clustered, around a central topic or term.

Cognitive Framework: the organization of one's schemata into a consistent system; everything one knows as it is organized in one's brain.

Coherent Reading: continuous reading of meaningful text for an extended period of time.

Computer-Mediated: any application of the computer that places the immediate display of written text under the direct control of a computer program. Helps to provide a more comprehensive analysis of how the computer interacts with the entire spectrum of written language processes (Reinking, 1986).

Concrete Operational Thought: the kind of thinking described by Jean Piaget as being dependent upon direct interaction with the real, concrete world; pertains to the thinking typically found in children from 7 to 11 years of age and is characterized by reversibility.

Constructivist View: belief that readers create or construct a text by using stored knowledge about the topic and language in general; reading is viewed as an interaction between a reader and the text.

Cooperative Group Learning: an instructional framework in which students work on learning tasks in small groups. Four procedural steps are involved: (a) the teacher defines a learning task; (b) the teacher assigns students to groups; (c) students complete the learning task together through a cooperative group activity; (d) students share their results with other groups (Leu & Kinzer, 1991).

Cross-Curricular: cutting across disciplines, for example, mathematics, social studies, and science, usually included in thematic units where instruction about a topic includes many content areas.

Daily Response to Reading: written reaction to what is read every day through, for example, journals and log sheets.

Database Program: a computer program that contains a large organized collection of related information, for example, a collection of facts related to the 41 presidents of the United States.

Decoding: identifying words (not necessarily with understanding) from the text.

Deep Structure: the underlying meaning of a text; for example, the sentences, "John hit the ball" and "The ball was hit by John" both mean the same thing (deep structure) although their surface structure is different.

Desktop Publishing: use of technology to produce publication-quality printed documents, historically achieved only by typesetting equipment. Desktop publishing systems include computers and peripherals, laser printers, and publishing software (Bitter, 1989).

Directed Reading Activity (DRA): a step-by-step process of dealing with a reading lesson under the guidance of a teacher; usually involves preparation, reading (oral and silent), and followup activities.

Directed Reading-Thinking Activities (DR-TA): a step-by-step process of dealing with a reading lesson in which the students set their own purposes for reading by making predictions, read to verify their predictions, and discuss to check their verifications.

Drop Everything and Read (DEAR): type of Sustained Silent Reading in which students (and the teacher) spend part of the school day reading books of their own choosing.

Dynamic Text: the ability to adjust the contents to the interests and needs of the user. Technology, because of its ability to store user-inputted information, can automatically provide students with varied options for interacting with text; for example, when encountering an unfamiliar word, the reader can request a definition and receive it via a "window" on the screen.

Efferent Reading: a type of reading in which the reader focuses on what can be taken from the reading—the information to be acquired, the logical solution to a problem, the actions to be carried out (Rosenblatt, 1978).

Emergent Literacy: the view that children "emerge" into readers and writers by being exposed to meaningful print that others read to and with them until they can read and write on their own.

Empowerment: the participation of teachers in school decision-making areas such as curriculum, organization, hiring, and choice of materials for instruction.

Frames: a type of graphic organizer that indicates the organization of important content (main ideas and the relationships connecting those ideas) in a text (Armbruster, 1991).

Generating Questions: a metacomprehensive strategy in which students create their own questions to cover material they are about to read.

Genre: a form or type of literary and other artistic content, for example, poetry or biography.

Grapheme: a letter or a written or printed symbol that stands for a phoneme or sound, for example, the word *cat* has three graphemes, *c, a, t.*

Graphic Organizer: a visual representation of how information, concepts, and content are organized and related to each other.

Graphophonic Cues: letter-sound relationships (such as *c* representing /k/ in *kite*) that help us read.

Guided Reading Procedure (GRP): a highly structured reading comprehension strategy in which students gather information and organize it around important ideas. Students read to remember all that they can, rereading the same text to correct inconsistencies and add further information. Students' remembrances are recorded in some kind of outline before they synthesize their ideas through discussion (Manzo, 1975).

Holophrases: one-word utterances usually made by young children between the ages of one and two that stand for entire phrases or sentences (*Up* can mean "Pick me up" or "I want that toy up there"); by two, children expand utterances to two words, with a few "pivot" words such as *Want* and *Like* being combined with a large open class of words they can say, for example, "Want milk," "Want juice," "Want doggie," "Want hug."

Hypertext: computer capability that links information on the screen to stacks of related information so that students can access pertinent material at will rather than follow a fixed path; the electronic equivalent of a reference library.

Icon Menu: series of pictures or graphics representing computer commands (for example, a pic-

ture of a printer would represent the command, *print*).

Immersion Literacy: learning to read by being surrounded by meaningful print that others read to and for children until they can read for themselves.

Independent Reading: opportunity for students to read self-selected books on their own, taking responsibility to work through the challenges of the text.

Individualized Reading (IR): an approach to teaching reading that was popular in the 1950s and 1960s; emphasized self-selection of materials (usually trade books) and self-pacing of oneself in reading; understanding was assessed during small-group and individual conferences with the teacher.

Inquiry-Oriented Approach: an instructional method in which students use their own initiative, in combination with teacher guidance, to investigate ideas through reading, writing, speaking, and listening.

Integrated Instructional System (IIS): computer-managed, comprehensive skill-oriented software programs, typically used in school districts that emphasize centralized decision making, accountability, and uniform coverage of mandated curricula.

Interactive Story: reading passage, typically on the computer, that requests information from the user and responds to the user according to the information supplied.

K-W-L: a guided reading procedure for helping students to read for a purpose by assessing what they *know* (K), what they *want* (W) to learn, and what they *learned* (L) as a result of reading.

Language Experience Approach (LEA): an approach to learning to read in which the students' own words are written down and used as materials of instruction for reading, writing, speaking, and listening.

Learning Center: a location within a classroom with a variety of instructional materials that have clearly defined objectives, directions, and self-checking tools for learning; for example, a writing center would contain several types of paper and writing implements plus writing prompts and aids (dictionaries; thesauruses).

Learning Log: journal/diary for recording content area learning experiences.

Literacy: the ability to read and write a language.

Literature-Based Classroom: instructional environment that uses trade books as the centerpiece for learning.

Literature-Based Guides: lesson plans that help to organize and provide ideas for working with trade books.

Literature Circles: groups of students who read and discuss books together; they may all read the same book or different books; appears in work by Harste, Short, and Burke (1988).

Long-Term Memory (LTM):   the aspect of memory that lasts over a long period of time; develops from continued or repeated short-term memory inputs and has great capacity; when reading, information from short-term memory is "chunked" into long-term memory, and we remember the "gist" rather than the details.

Management System: method for keeping track of all the data collected about students' academic performance.

Metacognition: may be loosely defined as "thinking about thinking" or the awareness and monitoring of one's thinking processes.

Metacomprehension: metacognition as it pertains to comprehending and learning from text; planning, monitoring, and regulating a reading/learning task by applying appropriate strategies as needed.

Metalinguistic Awareness: understanding the concepts about language (for example, a word, a sentence, and letter-sound correspondences) that are important in learning to read and write.

Mini-lesson: short, focused lesson on a particular skill or convention, for example, a phonics lesson on the sound of the letter *m* in *my, mother,* and *milk*; or a lesson on when to use the exclamation point. Mini-lessons are based on students' needs, as observed from previous activities.

Multimedia: combination of media for learning, for example, audio (sound, music, speech), video, and print, in which a microcomputer can be at the hub of the system.

Narrative Text: form of writing in which an author tells a story, actual or fictional, in prose or verse.

National Assessment of Educational Progress (NAEP):   the national government's monitoring of the educational level of a carefully selected sampling of American students at benchmark ages (9, 13, and 17); assessments were started in 1970 and are done on reading and writing approximately every 5 years.

Network: a type of graphic organizer that depicts the interrelationships between ideas; also used to refer to "literacy networks" in which groups of educators meet to share ideas.

Nonvisual Information: information that is stored in one's brain that helps one read print; it can be linguistic knowledge, knowledge of the topic, or general knowledge gained from a lifetime of experiences and experiments.

Off-Line: any material not presented on the computer screen.

On-Line: any material presented on the computer screen.

Phoneme: the smallest unit of sound that makes a difference in a language; for example, *pan* and *pin* differ by one phoneme (medial vowel).

Portfolio: a collection of samples of a student's work, for example, dated writing pieces, tapes of oral reading, and journal entries.

Prior Knowledge: all the information that is stored in one's brain; it comes from all the experiences a person has been through and forms the knowledge network one uses to understand new concepts and information.

Process-Oriented: focus on noticing and valuing what the student does during reading, writing, listening, and speaking rather than just the final or end product created. Ongoing assessment is usually practiced in a process-oriented classroom.

Progressive Writing: a cooperative group-writing experience in which students experience each stage of the writing process: prewriting, writing, revising, editing, and creating final copy.

Psycholinguistics: the interdisciplinary field of psychology and linguistics; includes areas such as language acquisition, rules for generating language, and discourse analysis.

Readability: objective estimate or prediction of comprehensibility of material, usually in terms of reading grade level, based upon selected and quantified variables in text, usually some index of vocabulary difficulty and sentence length.

Reading Aloud: a time when the teacher orally reads to the entire class from a book or other interesting resource.

Reading Workshop: a time in the school day when students read books chosen either by them or the teacher; they usually discuss their reading in groups and/or respond by writing in journals or doing other post-reading activities such as art projects, creative dramatics, or related writing projects.

Recursive Process: used in the writing process literature; going both backward and forward during the process of composing.

Response (or Reading) Log: diary or journal in which students react to what they read. Sometimes, teachers use ideas or prompts to guide students' reactions; at other times, a response log is totally open-ended.

Schemata: conceptual system for understanding things, for example, schema for going to a restaurant; also sometimes called *script* as in "*script* for going to a restaurant."

Schema Theory: a way of explaining how knowledge is organized in the brain and how this stored knowledge aids comprehension and learning; a schema (*schemata* is the plural form) represents all the information that summarizes what one knows about a concept; according to schema theory, comprehension depends on a person's schemata and how one relates new information to stored information.

Scientific Literacy: the ability to read and write about science concepts and content.

Scope and Sequence: a curriculum plan, usually in chart form, in which instructional objectives and skills are arranged according to the levels at which they are taught, usually found in basal reader systems.

Semantic Cues: meaning cues; evidence from the meaning of the whole text that helps one identify an unknown word.

Semantic Mapping: a type of graphic organizer in which main ideas and related supporting details are displayed visually.

Shared Book Reading: reading situation in which a student or group of students sees the text, observes the teacher reading the text with fluency and expression, and is invited to read along.

Short-Term Memory (STM): the aspect of memory that has limited capacity and lasts very briefly; when reading, ideas are stored briefly in short-term memory until "big ideas" are moved into long-term memory.

Simulations: the creation of realistic situations by duplicating actual situations as closely as possible.

Site-Based Management: committees of administrators, teachers, and parents assume budgetary, organizational, and curricular responsibility for their school.

Skillwork: paper-and-pencil tasks in workbooks and skill practice books found in basal materials to help with specific skill instruction.

Sociolinguistics: the interdisciplinary field of sociology and linguistics; the study of language as it develops in various social settings; for example, social class, regional, and ethnic dialects.

Standardized Tests: tests with specified tasks and procedures so that comparable measurements may be made in different geographical areas. Norms on a reference group, ordinarily drawn from many schools or communities, are provided.

Story Graph: a type of graphic organizer that plots specific story elements from the beginning to the end of the story.

Story Grammar: the structure of a narrative that usually has chronological links from a beginning, through episodes and outcomes, to an ending; stories typically have characters, setting, plot, and theme.

Structured Overview: a type of graphic organizer in which important concepts of a topic or unit of study are put into a visual pattern to show relationships between the concepts and/or vocabulary.

Study Skills: techniques and strategies (for example, following directions and interpreting graphic aids) that help a person read or listen for specific purposes.

Surface Structure: what is actually written; the print that the eye sees as opposed to the deep structure which is what the print means; the two sentences—"John hit the ball" and "The ball was hit by John"—have different surface structures but the same deep structure.

Sustained Silent Reading (SSR): time period during the school day when students (and the teacher) read books of their own choosing.

Syntactic Cues: evidence from the knowledge of the grammar of a language that helps one to identify a word from the way it is used in connected discourse.

Technology: broad range of computerized tools (microcomputers, video disks, optical disks, CD-ROM disks) to make work easier and more productive.

Text Structure: how reading material is organized to signal different messages to the reader. The two most common types of text structure—narrative and expository—have very different structures. Narrative text usually has a time-order sequence involving one or more main characters. Expository text is organized to show, for example, cause-effect relationships, comparison/contrasts, and problem/solution of concepts and events.

Thematic Unit: a series of organized lesson plans in which the materials and strategies (which may or may not cut across curricular areas) relate to a major idea, proposition, or broad topic (for example, endangered species).

Thinking Aloud: a metacomprehensive strategy for reading in which students verbally express and share their thoughts as they read.

Top-Down: a reference to initiatives for change in the schools that start with the administrators; also can refer to an approach to teaching reading and writing by starting with whole stories and texts.

Topical Net: a type of graphic organizer in which the main idea serves as the hub for a number of related ideas.

Trade Book: a bound, library book that contains an entire literary composition of a specific genre.

Transaction Model: a way of looking at instruction in which students learn by interacting between the known and the unknown, the focus is on the relationship between the reader and the text.

Transmission Model: a way of looking at instruction in which teachers transmit discrete knowledge and skills to students; in reading, the focus is on teaching isolated skills.

Venn Diagram: a type of graphic organizer that shows the similarities and differences between two or three ideas.

Visual Information: what the eye actually sees during reading; the surface structure of a text.

Voluntary Reading: reading done by students on their own initiative; not required or prescribed by the teacher.

Weave: a type of graphic organizer to show how various ideas or elements connect to form a whole.

Webbing (or Web): graphic representation or visual display of categories of information and their relationships.

Whole Language: philosophy of teaching and learning based on the assumption that children learn to read and write through encounters with real text rather than from sets of practice exercises.

Workshop Approach: teaching in a studio atmosphere in which students learn to read by reading and write by writing with feedback from teachers and peers, similar to the way artists learn their craft.

Writing Workshop: a time during the school day devoted to writing; students write from their own topic lists and share their writing with others to get feedback, revising if needed after conferences; writing is usually stored in folders, and students continue pieces until finished; certain pieces are selected to be revised and edited so they can be "published" in some form for others to read; the term is frequently used by Donald Graves (1983).

References

Armbruster, B. B. (1991). Framing: A technique for improving learning from science texts. In C. M. Santa & D. E. Alvermann (Eds.), *Science learning: Processes and applications* (pp. 104–113). Newark, DE: International Reading Association.

Bitter, G. G. (1989). *Microcomputers in education today.* Watsonville, CA: Mitchell Publishing.

Flake, J. L., McClintock, C. E., & Turner, S. V. (1990). *Fundamentals of computer education* (2nd ed.). Belmont, CA: Wadsworth.

Graves, D. (1983). *Writing: Teachers and students at work.* Portsmouth, NH: Heinemann.

Harris, T. L., & Hodges, R. E. (Eds.). (1981). *A dictionary of reading and related terms.* Newark, DE: International Reading Association.

Harste, J. C., Short, K. G., & Burke, C. (1988). *Creating classrooms for authors: The reading-writing connection.* Portsmouth, NH: Heinemann.

Leu, D. J. & Kinzer, C. K. (1991). Effective reading instruction, K–8 (2nd ed.). New York: Merrill/Macmillan.

Manzo, A. V. (1975). Guided reading procedure. *Journal of Reading, 18,* 287–291.

Reinking, D. (1986). Six advantages of computer-mediated text for reading and writing instruction. *The Reading Instruction Journal, 29*(3), 8–16.

Rosenblatt, L. (1978). *The reader, the text, and the poem.* Carbondale, IL: Southern Illinois University Press.

Author Index

Subject Index

Trade Book Index

About the Authors

Shelley B. Wepner

Joan T. Feeley

Shelley B. Wepner is chairperson and associate professor in the Department of Curriculum and Instruction at William Paterson College, Wayne, New Jersey, where she teaches undergraduate courses in content area reading and graduate courses in reading and technology and administration and supervision of reading programs. She earned her B.S. from the University of Pittsburgh and M.S. and Ed.D. degrees from the University of Pennsylvania. Prior to her higher education teaching experiences, she was a reading teacher (grades 5–8), a reading resource teacher (grades K–6), a Title 1 teacher (grades K–4), a reading/language arts teacher (grades 7 and 8), a curriculum coordinator (grades K–8), and a Supervisor of Curriculum and Instruction (grades K–8). Shelley has published in, among other journals, *The Reading Teacher,* the *Journal of Reading, Reading Psychology, The Computing Teacher, Journal of Developmental Education, Reading World, Reading Horizons, Special Services in the Schools,* and *Teaching, preK–8.* Her books include *Using Computers in the Teaching of Reading, The Administration and Supervision of Reading Programs,* and *Process Reading and Writing: A Literature-Based Approach.* She also has authored/coauthored three software packages, two of which won national awards, including "top five" in the country. Former editor of *The Reading Instruction Journal,* and coauthor of *Literature Lesson Links,* a series of 45 literature-based plans that are coordinated with software, she currently is the department editor for the Technology Links to Literacy column for *The Reading Teacher.*

Joan T. Feeley is coordinator of the graduate Reading Program and professor in the Department of Curriculum and Instruction at William Paterson College, Wayne, New Jersey, where she teaches undergraduate courses in emergent literacy and graduate courses in research and psycholinguistics. Having received her Ph.D. from New York University, she taught at NYU and Seton Hall University before coming to William Paterson. Beginning her career as a high school teacher of English and French, she has also taught in elementary schools in New York City and suburban New Jersey. Besides articles and reviews for journals, such as *The Reading Teacher,* the *Journal of Reading, Language Arts, Reading World, Day Care and Early Education, Journal of Developmental Education,* and *The Reading Instruction Journal,* Joan has coauthored a chapter, "Research on Language Learners: Development in the Elementary Years," in *The Handbook of Research on Teaching the English Language Arts.* Her books include *Using Computers in the Teaching of Reading, The Administration and Supervision of Reading Programs,* and *Process Reading and Writing: A Literature-Based Approach.* A past president of the North Jersey Council of the International Reading Association, she received the Distinguished Service Award from the New Jersey Reading Association.